SINGAPORE
MALAY/MUSLIM
COMMUNITY
1819–2015

ISEAS – Yusof Ishak Institute (formerly the Institute of Southeast Asian Studies) was established as an autonomous organization in 1968. It is a regional centre dedicated to the study of socio-political, security and economic trends and developments in Southeast Asia and its wider geostrategic and economic environment. The Institute's research programmes are the Regional Economic Studies (RES, including ASEAN and APEC), Regional Strategic and Political Studies (RSPS), and Regional Social and Cultural Studies (RSCS).

ISEAS Publishing, an established academic press, has issued more than 2,000 books and journals. It is the largest scholarly publisher of research about Southeast Asia from within the region. ISEAS Publishing works with many other academic and trade publishers and distributors to disseminate important research and analyses from and about Southeast Asia to the rest of the world.

SINGAPORE MALAY/MUSLIM COMMUNITY 1819–2015

A BIBLIOGRAPHY

EDITED BY
HUSSIN MUTALIB.
ROKIAH MENTOL
SUNDUSIA ROSDI

ISEAS YUSOF ISHAK INSTITUTE

First published in Singapore in 2016 by
ISEAS – Yusof Ishak Institute
30 Heng Mui Keng Terrace
Singapore 119614

E-mail: publish@iseas.edu.sg • Website: bookshop.iseas.edu.sg

ISEAS Library Cataloguing-in-Publication Data

Singapore Malay/Muslim Community, 1819-2015 : A Bibliography / editors, Hussin
Mutalib, Rokiah Mentol and Sundusia Rosdi.
   1.   Malays (Asian people)—Singapore—Bibliography.
   2.   Muslims—Singapore—Bibliography.
   I.   Hussin Mutalib.
   II.   Rokiah Mentol.
   III.   Sundusia Rosdi.
Z3254 M2S611   2016

ISBN 978-981-4695-88-6 (soft cover)
ISBN 978-981-47-6223-6 (E-book PDF)

Typeset by International Typesetters Pte Ltd
Printed in Singapore by Markono Print Media Pte Ltd

CONTENTS

INTRODUCTION

Objectives and Significance of this Bibliography

The principal aim of this Bibliography is to compile all available, useful information and resource lists about Singapore's Malay/Muslim community into one document. This will enable anyone who are keen to know about the different aspects of the community, easy access to the compilation. Like other ethnic Singaporeans living in this global city-state, Malays/Muslims are also experiencing a rapid transformation in their lives — educationally, politically, economically, culturally and socially. It is thus important that these changes be captured and documented so that the huge reservoir of information about the various facets of their life can be preserved and made available to anyone interested, be they serious researchers and academics, or the general public.

This realization to scholastically preserve and document a bibliography about the Republic's Malay/Muslim community (which did not exist before) led to our formation of a Working Committee in the early 1990s. We met and deliberated for many months as to how best to go about researching and compiling such a bibliography. The result was the successful publication of the *Singapore Malay/Muslim Community, 1819–1994: A Bibliography* in 1995, by the National University Singapore (NUS).

Since then, many new materials about the community have been produced, reflecting the developments, achievements and challenges faced by the community during the last two decades or so. Hence, this latest academic enterprise by the present Editors and Compilers, the majority of whom are senior librarians who have served the national and university libraries in this Republic for many years, and a senior academic with NUS who initiated the earlier 1995 project. The objective this time around, however, was to produce a bibliography that would not only merely update the previous publication by accommodating these new materials, but also collate and expand its scope and coverage as exhaustively as possible to encompass many different sources (print or non-print materials), such as microforms, documentaries, electronic resources and other media forms. After much painstaking, three-year effort, we now see the publication of this new Bibliography — *Singapore Malay/Muslim Community, 1819–2015: A Bibliography* — which we believe (humbly!) to be the one and only comprehensive bibliography of its kind available anywhere.

It is our earnest hope that this latest publication would be an indispensable, significant reference guide to scholars and researchers in particular and also the general public who are interested in any aspect of the development of Singapore's Malay/Muslim community, then and now — from the time of Stamford Raffles in 1819 to today (2015).

Scope, Coverage and Sources

The materials in this present collection cover a wide and rich repertoire of information about the Republic's Malay/Muslim community — prints and non-prints, such as books and book chapters, journal articles (local, regional and international), microforms, conference proceedings and papers presented at seminars, symposiums and talks, academic dissertations submitted to both local and foreign universities, audio and video recordings, and online and electronic resources. (Newspapers, newspaper articles and book reviews are, however, excluded.)

To enable researchers and readers to have a deeper understanding of the community, "community" publications that we regard as useful for the non-specialist, popular readers, such as annual reports and "news and views" about the Malay/Muslim community that were published in various Malay/Muslim community magazines and related publications, are also included. While our focus is on the ethnic "Malays", but in order to ensure a larger catchment of literature, we define the term liberally and broadly so as to also include Muslims of non-Malay descent, such as Indian Muslims, Arabs, and Muslim converts.

Covering a period of about two centuries — from the arrival of Stamford Raffles in Singapore in 1819 until the present (2015) — this Bibliographic compendium not only contains both published and unpublished works in English, but also Malay (including in *Jawi* script). The date 1819 was chosen as the starting point of this bibliography coverage, given its significance as the founding date of modern Singapore.

The main sources of reference used by the Editors include the following: the *Index to Articles relating to Singapore, Malaysia, Brunei, ASEAN: Humanities and Social Sciences*, compiled by the National University of Singapore; the *Singapore Periodical Index*, compiled by the National Library Board; the lists of dissertations, theses and academic exercises submitted to the National University of Singapore and its predecessor, the University of Singapore; and the online catalogues of the five main libraries — the libraries of the National University of Singapore (NUS), the Institute of Southeast Asian Studies (ISEAS), the National Library Board (NLB), the Nanyang Technological University (NTU), and the National Institute of Education (NTU/NIE). These libraries are chosen for the obvious reason that they are established libraries and have a sizeable collection of materials on Singapore and the Malay/Muslim community. The holdings of the titles are indicated with the abbreviations of the libraries.

Other sources consulted are *WorldCat*, the online catalogues of some libraries outside Singapore, and bibliographies of books, academic dissertations and journal articles.

Classification and Organization

The numerous information here are classified according to a broad range of themes and sub-themes. The goal is to try to capture as many diverse aspects of the community's life as possible, including their history, religion, culture, literature, education, ethnicity, health, law and many others.

In classifying this Bibliography, the Editors were guided in the main by the latest 16th edition of the *Chicago Manual Style* (an academic standard for citation format), the *Library of Congress Name Authority* and the *Library of Congress Subject Headings* (the internationally recognized reference for name and topical headings) with some slight modifications in the citations of Malay, Arab and Chinese names to reflect local practice. Given their inter-relatedness, some of the subject classifications contain multiple entries. For the benefit of users, a List of Journals Cited is also provided.

In terms of organization (arrangement) of entries, the items are placed alphabetically (by author or title) under the following order of broad subject categories:

Bibliographies, Catalogues and Indexes
Biography
Culture
Demography
Economics
Education
Ethnology
Health
History
Journalism, Mass Media and Publishing
Language
Law
Literature
Politics
Religion
Sociology
Special Localities

For the convenience of readers and researchers, each subject category (except the first two) is further sub-divided into finer or more specialized sub-categories. For example, the subject category "Sociology" is sub-categorized into "Social Structure", "Family, Kinship and Marriage", "Women", "Youth", "Children and the Elderly", "Social Integration", "Social Policy and Conditions", "Social Problems and Services", and "Self-Help Groups".

The Editors decided on the seventeen broad subject categories to reflect the content of the Bibliography. The categories are based on two library classification systems: Dewey Decimal Classification (DDC) System and Library of Congress Classification (LCC) System. Both systems organize materials by discipline or field of study. The broad subject categories in this Bibliography are a selection of subject headings or divisions from both the DDC and LCC Systems. As the resources compiled and listed in this Bibliography are from diverse libraries, including public library (National Library Singapore), research library (ISEAS Library) and academic libraries (National University of Singapore Library, Nanyang Technological University Library, etc.), the Editors felt it is appropriate to use the combined subject classifications of the DDC and LCC systems.

Information about the location of the works cited in the Bibliography that are available in the five local libraries is given at the end of the citations. Other relevant works found outside the five libraries are also included but without indicating their locations. We are confident that academics and researchers in particular and the general public who are serious enough to delve into the subjects of their interest, should have little difficulty in searching these works that are stored in other libraries, either within or outside Singapore.

To further facilitate usage of this Bibliography, a *Name Index* is provided. This index lists alphabetically names of authors, compilers, editors, creators and any other individuals involved in producing the works. It also lists the main personalities highlighted in the cited works. It is hoped that this Name Index would serve as a useful reference tool to enable users of this Bibliography find works by the authors of their interest.

Again, having the interest of readers and researchers in mind, a *Directory of Singapore Malay/Muslim Organizations* is also provided. This Directory lists the main and currently active Malay/Muslim organizations especially in the educational, social, cultural and welfare areas.

Limitations and Challenges Encountered

Now that this Bibliography is ready, as Editors and Compilers, we sincerely believe it is sufficiently expansive and comprehensive. For perspective, we could in fact produce an even more holistic and complete compendium, but some of the limitations and challenges that we encountered during the long process of preparing this Bibliography prevented us from doing so. Perhaps, we could share some of these challenges with the readers.

The first is the problem of getting access to works that are either supposed to be in the libraries holdings but somehow were not available on the shelves during several checks or visits, or materials that were kept by the writers themselves or some Malay/Muslim organizations.

The second is the difficulty of identifying relevant Malay/Muslim works from the rich body of literature related to Singapore as a whole. A substantial amount of information about the Malays/Muslims may be buried in such works and go unnoticed unless discovered by accident or referred to in some writings. There are also general titles which may on the surface seem somewhat unrelated to the Malay/Muslim community when in fact, upon further scrutinizing, are indeed relevant.

The third challenge is the task of tracing the unpublished materials that are stored and scattered in the holdings of many different libraries, such as papers presented at various conferences, seminars, symposiums or talks organized either by various Malay/Muslim organizations in Singapore or by the government's ministries and agencies. For the record, the Malays have been the most active community in organizing such regular seminars that discuss their development, problems and progress in a rapidly changing Singapore.

The fourth is the earlier plan by the Editors to annotate the Bibliography. While admittedly this would be a bonus to researchers and readers of the Bibliography, after much deliberation and taking into account our limited resources and the time and effort that are required to do so, we decided not to proceed with this herculean task.

Finally, while we noted the benefits of producing an "online" database for this Bibliography for reasons that are obvious — updated, on-going sources and materials about the community can be uploaded more quickly; it will be more user-friendly and faster given the flexibility of searching through key words; and allowing for contributions from a larger pool of resources and expertise, including crowd sourcing — again, our limited resources was a determining factor impeding us from doing so. As it is, our current print format has taken us more than three years to see its fruition. Still, this online version should certainly be considered as a feasible future endeavour.

Acknowledgments

It is our earnest hope that this much updated and revised Bibliography would be able to serve the needs of academics and researchers in particular and the general public as a whole, in their quest to know more about Singapore's Malay/Muslim community since earlier times until today. For the more serious researchers and scholars, we hope that this Bibliography would enthuse them to do more substantial research on the community and publish the findings in whatever media they consider appropriate and effective, be it in print or electronic. If this can be done, future generation of scholars, researchers and others who are keen to know more about the various facets of life of this Republic's Malay/Muslim community, would stand to gain.

No doubt, a serious and coordinated compilation work of this nature is never easy to do. However, with the determined commitment, professionalism and perseverance exhibited by the entire team (Editors and Compilers) throughout this bibliographic endeavour, these challenges managed to be overcome. The help offered by others has also facilitated the final publication of this Bibliography. In this regard, we wish to especially acknowledge the financial grant from the National Heritage Board. The Prophet Muhammad Scholarship Fund Board also assisted us in the early preparatory phase of launching this project, for which we are indeed grateful. Finally, our appreciation also go to Ms Hashimah Johari and Ms Zaleha Othman — who were in the original team — for their support.

Editors

Hussin Mutalib, Ph.D.
Rokiah Mentol
Sundusia Rosdi

With the assistance of

Haslinda Md Yusof
Hasmidah Hosaimi
Norulashikin Jamain
Rohayah Mohd Lani
Zaleha Tamby
Zarinah Mohamed

SMMC BIBLIOGRAPHY WORKING COMMITTEE
(EDITORS AND COMPILERS)
2013–15

Hashimah Johari is a Senior Associate University Librarian at the National University of Singapore (NUS) Libraries. She is currently the Head of Central Library and Head of Access Services. She formerly worked as the Head of Research and Information Services for almost ten years and was the Coordinator for *Perind*, an indexing database of periodical articles on Singapore, Malaysia, Brunei and ASEAN produced by NUS Libraries. She obtained an M.A. in Malay Studies from the University of Singapore in 1985 and M.A. in Library and Information Studies from the University College of London in 1988.

Haslinda Md Yusof, B.A., is a Senior Librarian with the National Library Board (NLB), Singapore. She joined the National Library in 1988 as a Library Officer and obtained her Diploma in Library and Information Science in 1992 from the National Library, Singapore and the Library Association of Singapore. She has worked in public libraries, research library (Marine Fisheries Research Department Library), National Reference Library, Information Services, Lee Kong Chian Reference Library and is currently attached to the Resource Discovery and Management Division of NLB. From 2005 to 2009, Haslinda was involved in the *Aksara: The Passage of Malay Scripts Exhibition* Project. Her key deliverables for this project included a coffee table book, a gallery guide and a select bibliography.

Hasmidah Hosaimi is currently a Librarian with the National Library Board (NLB), Singapore. She holds a Bachelor's degree in Petroleum Engineering from the University of Technology, Malaysia in 1994. She joined NLB in 2006 as an Associate Librarian. Her expertise is in audio visual cataloguing.

Hussin Mutalib was the principal initiator and coordinator of the inaugural *Singapore Malay/Muslim Community, 1819–1994: A Bibliography*. A senior member of the Political Science Department at the National University of Singapore (NUS) since 1981, he is also a community activist, having served most of the major Malay/Muslim associations/institutions in this Republic, including AMP, MUIS, Mendaki, CCIS and Muhammadiyah and chairs the scholarship committee of LBKM, the academic committee of Muhammadiyah Islamic College and the Pergas' annual Assatizah Awards. At NUS, he teaches Contemporary Politics of Singapore and Malaysia, Islamic Political Thought, and Middle East Politics. An author of seven academic books (his latest being *Melayu Singapura*, 2015) and numerous articles in international journals, he has been a Fulbright Fellow/Visiting Professor to universities such as Harvard, Oxford, LSE, California (Berkeley), Cairo and Jordan.

Norulashikin Jamain was a Librarian at the National Library Board (NLB), Singapore. She worked in NLB from 1977 to 1989, and from 1999 to 2012. She holds a Bachelor's degree from the National University of Singapore in 1977, majoring in Malay Studies and Sociology. She obtained her Post-Graduate Diploma in Library and Information Science in 1984 from the National Library, Singapore and the Library Association of Singapore. She worked in public libraries, government department libraries, Acquisition Services and Resource Discovery and

Management Division of NLB. She was in the editorial teams for the NLB's publications *Bibliografi Masuri S.N.* (2008) and *Bibliografi Abdul Ghani Hamid* (2011), and was a co-compiler of *Rentas Tinta* (2003). She wrote a poetry collection *Perjalanan Waktu* (2005).

Rohayah Mohd Lani, B.A. (Hons) was a Collection Librarian (Singapore & Southeast Asia) at the Lee Kong Chian Reference Library, National Library Board (NLB), Singapore. She joined the National Library in 1980 and retired in 2015. She obtained her degree in Information & Library Studies from UCE in Birmingham, in 2003. She was a joint compiler and editor of *AKSARA : the passage of Malay scripts — a select bibliography* (2007) and *Bibliography MAS : Md. Ariff Ahmad* (2013). She also edited Malay articles published in *BiblioAsia* (2010–11) and *Jurnal Dakwah, Pergas* (2012) as well as two books entitled *Obor Ummah 2* (2014) and *Masyarakat Bawean Singapura La-A-Obě* (2015). Her short stories have appeared in *Berita Minggu* and she received an award "Anugerah Persuratan Singapura (Kategori Cerpen)" in 2009.

Rokiah Mentol, B.A. was a Principal Librarian at the National Library Board (NLB), Singapore. She joined the National Library in 1977 and retired in 2011. She holds a Bachelor's degree from the National University of Singapore in 1977, majoring in Economics and Sociology. She obtained her Post-Graduate Diploma in Library and Information Science in 1984 from the National Library, Singapore and the Library Association of Singapore. She has been a Librarian in public libraries, government department libraries, National Reference Library and Publishing and Research Division of NLB. Her domain research expertise is in library research, social services, official statistical publications and economics. She was in the editorial teams for the publication *National Directory of Scholars: Humanities and Social Sciences* (2007) and *Statistical Snapshots of Asia-Pacific Countries* (2007) and was one of the compilers for *Singapore Malay/Muslim Community, 1819–1994: A Bibliography* (1995).

Sundusia Rosdi, B.A. (Hons) was a Senior Librarian at the National Library Board (NLB), Singapore who joined the NLB in 1977 and retired in 2012. She holds a Bachelor's degree in History from the University of Malaya, Kuala Lumpur (1977) and a Post-Graduate Diploma in Librarianship from the University of Wales, UK (1981). She has worked in public libraries, research library and junior college libraries. Prior to her retirement, she was the Project Manager of NLB's project, *Index to Singapore Information from 2006–2012*. Her articles on the Malay community and literature have appeared in *Berita Minggu*, *BiblioAsia* (NLB's academic journal), and Singapore Islamic Scholars & Religious Teachers Association's (Pergas) newsletters and journal since 1997. She was also the compiler and editor of three books entitled: *Obor Ummah 2* (2014), *Footprints of Muslim's Scholars and Heritage: A Select Bibliography — 1914–2014* (2014) and *Masyarakat Bawean Singapura La-A-Obĕ* (2015).

Zaleha Othman, M.A. is a Senior Librarian at the National University of Singapore (NUS) Libraries. She obtained an M.A. (Librarianship) degree from the University of Sheffield in 1987.

Zaleha Tamby, B.A. was a Senior Librarian with the Institute of Southeast Asian Studies (ISEAS) and retired in December 2012. She is now working on contract as a Special Librarian at the same Institute. She holds a Bachelor's degree in Economics from the University of Malaya, Kuala Lumpur, and a Post-Graduate Diploma in Library and Information Science from the Library Association, UK. Her other works are *Cambodia: A Bibliography* (1982), *The Future of Southeast Asia and the Asia-Pacific: A Special Select Bibliography in Celebration of the 25th Anniversary of the Institute of Southeast Asian Studies, Singapore* (1993), and some other select bibliographies including *Islam, Politics and the State in Southeast Asia* (online, 2011). Her latest work is the *Toshio Egawa Collection in the ISEAS Library: A Catalogue* (2014).

Zarinah Mohamed, M.A. is a Librarian at the Information Resource Centre, Singapore Press Holdings. She also previously worked at the National University of Singapore (NUS) Libraries. She obtained her M.A. in Library and Information Studies from University College London

SINGAPORE MALAY/MUSLIM COMMUNITY 1819–2015

1819–2015

A BIBLIOGRAPHY

BIBLIOGRAPHIES, CATALOGUES
AND INDEXES

1. Ainon Kuntom. "Malay Newspapers, 1876–1973: A Historical Survey of the Literature". Academic exercise, Pusat Pengajian Ilmu Kemanusiaan, Universiti Sains Malaysia. 1974. 84 pp. NLB, NUS.

2. *An Annotated Bibliography of Statistical Publications.* Singapore: Department of Statistics, 1983–86. ISEAS, NLB, NUS. Previously published: Singapore: National Statistical Commission of Singapore, 1972–82. ISEAS, NLB, NUS.

3. *ASAS 50: Senarai Awal.* Kuala Lumpur: Dewan Bahasa dan Pustaka, 1980. 12 pp. ISEAS, NLB

4. Azizah Sidek and V. Perumbulavil. *Prominent Singaporeans: Sources of Information.* Singapore: Reference Services Division, National Library, 1993. 39 pp. ISEAS, NLB, NTUNIE, NUS.

5. Challis, Joyce, comp. *Annotated Bibliography of Economic and Social Materials in Singapore. Part 1, Government Publications.* Singapore: Economic Research Centre, University of Singapore, 1969. 86 pp. NUS. Previously published: Singapore: Economic Research Centre, University of Singapore, 1967. 78 pp. ISEAS, NLB, NTUNIE.

6. Challis, Joyce, comp. *Annotated Bibliography of Economic and Social Materials in Singapore and West Malaysia: Non-Government Publications.* Singapore: Economic Research Centre, University of Singapore, 1969. 241 pp. ISEAS, NLB, NTUNIE, NUS.

7. Cheeseman, Harold Robinson. *Bibliography of Malaya: Being a Classified List of Books Wholly or Partly in English Relating to the Federation of Malaya and Singapore.* London: Longman for the British Association of Malaya, 1959. 234 pp. ISEAS, NLB, NTUNIE, NUS.

8. Chen S.J., Peter and Tai Ching Ling. *Social Development in Singapore: A Selected Bibliography.* Singapore: Chopman Enterprises, 1976. 74 pp. ISEAS, NLB, NTUNIE, NUS.

9. Cheung Po Lo, Paul, ed. *A Guide to Singapore Official Statistics.* Singapore: Department of Statistics, 1999. 142 pp. ISEAS, NLB, NTUNIE, NUS.

10. *A Decade of Singapore Creative Writing in English, Malay and Tamil 1976–1985: A Select Booklist.* Singapore: Reference Services Division, National Library, 1986. 42 pp. ISEAS, NLB, NTUNIE, NUS.

11.   Ding Choo Ming. *Bibliografi Sastera Kreatif Melayu = A Bibliography of Malay Creative Writings*. Bangi, Selangor: Perpustakaan Universiti Kebangsaan Malaysia, 1980. 497 pp. ISEAS, NLB, NUS.

12.   Ding Choo Ming. *A Bibliography on Malay Sajak, 1980–1984*. Bangi, Selangor: Perpustakaan Tun Seri Lanang, Universiti Kebangsaan Malaysia, 1987. 127 pp. ISEAS, NLB, NUS.

13.   Dinsman. "Buku-Buku Drama Melayu, 1951–1974". *Dewan Bahasa* 19, no. 1 (January 1975): 63–71. NLB, NUS.

14.   *Dissertations, Theses and Academic Exercises Submitted to the National University of Singapore 1981–1982*. Singapore: National University of Singapore Library, 1983. 129 pp. ISEAS, NLB, NTUNIE, NUS.

15.   *Dissertations, Theses and Academic Exercises Submitted to the National University of Singapore 1983–1987*. Singapore: National University of Singapore Library, 1989. 558 pp. ISEAS, NLB, NTUNIE, NUS.

16.   *Dissertations, Theses and Academic Exercises Submitted to the University of Singapore and Deposited in the University of Singapore Library 1947–1976*. Singapore: University of Singapore Library, 1977. 341 pp. ISEAS, NLB, NTUNIE, NUS.

17.   *Dissertations, Theses and Academic Exercises Submitted to the University of Singapore and Deposited in the University of Singapore Library. Supplement 1977–78*. Singapore: University of Singapore Library, 1980. 100 pp. ISEAS, NLB, NTUNIE, NUS.

18.   *Harun Aminurrashid: Satu Bibliografi = Harun Aminurrashid: A Bibliography*. Bangi, Selangor: Perpustakaan Tun Seri Lanang, Universiti Kebangsaan Malaysia, 1982. 7 pp. ISEAS, NLB, NUS.

19.   Hussin Mutalib. "Muslim Social Science Studies in Singapore". Paper presented at the ASEAN Forum for Muslim Social Scientists, held under the auspices of the Foundation for Democracy and Development Studies in Bangkok in 1988. 21 pp. Published under the title: "Muslim Studies in Singapore". In *Muslim Social Science in ASEAN*, edited by Omar Farouk Bajunid. Kuala Lumpur: Yayasan Penataran Ilmu: Penerbit Universiti Malaya, 1994. ISEAS, NLB, NUS.

20.   Hussin Mutalib. "Singapore Malays, 1819–1994: A Bibliographic Survey". *Southeast Asian Journal of Social Science* 24, no. 2 (1996): 22–48. First

presented at the Department of Malay Studies' Seminar, National University of Singapore, 17 August 1995. ISEAS, NTUNIE.

21. Hussin Mutalib et al., eds. *Singapore Malay/Muslim Community 1819–1994: A Bibliography*. Singapore: Centre for Advanced Studies, National University of Singapore, 1995. 249 pp. ISEAS, NLB, NTUNIE, NUS.
(Compilers and Editors: Hussin Mutalib, Hashimah Johari, Rokiah Mentol, Zaleha Othman and Zaleha Tamby).

22. Juffri Supaat, Saliyah Sapeon, and Sukinah Suradi. *Bibliografi Abdul Ghani Hamid*. Penyunting, Norulashikin Jamain, Mazelan Anuar. Singapore: National Library Board, 2011. 200 pp. NLB.

23. Juffri Supaat, Saliyah Sapeon, and Sukinah Suradi. *Bibliografi Masuri S. N. (1927–2005)*. Penyunting, Norulashikin Jamain, Noryati A. Samad. Singapore: National Library Board, 2008. 176 pp. ISEAS, NLB, NTUNIE, NUS.

24. Juffri Supaat, Saliyah Sapeon, and Sukinah Suradi. *Bibliografi Muhammad Ariff Ahmad*. Penyunting, Rohayah Md. Lani, Juffri Supa'at. Singapore: National Library Board, 2012. 288 pp. NLB, NTUNIE.

25. Juffri Supaat, Saliyah Sapeon, and Sukinah Suradi. *Bibliografi Sastera Melayu Singapura (1965–2009) = Bibliography of Singapore Malay Literature (1965–2009)*. Penyunting, Juffri Supa'at. Singapore: National Library Board, 2011. 598 pp. NLB, NTUNIE, NUS.

26. Karni, Rahadi S. *Bibliography of Malaysia and Singapore*. Kuala Lumpur: Penerbit Universiti Malaya, 1980. 649 pp. ISEAS, NLB, NTUNIE, NUS.

27. Kartini Saparudin, comp. *The Hadhrami Arabs in Southeast Asia with Special Reference to Singapore: An Annotated Bibliography*. Editor, Noryati Abdul Samad. Singapore: National Library Board, 2010. 320 pp. ISEAS, NLB, NUS.

28. *Katalog Manuskrip Melayu di Singapura*. Kuala Lumpur: Perpustakaan Negara Malaysia, 1993. 41 pp. ISEAS, NLB, NUS.

29. Kee Yeh Siew. *Singapore: A List of Publications and Periodical Articles Arranged by Subjects*. Wellington: Library School, National Library Service, 1962. 32 pp. NLB.

30.   Lim, Beda. *Malaya: A Background Bibliography*. Singapore: Malayan Branch of Royal Asiatic Society, 1962. 199 pp. ISEAS, NLB, NUS.

31.   Lam Bee Goh. *Communities of Singapore: A Catalogue of Oral History Interviews. Part 3, Malays*. Singapore: Oral History Department, 1996. ISEAS, NLB, NTUNIE, NUS.

32.   Lim Bee Lum and Ngiam Tee Liang. *A Select Bibliography on Social Issues, Social Services and Social Work in Singapore and Malaysia*. Singapore: Department of Social Work, National University of Singapore, 1984. 82 pp. ISEAS, NLB, NTUNIE, NUS.

33.   Lim Pui Huen, Patricia. *The Malay World of Southeast Asia: A Select Cultural Bibliography*. Singapore: Institute of Southeast Asian Studies, 1986. 456 pp. ISEAS, NLB, NTUNIE, NUS.

34.   *PERIND: Index to Articles Relating to Singapore, Malaysia, Brunei & ASEAN*. Singapore: National University of Singapore Library, 1984. Previously produced in print under the title: *Index to Periodical Articles Relating to Singapore, Malaysia, Brunei, ASEAN: Humanities & Social Sciences*. ISEAS, NLB, NTUNIE, NUS.

35.   Perret, Daniel. *Sejarah Johor-Riau-Lingga sehingga 1914: Sebuah Esei Bibliografi*. Malaysia: Kementerian Kebudayaan, Kesenian dan Pelancongan École française d'Extrême-Orient, 1998. 460 pp. NLB.

36.   Putten, Jan van der and Suryadi Sunari. *Yang Menulis = They Who Write*. Singapore: National Library Board, 2013. 84 pp. NLB, NTU, NTUNIE, NUS.

37.   Roff, William R. *Autobiography and Biography in Malay Historical Studies*. Singapore: Institute of Southeast Asian Studies, 1972. 21 pp. ISEAS, NLB, NUS.

38.   Roff, William R. *Bibliography of Malay and Arabic Periodicals Published in the Straits Settlements and Peninsular Malay States 1876–1941: With an Annotated Union List of Holdings in Malaysia, Singapore and the United Kingdom*. London: Oxford University Press, 1972. 74 pp. ISEAS, NLB, NUS.

39.   Roff, William R. *Guide to Malay Periodicals, 1876–1941: With Details of Known Holdings in Malaya*. Singapore: Eastern Universities Press, 1961. 46 pp. ISEAS, NLB, NUS.

40.   Rugayah Abdul Rashid. *Bibliografi Sastera Kreatif Melayu, 1920–1967.* 3 vols. Kuala Lumpur: ¯abatan Pengajian Melayu, Universiti Malaya, 1977–79. ISEAS, NLB.

41.   Safian Hussain, Siti Aisah Murad, and Fadzil Agussalim. *Bibliografi Sastera Melayu Moden 1925–1980.* Kuala Lumpur: Dewan Bahasa dan Pustaka, 1985. 245 pp. ISEAS, NLB, NTUNIE, NUS.

42.   Saw Swee-Hock. *Bibliography of Singapore Demography.* Singapore: Institute of Southeast Asia Studies, 2005. 173 pp. ISEAS, NLB, NTUNIE, NUS.

43.   Saw Swee-Hock and Cheng Siok Hwa. *A Bibliography of the Demography of Singapore.* Singapore: University of Education Press, 1975. 120 pp. ISEAS, NLB, NTUNIE, NUS.

44.   *Singapore Conference Index, 1970–1982: Holdings of Singapore Proceedings in the NUS Library.* Singapore: National University of Singapore Library, 1983. 234 pp. NLB, NTUNIE, NUS.

45.   *Singapore National Bibliography.* Singapore: National Library, 1969–93. From July 1993, published in CD-ROM, updated semi-annually. ISEAS, NLB, NTUNIE, NUS.

46.   *Singapore Periodical Index.* Singapore: National Library, 1974–2006. Also published in CD-ROM. ISEAS, NLB, NTUNIE, NUS.

47.   Sundusia Rosdi, comp. *Footprints of Muslim Scholars' Heritage in Singapore: A Select Bibliography.* Editor, Rohayah Mohd. Lani. Singapore: PERGAS, 2014. 75 pp. ISEAS, NLB.

48.   *Transition to Nationhood: A Resource Guide to Singapore's Merger and Separation.* Singapore: National Library Board, 1999. 1 CD-ROM. ISEAS, NLB, NTU, NTUNIE, NUS.

49.   Turnbull, C.M. "Bibliography of Writings in English on British Malaya, 1786–1867". *JMBRAS* 33, pt. 3 (1960): 1–424. ISEAS, NLB, NTUNIE, NUS.

50.   University of Singapore Library. *Catalogue of the Singapore/Malaysia Collection.* Boston: G.K. Hall, 1968. 757 pp. ISEAS, NLB, NUS.

51.   University of Singapore Library. *Catalogue of the Singapore/Malaysia Collection: Supplement, 1968/1972.* Singapore: Singapore University Press, 1974. 324 pp. ISEAS, NLB, NTUNIE, NUS.

52.   Wicks, Yoke-Lan. "Bibliography on Malay Culture in Singapore". In *Report of the Preliminary Meeting of Bibliographers of the Bibliography on Malay Culture held at the Institute of Southeast Asian Studies, Singapore, 23-25 June 1976*. Singapore: Singapore National Commission for UNESCO, 1976. ISEAS, NLB, NUS.

53.   Zainab Awang Ngah. "Malay Comic Books Published in the 1950's". *Kekal Abadi* 3, no. 3 (September 1984): 4–11. ISEAS, NLB, NUS. Also published under the same title: *Singapore Book World* 16, no. 2 (1986): 19–28. NLB, NTUNIE, NUS.

BIOGRAPHY

54.   A. Karim Haji Abdullah (Abdul Karim Haji Abdulllah), ed. *A. Samad Ismail: Ketokohan dan Kewartawanan*. Kuala Lumpur: Dewan Bahasa dan Pustaka, 1991. 441 pp. ISEAS, NLB, NUS.

55.   A.R. Zahari (Ab. Rashid Zahari). "Abdullah Munsyi: Who was He?" *Jurnal Biografi Malaysia* 1 (June 2005): 48–76. NLB.

56.   "A. Samad Ismail (1924–2008): Tokoh Wartawan dan Nasionalis". In *Ensiklopedia Sejarah dan Kebudayaan Melayu*, vol. 1, pp. 15–16. Kuala Lumpur: Dewan Bahasa dan Pustaka, 1994. NLB, NTUNIE, NUS.

57.   A. Samad Ismail (Abdul Samad Ismail). *Memoir A. Samad Ismail di Singapura*. Bangi, Selangor: Universiti Kebangsaan Malaysia, 1993. 275 pp. ISEAS, NLB, NTUNIE, NUS.

58.   A. Samad Ismail (Abdul Samad Ismail). "Penghulu Keluarga". *Dewan Budaya* 14, no. 10 (October 1992): 20–22. ISEAS, NLB, NTUNIE, NUS.

59.   A. Samad Ismail (Abdul Samad Ismail). "Utusan Melayu dan Saya". In *Cenderamata Genap 25 Tahun Utusan Melayu Akhbar Kebangsaan Melayu yang dipunyai dan diusahakan oleh Bangsa Melayu 29 Mei 1939–29 Mei 1964*, disusun oleh Rusdin Yaakub dan Abdul Malik Haji Abdullah, 7–23. Kuala Lumpur: Utusan Melayu Press, 1964. ISEAS, NLB.

60.   A. Talib Samat. "Ahmad Lutfi: Penulis, Penerbit dan Pendakwah". *Dewan Sastera* 21, no. 5 (May 1991): 89–91. NLB, NTUNIE, NUS.

61.   Abd. Ghani Said (Abdul Ghani Said). "As Sayid Habib Nuh: Peranannya Tersembunyi". In *7 Wali Melayu*. Kuala Lumpur: Penerbitan Hikmah, 1993. ISEAS, NLB.

62.   Abdul Aziz Bari. "Ahmad Ibrahim and the Islamization of Law in Malaysia". In *Monograph on Selected Malay Intellectuals*, compiled by Mohamad @Md. Som Sujimon. Kuala Lumpur: International Islamic University Malaysia, 2003. ISEAS, NLB, NUS.
(Discusses Natrah's case in Singapore).

63.   Abdul Ghafar Ibrahim. "Masuri S.N. (Singapura)". In *Dialog Seniman Dunia*. Shah Alam: Pustaka Dini, 2010. NLB, NTUNIE.

64.   Abdul Ghani Hamid. "Masuri S.N.". In *Jati Diri: Citra Seni di Singapura = Selves: The State of the Arts in Singapore*, edited by Kwok Kian Woon, Arun Mahizhnan, and T. Sasitharan. Singapore: National Arts Council, 2002. NLB, NUS.

65.   "Abdul Ghani bin Abdul Hamid, Cultural Medallion Recipient, 1999, Literature". Produced by National Library Board, Singapore, in collaboration with National Arts Council, Singapore. 2007 [released in 2009]. 1 videodisc. 18 min. NLB.

66.   Abdul Halim Abdul Karim. "Haji Mohamad Sanusi Mahmood: The First Mufti of Singapore". Paper presented at a Workshop on the Education of Southeast Asian Islamic Leadership, Singapore, 19–20 May 2005. ISEAS.

67.   "Abdul Hamid Jumat". In *Ensiklopedia Sejarah dan Kebudayaan Melayu*, vol. 1, pp. 33–34. Kuala Lumpur: Dewan Bahasa dan Pustaka, 1994. NLB, NTUNIE, NUS.

68.   Abdul Monir Yaacob et al. *Permata Pengislahan Perundangan Islam: Biografi Profesor Emeritus Tan Sri Datuk Ahmad Mohamed Ibrahim*. Kuala Lumpur: MPH & IKIM, 2007. 203 pp. NLB, NUS.

69.   Abdul Rahman Haji Ismail. "Syed Sheikh Al-Hadi: Penggerak Kebangkitan Melayu Abad ke-20". In *Syed Syeikh Al-Hadi Cendekia dan Sasterawan Ulung*, edited by Eric Taliagozzo. Pulau Pinang: Penerbit Universiti Sains Malaysia, 2003. NLB.

70.   Abdul Rahman Mohamed. *Travelog Seorang Da'i*. Kuala Lumpur: Telaga Biru, 2009. 277 pp. NLB.

71.   "Abdul Samad Pagek (1905–1952): Ahli Perubatan". In *Ensiklopedia Sejarah dan Kebudayaan Melayu*, vol. 1, pp. 53–54. Kuala Lumpur: Dewan Bahasa dan Pustaka, 1994. NLB, NTUNIE, NUS.

72.   Abdullah Hussain. *Harun Aminurashid: Pembangkit Semangat Kebangsaan*. Kuala Lumpur: Dewan Bahasa dan Pustaka, 1982. 412 pp. ISEAS, NLB, NTUNIE, NUS.

73.   Abdullah Hussain. *P. Ramlee: Kisah Hidup Seniman Agung*. Petaling Jaya: Pena, 1984. 261 pp. ISEAS, NLB, NUS.

74.   "Abu Bakar Maidin: Seorang Tokoh". In *Inspiration: Madrasah Al-Maarif Al-Islamiah 50th Anniversary and Official Opening Ceremony, 15th March 1987*. Singapore: Madrasah Al-Maarif Al-Islamiah, 1987. NLB, NUS.

75.   *Abu Bakar Maidin: Singapore's Global Muslim: His Life, Times and Deeds*. Singapore: Jamiyah Singapore, 2012. 473 pp. NLB, NUS.

76. *Abu Bakar Maidin's Global Photo-Journey: A Nostalgic Bouquet of Memories.* Singapore: Jamiyah Singapore, 2012. 211 pp. NLB, NUS.

77. Ahmad Sarji. *P. Ramlee: Erti yang Sakti.* Kuala Lumpur: Pelanduk Publications, 1999. 400 pp. ISEAS, NLB, NTUNIE, NUS.

78. Ahmad Solhan. *Sasterawan A. Ghani Hamid: Suatu Transkripsi.* 1988. 44 pp. NLB.
(Interview with A. Ghani Hamid).

79. Aimi Jarr. *Jejak Terbilang.* Ampang, Selangor: Perbadanan Kemajuan Filem Nasional Malaysia, 2007. 297 pp. NUS.

80. Alatas, Syed Farid. "Ideology and Utopia in the Thought of Syed Shaykh Al-Hady". Working Papers no. 172. Singapore: Department of Sociology, National University of Singapore, 2005. 31 pp. NLB, NUS.

81. Al-Hady, Syed Mohamed Alwi. "Syed Shaykh: Through the Prism of a Child's Eyes and the al-Hady Clan". In *The Real Cry of Syed Shaykh Al-Hady*, edited by Alijah Gordon. Kuala Lumpur: Malaysia Sociological Research Institute, 1999. ISEAS, NLB, NTUNIE, NUS.

82. Ali Hainin. "Penggumulan Tokoh-Tokoh dan Penjanaan Pemikiran Gerakan di Kalangan Muhammadiyah Singapura". *Suara Muhammadiyah* 1 (1999): 35–41. ISEAS, NLB, NUS.

83. Ali Salim. "A Pioneer in Malay Journalism". In *A. Samad Ismail: Journalism and Politics,* compiled and edited by Cheah Boon Kheng. Kuala Lumpur: Utusan Publications, 2000. ISEAS, NLB, NTU, NTUNIE.

84. Alsagoff, Syed Mohsen. *The Alsagoff Family in Malaysia A. H. 1240 (A. D. 1824) to A. H. 1382 (A. D. 1962).* Singapore: The author, 1963. 50 pp. NUS.

85. Alsagoff, Syed Mohsen. "The Arab Pioneers of Singapore: The Alsagoff Family". In *Commercial Directory and Guide: Malaya.* Kuala Lumpur: [s.n.], 1959. NLB, NUS.

86. Anis Mohamed. "Muzik Terus Bergetar di Jiwa". *Dewan Budaya,* no. 7 (July 2004): 6–7. NLB, NTUNIE, NUS.
(On Kassim Masdor).

87. Anis Mohamed. "Yusnor Ef Malar Segar Hingga Kini". *Dewan Budaya,* no. 11 (November 2004): 6–7. NLB, NTUNIE, NUS.

88.   Anuar Nor Arai. "Dendam Seorang Penyair". *Dewan Sastera* 19, no. 3 (March 1989): 68–72. NLB, NTUNIE, NUS. (On Noor S. I.).

89.   Anuar Nor Arai. "Dua Penyair Si Umat Singapura: dari Jalan Permulaan, ke Danau Sukma". *Dewan Sastera* 19, no. 12 (December 1989): 14–18. NLB, NTUNIE, NUS. (On Mohamed Latiff Mohamed and S. Markasan (Suratman Markasan)).

90.   Al-Attas, Syed H.M. (Hassan Muhammad). *Nota Kembara Seorang Abid: Sekelumit Riwayat Habib Muhammad bin Salem al-Attas dan Tebaran Anak Hadhrami.* Singapore: Masjid Ba'Alwi, 2010. 155 pp. NLB.

91.   Aziz Sattar. *Meredah Gelombang Seni: Sebuah Memoir,* edited by Mohamad Saleeh Rahamad dan Ruzita Alias. Ampang, Selangor: Finas, [2007?]. 227 pp. ISEAS, NLB.

92.   Azlan Mohamed Said. *Musika: Malaya's Early Music Scene = Arena Muzik Silam di Malaya,* edited by Juffri Supa'at. Singapore: Azlan Mohamed Said, 2013. 256 pp. ISEAS, NLB, NTUNIE, NUS.

93.   Balamurugam, Anasuya et al. "Abdul Ghani Hamid (1933–2014)". In *Singapore Literary Pioneers Gallery Guide = Panduan Galeri Perintis Sastera Singapura.* Singapore: National Library Board, 2006. ISEAS, NLB, NUS.

94.   Balamurugam, Anasuya et al. "Harun Aminurrashid (1907–1986)". In *Singapore Literary Pioneers Gallery Guide = Panduan Galeri Perintis Sastera Singapura.* Singapore: National Library Board, 2006. ISEAS, NLB, NUS.

95.   Balamurugam, Anasuya et al. "Mahmud Ahmad (1906–1976)". In *Singapore Literary Pioneers Gallery Guide = Panduan Galeri Perintis Sastera Singapura.* Singapore: National Library Board, 2006. ISEAS, NLB, NUS.

96.   Balamurugam, Anasuya et al. "Masuri S.N. (1927–2005)". In *Singapore Literary Pioneers Gallery Guide = Panduan Galeri Perintis Sastera Singapura.* Singapore: National Library Board, 2006. ISEAS, NLB, NUS.

97.   Balamurugam, Anasuya et al. "Muhammad Ariff Ahmad, (1924–)". In *Singapore Literary Pioneers Gallery Guide = Panduan Galeri Perintis*

Sastera Singapura. Singapore: National Library Board, 2006. ISEAS, NLB, NUS.

98.   Balamurugam, Anasuya et al. "Noor S. I. (Ismail Omar), 1933–1990". In *Singapore Literary Pioneers Gallery Guide = Panduan Galeri Perintis Sastera Singapura*. Singapore: National Library Board, 2006. ISEAS, NLB, NUS.

99.   Balamurugam, Anasuya et al. "Suradi Parjo (1926–1996)". In *Singapore Literary Pioneers Gallery Guide = Panduan Galeri Perintis Sastera Singapura*. Singapore: National Library Board, 2006. ISEAS, NLB, NUS.

100.   Balamurugam, Anasuya et al. "Suratman Markasan, (1930–)". In *Singapore Literary Pioneers Gallery Guide = Panduan Galeri Perintis Sastera Singapura*. Singapore: National Library Board, 2006. ISEAS, NLB, NUS.

101.   Baharuddin Zainal et al, comps. *A Biography of Malaysian Writers*. Kuala Lumpur: Dewan Bahasa dan Pustaka, 1985. 319 pp. ISEAS, NLB, NTUNIE, NUS

102.   "Balasungkawa: Prof. Tan Sri Ahmad Ibrahim". *Warita Kita* 120 (March–April 1999): 12. ISEAS, NLB, NUS.

103.   Buang Omar Junid. "Pengalaman Saya". *Petir: Organ of the People's Action Party* 3 (December 1980): 72–73. ISEAS, NLB, NTUNIE, NUS.

104.   Chamil Wariya. "Leftenan Datuk Adnan Saidi". In *50 Ikon Bangsa*. Kuala Lumpur: Media Global Matrix, 2008. ISEAS, NLB.

105.   Chamil Wariya. "Tan Sri P. Ramlee: Seniman Terbilang, 1929–1973". In *50 Ikon Bangsa*. Kuala Lumpur: Media Global Matrix, 2008. ISEAS, NLB.

106.   Chamil Wariya. "Yusof Ishak: Pengasas Suara Keramat Bangsa, 1910–1970". In *50 Ikon Bangsa*. Kuala Lumpur: Media Global Matrix, 2008. ISEAS, NLB.

107.   "Champion of Muslim Women". *The Voice* (July 1993): 10–11. NLB. (On Mehrun Siraj, a lawyer).

108.   Cheah Boon Kheng, comp. and ed. *A. Samad Ismail: Journalism and Politics*. Kuala Lumpur: Utusan Publications, 2000. 332 pp. ISEAS, NLB, NTU, NTUNIE, NUS.

109.   Chew, Melanie. *A Biography of President Yusof bin Ishak*. In collaboration with the National Archives of Singapore. Singapore: Singapore National Printers for Board of Commissioners of Currency, 1999. 197 pp. ISEAS, NLB, NUS.

110.   Chia Poteik. "Interview with SBC Orchestra Leader Ahmad Jaafar: Composer and Orchestra Leader". *Petir: Organ of the People's Action Party* 11 (December 1981): 30–32. ISEAS, NLB, NTUNIE, NUS. Also published in Malay under the title: "Wawancara dengan Ahmad Jaafar, Pemimpin Orkes SBC: Penggubah dan Pemimpin Orkes". *Petir: Organ of the People's Action Party* 11 (December 1981): 34–35. ISEAS, NLB, NTUNIE, NUS.

111.   Cheong Suk Wai et al. "All at the Same Level at the Negotiation Table". In *Living the Singapore History: Celebrating Our 50 Years: 1965–2015*. Singapore: National Library Board, 2015. ISEAS, NLB.
        (On Abdul Rahman Mahbob, a veteran union leader).

112.   Cheong Suk Wai et al. "Do You Know the Satay Man? He Has Moved". In *Living the Singapore History: Celebrating Our 50 Years: 1965–2015*. Singapore: National Library Board, 2015. ISEAS, NLB.
        (On Ngalirdjo Mungin, a satay hawker).

113.   Cheong Suk Wai et al. "First First Lady: I Wanted to Do More Smile". In *Living the Singapore History: Celebrating Our 50 Years: 1965–2015*. Singapore: National Library Board, 2015. ISEAS, NLB.
        (On Puan Noor Aishah Mohd. Salim, the first First Lady).

114.   Cheong Suk Wai et al. "My Novel is about Who We Are". In *Living the Singapore History: Celebrating Our 50 Years: 1965–2015*. Singapore: National Library Board, 2015. ISEAS, NLB.
        (On Isa Kamari, an architect and novelist).

115.   Cheong Suk Wai et al. "No, We Don't Have Hairy Legs". In *Living the Singapore History: Celebrating Our 50 Years: 1965–2015*. Singapore: National Library Board, 2015. ISEAS, NLB.
        (On Zaibun Siraj, a founding member of AWARE).

116.   Cheong Suk Wai et al. "Shot by Botak, the Cop Killer". In *Living the Singapore History: Celebrating Our 50 Years: 1965–2015*. Singapore: National Library Board, 2015. ISEAS, NLB.
        (On Abd Rahman Khan Gulap Khan, a veteran police officer).

117. Cooper, Arthur Egerton. 'Munshi Abdullah". *Malaya* 11 (1953): 652–53. NLB, NUS.

118. *Directory of the State of Singapore 1960–61: Including Trade Index and Biographical Section.* London: Diplomatic Press and Publisher, 1961. 168 pp. NLB, NUS.

119. Djamal Tukimin. "Mahmud Ahmad — Membongkarkan Rahsia Pengaryaannya". *Sekata* 2, no. 2 (2001): 20–24. ISEAS, NLB, NTUNIE, NUS.

120. Djamily, Bachtiar. *Menyorot Karir, Peranan, Latar Belakang A. Samad Ismail.* Kuala Lumpur: Pustaka Budiman, 1985. 261 pp. NLB, NUS.

121. Dorset, J.W., comp. *Who's Who in Malaya 1918.* Singapore: Dorset & Co., 1918. 134 pp. NLB. NUS.

122. "Ensaikelopedia Sastera: Hamzah". *Dewan Bahasa* 9, no. 10 (October 1965): 465–69. NLB, NUS.
    (On Hamzah Hussin).

123. Fadhullah Jamil. "Syed Sheikh Al-Hadi: Pemikirannya Terhadap Islam dan Perubahan". In *Syed Syeikh Al-Hadi: Cendekia dan Sasterawan Ulung*, edited by Sohaimi Abdul Aziz. Pulau Pinang: Penerbit Universiti Sains Malaysia, 2003. NLB.

124. Faridah Abdul Rashid. *Biography of the Early Malay Doctors 1900–1957, Malaya and Singapore.* Bloomington, IN: Xibris Corporation, 2012. 964 pp. NLB.

125. Faridah Abdul Rashid. *Research on the Early Malay Doctors 1900–1957, Malaya and Singapore.* Bloomington, IN: Xibris Corporation, 2012. 392 pp. NLB.

126. Farrer, D.S. "The Healing Arts of the Malay Mystic". *Visual Anthropology Review* 24, issue 1 (Spring 2008): 29–46. NUS.
    (On Mohammad Din Mohammad).

127. Fatimah Zainal. "Masuri S. N. Karyawan Tamu DBP". *Dewan Sastera* 28, no. 1 (January 1998): 54–55. NLB, NTUNIE, NUS.

128. Filzah A. Hadi. "One with the Workers". *Karyawan: Professionals for the Community* (August 1994): 14, 17. ISEAS, NLB, NTUNIE, NUS.
    (On Halimah Yaacob)

129.   Firdaus Hj. Yahya, Wan Hussin Hj. Zoohri, and Mohd. Raman Daud, eds. *Obor Ummah: Jejak Tokoh Agama Islam di Singapura*. Singapore: Persatuan Ulama dan Guru-guru Agama Singapura: Lembaga Biasiswa Kenangan Maulud, 2011. 154 pp. ISEAS, NLB.

130.   Freitag, Ulrike. "Arab Merchants in Singapore: Attempt of a Collective Biography". In *Transcending Borders: Arabs, Politics, Trade and Islam in Southeast Asia*, edited by Huub de Jonge and N.J.G. Kaptein. Leiden: KITLV Press, 2002. ISEAS, NLB, NUS.

131.   Ghazali Ismail. *Tempat Jatoh Lagi di-Kenang*. Singapore: Penerbit Riwayat, 1968. 105 pp. ISEAS, NLB, NUS.

132.   Gibson-Hill, Carl Alexander. "The Date of Munshi Abdullah's First Visit to Singapore". *JMBRAS* 28, pt. 1 (1955): 191–95. ISEAS, NLB, NTUNIE, NUS.

133.   Goh Kai Ling. "Saya Sesuai Bermain Perseorangan: Wawancara dengan Zarinah Abdullah, Jaguh Badminton Wanita". In *Meneroka Hidup Baru: Cerita Veteran Sukan,* penyunting Phoon Kwee Hian. Singapore: Candid Creation Publishing, 2005. NLB.

134.   Gordon, Alijah, ed. *The Real Cry of Syed Shaykh al-Hady*. Kuala Lumpur: Malaysia Sociological Research Institute, 1999. 369 pp. ISEAS, NLB, NTUNIE, NUS.

135.   Gordon, Alijah, ed. "Syed Alwi Al-Hady: Biographical Outline and Family Trees". In *The Real Cry of Syed Shaykh al-Hady*. Kuala Lumpur: Malaysia Sociological Research Institute, 1999. ISEAS, NLB, NTUNIE, NUS.

136.   Gwee, Monica. *Iskandar Ismail: The Music Man*. Singapore: Epigram Book, 2013. 126 pp. ISEAS, NLB, NTUNIE, NUS.

137.   "H.M. Rohaizad". In *Ensiklopedia Sejarah dan Kebudayaan Melayu*, vol. 2, p. 823. Kuala Lumpur: Dewan Bahasa dan Pustaka, 1995. NLB, NTUNIE, NUS.

138.   "Habib Noh". In *Ensiklopedia Sejarah dan Kebudayaan Melayu*, vol. 2, p. 824. Kuala Lumpur: Dewan Bahasa dan Pustaka, 1995. NLB, NTUNIE, NUS.

139.   Hadijah Rahmat, Mana Sikana, and Kartini Anwar, eds. *Citra Murni Insan dalam Dunia Pendidikan: Sebuah Feskrip untuk Abbas Mohammad*

Shariff. Penolong editor, Roszalina Rawi. Singapore: Institut Pendidikan Nasional Singapura, Universiti Teknologi Nanyang, 2011. 179 pp. NLB, NTUNIE.

140. Hadijah Rahmat, Mukhlis Abu Bakar, and Roksana Abdullah, eds. *Masuri S. N.: Sasterawan Melayu di Persada Dunia.* Singapore: National Institute of Education, 2011. 593 pp. NLB.

141. Hafiz Zakariya. "Sayyid Shaykh Ahmad Al-Hadi's Contributions to Islamic Reformism in Malaya". In *The Hadhrami Diaspora in Southeast Asia: Identity Maintenance or Assimilation?*, edited by Ibrahim Abushouk Ahmed and Hassan Ahmed Ibrahim. Leiden and Boston: Brill, 2009. ISEAS, NLB, NTUNIE, NUS.

142. "Hamzah Hussin". In *Ensiklopedia Sejarah dan Kebudayaan Melayu,* vol. 2, p. 847. Kuala Lumpur: Dewan Bahasa dan Pustaka, 1995. NLB, NTUNIE, NUS.

143. Hamzah Hussin. *Memoir Hamzah Hussin: dari Keris Filem ke Studio Merdeka.* Bangi: Universiti Kebangsaan Malaysia, 2004. 127 pp. ISEAS, NLB, NTUNIE, NUS.

144. Harding, James and Ahmad Sarji. *P. Ramlee: The Bright Star.* Petaling Jaya, Selangor: MPH, 2011. 280 pp. NLB, NUS.

145. "Harun Aminurrashid". In *Ensiklopedia Sejarah dan Kebudayaan Melayu,* vol. 2, p. 854. Kuala Lumpur: Dewan Bahasa dan Pustaka, 1995. NLB, NTUNIE, NUS.

146. "Hassan Bandung". In *Ensiklopedia Sejarah dan Kebudayaan Melayu,* vol. 2, p. 866. Kuala Lumpur: Dewan Bahasa dan Pustaka, 1995. NLB, NTUNIE, NUS.

147. "Haul Sheikh Omar Alkhatib". *Al-Mahjar: A Publication of the Arab Association of Singapore* 3, no. 2 (1998): 2. NLB.

148. Hidayah Amin. *Gedung Kuning: Memories of a Malay Childhood.* Singapore: Singapore Heritage Society and Helang Books, 2010. 227 pp. ISEAS, NLB, NTUNIE, NUS.

149. Hidayah Amin. "Haji Yusoff 'Tali Pinggang' — Patriarch of Gedung Kuning and Pioneering Malay Entreprenuer". *Karyawan: Professionals for the Community* 9, issue 2 (January 2009): 34–36. ISEAS, NLB, NTUNIE, NUS.

150.   Hidayah Amin. *The Mango Tree*, illustrated by Idris Ali. Singapore: Helang Books, 2013. 32 pp. NLB.

151.   Holmberg, Erik. "Sheikh Salim bin Mohamed bin Talib". In *Hadhrami Arabs Across the Indian Ocean: Contributions to Southeast Asian Economy and Society*, edited by Syed Farid Alatas. Singapore: National Library Board, 2010. ISEAS, NLB, NUS.

152.   Ibrahim Ahmad. "Harun Aminurrashid". *Pelita Bahasa* 2, no. 8 (August 1990): 40–41. NLB, NUS.

153.   Ibrahim Ariff and Andik Marinah Ibrahim. *The Past Malay Entreprenuers in Singapore*. Singapore: Daing Pasandri Achiever Avenue, 2015. 98 pp. NLB.

154.   *Ikon Wanita*. Penerbit, Brett Azeem Patterson; pengarah, Mohamad Sanif Olek; penulis skrip dan pengkaji, Noridah Kamari et al. Singapore: Mediacorp TV 12, 2003. 8 videocassettes. 192 min. NLB.
        (Documentary series that give insights into the lives of successful Malay/Muslim women of Singapore who have risen from their humble beginnings and defied stereotypes along the way).

155.   Ilya Romiza Hj. Suri. "Za'ba and His Ideas on Revival of Islam". In *Monograph on Selected Malay Intellectuals*, compiled by Mohamad @ Md. Som Sujimon. Kuala Lumpur: Research Centre, International Islamic University Malaysia, 2003. ISEAS, NLB, NUS.

156.   "Isa Kamari". *Dewan Sastera* (July 1999): 100. NLB, NUS.

157.   Ismail Hussein. "Post-War Malay Writers in Singapore". *The Malayan Undergrad* 11, no. 2 (November 1959): 6, 11; no. 3 (December 1959): 6–7. ISEAS, NUS.

158.   "Jahlelawati". In *Ensiklopedia Sejarah dan Kebudayaan Melayu*, vol. 2, pp. 1010–11. Kuala Lumpur: Dewan Bahasa dan Pustaka, 1995. NLB, NTUNIE, NUS.

159.   Jamilah Othman. "Sayyid Syakh al-Hadi: His Roles in the Transformation of Muslim Societies in Peninsular Malaya and the Straits Settlements during the Later Half of the Nineteenth & Early Twentieth Centuries". MA dissertation, Department of Malay Studies, National University of Singapore, 1986. 128 pp. NUS.

160. Johar Buang. *70 tahun Suratman Markasan*. Singapore: Haji Hashim, 2001. 463 pp. NLB.

161. "Johari Salleh". In *Ensiklopedia Sejarah dan Kebudayaan Melayu*, vol. 2, pp. 1044–45. Kuala Lumpur: Dewan Bahasa dan Pustaka, 1995. NLB, NTUNIE, NUS.

162. Johari Salleh. *Memoir Johari Salleh: Tegar Meladeni Industri Muzik*. Bangi, Selangor: Universiti Kebangsaan Malaysia, 2008. 465 pp. ISEAS, NLB.

163. Joseph, K.T. "Sultan Ali Iskandar Shah of Johore". *Malayan Historical Journal* 2, no. 2 (1955): 108–14. ISEAS, NLB, NUS.

164. Juffri Supa'at. "Sumbangsih MAS: An Exhibition on Muhammad Ariff Ahmad". *BiblioAsia* 9, no. 1 (April–June 2013): 44–47. NLB, NTUNIE, NUS.

165. Junaidah Ahmad Ghazali. "Liaw Yock Fang". *Pelita Bahasa* 9, no. 12 (December 1997): 57. NLB, NUS.

166. Junaidah Ahmad Ghazali. "Mahmud Ahmad". *Pelita Bahasa* 13, no. 9 (September 2001): 57. NLB, NUS.

167. Junaidah Ahmad Ghazali. "Muhammad Ariff Ahmad". *Pelita Bahasa* 14, no. 10 (October 2002): 59. NLB, NUS.

168. Kalam Hamidi. *Fatamorgana Kembara dari Nusantara ke Eropah*. Bangi: Universiti Kebangsaan Malaysia, 2003. 577 pp. ISEAS, NLB, NUS.

169. Kalam Hamidi. *Memoir Kalam Hamidi: dari Panggung Victoria ke Istana Budaya*. Bangi, Selangor: Universiti Kebangsaan Malaysia, 2001. 178 pp. ISEAS, NLB, NUS.

170. "Kalam Hamidi (1936–): Aktivis Pentas Singapura". In *Ensiklopedia Sejarah dan Kebudayaan Melayu*, vol. 2, p. 1071. Kuala Lumpur: Dewan Bahasa dan Pustaka, 1994. NLB, NTUNIE, NUS.

171. "Kamariah Noor". In *Ensiklopedia Sejarah dan Kebudayaan Melayu*, vol. 2, p. 1072. Kuala Lumpur: Dewan Bahasa dan Pustaka, 1995. NLB, NTUNIE, NUS.

172. "Kassim Masdor". In *Ensiklopedia Sejarah dan Kebudayaan Melayu*, vol. 2, p. 1111. Kuala Lumpur: Dewan Bahasa dan Pustaka, 1995. NLB, NTUNIE, NUS.

173.   "Keluarga Musik". *Mekar* (July 1980): 28–29, 31. NLB, NUS.
       (On Nona Asiah).

174.   Keris Mas. "A. Samad Ismail…Aku ini Binatang Jalang…Tak
       Mungkin Terbuang". *Dewan Sastera* 17, no. 9 (September 1987): 42–44.
       NLB, NUS.

175.   Keris Mas. "A. Samad Ismail: Pemikir yang Tajam, Tokoh Politik yang
       Dinamik". *Dewan Sastera* 17, no. 9 (September 1987): 48–49. NLB,
       NTUNIE, NUS.

176.   Knehtl, Irena. "Ms Zahra Al-Junied, Senior Librarian & Exhibition
       Coordinator on Hadhrami Diaspora in Singapore". *Yemen Post*. Available
       at <http://www.yemenpost.net/Detail123456789.aspx?ID=3&SubID=
       460%MainCat=4>.

177.   Koh, Cindy. "Encik Sarkasi". *Petir: Organ of the People's Action Party*
       (November 1989): 39–41. ISEAS, NLB, NTUNIE, NUS.
       (On Sarkasi Said).

178.   Kon, Stella. *President Yusof bin Ishak and the Portrait Notes*. Singapore:
       SNP Pub., 1999. 85 pp. NLB.

179.   Kwa Chong Guan. "Cresent and 'Hammer and Sickles' in Malaysia:
       The Case of Samad Ismail". MA dissertation, University of Kent at
       Canterbury, 1978. 81 pp. NUS.

180.   "Leftenan Muda Adnan Saidi". In *Ensiklopedia Sejarah dan Kebudayaan
       Melayu*, vol. 2, pp. 1338–39. Kuala Lumpur: Dewan Bahasa dan Pustaka,
       1995. NLB, NTUNIE, NUS.

181.   Leong, Stephen. "The Malay Women Entrepreneur of the Year". *The
       Veteran* 6 (August 2000): 192–93. NLB.
       (On Nooraini Nordin).

182.   *Living the Singapore History: Celebrating Our 50 Years: 1965–2015*.
       Singapore: National Library Board, 2015. ISEAS, NLB.

183.   Lopez, Bruno. "Yusof bin Ishak: Journalist and Head of State". Academic
       exercise, National University of Singapore, 1988. 101 pp. NUS.

184.   Low, Sylvia. "Dance Stalwart Madam Som Said". *Instep NAC and the Arts*
       (May/June 2006): 7. NLB.

185.   *Majulah! The Film Music of Zubir Said*. Singapore: National Museum of
       Singapore, 2012. 111 pp. NLB.

186. "Maliki Osman: The Science of Connecting — Conversation". *Petir: Organ of the People's Action Party* (October 2013): 15–17. ISEAS, NLB, NTUNIE, NUS.

187. "Maria Menado". In *Ensiklopedia Sejarah dan Kebudayaan Melayu*, vol. 3, p. 1463. Kuala Lumpur: Dewan Bahasa dan Pustaka, 1998. NLB, NTUNIE, NUS.

188. "Mariam Rahim". In *Ensiklopedia Sejarah dan Kebudayaan Melayu*, vol. 3, p. 1464. Kuala Lumpur: Dewan Bahasa dan Pustaka, 1998. NLB, NTUNIE, NUS.
    (On seniwati Mariam).

189. Marina Marican. "Sayed Shaikh al-Hadi dan Pendapat2nya mengenai Kemajuan Kaum Perempuan Sebagai Tersiar dalam Majalah Al-Ikhwan". Academic exercise, Universiti Malaya, 1960. 1 microfilm reel. NUS.

190. "MAS". In *Ensiklopedia Sejarah dan Kebudayaan Melayu*, vol. 3, p. 1466. Kuala Lumpur: Dewan Bahasa dan Pustaka, 1998. NLB, NTUNIE, NUS.
    (On Muhammad Ariff Ahmad).

191. "Masuri S. N.". In *Ensiklopedia Sejarah dan Kebudayaan Melayu*, vol. 3, p. 1475. Kuala Lumpur: Dewan Bahasa dan Pustaka, 1998. NLB, NTUNIE, NUS.

192. Mazelan Anuar. "Mohamed Eunos Abdullah: The Father of Malay Journalism". *BiblioAsia* 11, no. 2 (July–September 2015): 32–35. ISEAS, NLB, NTU, NTUNIE, NUS.

193. Mazlan Ibrahim, Jawiah Dakir, and Muhd. Najib Abdul Kadir. "Tafsir 'Abr Al-Athir: Ahmad Sonhadji Mohamad Milatu". In *Pengenalan Tokoh-Tokoh dan Kitab Tafsir Melayu Ulama Nusantara*. Bangi, Selangor: Universiti Kebangsaan Malaysia, 2013. NLB.

194. Mazlan Nordin. *Tokoh dan Akhbar Melayu: Penebus Peminggiran Melayu*. Bangi, Selangor: Universiti Kebangsaan Malaysia, 2009. 106 pp. ISEAS, NLB, NUS.

195. Md. Said A. Hadi. *28 Tokoh-tokoh Islam yang Terkemuka*. Johor Baru: Jabatan Agama Johor, 1977. 400 pp. ISEAS, NLB.
    (Bab no. 13: Fadhlullah Suhaimi).

196.   Melan Abdullah. "Samad in Love and War". In *A. Samad Ismail: Journalism & Politics,* compiled and edited by Cheah Boon Kheng. Kuala Kumpur: Utusan Publications, 2000. ISEAS, NLB, NTU, NTUNIE.

197.   "Mengenal Pengasas Madrasah Al-Maarif Al-Islamiah". In *Inspiration: Madrasah Al-Maarif Al-Islamiah 50th Anniversary and Official Opening Ceremony, 15th March 1987.* Singapore: Madrasah Al-Maarif Al-Islamiah, 1987. NLB, NUS.

198.   Mohamad Ghouse Khan Suratee, ed. *The Grand Saint of Singapore: The Life of Habib Nuh Bin Muhammad Al-Habshi.* Singapore: Masjid Al Firdaus, 2008. 63 pp. NLB, NUS. Also published in Malay under the title: *Lambang Terukir: dalam Mengisahkan Manaqib Habib Noh bin Muhamad Alhabsyi yang Syahir.* Susunan Unit Dakwah Masjid Al Firdaus. Singapore: Masjid Al Firdaus, 2010. 81 pp. NLB, NUS.

199.   Mohamad Saleeh Rahamad. *Ahmad Mahmood: Bintang di Langit Seni.* Ampang, Selangor: Perbadanan Kemajuan Filem Nasional Malaysia, 2010. 148 pp. ISEAS, NLB.

200.   Mohamed Fazil Aris. "Masuri S.N.: Karya dan Falsafah Kesusasteraan". Academic exercise, Department of Malay Studies, National University of Singapore, 1994. 55 pp. NUS.

201.   "Mohamed Latiff Mohamed". In *Ensiklopedia Sejarah dan Kebudayaan Melayu,* vol. 3, p. 1544. Kuala Lumpur: Dewan Bahasa dan Pustaka, 1998. NLB, NTUNIE, NUS.

202.   Mohamed Pitchay Gani Mohamed Abdul Aziz, ed. *Dari Gerhana ke Puncak Purnama: Biografi Asas '50: 55 Tahun dalam Persuratan.* Singapore: Angkatan Sasterawan '50, 2005. 322 pp. NLB, NTUNIE, NUS.

203.   Mohamed Pitchay Gani Mohamed Abdul Aziz, ed. *Leksikon: Direktori Penulis Melayu Singapura, Pasca 1965.* Singapore: Angkatan Sasterawan '50: National Library Board, 2005. 216 pp. NLB, NTUNIE, NUS.

204.   Mohamed Pitchay Gani Mohamed Abdul Aziz. "Portrait of Poetry in Art". *BiblioAsia* 2, no. 3 (October 2006): 16–19. NLB, NTUNIE, NUS.
        (On A. Ghani Hamid).

205.   Mohd Asa'ad Mohd Arshad, comp. *Mutiara Keluarga Haji Mohd. Arshad Haji Mahmood (Al-Arham): Senarai Nama-nama Keluarga Kita di*

Singapura, Malaysia dan Indonesia, edited by Hj Mohd Gazali Hj Mohd Arshad. Singapore: [s.n.]. 2004. 49 pp. NLB.

206. "Mohd. Eunos Abdullah". In *Ensiklopedia Sejarah dan Kebudayaan Melayu*, vol. 3, p. 1555. Kuala Lumpur: Dewan Bahasa dan Pustaka, 1998. NLB, NTUNIE, NUS.

207. Mohd. Naim Daipi. "Sedikit tentang Harun Aminurrashid: Cikgu Harun Guruku". *Sasterawan* 2 (July 1980): 23–28. NLB.

208. Mohd Shukri Mohd Arif. "Saya Memperjuangkan Hak dan Kebenaran". *Dewan Masyarakat* 43, no. 11 (November 2005): 22–23. ISEAS, NLB, NTUNIE, NUS.
(On A. Samad Ismail).

209. Mohd. Taha Suhaimi, Ustaz Haji, comp. *Sejarah Hidup Syeikh Muhammad Suhaimi*. Singapore: PERPENSIS, 1994. 116 pp. NLB.

210. "Mohd. Taib Osman". In *Ensiklopedia Sejarah dan Kebudayaan Melayu*, vol. 3, p. 1564. Kuala Lumpur: Dewan Bahasa dan Pustaka, 1998. NLB, NTUNIE, NUS.

211. Mohd. Zamberi A. Malek. *Suria Kencana: Biografi Jins Shamsudin*. Bangi, Selangor: Universiti Kebangsaan Malaysia, 1998. 357 pp. ISEAS, NLB, NUS.

212. Mohd. Zamberi A. Malek. *Jins Shamsudin: Kembara Seorang Seniman*. Ampang, Selangor: Perbadanan Kemajuan Filem Nasional Malaysia, 2007. 299 pp. ISEAS NLB, NUS.

213. "Monuments: The Alsagoff Family". *Treasures of Time* (December–January 2003): 10–13. NLB, NTUNIE.

214. "Muhammad Ariff Ahmad, Cultural Medallion Recipient, 1987, Literature". Produced by the National Library Board Singapore, in collaboration with the National Arts Council Singapore. 2010. 1 videodisc. 20 min. NLB.

215. Muhammad Ariff Ahmad. *Perjalanan Mas: Memoir Muhammad Ariff Ahmad*. Disunting oleh Mohd. Raman Daud. Singapore: Angkatan Sasterawan '50, 2003. 208 pp. NLB, NTUNIE, NUS.

216. Muhammad Hasanyn. *Di Kampung, di Kota*. Singapore: Muslimmedia Bookshop, 2007. 127 pp. NLB, NTUNIE.

217.   Muhammad Mubarak Habib Mohamed. "The Role of Syed Ahmad Bin Muhammad Semait in Disseminating Islamic Teachings in Modern Singapore: His Approach and Methodology". MA dissertation, International Islamic University, Malaysia, 2013. 105 pp.

218.   "Munsyi Muhammad Said Dada Muhyiddin". In *Ensiklopedia Sejarah dan Kebudayaan Melayu*, vol. 3, p. 1590. Kuala Lumpur: Dewan Bahasa dan Pustaka, 1998. NLB, NTUNIE, NUS.
(Writer of Sekola Melayu).

219.   Mustafa Abdullah. "Khazanah Tafsir di Nusantara: Penelitian Terhadap Tokoh-Tokoh dan Karya Tafsir di Malaysia, Singapura, Thailand dan Brunei Darus Salam". In *International Seminar on Research in Islamic Studies: Addressing Contemporary Challenges & Future Prospects*, vol. 2. (On Ustaz Ahmad Sonhadji Mohamad).

220.   *National Directory of Scholars: Humanities and Social Sciences Research*. Singapore: National Library Board, 2007. 600 pp. ISEAS, NLB, NTUNIE, NUS.

221.   Ng Lai Lian. "Bertolak Semula dari Dasar Lembah: Wawancara dengan Azman Abdullah, Bekas Juara Bina Badan Dunia". In *Meneroka Hidup Baru: Cerita Veteran Sukan*, penyunting Phoon Kwee Hian. Singapore: Candid Creation Publishing, 2005. NLB, NTUNIE.

222.   Ng Lai Lian. "Hidup untuk Bola Sepak: Wawancara dengan Fandi Ahmad, Wira Veteran Bola Sepak Melayu". In *Meneroka Hidup Baru: Cerita Veteran Sukan*, penyunting Phoon Kwee Hian. Singapore: Candid Creation Publishing, 2005. NLB, NTUNIE.

223.   Ng Lai Lian. "Kuat Menghentam Berani Mencinta: Wawancara dengan Saiedah Bte Said, Srikandi Silat Melayu". In *Di Sebalik Kilauan Emas: Cerita Bintang Sukan Singapura*, penyunting Chan Meow Wah. Singapore: Candid Creation Publishing, 2005. NLB.

224.   Ni'mah Ismail. *Fadhlullah Suhaimi*. Susunan Mustaffa Suhaimi. Ulu Kelang, Selangor: Progressive Publishing, 1998. 229 pp. NLB.
(On Kiayi Fadhlullah Suhaimi, ulama and founder of Madrasah Al-Maarif Al-Islamiah).

225.   "Noor S. I. (Ismail Haji Omar, 1933–1990): Penyair Singapura". In *Ensiklopedia Sejarah dan Kebudayaan Melayu*, vol. 3, pp. 1630–31. Kuala Lumpu: Dewan Bahasa dan Pustaka, 1994. NLB, NTUNIE, NUS.

226. Norman Suratman. *Menyongsong Arus: Biografi Ustaz Ahmed Sonhadji Mohamad*. Singapore: Pustaka ASB, 1997. 201 pp. NLB.

227. Norshahril Saat. *Yusof Ishak: Singapore's First President*. Singapore: Institute of Southeast Asian Studies, 2015. 120 pp. ISEAS, NLB, NTUNIE, NUS.

228. Oehler, Shirley. "Abdullah Tarmugi". *Petir: Organ of the People's Action Party* (January/February 2002): 24. NLB.

229. Osman Jantan. "Jasawan Pendidik yang Gigih Syed Abu Bakar bin Taha Alsagoff". *Fajar Islam* 1, no. 1 (1974): 51–54. ISEAS, NLB, NUS.

230. Othman Puteh. "Pengkritik pada Era ASAS 50 (Bahagian Akhir)". *Dewan Sastera* (August 1999): 63–64. NLB, NUS.
     (On Hamzah Hussin).

231. "Othman Wok". In *Ensiklopedia Sejarah dan Kebudayaan Melayu*, vol. 3, p. 1680. Kuala Lumpur: Dewan Bahasa dan Pustaka, 1998. NLB, NTUNIE, NUS.

232. Othman Wok. "Bila Yusuf Marah Utusan Melayu Senyap Sunyi". In *Di Sebalik Jendela Utusan: Suara Keramat Ulang Tahun yang ke 50, 1939–1989*. Kuala Lumpur: Utusan Melayu Berhad, 1989. ISEAS, NLB, NUS.
     (On Yusof Ishak).

233. Othman Wok. *Never in My Wildest Dream*. Singapore: Raffles, 2000. 233 pp. ISEAS, NLB, NTUNIE, NUS.

234. "Othman Wok: An Architect of the Multi-Racial Concept". *Petir: Organ of the People's Action Party* 9 (May 1981): 42–47. ISEAS, NLB, NTUNIE, NUS. Also published in Malay under the title: "Othman Wok: Salah Seorang Pelopor Konsep Masyarakat Berbilang Bangsa". *Petir: Organ of the People's Action Party* 5 (June 1981): 36–41. ISEAS, NLB, NTUNIE, NUS.

235. "P. Ramlee". In *Ensiklopedia Sejarah dan Kebudayaan Melayu*, vol. 3, p. 1683. Kuala Lumpur: Dewan Bahasa dan Pustaka, 1998. NLB, NTUNIE, NUS.

236. Pearson, H.F. "Syed Omar bin Ali Al-Junied: Merchant". In *People of Early Singapore*. London: University of London Press, 1955. NLB, NTUNIE, NUS.

237.   *Perintisku, Singapuraku.* Singapore: Berita Harian, Singapore Press Holdings, 2015. 143 pp. NLB.

238.   Qiao Bo. "Silat Membawakannya Senyum Terceria: Wawancara dengan Saifuddin, Jaguh Muda Silat Melayu". In *Cerita Tunas Sukan Singapura dan Perspektif Sukan Singapura*, penyunting Phoo Kwee Hian. Singapore: Candid Creation Publishing, 2006. NLB.

239.   "R. Azmi". In *Ensiklopedia Sejarah dan Kebudayaan Melayu*, vol. 4, p. 2008. Kuala Lumpur: Dewan Bahasa dan Pustaka, 1999. NLB, NTUNIE, NUS.

240.   "R. Ismail". In *Ensiklopedia Sejarah dan Kebudayaan Melayu*, vol. 4, pp. 2008–9. Kuala Lumpur: Dewan Bahasa dan Pustaka, 1999. NLB, NTUNIE, NUS.

241.   Radzi Sapiee. *Jejak Keluarga Yakin: Satu Sketsa Sejarah.* Kajang, Selangor: Wasilah Merah Silu Enterprise, 2011. 240 pp. NLB.

242.   "Rafeah Buang". In *Ensiklopedia Sejarah dan Kebudayaan Melayu*, vol. 4, pp. 2011–12. Kuala Lumpur: Dewan Bahasa dan Pustaka, 1999. NLB, NTUNIE, NUS.

243.   Raja Yusuf Arifin. "Yusnor Ef Seniman Versatil". *Dewan Budaya*, no. 9 (September 2007): 24–25. NLB, NTUNIE, NUS.

244.   Raja Zainal Abidin Zahid. "Malay Personal Names: Singapore, 1872–1883 and 1951–1955". Academic exercise, Department of Malay Studies, University of Malaya, 1957. 42 pp. NUS.

245.   Ramlee Ismail. *Kenangan Abadi P. Ramlee.* Kuala Lumpur: Adhicipta, 1988. 230 pp. ISEAS, NLB, NUS.

246.   Ramli Sarip. "Hilang Budaya Rapuh Agama". *Dewan Budaya*, no. 4 (April 2007): 50–52. NLB, NTUNIE, NUS.

247.   Ramli Sarip. "Ramadan Pergi Pusara Menanti". *Dewan Budaya*, no. 1 (January 2007): 49–51. NLB, NTUNIE, NUS.

248.   Ramli Sarip. "Rock Bukan Sekadar Laungan Suara: Bidang Seni Tiada Garis Terakhir". *Dewan Budaya*, no. 11 (November 2004): 8–9. NLB, NTUNIE, NUS.

249.   Rashidah Ismail. *Memoir Rashidah Ismail: Pendeta Za'ba dan Kisah Silam.* Bangi, Selangor: Penerbit Universiti Kebangsaan Malaysia, 2009. 333 pp. ISEAS, NLB.

250. *Recollections: People and Places.* Singapore: Oral History Department, 1990. 58 pp. ISEAS, NLB, NTUNIE, NUS.

251. Rohana Zubir. *Zubir Said: The Composer of Majulah Singapura.* Singapore: Institute of Southeast Asian Studies, 2012. 279 pp. ISEAS, NLB, NTUNIE, NUS.

252. "Rokiah Wanda". In *Ensiklopedia Sejarah dan Kebudayaan Melayu*, vol. 4, p. 2063. Kuala Lumpur: Dewan Bahasa dan Pustaka, 1999. NLB, NTUNIE, NUS.

253. *Romantika Pujangga R. Ismail: Biografi & MTV Karaoke.* Penerbit album, Baharudin Ismail. Singapore: Life Record Industries, 2006. 1 videodisc. 50 min. NLB.

254. "Rosiah Chik". In *Ensiklopedia Sejarah dan Kebudayaan Melayu*, vol. 4, p. 2063. Kuala Lumpur: Dewan Bahasa dan Pustaka, 1999. NLB, NTUNIE, NUS.

255. Rosnah Baharudin. *Biografi A. Samad Said: Memberi Hati Nurani.* Kuala Lumpur: Institut Terjemahan & Buku Malaysia Berhad, 2012. 395 pp. NLB.

256. Rosnani Hashim. "Munshi Abdullah, an Early Critic of Malay Language, Culture, and Society". In *Reclaiming the Conversation: Islamic Intellectual Tradition in the Malay Archipelago*, edited by Rosnani Hashim. Kuala Lumpur: The Other Press, 2010. NLB, NTUNIE, NUS.

257. Rosnani Hashim. "Pendeta Za'ba, Education for the Upliftment of the Malays". In *Reclaiming the Conversation: Islamic Intellectual Tradition in the Malay Archipelago*, edited by Rosnani Hashim. Kuala Lumpur: The Other Press, 2010. NLB, NTUNIE, NUS.

258. S. Markasan (Suratman Markasan). "Lima Penulis Cerpen Produktif Singapura Dewasa ini". Kertas kerja yang dibentang dalam Pertemuan Penulis Singapura IV, 23–24 September 1989. NUS.

259. "S. Sudarmaji". In *Ensiklopedia Sejarah dan Kebudayaan Melayu*, vol. 4, p. 2082. Kuala Lumpur: Dewan Bahasa dan Pustaka, 1999. NLB, NTUNIE, NUS.

260. "Saadiah". In *Ensiklopedia Sejarah dan Kebudayaan Melayu*, vol. 4, p. 2063. Kuala Lumpur: Dewan Bahasa dan Pustaka, 1999. NLB, NTUNIE, NUS.
(On Saadiah, an actress).

261.   Saadiah Said. "Penglibatan Keluarga Alsagoff dalam Ekonomi Johor, 1876–1926". *Jauhar: Jurnal Sejarah Johor* 2 (1983): 5–60. NUS.

262.   "Said Zahari". In *Ensiklopedia Sejarah dan Kebudayaan Melayu*, vol. 4, p. 2094. Kuala Lumpur: Dewan Bahasa dan Pustaka, 1999. NLB, NTUNIE, NUS.

263.   Said Zahari. *Dalam Ribuan Mimpi Gelisah: Memoir*. Kuala Lumpur: Utusan Publications & Distributors, 2006. 290 pp. ISEAS, NLB, NUS.

264.   Said Zahari. *Dark Clouds at Dawn: A Political Memoir*. Kuala Lumpur: Insan, 2001. ISEAS, NLB, NUS.

265.   Said Zahari. *The Long Nightmare: My 17 Years as a Political Prisoner*. Kuala Lumpur: Utusan Publications & Distributors, 2007. 186 pp. ISEAS, NLB.

266.   Said Zahari. *Meniti Lautan Gelora: Sebuah Memoir Politik*. Kuala Lumpur: Utusan Publications, Universiti Kebangsaan Malaysia, 2001. 374 pp. ISEAS, NLB, NUS.

267.   Saleha Salleh. "The Many Old Faces of Jorah". *Citizen* 8, no. 9 (1 May 1979): 11–13. NLB.
       (On Jorah Ahmad, a dramatist).

268.   Saleha Salleh. "'Pak Long' an Old Bangsawan Actor". *Citizen* 7, no. 17 (1 September 1978): 16. NLB.
       (On Haji Shariff Medan).

269.   "Salleh Kamil". In *Ensiklopedia Sejarah dan Kebudayaan Melayu*, vol. 4, pp. 2106–7. Kuala Lumpur: Dewan Bahasa dan Pustaka, 1999. NLB, NTUNIE, NUS.

270.   "Salmi Manja". In *Ensiklopedia Sejarah dan Kebudayaan Melayu*, vol. 4, p. 2109. Kuala Lumpur: Dewan Bahasa dan Pustaka, 1999. NLB, NTUNIE, NUS.

271.   Salmiah Ismail. "Noor S.I.". *Dewan Sastera* 26, no. 7 (July 1986): 29–31. NLB, NTUNIE, NUS.

272.   "Saloma". In *Ensiklopedia Sejarah dan Kebudayaan Melayu*, vol. 4, p. 2110. Kuala Lumpur: Dewan Bahasa dan Pustaka, 1999. NLB, NTUNIE, NUS.

273. "Sang Nila Utama (??–1348): Raja Pertama Kerajaan Temasik". In *Ensiklopedia Sejarah dan Kebudayaan Melayu*, vol. 4, p. 2114. Kuala Lumpur: Dewan Bahasa dan Pustaka, 1999. NLB, NTUNIE, NUS.

274. "Sayyid Abu Bakar Abdullah". In *Ensiklopedia Sejarah dan Kebudayaan Melayu*, vol. 4, p. 2152. Kuala Lumpur: Dewan Bahasa dan Pustaka, 1999. NLB, NTUNIE, NUS.

275. "Secebis Riwayat Hidup Mudir Kedua 1951–1962: Assaiyid Abdullah bin Sheikh bin Muhammad Balfaqih". In *Perayaan Jubli Emas Sekolah Ugama Aljunied (1927–1977): Cenderamata*. Singapore: Madrasah Al-Junied, 1977. NLB.

276. "Segelintir Kisah Hidup Mudir Pertama, 1927–1951: Assaiyyid Abu Bakar bin Taha bin Abdul Kadir". In *Perayaan Jubli Emas Sekolah Ugama Aljunied (1927–1977): Cenderamata*. Singapore: Madrasah Al-Junied, 1977. NLB.

277. "Selingkar Kisah Hidup Mudir Ketiga 1963–1967: Assaiyyid Muhammad bin Alwi Alidrus". In *Perayaan Jubli Emas Sekolah Ugama Aljunied (1927–1977): Cenderamata*. Singapore: Madrasah Al-Junied, 1977. NLB.

278. "Seorang Pemimpin yang Tak Terkenal dan Beberapa Keistimewaanya". *Mastika Keluaran Istimewa Merdeka* (Ogos 1957): 102–3, 106. NLB. (On Ahmad Ibrahim, a politician and Member of Parliament in 1960s).

279. "Seorang Usahawan yang Berjaya — Mohamed Salleh Marican". *Citizen* (June 1991): 11. NLB.

280. Sevea, Terenjit. "Empire in the Service of Ecstatic Islam: A Majzub in Colonial Singapore". In *Hadhrami Arabs Across the Indian Ocean: Contributions to Southeast Asian Economy and Society*, edited by Syed Farid Alatas. Singapore: National Library Board, 2010. 96 pp. ISEAS, NLB, NUS.

281. "7 Magnificient Composers = 7 Tokoh Musik". Penyunting, Mohd Raman Daud. Singapore: PERKAMUS, 2002. 211 pp. NLB, NTUNIE.

282. Shamsuddin Jaafar, comp. *Wajah: Biografi Penulis*. Kuala Lumpur: Dewan Bahasa dan Pustaka, 2005. 796 pp. ISEAS, NLB, NTUNIE, NUS.

283. "Sharif Medan". In *Ensiklopedia Sejarah dan Kebudayaan Melayu*, vol. 4, p. 2221. Kuala Lumpur: Dewan Bahasa dan Pustaka, 1999. NLB, NTUNIE, NUS.

284. "Sharifah Aini". In *Ensiklopedia Sejarah dan Kebudayaan Melayu*, vol. 4, p. 2220. Kuala Lumpur: Dewan Bahasa dan Pustaka, 1999. NLB, NTUNIE, NUS.

285. Sharifah Hamzah. *Kampung Memories: A Life's Journey, Revisited.* Singapore: Sharifah Hamzah, 2011. 153 pp. ISEAS, NLB, NUS.

286. "Siput Sarawak". In *Ensiklopedia Sejarah dan Kebudayaan Melayu*, vol. 4, p. 2238. Kuala Lumpur: Dewan Bahasa dan Pustaka, 1999. NLB, NTUNIE, NUS.

287. Siti Noorasikin Tumiran, Ezad Azraai Jamsari, and Kaseh Abu Bakar. "Personaliti Termasyhur Singapura: Syed Mohamed bin Ahmed Alsagoff". In *Prosiding Nadwah Ulama Nusantara (NUN) IV, 25–26 November 2011.* Bangi, Selangor: Universiti Kebangsaan Malaysia, 2011. (On ulama and founder of Madrasah Alsagoff Al-Arabiah).

288. "Siti Tanjong Perak". In *Ensiklopedia Sejarah dan Kebudayaan Melayu*, vol. 4, p. 2251. Kuala Lumpur: Dewan Bahasa dan Pustaka, 1999. NLB, NTUNIE, NUS.

289. Skinner, C. "Transitional Malay Literature. Part 1, Ahmad Rijaluddin and Munshi Abdullah". *Bijdragen Tot De Taal-, Land- En Volkenkunde* 134, no. 4 (1978): 466–87. ISEAS, NUS.

290. Sudar Majid. "The Malay Artist". *Singapore Artist* 1, no. 2 (December 1954): 3–9. NLB, NUS.

291. Suhaimi Haji Muhammad. "Kembalinya Seorang Penulis dan Nasionalis Tulen: Harun Aminurashid, 1907–1986". *Dewan Sastera* 16, no. 12 (December 1986): 50–51. NLB, NTUNIE, NUS.

292. "Sukar Surif: Photographer, Artist". *Intisari* 2, no. 3 (1968): 7–8. ISEAS, NLB, NUS.

293. Sulaiman Jeem. *Kembara Hidup: Sebuah Memoir.* Singapore: Penerbitan Wisma, 2008. 116 pp. NLB.

294. Sulaiman Jeem and Abdul Ghani Hamid, eds. *Aktivis Melayu/Islam di Singapura.* Singapore: Persatuan Wartawan Melayu Singapura, 1997. 466 pp. ISEAS, NLB, NTUNIE, NUS.

295. Sulaiman Jeem and Abdul Ghani Hamid. *Mengenang Pak Zubir.* Singapore: Pustaka Melayu, 1988. 188 pp. ISEAS, NLB, NTUNIE, NUS.

296. Sulaiman Jeem and Abdul Ghani Hamid. *Ya'acob Mohamed: (dalam API, PKMM, UMNO, PAP)*. Singapore: Penerbitan Wisma, 1990. 280 pp. ISEAS, NLB, NUS.

297. Sundusia Rosdi. "Harun Aminurrashid". *BiblioAsia* 3, no. 2 (July 2007): 4–10. NLB, NUS.

298. Sundusia Rosdi. "Harun Aminurrashid (Tuan Haji Harun Bin Haji Mohd Amin)". In *Sastera & Sasterawan*, edited by Khoo Kay Kim and Mohd Fadzil Othman. Kuala Lumpur: Persatuan Sejarah Malaysia, 1984. ISEAS, NLB, NUS.

299. Sundusia Rosdi, comp. *Obor Ummah: Jejak Tokoh Agama Islam di Singapura, Siri 2*. Singapore: Persatuan Ulama dan Guru-guru Agama Singapura, 2014. 154 pp. ISEAS, NLB.

300. Sundusia Rosdi. "Sumbangan Cendekiawan Peranakan Arab dalam Persuratan Melayu". *BiblioAsia* 5, no. 4 (January 2010): 4–9. NLB, NTUNIE, NUS.

301. "Suratman Markasan". In *Ensiklopedia Sejarah dan Kebudayaan Melayu*, vol. 4, p. 2238. Kuala Lumpur: Dewan Bahasa dan Pustaka, 1999. NLB, NTUNIE, NUS.

302. Suryahti A. Latiff. "Making a Mark". *Karyawan: Professionals for the Community* (March 1995): 12–13. ISEAS, NLB, NTUNIE, NUS. (On Rahim Leyman).

303. Suryahti A. Latiff. "Young and Confident". *Karyawan: Professionals for the Community* (December 1994): 12–13. ISEAS, NLB, NTUNIE, NUS. (On Roslima Saad and Saifuddin Sidek).

304. Syed Zakir Hussain. *Keeping the Faith: Syed Isa Semait Mufti of Singapore 1972–2010*. Singapore: Straits Times Press, 2012. 199 pp. ISEAS, NLB, NUS.

305. Syed Zakir Hussain. *The Next Wave: 25 Stories of Excellence*. Singapore: Yayasan MENDAKI, 2007. 99 pp. NLB.

306. Tan, Linda. "Syed Shaykh: His Life and Times". In *The Real Cry of Syed Shaykh Al-Hady*, edited by Alijah Gordon. Kuala Lumpur: Malaysia Sociological Research Institute, 1999. 369 pp. ISEAS, NLB, NUS.

307. Tan S.H. "The Life and Times of Sayyid Shaykh Al-Hadi". Academic exercise, University of Malaya, Singapore, 1961. 133 pp. NUS.

308. Trail, H.F. "An Indian Protagonist of the Malay Language: Abdullah Munshi: His Race and His Mother Tongue". *JMBRAS* 52, no. 2 (1979): 67–83. ISEAS, NLB, NTUNIE, NUS.

309. Trekker, Pat. "The Arab Pioneers of Singapore". *Beam* (November 1995): 10–11. NLB, NUS.

310. "Tribute to Haji Yaacob Mohamed". *Petir: Organ of the People's Action Party* (October 1982): 36. ISEAS, NLB, NTUNIE, NUS. Also published in Malay under the title: "Tanda Penghormatan Buat Haji Yaacob Mohamed". *Petir: Organ of the People's Action Party* (October 1989): 37. ISEAS, NLB, NTUNIE, NUS.

311. Tuminah Sapawi. "The Write Way". *Arts Magazine* (September/October 1998): 32–33. NLB, NUS.
     (On Hadijah Rahmat).

312. "Wahid Satay". In *Ensiklopedia Sejarah dan Kebudayaan Melayu*, vol. 4, p. 2574. Kuala Lumpur: Dewan Bahasa dan Pustaka, 1999. NLB, NTUNIE, NUS.

313. *Wajah Pendatang*. Penerbit, Mohamad Sanif Olek, Mufreha Hj Maarof, Muhamad Yusoff Ahmad; pengarah, Wahida Wahid, Communication 2000. Singapore: MediaCorp TV12, 1998. 8 videocassettes. 200 min. NLB.
     (Orang Minangkabau, Jawa, Bawean dan Bugis).

314. *Wajah-Wajah Perintis*. Penerbit Eksekutif, Yusuf Ismail, Mohd. Yusoff Ahmad, MYI International Communication 2000; penulis skrip, Yusnor Ef, Mohd Raman Daud, Julina Khusaini. Singapore: MediaCorp TV 12 Suria, 1999. 3 videocassettes. 75 min. NLB.
     (On Ambo Sooloh, Syed Omar Ali and Mohd. Javad Namazie).

315. "Waliullah: Habib Noh". *Inabah* 13, no. 6 (May 2002): 109–10. NLB.

316. Wan Hussin Zoohri. *Memories and Musings*. Singapore: Wan Hussin Zoohri, 2015. 276 pp. NLB.

317. Wan Hussin Zoohri and Harun A. Ghani. "An Interview with Dr. Haji Yaacob Mohamed: Recipe for Racial Harmony". *Petir: Organ of the People's Action Party* 10 (September 1981): 36–39. ISEAS, NLB, NTUNIE, NUS.

318. Wan Hussin Zoohri and Harun A. Ghani. "An Interview with Mr Masuri S.N.: Poet Masuri on Our Cultural Development". *Petir: Organ of the*

People's Action Party 12 (March 1982): 37–40. ISEAS, NLB, NTUNIE, NUS. Also published in Malay under the title: "Wawancara dengan Cikgu Masuri S.N., BBM: Penyair Ulung Kita". *Petir: Organ of the People's Action Party* 8 (March 1982): 33–37. ISEAS, NLB, NTUNIE, NUS.

319. Wan Hussin Zoohri and Harun A. Ghani. "An Interview with Rahmat Kenap: Common Interest, Not Communal Intrigue". *Petir: Organ of the People's Action Party* 10 (September 1981): 44–49. ISEAS, NLB, NTUNIE, NUS. Also published in Malay under the title: "Wawancara [dengan] Hj. Rahmat Kenap: Kepentingan Bersama, Bukan Muslihat Perkauman". *Petir: Organ of the People's Action Party* 6 (October 1981): 32–37. ISEAS, NLB, NTUNIE, NUS.

320. "When Duty Calls, You Just Do It: Madam Halimah Yacob as a Speaker of Parliament — Conversation". *Petir: Organ of the People's Action Party* (April 2013): 15–17. ISEAS, NLB, NTUNIE, NUS.

321. *Who's Who in Malaya.* Singapore: Dorset & Co., 1918–1939. NLB.

322. *Who's Who in Malaya 1925: A Biographical Record of Prominent Members of Malaya's Community in Official, Professional and Commercial Circles.* Singapore: Julius S. Fisher, 1925. 1 microfilm reel. ISEAS.

323. *Who's Who in Malaya, 1939: A Biographical Record of Prominent Members of Malaya's Community in Official, Professional and Commercial Circles.* Singapore: Fishers Ltd. 1939. 148 pp. ISEAS.

324. *Who's Who in Malaya & Malayan Year Book 1947–1948.* Kuala Lumpur: Das & Sons, [1949?]. 340 pp. NLB, NUS.

325. *Who's Who in Malaysia.* Kuala Lumpur: Solai Press, 1956–1967. ISEAS (1959/60), NLB, NUS.
(Published in 1956–60 under the title: *Leaders of Malaya and Who's Who.* Continued by *Who's Who, Malaysia and Singapore*).

326. *Who's Who in Malaysia... & Profiles of Singapore 1982.* Kuala Lumpur: Who's Who Publications, 1981. ISEAS, NTUNIE, NUS. Continued by *Who's Who in Malaysia & Singapore.*

327. *Who's Who in Malaysia & Singapore 1979–1980.* Kuala Lumpur: Who's Who Publications, 1980. NTUNIE, NUS. Continued by *Who's Who in Malaysia... & Profiles of Singapore.*

328.   *Who's Who in Malaysia & Singapore.* Petaling Jaya, Selangor: Who's Who
        Publications, 1983–. ISEAS, NLB, NUS.

329.   *Who's Who in Malaysia and Guide to Singapore 1973/1974–1977/1978.*
        Kuala Lumpur: J. Victor Morais, 1974–78. NUS. Continued by *Who's
        Who in Malaysia, Singapore & Brunei.*

330.   *Who's Who in Malaysia, Singapore & Brunei 1978–1979.* Kuala
        Lumpur: Who's Who Publications, 1979. ISEAS, NLB, NTUNIE, NUS.
        Continued by *Who's Who in Malaysia and Singapore.*

331.   *Who's Who in Singapore Legislative Assembly Election, 1959.* Singapore:
        Tan Hock Lim, 1959. 56 pp. NLB, NUS.

332.   *Who's Who, Malaysia and Singapore 1969–1971/1972.* Kuala Lumpur:
        J. Victor Morais, 1970–72. NUS. Continued by *Who's Who in Malaysia
        and Guide to Singapore.*

333.   Y. A. Talib (Yusof A. Talib). "Munshi Abdullah's Arab Teachers". *JMBRAS*
        63, pt. 2 (1990): 27–34. ISEAS, NLB, NTUNIE, NUS.

334.   Yahya Ismail. "Biografi tentang Abdullah Munshi". *Bahasa* 8, no. 12
        (December 1964): 547–52. NLB, NUS.

335.   Ying Lei. "Tak Kenal Lelah Memupuk Atlet Baru: Wawancara dengan
        Veteran Sheikh Alau'ddin Yacoob Marican". In *Meneroka Hidup Baru:
        Cerita Veteran Sukan,* penyunting Phoon Kwee Hian. Singapore: Candid
        Creation Publishing, 2005. NLB.

336.   Yusof Hj. Wanjor, comp. *Profil Haji A. Wanjor Tokoh Muslim Singapura
        1902–1979.* [S.l.: s.n.], 2009. 34 pp. NLB.

337.   "Yusuf Ishak". In *Ensiklopedia Sejarah dan Kebudayaan Melayu,* vol. 4,
        p. 2609. Kuala Lumpur: Dewan Bahasa dan Pustaka, 1999. NLB,
        NTUNIE, NUS.

338.   Zabha (Zainal Abidin Haji Alias). "Tun Yusuf Ishak Yang Saya Tau".
        In *Cenderamata Genap 25 Tahun Utusan Melayu Akhbar Kebangsaan
        Melayu yang dipunyai dan diusahakan oleh Bangsa Melayu, 29 Mei
        1939–29 Mei 1964,* susunan Rusdin Yaakub dan A. Malik Abdullah.
        Kuala Lumpur: Utusan Melayu Press, 1964. ISEAS, NLB.

339.   "Zahara Zaaba". In *Ensiklopedia Sejarah dan Kebudayaan Melayu,*
        vol. 4, p. 2613. Kuala Lumpur: Dewan Bahasa dan Pustaka, 1999. NLB,
        NTUNIE, NUS.

340. Zakaria Buang. "Poetry is His Cup of Tea: Interview with Mr Masuri Salikun, Malay Poet". *Mirror* 24, no. 2 (January 1988): 13–14. ISEAS, NLB, NUS.

341. Zubir Ali. "Hamzah Dolmat: Hilang Tak Berganti". *Dewan Budaya* 9, no. 8 (Ogos 1987): 56. NLB, NUS.

342. *Zubir Said: His Songs.* Singapore: Times Books International, 1990. 120 pp. ISEAS, NLB, NTUNIE, NUS.

343. Zulkifli Khair. "Sumbangan Besar Sonhadji". *Dewan Masyarakat* 48, no. 10 (October 2010): 41–43. NLB.
(On Ahmad Sonhadji Mohamad).

344. Zulkifli Ramli. "Isa Kamari Kembara Kerohanian dalam Cinta Arafah". *Dewan Budaya*, no. 4 (April 2007): 24–25. ISEAS, NLB, NTUNIE.

CULTURE

- *Cultural Policy and Heritage*
- *Manners and Customs*
- *Beliefs and Values*
- *Traditional Medicine*
- *Clothing, Food and Cooking*
- *Art*
- *Architecture*
- *Performing Arts*
- *Sports and Recreation*
- *Cultural Organizations*

Cultural Policy and Heritage

345. Abdul Halim Aliman. "A National Singapore Culture: Official Perception and Malay Response". Academic exercise, Department of Sociology, National University of Singapore, 1981. 83 pp. NUS.

346. Abdul Samad Ismail, Zubir Said and Harun Aminurrashid. *Ceramah-Ceramah Kebudayaan*. Singapore: Geliga, 1957. 58 pp. NLB.

347. "The Guardians of Malay Cultural Heritage". *Citizen* (August 1955): 6. NLB.

348. Hardwick, Patricia A. "Horsing around Melayu: Kuda Kepang, Islamic Piety and Identity Politics at Play in Singapore's Malay Community". *JMBRAS* 87, pt. 1 (2014): 1–19. ISEAS, NLB.

349. Henkel, David. "Status, Wealth & Utility — the Material Culture". In *Malay Heritage of Singapore*, edited by Aileen T. Lau and Bernhard Platzdasch. Singapore: Suntree Media in association with Malay Heritage Foundation, 2010. ISEAS, NLB, NTUNIE, NUS.

350. Lee Khoon Choy. *National Culture in a Multi-Racial Society*. Singapore: Ministry of Culture, 1967. 18 pp. ISEAS, NLB.

351. Mahmud Ahmad, 1906–76. "Kemajuan Singapura". In *Teras Kebudayaan Nasional*. Singapore: Penerbit Qalam, 1958. NLB, NTUNIE, NUS.

352. "Malay Cultural Month: Top Marks for Malay Village". *Petir: Organ of the People's Action Party* (March 1990): 39–40. ISEAS, NLB, NTUNIE, NUS. Also published in Malay under the title: "Bulan Budaya Melayu: Markah Tertinggi diberikan Buat Perkampungan Melayu". *Petir: Organ of the People's Action Party* (March 1990): 41–42. ISEAS, NLB, NTUNIE, NUS.

353. "The Malay Heritage Centre". *Economic Bulletin* 30, no. 5 (May 2001): 2–4. ISEAS.

354. Miksic, John N. "Malays, Trade & Artefacts in Ancient Singapore". In *Malay Heritage of Singapore*, edited by Aileen T. Lau and Bernhard Platzdasch. Singapore: Suntree Media in association with Malay Heritage Foundation, 2010. ISEAS, NLB, NTUNIE, NUS.

355. Yuen, Belinda. "Reclaiming Cultural Heritage in Singapore". *Urban Affairs Review* 41, no 6 (2006): 830–54. NTUNIE, NUS.

Manners and Customs

356. A. Ghani Hamid. *Laluan Budaya*. Singapore: ASAS 50, 2011. 437 pp. NLB, NTUNIE.

357. Abbas Mohd Shariff. *Adab Orang Melayu*. Singapore: Alfa Media, 2004. 190 pp. NLB.

358. Abbas Mohd Shariff. "Penghakisan Nilai-Nilai Budi Bahasa dan Budi Pekerti dalam Masyarakat Melayu: Pengalaman Singapura". Paper presented at a Persidangan Antarabangsa Bahasa, Sastera dan Kebudayaan Melayu ke 2, anjuran Jabatan Bahasa dan Kebudayaan Melayu, Kumpulan Akademik Bahasa dan Kebudayaan Asia, Institut Pendidikan Nasional, Universiti Teknologi Nanyang, Singapura, 1–3 September 2002. 18 pp. ISEAS, NLB.

359. Alwi Alhady. *Adab-Tertib: (dalam Pergaulan dan Champoran): Chara Barat dan Chara Melayu*. Singapore: Malaysia Publications, 1965. 92 pp. NLB.

360. Ahmad Mattar. "Let Us Preserve Our Traditions and Keep Them Alive". *Speeches* 13, no. 3 (May/June 1989): 18–20. ISEAS, NLB, NTUNIE, NUS.

361. Akbur, Peer M. "Why Do Muslims Wear the Songkok?" *Mirror* 27, no. 6 (15 March 1991): 10. ISEAS, NLB, NUS.

362. Ali Ibrahim. "Nature's Bounty — the Love of Plants". In *Malay Heritage of Singapore*, edited by Aileen T. Lau and Bernhard Platzdasch. Singapore: Suntree Media in association with Malay Heritage Foundation, 2010. ISEAS, NLB, NTUNIE, NUS.

363. Alimashor, Sharifah Maheran and A. Latif Othman. "Baju Kurong: The Dress from Telok Belanga". *ASEAN Review* 1, no. 2 (1976): 24. ISEAS, NLB, NUS.

364. *Arena*. Singapore: Arena Pub., 1971–72. NUS.

365. *Budaya: Penyambung Lidah Majlis Pusat*. Singapore: Majlis Pusat, 1981–. NLB, NUS. Continues *Warta Majlis*. Singapore: Majlis Pusat Singapura, 1972–76. ISEAS, NLB, NUS.

366. *Gateway to Malay Culture*. Singapore: Asiapac, 2003. 150 pp. ISEAS, NLB, NTUNIE, NUS.

367.   Hadijah Rahmat. "Community Spirit & Kampung Life". In *Malay Heritage of Singapore*, edited by Aileen T. Lau and Bernhard Platzdasch. Singapore: Suntree Media in association with Malay Heritage Foundation, 2010. ISEAS, NLB, NTUNIE, NUS.

368.   Hadijah Rahmat. "Membina Minda dan Budaya Melayu Baru Melalui Perekayasaan Pendidikan Bangsa". *Jurnal e-Utama* 1 (2008): 8–23. NTUNIE.

369.   Hadijah Rahmat. "Meningkat Tahap Pemahaman dan Penghargaan terhadap Kebudayaan Melayu". *Karyawan: Professionals for the Community* 3 (September–November 1997): 10–13. ISEAS, NLB, NTUNIE, NUS.

370.   Hamzah Muhat. "Penilaian Adat Persandingan Melayu dan Kesannya Pada Masa Hadapan". Research exercise, Department of Malay Studies, National University of Singapore, 1991. 52 pp. NUS.

371.   Haniah Abdul Hamid. "Entering Life, Entering Death: The Case of the Malays in Singapore". Academic exercise, Department of Sociology, National University of Singapore, 1992. 72 pp. NUS.

372.   Hidayah Amin. *Malay Weddings Don't Cost $50 and Other Facts about Malay Culture*. Editor, Lee Seow Ser. Singapore: Helang Books, 2014. 224 pp. ISEAS, NLB, NTUNIE, NUS.

373.   "In Search of History, Traditions and Values". *Pointer*, no. 591 (1993): 18–39. NLB.

374.   Lee Jake Hool. "Conceptions of Death in Singapore". Academic exercise, Department of Sociology, National University of Singapore, 1989. 48 pp. NUS.

375.   Lee Khum Thong. "Malay Skateboarders: From Mat Rockers to Mat Skaters". Academic exercise, Department of Sociology, National University of Singapore, 2004. 45 pp. NUS.

376.   Leo, John. "Malay Vows in Marriage". *Singapore Paraplegics* (August 1980): 25–31. NLB, NUS.

377.   Li, Tania (Joan Alexandra). "Cultural and Economic Change in the Singapore Malay Community". PhD dissertation, University of Cambridge, 1986. 336 pp. ISEAS, NLB, NUS.

378. Li, Tania (Joan Alexandra). *Malays in Singapore: Culture, Economy and Ideology.* Singapore: Oxford University Press, 1989. 206 pp. ISEAS, NLB, NTU, NTUNIE, NUS. Also published in Malay under the title: *Orang Melayu di Singapura: Budaya, Ekonomi, dan Ideologi.* Penterjemah, Abdul Rahman Haji Embong. Kuala Lumpur: S. Abdul Majeed, 1995. 274 pp. NLB, NUS.

379. Maarof Salleh. *Islam, Songkok & Bahasa: Awasi Rasa Ghairah yang Boleh Membunuh.* Selangor: Kemilau Publika, 2014. 329 pp. NLB.

380. "A Malay Wedding". *Goodwood Journal* (4th Quarter 1975): 4–5. NLB.

381. Mat Rofa Ismail and Kamel Ariffin Mohd Atan. "Mathematics in the Malay World Prior to the Arrival of Western Mathematics". *Procedia - Social and Behavioral Sciences* 8 (2010): 729–34. NUS.

382. Muhammad Ariff Ahmad. *Bicara Tentang Adat dan Tradisi.* Singapore: Pustaka Nasional, 1993. 201 pp. ISEAS, NLB, NTUNIE, NUS.

383. Muhammad Ariff Ahmad. *Nilam: Nilai Melayu Menurut Adat.* Singapore: Majlis Pusat Pertubuhan-Pertubuhan Budaya Melayu Singapura, 2007. 347 pp. NLB, NTUNIE.

384. Muhammad Ariff Ahmad. "Singapura dalam Konteks Dunia Melayu". In *Dunia Melayu*, edited by Mohd. Yusof Hasan. Kuala Lumpur: Dewan Bahasa dan Pustaka, 1991. NTUNIE, NUS.

385. Nadwah Sastera. *Dinamika Budaya.* Singapore: Majlis Pusat, 1991. 446 pp. ISEAS, NLB, NTUNIE, NUS.

386. Noor Wahidah Rusmani. "Adat Perpatih in Transition: A Case Study Spanning Negri Sembilan and Singapore". Research exercise, Department of Malay Studies, National University of Singapore, 1994. 1 vol. (various pagings). NUS.

387. Nor-Afidah Abd. Rahman. "Kampong Living A-Z". *BiblioAsia* 9, no. 4 (January–March 2014): 20–27. NLB, NTUNIE, NUS.

388. *Pameran Pesta Budaya Melayu ... '81, [Singapura] = Malay Cultural Festival Exhibition ... '81, [Singapore].* Organized by Majlis Pusat Pertubuhan-Pertubuhan Budaya Melayu Singapura, 1981. 1 vol. (various foliations). NUS.

389. *Perkhemahan Adab dan Kesantunan: 16 & 17 Mac 2012, Kelab Masyarakat Kampong Ubi.* Anjuran Majlis Bahasa Melayu Singapura. Singapore: Majlis Bahasa Melayu Singapura, 2012. 87 pp. NLB, NTUNIE.

390.   *Pesta Budaya Melayu: [Buku Cenderamata].* Singapore: Majlis Pusat Pertubuhan-Pertubuhan Budaya Melayu Singapura, 1981. 41 pp. NLB.

391.   *A Pictorial Illustration on Malay Customs and Practices.* Singapore: Ministry of Community Development, 1990. 12 pp. NLB, NUS.

392.   Rosman Kass. "Some Malay Customs, Beliefs and Practices and Their Effect on Health and Happiness". Academic exercise, Department of Social Medicine and Public Health, University of Malaya, Singapore, 1962. 1 microfilm reel. NUS.

393.   S. Markasan (Suratman Markasan). *Bangsa Melayu Singapura dalam Transformasi Budayanya.* Singapore: Anuar Othman & Associates Media Enterprise, 2005. 213 pp. NLB, NTUNIE, NUS.

394.   S. Markasan (Suratman Markasan). "Budaya Melayu dalam Masyarakat Kosmopolitan". *Dewan Budaya* 9, no. 1 (January 1987): 50–52. ISEAS, NLB, NTUNIE, NUS.

395.   S. Markasan (Suratman Markasan). "Hari Depan Kebudayaan Melayu/ Islam di Singapura". Kertas kerja yang dibentang, di Tekengong, Acheh, pada 20–24 Januari 1986. NLB.

396.   S. Markasan (Suratman Markasan). "Orang Melayu Singapura dengan Kebudayaannya". *Dewan Budaya* 6, no. 1 (January 1984): 19–21. ISEAS, NLB, NTUNIE, NUS.

397.   S. Markasan (Suratman Markasan). "Warisan Budaya Melayu Dalam Masyarakat Kosmopolitan". In *Tamadun Melayu*, edited by Ismail Hussein and Aziz Deraman dan Abd. Rahmat Al-Ahmadi. Kuala Lumpur: Dewan Bahasa dan Pustaka, 1989. ISEAS, NLB, NUS.

398.   S. Singaravelu. "The Malay-Tamil Cultural Contacts with Special Reference to the Festival of 'Mandi Safar'". *Asian Folklore Studies* 45, no. 1 (1986): 67–78. ISEAS, NTUNIE, NUS.

399.   Sabariah Abdullah. "Kajian terhadap Upacara-Upacara Adat Berhubung dengan Kelahiran, Perkahwinan dan Kematian di dalam Masyarakat Melayu Singapura". Academic exercise, Department of Malay Studies, National University of Singapura, 1994. 46 pp. NUS.

400.   Seminar Kebudayaan Melayu (1978: Singapura). "Kertas-Kertas Kerja Seminar Kebudayaan Melayu". Anjuran Majlis Pusat Pertubuhan-Pertubuhan Budaya Melayu dengan Kerjasama Kesatuan Guru-Guru Melayu Singapura, pada 23–25 Disember 1978. 125 pp. ISEAS, NUS.

401. Shamsudin Raduan. "Exploration of an Emerging Sub-Culture among Malay Men". Research exercise, Department of Malay Studies, National University of Singapore, 1994. 68 pp. NUS.

402. Singapore Broadcasting Corporation. *An Introduction to Malay Customs and Beliefs*. Producer, Agnes Lim Siew Chin. Singapore: SBC, 1992. 1 videocassette (VHS, PAL). 30 min. NLB.

403. Singapore Broadcasting Corporation. *A Malay Marriage: A Community Affair*. Singapore: SBC, 1988. 1 videocassette (VHS, PAL). 30 min. NLB.

404. Siti Nur Azrina Mohd Nazri et al. *Journeys: Rediscovering the Malay Legacy*. Editor-in-chief, Syed Hassan Bin Syed Nashir Alsagoff. Singapore: Malay Language & Cultural Club, Singapore Management University, 2006. 139 pp. ISEAS, NLB, NTUNIE, NUS.

405. *Some Aspects of Malay Customs and Practices = Beberapa Aspek Adat dan Amalan Melayu*. Singapore: Majlis Pusat Pertubuhan-Pertubuhan Budaya Melayu Singapura, 1990. 60 pp. ISEAS, NLB, NTUNIE, NUS.

406. Talib, Khaled. "Land Acquisition Bungled Arab Lifestyle". *Al-Mahjar: A Publication of the Arab Association of Singapore* 3, no. 1 (1998): 5–6. NLB, NUS.

407. Tham Seong Chee. *Budaya Melayu, Budaya Cina dan Islam: Mencari Sintesis dan Imbangan dalam Proses Pembudayaan Islam di dalam Masyarakat Majmuk*. Seminar Papers, no. 15. Singapore: Department of Malay Studies, National University of Singapore, 1994. 13 pp. ISEAS, NLB, NUS.

408. Tschacher, Torsten. "Rational Miracles, Cultural Rituals and the Fear of Syncretism: Defending Contentious Muslim Practice among Tamil-Speaking Muslims". *Asian Journal of Social Science* 37, no. 1 (2009): 55–82. ISEAS, NLB, NTUNIE.

409. Wan Alfida Suleiman. "Suatu Kajian tentang Mak Andam Masa Kini di Singapura". Academic exercise, Department of Malay Studies, National University of Singapore, 1994. 50 pp. NUS.

410. Yaacob Ibrahim. "Openness is the Malay Way". *Petir: Organ of the People's Action Party* (July/August 2010): 6–7. ISEAS, NLB, NTUNIE, NUS.

Beliefs and Values

411. Bedlington, Stanley. "Malays of Singapore: Values in Conflict?" *Sedar* 3 (1971): 43–55. ISEAS, NLB, NUS.

412. *An Essential Guide to Pantang! Taboos and Superstitions of Singapore & Malaysia.* Singapore: Gartbooks, 2009. 109 pp. ISEAS, NLB, NUS.

413. Evers, Hans-Dieter. "Reports on the Kuburan Keramat of Singapore: Fieldnotes". 1972. 1 vol. (various pagings). ISEAS.

414. Harun Aminurrashid. *Mengesan Jejak Pelayaran Abdullah Munshi.* Singapore: Pustaka Melayu, 1966. 207 pp. NLB, NTUNIE, NUS.

415. Henkel, David. "Magic, Might & Myth — Traditional Weapons". In *Malay Heritage of Singapore*, edited by Aileen T. Lau and Bernhard Platzdasch. Singapore: Suntree Media in association with Malay Heritage Foundation, 2010. ISEAS, NLB, NTUNIE, NUS.

416. Kau Ah Keng and Charles Yang. *Values and Lifestyles of Singaporeans: A Marketing Perspective.* Singapore: Singapore University Press, 1991. 248 pp. ISEAS, NLB, NTUNIE, NUS.

417. Lee L.M., Raymond. "The Social Meaning of Mass Hysteria in West Malaysia and Singapore". PhD dissertation, University of Massachusetts, 1979. Ann Arbor, Mich.: University Microfilms International, 1985. 280 pp. ISEAS, NUS.

418. Liyana Taha. "Life in Death: The Case of Keramats in Singapore". *BiblioAsia* 8, no. 4 (January–March 2013): 14–19. NLB, NTUNIE, NUS.

419. Mohamed Nahar Ros. "Sacred Places: Keramats in Singapore". Academic exercise, Department of Geography, National University of Singapore, 1984. 90 pp. NUS.

420. Mohd Zain Mabmood. "A Study of Keramat Worship with Special Reference to Singapore". Academic exercise, University of Malaya, Singapore, 1959. 53 pp. NUS.

421. Muhammad Ariff Ahmad. "Nilai-Nilai Hidup Orang Melayu". *Mekar* (January 1980): 24–25. NLB, NUS.

422. *Nagore Durgha Shrine Preservation Guidelines.* Singapore: Preservation of Monuments Board. 1991. 2 vols. NLB, NUS.

423.   Ow, R. and N.H.B. Saparin. "Malay Muslim Worldviews: Some Thoughts for Social Work Practice in Singapore". *Journal of Religion & Spirituality in Social Work: Social Thought* 33, no. 1 (2014): 73–94. NUS.

424.   River, Philip J. "Keramat in Singapore in the Mid-twentieth Century". *JMBRAS* 76, pt. 2 (2003): 93–119. ISEAS, NLB, NTUNIE, NUS.

425.   Suen-Oltmanns, Angela. "A Historical Survey of the Keramat Phenomenon: With Special Reference to Singapore". Academic exercise, Department of History, National University of Singapore, 1994. 91 pp. NUS.

426.   Suhana Khairudin. "Malay Sense of Value with Special Reference to the Home and Its Environs". Research exercise, Department of Malay Studies, National University of Singapore, 1994. 29 pp. NUS.

427.   Winstedt, Richard O. "Karamat: Sacred Places and Persons in Malaya". *JMBRAS* 2, pt. 3 (December 1924): 264–79. ISEAS, NLB, NTUNIE, NUS.

428.   Zuraihan Isahak. "Cultural Practice vs Religious Injunctions in Adaptation and Change in Malay Culture (with Special Reference to Keramat Worship in Singapore)". Research exercise, Department of Malay Studies, National University of Singapore, 1992. 66 pp. NUS. Published under the title: *Cultural Practice versus Religious Junctions: A Study of* Keramat *Worship in Singapore*. Culture Series, no. 1. Singapore: Department of Malay Studies, National University of Singapore, 1995. 35 pp. ISEAS, NUS.

Traditional Medicine

429.   Audi Yudasmara et al. "Bomoh". *Bulletin Saujana* 1 (2000): 51–64. NLB, NUS.

430.   Kamsiah Abdullah. "The Magical, Herbs & Healing". In *Malay Heritage of Singapore*, edited by Aileen T. Lau and Bernhard Platzdasch. Singapore: Suntree Media in association with Malay Heritage Foundation, 2010. ISEAS, NLB, NTUNIE, NUS.

431.   Mastura A. Rahman. "The Practice of Traditional Cures among the Malay Society in Singapore". Research exercise, Department of Malay

Studies, National University of Singapore, 1992. 47 pp. NUS. Published under the title. *The Practice of Traditional Cures among the Malays in Singapore.* Culture Series, no. 2. Singapore: Department of Malay Studies, National University of Singapore, 1996. 40 pp. ISEAS, NTUNIE.

432. Robert, Katherine. "The Role of Malay Magicians and Medicine Men: A Study of Their Practice, Their Clients and Their Relation to Their Clients to Singapore". Academic exercise, Department of Social Studies, University of Malaya, Singapore, 1959. 119 pp. NUS.

433. Sa'adah Yusof. "Cultural Appraisal of Flora: Malay Folk Medicine in Singapore". Academic exercise, Department of Geography, National University of Singapore, 1988. 172 pp. NUS.

434. Siti Hanifah Mustapha. "Malay Magic and Folk Medicinal Practice among the Malays in Singapore". MA dissertation, Department of Malay Studies. University of Singapore, 1978. 168 pp. NUS.

435. Siti Hanifah Mustapha. "The Role of Bomohs and Functions of Magic in Singapore". In *Society of Malay Culture, 26th Anniversary Souvenir Programme, 1979 = Persatuan Kebudayaan Melayu, Ulang Tahun ke-26 Cenderamata.* Singapore: Persatuan Kebudayaan Melayu, 1980. NLB, NUS.

436. Tuschinsky, C. "Balancing Hot and Cold – Balancing Power and Weakness: Social and Cultural Aspects of Malay Jamu in Singapore". *Social Science & Medicine* 41, no. 11 (1995): 1587–95. NTUNIE, NUS.

Clothing, Food and Cooking

437. *2007 Rasa-Rasa WARNA.* Singapore: MediaCorp Radio WARNA 94.2FM, 2007. 112 pp. NLB.

438. Aini Salim. *Biskut dan Kek Singapura.* Kuala Lumpur: Utusan Publications, 2009–13. 3 vols. NLB.

439. Asmah Laili. *Mintak Ampun Sedapnya….* Singapore: Q-Zeen, 2003. 150 pp. NLB.

440. Asmah Laili. *Mintak Ampun Sedapnya…Ooo…Lala….* Singapore: Q-Zeen, 2004. 150 pp. NLB.

441. Aziza Ali. *Sambal Days, Kampong Cuisine*. Editor, Koh Buck Song. Singapore: Ate Media, 2013. 142 pp. ISEAS, NLB, NUS.

442. Chef Bob. *Aroma oleh Chef Bob Pasti Gorjas!* Singapore: Chef Bob & Wan's World Creative Works, 2015. 122 pp. NLB.

443. Devasahayam, Theresa. "Food, Ethnicity and Religion: What and Why do People Eat in Singapore". Academic exercise, Department of Sociology, National University of Singapore, 1987. 152 pp. ISEAS, NUS.

444. *Kearah Pemakanan yang Sihat: Satu Panduan Penyajian di Majlis-Majlis Melayu*. Singapore: MOH Food & Nutrition Department, 2000. 63 pp. NLB, NTUNIE.

445. *Lazatnya...Recipes of Love: Cosmopolitan Cuisines*. Singapore: LBKM Scholarship Fund Board, 2010. 158 pp. NLB.

446. Nurdini Mohd Ariff. "Makanan dalam Kebudayaan Melayu". Research exercise, Department of Malay Studies, National University of Singapore, 1995. 37 pp. NUS.

447. *Resipi Pesta Perut*. Singapore: MediaCorp Radio WARNA 94.2FM, 2000. 145 pp. NLB.

448. Rita Zahara. *Malay Heritage Cooking*. Singapore: Marshall Cavendish Cuisine, 2012. 194 pp. NLB, NTUNIE.

Art

449. A. Ghani Hamid (Abdul Ghani Hamid). *Kegiatan Kolektif Pelukis-Pelukis Melayu*. Singapore: Angkatan Pelukis Aneka Daya, 1990. 8 pp. NLB, NUS.

450. A. Ghani Hamid. "Mendekati Sebahagian Falsafah dan Konsep Pelukis". In *Budaya: Penyambung Lidah Majlis Pusat Pertubuhan-Pertubuhan Budaya Melayu Singapura*. Bil 2 (1983): 8–12. NLB, NUS.

451. Alfred, E.R. "Boats of Singapore". *JMBRAS* 60, pt. 2 (1987): 99–114. ISEAS, NLB, NTUNIE, NUS.

452. *Definitive Exhibition of Malay Arts & Crafts, British Council Centre, Stamford Road Singapore, July 21st to 29th, 1951*. Singapore: Craftsman Press, 1951. 1 vol. NLB.

453. Foo Kwee Horng. "A Brief History of Woodcuts in Singapore". *BiblioAsia* 2, issue 3 (October 2006): 30–34. NLB, NTUNIE.

454. Lai Chee Kien. "Thoughts about Nature: A Conversation with Iskandar Jalil". *Singapore Architect* 203 (1999): 128–31. NLB, NUS.

455. Lee Chor Lin. "Batik in Singapore". In *Batik: Creating an Identity*. Singapore: National Museum, 1991. ISEAS, NLB, NTUNIE, NUS.

456. Loy Kwee Wah. "Geylang Serai Arts and Craft Centre". Academic exercise, National University of Singapore, 1985. 130 pp. NUS.

457. *Pameran Photografi Melayu Sa-Malaysia yang Pertama*. Singapore: Perkumpulan Penggambar-Penggambar Melayu Singapura, 1963. 44 pp. NLB.

458. Seng Yu Jin. "Artistic Expressions & Fine Art". In *Malay Heritage of Singapore*, edited by Aileen T. Lau and Bernhard Platzdasch. Singapore: Suntree Media in association with Malay Heritage Foundation, 2010. ISEAS, NLB, NTUNIE, NUS.

459. Sheares, Constance. *Batik in Singapore*. Singapore: National Museum, 1975. 13 pp. ISEAS, NLB, NTUNIE, NUS.

460. Sullivan, Frank. "Pictures of Straw". *Singapore Artist* 1, no. 3 (March 1955): 38–49. ISEAS, NLB, NUS.

461. Winstedt, R.O. (Richard O.). "Muslim Tombstone in Raffles Museum". *JMBRAS* 10, pt. 1 (1932): 6–8. ISEAS, NLB, NTUNIE, NUS.

Architecture

462. Edwards, Norman. *The Singapore House Residential Life, 1819–1939*. Singapore: Oxford University Press, 1990. 281 pp. ISEAS, NLB, NTUNIE, NUS.

463. Imran Tajudeen. "For Body & Soul — Architecture of Houses & Mosques". In *Malay Heritage of Singapore*, edited by Aileen T. Lau and Bernhard Platzdasch. Singapore: Suntree Media in association with Malay Heritage Foundation, 2010. ISEAS, NLB, NTUNIE, NUS.

464. Imran Tajudeen. "Sejarah Kota dan Senibina Masyarakat Pedagang Bugis/Makassar di Singapura 1811–1940". In *Prosiding Konvensyen*

Antarabangsa Diaspora Bugis: Sejarah Budaya Seni Bina — International Convention Bugis Diaspora, 25–28 November, 2011, Universiti Teknologi Malaysia, edited by Mohamad Tajuddin Mohamad Rasdi. Johor: Pusat Kajian Alam Bina Dunia, 2011. NLB.

465. Kwa Chong Guan and Tisa Ng. "Country Report of Singapore for SPAFA Workshop". In *Workshop on Community-Based Conservative and Maintenance of Historic Buildings/Living Monuments (S-W111), Bangkok, Thailand, August 23–30, 1987: Final Report*. Bangkok: SPAFA Regional Centre Office, 1988. ISEAS, NLB, NUS.

466. Lee, Edwin. *Historic Buildings of Singapore*. Singapore: Preservation of Monuments Board, 1990. 97 pp. ISEAS, NLB, NTUNIE, NUS.

467. Quek Poh Lian, Lena. "The Muslim Converts Association (Darul Arqam) Islamic Centre of Singapore: The Transformation and Translation of Islamic Design Principles". Academic exercise, National University of Singapore, 1988. NUS.

468. Thew Kim Lean. *Malay Influences in Architecture: Focus on West Malaysia and Singapore*. Singapore: University of Singapore, 1979. 181 pp. NUS.

469. Zulkifli Mohammed. "Geylang Serai Malay Village: Linking the Past with the Future". *Petir: Organ of the People's Action Party* (February 1990): 18–19. ISEAS, NLB, NTUNIE, NUS. Also published in Malay under the title: "Perkampungan Melayu Geylang Serai: Menghubungkan Masa Silam dengan Masa Depan". *Petir: Organ of the People's Action Party* (February 1990): 42–43. ISEAS, NLB, NTUNIE, NUS.

Performing Arts

470. A. Ghani Hamid. *Reaksi: Antologi Esei dan Puisi*. Singapore: Angkatan Pelukis Aneka Daya, 1990. 201 pp. NLB, NUS.

471. Abdul Aziz H.M. "Juara Yang Takut Jadi Juara". *Dewan Budaya* 11, no. 5 (May 1989): 42–43. NLB, NUS.

472. Abdul Muthalib Hassan. "Winning Hearts and Minds: Representations of Malays and their Milieu in the Films of British Malaya". *South East Asia Research* 17, no. 1 (March 2009): 47–63. ISEAS, NLB, NTUNIE, NUS.

473. Ahmad Azmi. *Panduar Bermain Seni Hadrah Kompang*. Singapore: Persatuan Hadrah dan Kompang Singapura, 1990. 100 pp. ISEAS, NLB, NUS.

474. Ahmad Azmi Haji Mohamed Ishak. *Rentak Rebana: Sejarah dan Perkembangan di Singapura*. Penyunting, Hartinah Ahmad, Samsudin Said. Singapore: Perkumpulan Seni Singapura, 2015. 176 pp. NLB.

475. Ahmad Jaafar. "Masyarakat Harus Dididik Nikmati Muzik: Wawancara Mohd Raman Daud". In *Budaya: Penyambung Lidah Majlis Pusat. Pertubuhan-pertubuhan Budaya Melayu Singapura*. Bil 2 (1983): 4–6. NLB, NUS.

476. Alatas, Syed Farid. "Music and Worship in Islam: Zafin among the Arabs of Southeast Asia". In *Hadhrami Arabs Across the Indian Ocean: Contributions to Southeast Asian Economy and Society*. Singapore: National Library Board. 2010. ISEAS, NLB, NUS.

477. Aljunied, Syed Muhd Khairudin. "Films as Social History — P. Ramlee's 'Seniman Bujang Lapck' and Malays in Singapore". *Heritage Journal* 2, no. 1 (2005): 1–21. NLB, NTUNIE, NUS.

478. Barnard, Timothy F. "Chickens, Cakes and Kitchen: Food and Modernity in Malay Films of the 1950s and 1960s". In *Reel Food: Essays on Food and Film*, edited by Anne L. Bower. New York: Routledge, 2004. NUS.

479. Barnard T.P. (Timothy P.). "Decolonization and the Nation in Malay Film, 1955–1965". *South East Asia Research* 17, no. 1 (2009): 65–86. ISEAS, NLB, NTUNIE, NUS.

480. Barnard, Timothy P. "Film Melayu: Nationalism, Modernity and Film in a Pre-World War Two Malay Magazine". *Journal of Southeast Asian Studies* 41, issue 01 (February 2010): 47–70. ISEAS, NLB, NTU, NTUNIE, NUS.

481. Barnard, Timothy P. "Sedih Sampai Buta: Blindness, Modernity and Tradition in Malay Films of 1950s and 1960s". *Bijdragen tot de Taal, Land- en Volkenkunde* 161, no. 4 (2005): 433–51. ISEAS, NLB, NTUNIE, NUS.

482. "Bringing Back the Ghazal — Malay Ghazal Singing Competition". *Citizen* (April 1987): 20. NLB.

483. Chua Soo Pong. *Singapore Malay Dance: Dynamics of Expressive Culture.* Report, no. 9. Singapore: Teaching and Research Exchange Fellowships, Southeast Asian Studies Program, Institute of Southeast Asian Studies, 1991. 12 pp. ISEAS, NUS.

484. Djamal Tukimin. *Arus Teater Singapura: Sebuah Antologi Esei Teater.* Singapore: Pustaka Nasional, 2007. 163 pp. ISEAS, NLB, NTUNIE.

485. Djamal Tukimin. "Development of Malay Theatre in Singapore". *Singa* 20 (June 1990): 167–84. ISEAS, NLB, NTUNIE, NUS.

486. Djamal Tukimin. "Perkembangan Teater Singapura: Sebuah Komentar". Paper presented at a Pertemuan Jalan Permulaan Puisi-Teater, Singapore, 26–28 March 1985. 7 pp. NLB.

487. Hadijah Rahmat. *Munsyi: Drama Sejarah Sempena 200 Tahun Kelahiran Munsyi Abdullah bin Sheikh Abdul Kadir (1796–1854).* Singapore: Teater Kami, 1998. 80 pp. NLB, NTUNIE.

488. Hadijah Rahmat. "Wajah Sosial Melayu dari Cermin TV Singapura". In *Gerimis di Hati: Drama TV.* Singapore: Perkumpulan Seni: Suria MediaCorp, 2013. NLB.

489. Hamed Ismail et al. *Gerimis di Hati: Drama TV.* Singapore: Perkumpulan Seni: Suria MediaCorp, 2013. 555 pp. NLB.

490. Hardwick, Patricia A. "Horsing around Melayu: Kuda Kepang, Islamic Piety and Identity Politics at Play in Singapore's Malay Community". *JMBRAS* 87, pt. 1 (2014): 1–19. ISEAS, NLB.

491. Hashim Yusof. *Drama di Radio.* Singapore: Hashim Yusof, 2002. 72 pp. NLB, NTUNIE.

492. Hassan Abdul Muthalib. "'Winning Hearts and Minds': Representations of Malays and their Milieu in the Films of British Malaya". *South East Asia Research* 17, no. 1 (2009): 47–63. NTUNIE, NUS.

493. Hazlan Mohd. Aris. "Suatu Kajian tentang Gamelan di Singapura: Pendekatan dan Sudut Asalan, Sosiologikal dan Keagamaan". Research exercise, Department of Malay Studies, Universiti Nasional Singapura, 1994. 73 pp. NUS.

494. "Introducing PA's Malay Combo Band". *Citizen* (April 1986): 16. NLB.

495. *Irama.* Singapore: Persatuan Seni Muzik Malayu, Singapura, 1976–. NLB.

496. Jamil Sulong, Datuk. *Tiada Kata Secantik Bahasa*. Ampang, Selangor: Perbadanan Kemajuan Filem Nasional Malaysia, 2008. 150 pp. NUS.

497. Johari Shariff and Ubaidullah Mustaffa. *Nostalgia Filem Melayu Klasik*. Editor, Ruzita Alias. Ampang, Selangor: Perbadanan Kemajuan Filem Nasional Malaysia, 2005. 218 pp. ISEAS, NLB.

498. *Lagu-Lagu Kita = Our Songs*. Singapore: Jabatan Kesenian, Kesatuan Guru-Guru Melayu Singapura, 1981. 1 score (51 pp.). NLB, NUS.

499. *Lagu-Lagu Kita = Our Songs*. Singapore: Jabatan Kesenian, Kesatuan Guru- Guru Melayu Singapura, 1982. 1 sound cassette. NLB.

500. Lim Kay Tong. "Into the World of Malay Movies". In *Cathay: 55 Years of Cinema*. Singapore: Cathay Organisation, 1991. NLB, NTUNIE, NUS.

501. Lim Kean Bon. "Performing Whose Identity: Singapore Malay Theatre and the Politics of Malayness". Academic exercise, Department of Sociology, National University of Singapore, 2008. 75 pp. NUS.

502. Lockard, Craig A. "Reflections of Change: Sociopolitical Commentary and Criticism in Malaysian Popular Music since 1950". *Crossroads: An Interdisciplinary Journal of Southeast Asian Studies* 6, no. 1 (1991): 1–112. ISEAS, NLB, NTUNIE, NUS.

503. "The Making of Malay Theatre". *Art Magazine* (September/October 2001): 36. NLB.

504. "Menyingkap Tirai untuk Orkestra Melayu Persatuan Rakyat". *Citizen* (November 1991): 8. NLB.

505. Mohd Raman Daud and Yusnor Ef. "The Big Screen". In *Malay Heritage of Singapore*, edited by Aileen T. Lau and Bernhard Platzdasch. Singapore: Suntree Media in association with Malay Heritage Foundation, 2010. ISEAS, NLB, NTUNIE, NUS.

506. Mohd. Zamberi A. Malek and Aimi Jarr. *Malaysian Films: The Beginning*. Ampang, Selangor: National Film Development Corporation Malaysia, 2005. 217 pp. ISEAS, NLB, NUS.
      ("'Malaysian Films: The Beginning' covers that special early years of Malay filmmaking in Singapore, then still part of Malaya and then Malaysia until 1965", p. vii).
      (Also published in Malay under the title: *Bermulanya Filem Melayu*. Ampang, Selangor: Perbadanan Kemajuan Filem Nasional Malaysia, 2009. 108 pp. NLB, NUS).

507. Muhammad Ariff Ahmad and Mohd Raman Daud. "Rhythm & Dance". In *Malay Heritage of Singapore*, edited by Kamsiah Abdullah, Aileen T. Lau and Bernhard Platzdasch. Singapore: Suntree Media in association with Malay Heritage Foundation, 2010. ISEAS, NLB, NTUNIE, NUS.

508. Muhamad Zain Haji Hamzah. *Mengenai Musik Melayu: Beberapa Pendapat.* [Disusun oleh] Mohd Zain Haji Hamzah; Kumpulan Cheramah2 Radio oleh Zubair Said [dan lain2]. Singapore: Radio Singapura Bahagian Melayu, 1960. 70 pp. NLB.

509. Nadiputra. *Muzika Lorong Buang Kok.* English translation by Nazry Bahrawi. Singapore: Cokelat, 2012. 156 pp. NLB.

510. Nazri Othman. "A Sociological Study of Kuda Kepang in Singapore". Academic exercise, Department of Sociology, National University of Singapore, 1994. 79 pp. NUS.

511. Nongchik Ghani. "Malay Dances: History and Development". In *Dance in Singapore: A Historical Perspective: A Photographic Exhibition, 2nd–5th April 1981, National Theatre Foyer.* Singapore: National Theatre Trust, [1981?]. 60 pp. NLB, NUS.

512. Nor-Afidah Abd. Rahman and Michelle Heng. "The Golden Age of Malay Cinema". *BiblioAsia* 11, no. 1 (April–June 2015): 12–19. ISEAS, NLB, NIE, NUS.

513. Norlina Mohamed. "The Making of Malay Theatre: The Malay Theatre Scene is Active and Talented, but Where is the Support?" *Arts Magazine* (November–December 2001): 36–39. NLB.

514. "Orkestra Melayu Singapura Dazzles". *Citizen* (June 1994): 4–5. NLB.

515. Rahmah Bujang. "Sejarah Perkembangan Drama Bangsawan di Tanah Melayu dan Singapura". MA dissertation, Fakulti Sastera & Sains Sosial, Universiti Malaya, 1972. 356 pp. NUS. Published under the same title: Kuala Lumpur: Dewan Bahasa dan Pustaka, 1975. 159 pp. ISEAS, NLB, NTUNIE, NUS.

516. Ramli Sarip. "Akrabnya Alam Hidup dengan Alam Seni". *Dewan Budaya* no. 5 (May 2007): 50–52. ISEAS, NLB, NTUNIE, NUS.

517. Ramli Sarip. "Dahulu dengan Gaya Kini dengan Gerak". *Dewan Budaya* no. 3 (March 2007): 50–52. ISEAS, NLB, NTUNIE, NUS.

518. Ramli Sarip. "Kalau Sudah Tertulis di Loh Mahfuz". *Dewan Budaya* no. 9 (September 2006): 51–53. ISEAS, NLB, NTUNIE, NUS.

519. Ramli Sarip. "Kerja Seni = Tawakal". *Dewan Budaya* no. 7 (July 2006): 57–98. ISEAS, NLB, NTUNIE, NUS.

520. Ramli Sarip. "Litar Seni Ramli Sarip". *Dewan Budaya* no. 6 (June 2006): 56–58. ISEAS, NLB, NTUNIE, NUS.

521. Ramli Sarip. "Muzik Bahasa Hati". *Dewan Budaya* no. 6 (June 2007): 52–54. ISEAS, NLB, NTUNIE, NUS.

522. Ramli Sarip. "Seni Juga Satu Kebaktian". *Dewan Budaya* no. 8 (August 2006): 47–49. ISEAS, NLB, NTUNIE, NUS.

523. Ramli Sarip. "Tiada Darjat dalam Seni". *Dewan Budaya* no. 2 (February 2007): 49–51. ISEAS, NLB, NTUNIE, NUS.

524. Salleh Ghani. *Filem Melayu dari Jalan Ampas ke Ulu Kelang*. Ampang, Selangor: Perbadanan Kemajuan Filem Nasional Malaysia, 2011. 168 pp. ISEAS, NLB.

525. Salleh Ghani. *Sejarah Filem Melayu*. Kuala Lumpur: VariaPop Group, 1989. 134 pp. NLB.

526. Samsudin Said and Hartinah Ahmad, comps. *Tari Melayu Serampang 12: Sejarah & Perkembangan di dalam Perkumpulan Seni*. Singapore: Perkumpulan Seni Singapura, 2012. 68 pp. NLB.

527. "Seminar Teater: Bicara Teater Melayu Singapura 25 tahun: Tema, Arah dan Pemikiran, Pusat Drama". Anjuran Teater Kami, Singapura, 8hb Julai 1990. 1 vol. (various foliations). NLB, NUS.

528. Shaik Othman Sallim. "The Malay Opera". *Straits Chinese Magazine* 2, no. 8 (1898): 128–32. ISEAS, NLB, NUS.

529. Sharifah Masturah Syed Osman. "Dikir Barat in Kelantan and Singapore: Looking Beyond Its Superficiality". Academic exercise, Department of Southeast Asian Studies Programme, National University of Singapore, 1999. 61 pp. NUS.

530. Sharifah Zinjuaher H.M. Ariffin and Hang Tuah Arshad. *Sejarah Filem Melayu = The History of Malay Motion Pictures*. Kuala Lumpur: Sri Sharifah, 1980. 379 pp ISEAS, NLB, NTUNIE, NUS.

531.   Siti Rahimah Buang. "Selera Muzik Para Remaja Melayu Singapura Masakini". Academic exercise, Department of Malay Studies, National University of Singapore, 1993. 53 pp. NUS.

532.   Tan, Kenneth Paul. "Racial Stereotypes in Singapore Films". In *Race and Multiculturalism in Malaysia and Singapore,* edited by Daniel P.S. Goh et al. London & New York: Routledge, 2009. 240 pp. ISEAS, NLB, NTUNIE, NUS.

533.   Tan Meng Leng. "Bangsawan: A Lost Art?" *Citizen* 7, no. 17 (September 1978): 10–13. NLB.

534.   Tan Sooi Beng. "The 78 RPM Record Industry in Malaya Prior to World War II". *Asian Music* 28, no. 1 (Autumn–Winter 1996–97): 1–41. NLB, NTUNIE, NUS.

535.   Yusnor Ef. *Dendang Temasek: Lagu Melayu Asli Pembina Budaya.* Singapore: PERKAMUS, 2005. 96 pp. NLB, NTUNIE, NUS.

536.   Yusnor Ef. "Dondang Sayang — The Distinctive Heritage of the Malays". *Graduate* (August 2001): 42–43. NLB, NUS.

537.   Yusnor Ef. *Irama Juang PERKAMUS: 1992–2006.* Penyunting, Mohd. Raman Daud. Singapore: Persatuan Penyanyi dan Karyawan Muzik Melayu Singapura (PERKAMUS), 2007. 52 pp. NLB.

538.   Yusnor Ef. *Muzik Melayu, Sejak 1940-an.* Kuala Lumpur: YKNA Network Sdn. Bhd., 2011. 305 pp. NLB, NUS.

539.   Yusnor Ef. "P. Ramlee". In *SELVES: The State of Arts in Singapore.* Singapore: National Arts Council, 2002. NLB.

540.   Yusnor Ef. "Pleasure & Leisure — Music & Song". In *Malay Heritage of Singapore,* edited by Aileen T. Lau and Bernhard Platzdasch. Singapore: Suntree Media in association with Malay Heritage Foundation, 2010. ISEAS, NLB, NTUNIE, NUS.

541.   Zaidi Ismail dan Zuraini Hj. Abu Bakar. "Kembalikan Wajah Filem". *Dewan Budaya* 9 (September 2010): 61–65. NLB, NUS.

542.   Zubillaga-Pow, Jun. "The Dialectics of Capitalist Reclamation, or Traditional Malay Music in *fin de siècle* Singapore". *South East Asia Research* 22, no. 1 (March 2014): 123–39. ISEAS, NLB, NTUNIE, NUS.

543.   Zubir Said et al. *Mengenai Musik Melayu: Beberapa Pendapat: Kumpulan Cheramah-Cheramah Radio*. Disusun oleh Mohd. Zain Haji Hamzah. Singapore: Bahagian Melayu Radio, 1960. 70 pp. NLB.

Sports and Recreation

544.   Abdul Halim Kader, Abdul Sarip Naharawi, and Mohd. Seth Ismail. *Sepaktakraw: Sports of the Brave: Past, Present and Future*. Singapore: Abdul Halim Bin Kader, 2009. 242 pp. NLB.

545.   *Cahaya*. Singapore: Persatuan Pencak Silat Singapura, 1973–75. NLB, NUS.

546.   Farrer, Douglas. *Deathscapes of the Malay Martial Artist*. Working Papers, no. 174. Singapore: Department of Sociology, National University of Singapore, 2005. 35 pp. ISEAS, NLB.

547.   Ho Kong-Chong and Chua Beng Huat. *Cultural, Social and Leisure Activities in Singapore*. Census of Population 1990 Monograph, no. 3. Singapore: Department of Statistics, 1995. 83 pp. ISEAS, NLB, NTUNIE, NUS.

548.   "Kampong Games". In *Kampong Days: Village Life and Times in Singapore Revisited*. Singapore: National Archives, 1993. NLB, NTUNIE.

549.   Mastura Manap. "Malays are the Daredevils of Society…Singaporean Malay Bikers and the Rhetoric of Race". Academic exercise, Department of Sociology, National University of Singapore, 2008. 67 pp. NUS.

550.   Mohammad Noor Abdul Rahman. "*Persilatan di Singapura*". Academic exercise, Department of Malay Studies, National University of Singapore, 1992. 42 pp. NUS.

551.   *Suara Perpensis*. Singapore: Persatuan Penchak Silat Singapura, 1970–73. NLB, NUS.

552.   *Traditional Games*. Singapore: Curriculum Planning & Development Division, Ministry of Education, 1998. 33 pp. NLB.

553.   "Understanding Malay Traditional Games and Sports". *Citizen* (August 1995): 6. NLB.

Cultural Organizations

554. *32 tahun Majlis Pusat, 1969–2001.* Singapore: Majlis Pusat, 2001. 64 pp. NLB.

555. "Badan Budaya Melayu Geylang Serai". *Citizen* (November 1986): 12. NLB, NUS.

556. *Badan Kesenian Melayu = Board of Culture Society 11th Anniversary.* Singapore: Badan Kesenian Melayu, 1977. 1 vol. NUS.

557. Hidayah Amin. *A Journey of Giving: The LBKM Story.* Singapore: Lembaga Biasiswa Kenangan Maulud. 225 pp. NLB.

558. Juri Wari. "Majlis Pusat: Anggota-anggota Korporat Kami". *Citizen* (March 89): 22–23. NLB, NUS.

559. *Konvensyen '88 MP: Transkripsi.* Singapore: Majlis Pusat Pertubuhan-pertubuhan Budaya Melayu Singapura, 1988. 1 vol. (various foliations). NUS.

560. "Majlis Pusat". *Citizen* (March 1989): 22. NLB.

561. "MESRA Celebrates Achievements of Malay Community". *Citizen* (November 1995): 14–15. NLB.

562. Mohamed Pitchay Gani Mohamed Abdul Aziz, ed. *Dari Gerhana ke Puncak Purnama: Biografi ASAS 50, 55 Tahun dalam Persuratan.* Singapore: Angkatan Sasterawan '50, 2005. 326 pp. NLB, NTUNIE, NUS.

563. *Prima Seni = Perkumpulan Seni Singapura.* Singapore: Perkumpulan Seni, 2008. 186 pp. NLB.

564. "Sekitar Kerabat". In *Budaya: Penyambung Lidah Majlis Pusat.* Bil 2 (1983): 28–32. NLB, NUS.

565. *60 Years ASAS 50: Celebrating 6 Decades of Literary Excellence.* Singapore: Angkatan Sasterawan '50, 2010. 87 pp. NLB.

566. *Society of Malay Culture 26th Anniversary Souvenir Programme 1979 = Persatuan Kebudayaan Melayu Ulang Tahun Ke-26 Cenderamata.* Singapore: Persatuan Kebudayaan Melayu, 1979. 65 pp. NLB, NUS.

567. *Ulangtahun Majlis Pusat ke 34 = Majlis Pusat 34th Anniversary.* Singapore: Majlis Pusat, 2003. 40 pp. NLB.

568.   Zakir Hussain. *MESRA 20 years on = MESRA 20th Anniversary*. Singapore: People's Association, 2008. 200 pp. NLB.

569.   Zulkifli Mohammed. *Majlis Pusat: Contemporary Developments and Future Challenges*. Seminar Papers, no. 8. Singapore: Department of Malay Studies, National University Singapore, 1993. 9 pp. ISEAS, NUS.

DEMOGRAPHY

- *Population*
- *Fertility, Childbirth and Family Planning*
- *Mortality*

Population

570. Chen S.J., Peter. *Population Policy and Social Science Research on Population in Singapore.* Singapore: Chopmen Enterprises, 1977. 25 pp. ISEAS, NLB, NTUNIE, NUS.

571. Cheng Siok Hwa. "Demographic Trends". In *Singapore: Development Policies and Trends*, edited by Peter S.J. Chen. Singapore: Oxford University Press, 1983. ISEAS, NLB, NTUNIE, NUS.

572. Chew Seow Ting, Joab. "Demographic Aspects of the Aged Population: Ethnic Groups in Singapore, 1947–1989". Academic exercise, Department of Economics & Statistics, National University of Singapore, 1991. 76 pp. NUS.

573. Elinah Abdullah. "Malay/Muslim Patterns of Settlement and Trade in the First 50 Years". In *Malays/Muslims in Singapore: Selected Readings in History 1819–1965*, edited by Khoo Kay Kim, Elinah Abdullah and Wan Meng Hao. Subang Jaya, Selangor: Pelanduk Publications in cooperation with Centre for Research on Islamic and Malay Affairs, Singapore, 2006. ISEAS, NLB, NTUNIE, NUS.

574. Farish A. Noor (Farish Ahmad Noor). "The Use of Colonial Census, Racial Ideology and the Creation of a Racially Segregated Plural Colonial Economy in British Malaya". In *Diaspora: The Story of the South Asian Muslim Diaspora in Southeast Asia Today*, by Farish A. Noor. Kuala Lumpur: Malaysian Social Research Institute, 2013. ISEAS, NLB, NTU.

575. Fung Li Ning, Agnes. "Growth of Settlements in Rural Singapore (1819–1957)". MA dissertation, University of Singapore, 1962. 1 microfiche (62 pp.). NUS.

576. Iskandar Mydin. "City Lights: Pre-War Singapore's Allure for Rural Malays". *Heritage: An Annual Publication of the National Museum* 10 (1989): 5–12. NLB, NTUNIE, NUS.

577. Kahn, Joel S. "Making Race and Place in Colonial Singapore". In *Other Malays: Nationalism and Cosmopolitanism in the Modern Malay World.* Singapore: Asian Studies Association of Australia in association with Singapore University Press and NIAS Press, 2006. ISEAS, NLB, NTUNIE, NUS.

578.   Lee Hsien Loong. "Population Trends in Singapore". *Speeches* 11, no. 5 (September/October 1987): 56–65. ISEAS, NLB, NTUNIE, NUS.

579.   Lim Wui Jin, Anthony. "Future Implications of the Singapore Population: 1990–2050". Academic exercise, Department of Economics & Statistics, National University of Singapore, 1991. 74 pp. NUS.

580.   Loh Chee Harn, Jacqui. "The Arab Population of Singapore, 1819–1959". Academic exercise, University of Singapore, 1963. 1 microfilm reel. NUS.

581.   Malay States, Federated. Superintendent of Census. *British Malaya (the Colony of the Straits Settlements and the Malay States under British Protection, namely the Federated States of Perak, Selangor, Negri Sembilan and Pahang and the States of Johore, Kedah, Kelantan, Trengganu, Perlis and Brunei): A Report on the 1931 Census and on Certain Problems of Vital Statistics.* London: Crown Agents for the Colonies, 1932. 389 pp. ISEAS, NLB, NUS.

582.   Malaya (Federation). *Malaya, Comprising the Federation of Malaya and the Colony of Singapore: A Report on the 1947 Census of Population.* London: Crown Agents for the Colonies, 1949. 597 pp. ISEAS, NLB, NTUNIE, NUS.

583.   Neville, Warwick. "The Area Distribution of Population in Singapore". *The Journal of Tropical Geography* 20 (1965): 16–25. ISEAS, NLB, NUS.

584.   Neville, Warwick. "Singapore: Recent Trends in the Sex and Age Composition of a Community". *Population Studies* 17 (1963): 99–112. NTUNIE, NUS.

585.   *Population Trends 2014.* Singapore: Department of Statistics, 2014. 147 pp. NLB, NUS.

586.   Saw Swee-Hock. "Changing Population Structure". In *The Population of Singapore.* Singapore: Institute of Southeast Asian Studies, 2012. ISEAS, NLB, NTUNIE, NUS.

587.   Saw Swee-Hock. "The Changing Population Structure in Singapore during 1824–1962 (by Race, Sex and Age Groups)". *Malayan Economic Review* 9, no. 1 (April 1964): 90–101. ISEAS, NLB, NUS.

588.   Saw Swee-Hock. *Demographic Trends in Singapore.* Singapore: Department of Statistics, 1981. 75 pp. ISEAS, NLB, NTUNIE, NUS.

589. Saw Swee-Hock. "Migration". In *The Population of Singapore*. Singapore: Institute of Southeast Asian Studies, 2012. ISEAS, NLB, NTUNIE, NUS.

590. Saw Swee-Hock. *The Population of Singapore*. Singapore: Institute of Southeast Asian Studies, 2012. 362 pp. ISEAS, NLB, NTUNIE, NUS.

591. Saw Swee-Hock. "The Population of Singapore and Its Social Implications". MA dissertation, Department of Economics, University of Malaya, Singapore, 1961. 193 pp. NUS.

592. Saw Swee-Hock. *Singapore Population in Transition*. Philadelphia: University of Pennsylvania Press, 1970. 227 pp. ISEAS, NLB, NTUNIE, NUS.

593. Saw Swee-Hock and Cheng Siok Hwa. "Population Structure and Trends". In *Public Policy and Population Change in Singapore*, edited by Peter S.J. Chen and James T. Fawcett. New York: Population Council, 1979. ISEAS, NLB.

594. Sen, Mihir Kumar. "The Geographical Distribution of Population in Singapore, 1947–57 (with Economic Interpretation)". Academic exercise, University of Malaya, Singapore, 1959. 1 microfilm reel. NUS.

595. Shamsul Bahrin, Tunku. "The Growth and Distribution of the Indonesian Population in Malaya". *Bijdragen tot de taal land- en volkenkunde* 123 (1967): 267–86. ISEAS, NLB, NTUNIE, NUS.

596. Shamsul Bahrin, Tunku. "The Indonesians in Malaya: A Study of the Pattern of Migration to Malaya". MA dissertation, University of Sheffield, 1964. 1 microfilm reel. ISEAS, NUS.

597. Shantakumar, G. *The Aged Population of Singapore*. Census of Population 1990 Monograph, no. 1. Singapore: National Printers, 1994. 212 pp. ISEAS, NTUNIE.

598. Siebel, Maureen. "A Study of the Changes in the Malaysian Population of Singapore, 1819–1959". Academic exercise, University of Malaya, Singapore, 1960. Microform. NUS.

599. Singapore. Department of Statistics. *Census of Population 1980. Release no. 1*. [Compiled] by Khoo Chian Kim. Singapore: Department of Statistics, 1983. 50 pp. ISEAS, NLB, NTUNIE, NUS.

600. Singapore. Department of Statistics. *Census of Population 1980. Release no. 2, Demographic Characteristics*. [Compiled] by Khoo Chian Kim.

Singapore: Department of Statistics, 1983. 89 pp. ISEAS, NLB, NTUNIE, NUS.

601. Singapore. Department of Statistics. *Census of Population 1980. Release no. 3, Literacy and Education.* [Compiled] by Khoo Chian Kim. Singapore: Department of Statistics, 1983. 93 pp. ISEAS, NLB, NTUNIE, NUS.

602. Singapore. Department of Statistics. *Census of Population 1980. Release no. 4, Economic Characteristics.* [Compiled] by Khoo Chian Kim. Singapore: Department of Statistics, 1983. 303 pp. ISEAS, NLB, NTUNIE, NUS.

603. Singapore. Department of Statistics. *Census of Population 1980. Release no. 5, Geographic Distribution.* [Compiled] by Khoo Chian Kim. Singapore: Department of Statistics, 1983. 236 pp. ISEAS, NLB, NTUNIE, NUS.

604. Singapore. Department of Statistics. *Census of Population 1980. Release no. 6, Households and Houses.* [Compiled] by Khoo Chian Kim. Singapore: Department of Statistics, 1983. 129 pp. ISEAS, NLB, NTUNIE, NUS.

605. Singapore. Department of Statistics. *Census of Population 1980. Release no. 7, Income and Transport.* [Compiled] by Khoo Chian Kim. Singapore: Department of Statistics, 1983. 133 pp. ISEAS, NLB, NTUNIE, NUS.

606. Singapore. Department of Statistics. *Census of Population 1980. Release no. 8, Languages Spoken at Home.* [Compiled] by Khoo Chian Kim. Singapore: Department of Statistics, 1983. 147 pp. ISEAS, NLB, NTUNIE, NUS.

607. Singapore. Department of Statistics. *Census of Population 1980. Release no. 9, Religion and Fertility.* [Compiled] by Khoo Chian Kim. Singapore: Department of Statistics, 1983. 129 pp. ISEAS, NLB, NTUNIE, NUS.

608. Singapore. Department of Statistics. *Census of Population 1990: Advance Data Release.* Singapore: Department of Statistics, 1991. 71 pp. ISEAS, NLB, NTUNIE, NUS.

609. Singapore. Department of Statistics. *Census of Population 2000: Advance Data Release.* [Compiled] by Leow Bee Geok. Singapore: Department of Statistics, 2001. 208 pp. ISEAS, NLB, NTUNIE, NUS.

610. Singapore. Department of Statistics. *Census of Population 2000: Administrative Report.* [Compiled] by Leow Bee Geok. Singapore: Department of Statistics, Ministry of Trade and Industry, 2002. 188 pp. ISEAS, NLB, NTUNIE.

611.   Singapore. Department of Statistics. *Census of Population 2000. Statistical Release 1, Demographic Characteristics.* [Compiled] by Leow Bee Geok. Singapore: Department of Statistics, 2001. 142 pp. ISEAS, NLB, NTUNIE, NUS.

612.   Singapore. Department of Statistics. *Census of Population 2000. Statistical Release 2, Education, Language and Religion.* [Compiled] by Leow Bee Geok. Singapore: Department of Statistics, 2001. 130 pp. ISEAS, NLB, NTUNIE, NUS.

613.   Singapore. Department of Statistics. *Census of Population 2000. Statistical Release 3, Economic Characteristics.* [Compiled] by Leow Bee Geok. Singapore: Department of Statistics, 2001. 174 pp. ISEAS, NLB, NTUNIE, NUS.

614.   Singapore. Department of Statistics. *Census of Population 2000. Statistical Release 4, Geographic Distribution and Travel.* [Compiled] by Leow Bee Geok. Singapore: Department of Statistics, 2001. 164 pp. ISEAS, NLB, NTUNIE, NUS.

615.   Singapore. Department of Statistics. *Census of Population 2000. Statistical Release 5, Household and Housing.* [Compiled] by Leow Bee Geok. Singapore: Department of Statistics, 2001. 166 pp. ISEAS, NLB, NTUNIE, NUS.

616.   Singapore. Department of Statistics. *Census of Population 2010: Administrative Report.* Singapore: Department of Statistics, Ministry of Trade and Industry, 2011. 143 pp. ISEAS, NLB, NTUNIE.

617.   Singapore. Department of Statistics. *Census of Population 2010: Advance Census Release.* Singapore: Department of Statistics, Ministry of Trade and Industry, 2010. 36 pp. ISEAS, NLB, NTUNIE.

618.   Singapore. Department of Statistics. *Census of Population 2010. Statistical Release 1, Demographic Characteristics, Education, Language and Religion.* Singapore: Department of Statistics, 2011. 180 pp. ISEAS, NLB, NTU, NTUNIE, NUS.

619.   Singapore. Department of Statistics. *Census of Population 2010. Statistical Release 2, Households and Housing.* Singapore: Department of Statistics, 2011. 128 pp. ISEAS, NLB, NTUNIE, NUS.

620.   Singapore. Department of Statistics. *Census of Population 2010. Statistical Release 3, Geographic Distribution and Transport.* Singapore: Department of Statistics, 2011. 196 pp. ISEAS, NLB, NTUNIE, NUS.

621.   Singapore. Department of Statistics. *Profile of Singapore Resident Population, 1980–1991.* Singapore: Department of Statistics, 1992. 49 pp. ISEAS, NLB, NTUNIE, NUS.

622.   Singapore. Department of Statistics. *Report on the Census of Population 1957.* Singapore: Government Printer Office, 1964. 319 pp. ISEAS, NLB, NTUNIE, NUS.

623.   Singapore. Department of Statistics. *Report on the Census of Population 1970.* Singapore: Department of Statistics, 1973. 2 vols. ISEAS, NLB, NTUNIE, NUS.

624.   Singapore. Department of Statistics. *Singapore Census of Population 1990. Statistical Release 1, Demographic Characteristics.* [Compiled] by Lau Kak En. Singapore: Census of Population Office, Department of Statistics, 1992. 129 pp. ISEAS, NLB, NTUNIE, NUS.

625.   Singapore. Department of Statistics. *Singapore Census of Population 1990. Statistical Release 2, Households and Housing.* [Compiled] by Lau Kak En. Singapore: Census of Population Office, Department of Statistics, 1992. 186 pp. ISEAS, NLB, NTUNIE, NUS.

626.   Singapore. Department of Statistics. *Singapore Census of Population 1990. Statistical Release 3, Literacy, Languages Spoken and Education.* [Compiled] by Lau Kak En. Singapore: Census of Population Office, Department of Statistics, 1993. 165 pp. ISEAS, NLB, NTUNIE, NUS.

627.   Singapore. Department of Statistics. *Singapore Census of Population 1990. Statistical Release 4, Economic Characteristics.* [Compiled] by Lau Kak En. Singapore: Census of Population Office, Department of Statistics, 1993. 165 pp. ISEAS, NLB, NTUNIE, NUS.

628.   Singapore. Department of Statistics. *Singapore Census of Population 1990. Statistical Release 5, Transport and Geographic Distribution.* [Compiled] by Lau Kak En. Singapore: Census of Population Office, Department of Statistics, 1994. 201 pp. ISEAS, NLB, NTUNIE, NUS.

629.   Singapore. Department of Statistics. *Singapore Census of Population 1990. Statistical Release 6, Religion, Child Care, Leisure Activities.* [Compiled]

by Lau Kak En. Singapore: Census of Population Office, Department of Statistics, 1994. 166 pp. ISEAS, NLB, NTUNIE, NUS.

630. "Singapore Residents by Age Group, Ethnic Group and Sex, End June 2014". In *Yearbook of Statistics, Singapore, 2015*. Singapore: Department of Statistics, 2015. ISEAS, NLB, NTU, NTUNIE, NUS. Available at <http://www.singstat.gov.sg/docs/default-source/default-document-library/publications/publications_and_papers/reference/yearbook_2015/yos2015.pdf>.

631. Straits Settlements. *The Census of British Malaya, 1921*. [Compiled] by J.E. Nathan. London: Dunstable and Watford, 1922. 406 pp. ISEAS, NLB, NUS.

   (Report on 1921 census of the Straits Settlements, Federated Malay States and Protected States of Johore, Kedah, Perlis, Kelantan, Trengganu, and Brunei).

632. Straits Settlements. *Miscellaneous Numerical Returns [and] Straits Settlements Population [for the Year] 1871*. Singapore: [s.n.], 1871. 1 microfilm reel. NUS.

633. Straits Settlements. *Miscellaneous Numerical Returns [and] Straits Settlements Population 1881 (According to Census Taken in 1881)*. Singapore: [s.n.], 1881. 1 microfilm reel. ISEAS, NUS.

634. Straits Settlements. *Report on the Census of the Straits Settlements, Taken on the 5th April 1891*. [Compiled] by E.M. Merewether. Singapore: Government Printing Office, 1892. 1 microfilm reel. ISEAS, NLB, NUS.

635. Straits Settlements. *Report on the Census of the Straits Settlements Taken on the 1st March 1901*. [Compiled] by J.R. Innes. Singapore: Government Printing Office, 1901. 1 microfilm reel. ISEAS, NLB, NUS.

636. Straits Settlements. *Report on the Census of the Colony of the Straits Settlements, Taken on the 10th March, 1911*. [Compiled] by Hayes Marriott. Singapore: Government Printing Office, 1911. 1 microfilm reel. ISEAS, NLB, NUS.

637. Tan Mei Chang. "Female Population of Singapore 1980". Academic exercise, Department of Geography, National University of Singapore, 1986. 135 pp. NUS.

638. Thiruchelvan Selvadurai. "Some Observations on the Population of Singapore at the 1931 and 1947 Censuses". Academic exercise, Department of Economics, University of Malaya, Singapore, 1952. 87 pp. ISEAS, NUS.

639. Thomas, Margaret. "Must We Maintain the Racial Balance?" *Singapore Business* 13, no. 9 (September 1989): 8. ISEAS, NLB, NTU, NTUNIE, NUS.

640. Toh Mun Heng and Tay Boon Nga. *Households and Housing in Singapore*. Census of Population 1990 Monograph, no. 4. Singapore: Department of Statistics, 1995. 114 pp. ISEAS, NTUNIE.

641. Yap Mui Teng, ed. *Report of the IPS Forum on the Census Population 1990*. IPS Report Series, no. 4. Singapore: Institute of Policy Studies, 1991. 66 pp. NUS.

642. *Yearbook of Statistics, Singapore*. Singapore: Department of Statistics, 1968–. ISEAS, NLB, NTUNIE, NUS.

643. Yeh H.K. (Hua Kuo), Stephen. *Report on the Census of Malay Settlement Areas, Singapore, 1967*. Singapore: Economic Research Centre, University of Singapore, 1970. 148 pp. ISEAS, NUS.

Fertility, Childbirth and Family Planning

644. Anderson, Margaret Grace. "Family Planning in a Modernizing Malay Community in Singapore". PhD dissertation, University of Singapore, 1969. 1 microfilm reel. NUS.

645. Atputharajah V. "Some Aspects of Sexual Knowledge and Sexual Behaviour of Local Women, Results of a Survey: 1-General Sexual Knowledge and Attitude to Abortion, Pregnancy and Contraception". *Singapore Medical Journal* 25, no. 3 (1984): 135–40. NLB, NUS.

646. Chen A.J. et al. "Legalized Abortion: The Singapore Experience". *Studies in Family Planning* 16, no. 3 (1985): 170–78. ISEAS, NTUNIE, NUS.

647. Chen S.J., Peter. *Ethnicity and Fertility: The Case of Singapore*. Singapore: Chopmen Enterprise, 1979. 27 pp. ISEAS, NLB, NUS.

648. Chia K.S. et al. "Twin Births in Singapore: A Population-Based Study using the National Birth Registry". *Annals of the Academy of Medicine, Singapore* 33, no. 2 (2004): 195–99. NTUNIE, NUS.

649. *Family Planning Seminar for Community Leaders of Geylang Serai, Kampong Chai Chee, Kampong Kembangan and Kampong Ubi Constituencies [1974]: Report.* Singapore: Family Planning and Population Board, 1975. 30 pp. NLB, NUS.

650. Hassan, Riaz. *Ethnicity, Culture and Fertility: An Exploratory Study of Fertility and Sexual Beliefs.* Singapore: Chopmen, 1980. 188 pp. ISEAS, NLB, NTUNIE, NUS.

651. Hassan, Riaz. *A Preliminary Account of Social and Cultural Factors Affecting Fertility Behaviour in Singapore.* Singapore: UNPFA Law and Population Project, 1975. 106 pp. ISEAS, NLB, NUS.

652. Jones, Gavin W. "Fertility Transitions among Malay Populations of Southeast Asia: Puzzles of Interpretation". *Population and Development Review* 16, no. 3 (1990): 507–37. ISEAS, NTUNIE, NUS.

653. Kuo C.Y., Eddie and Chiew Seen Kong. *Ethnicity and Fertility in Singapore.* Singapore: Institute of Southeast Asian Studies, 1984. 180 pp. ISEAS, NLB, NTUNIE, NUS.

654. "Live-births by Ethnic Group and Sex". In *Yearbook of Statistics, Singapore, 2015.* Singapore: Department of Statistics, 2015. ISEAS, NLB, NTU, NTUNIE, NUS Available at <http://www.singstat.gov.sg/docs/default-source/default-document-library/publications/publications_and_papers/reference/yearbook_2015/yos2015.pdf>.
(Statistics of Live-births from 2008–14).

655. Neville, Warwick. "The Birth Rate in Singapore". *Population Studies* 32, no. 1 (1978): 113–33. NTUNIE, NUS.

656. Saw Swee-Hock. "Fertility Trends and Differentials". In *The Population of Singapore.* Singapore: Institute of Southeast Asian Studies, 2012. ISEAS, NLB, NTUNIE, NUS.

657. Singh, K., O. Viegas, and S.S. Ratnam. "Fertility Trends in Singapore". *Journal of Biosocial Science* 20, no. 4 (1988): 401–9. NUS.

658. Yeh H.K. (Hua Kuo), Stephen. *Some Observations on Fertility Decline in Singapore.* Reprint Monograph Series, no. 5. Singapore: Economic Research Centre, University of Singapore, 1967. 15 pp. ISEAS. Previous ed. published: Singapore: University of Singapore, 1966. 15 pp. NLB, NUS.

Mortality

659. Chia Boon-Hock et al. "Suicide Trends in Singapore: 1955–2004". *Archives of Suicide Research: Official Journal of the International Academy for Suicide Research* 14, no. 3 (2010): 276–83. NTUNIE, NUS.

660. Ko S.M. and E.H. Kua. "Ethnicity and Elderly Suicide in Singapore". *International Psychogeriatrics* IPA 7, no. 2 (1995): 309–17. NTUNIE, NUS.

661. Kua E.H. and W.F. Tsoi. "Suicide in the Island of Singapore". *Acta Psychiatrica Scandinavica* 71, no. 3 (1985): 227–29. NTUNIE, NUS.

662. Lum K.C. and H.P. Lee. "Standardised Mortality Ratios for Some Selected Causes among the Main Ethnic and Chinese Dialect Groups in Singapore, 1970". *Singapore Medical Journal* 22, no. 3 (1981): 144–49. NLB, NUS.

663. Saw Swee-Hock. "Mortality Trends and Differentials". In *The Population of Singapore*. Singapore: Institute of Southeast Asian Studies, 2012. ISEAS, NLB, NTUNIE, NUS.

664. Wai B.H. and K.E. Heok. "Parasuicide: A Singapore Perspective". *Ethnicity & Health* 3, no. 4 (1998): 255–63. NTUNIE, NUS.

665. Yeong C.T. et al. "Optimising Management of Stillbirths in Modern Singapore". *Singapore Medical Journal* 38, no. 8 (1997): 317–20. NUS.

ECONOMICS

- *Occupations, Employment and Income*
- *Business, Commerce and Industry*
- *Finance*
- *Economic Policy and Conditions*

Occupations, Employment and Income

666. A. Aziz Mahmood. "Employment Stability of Peons in Singapore". Academic exercise, Department of Economics, University of Malaya, Singapore, 1959. 1 microfilm reel (43 pp.). NUS.

667. A. Ghani Hamid (Abdul Ghani Hamid). "Malay Fishermen". In *Vanishing Trades of Singapore*, edited by Lo-Ang Siew Ghim and Chua Chee Huan. Singapore: Oral History Department, 1992. ISEAS, NLB, NTUNIE, NUS.

668. A. Ghani Hamid (Abdul Ghani Hamid). "Malay Masseuses". In *Vanishing Trades of Singapore*, edited by Lo-Ang Siew Ghim and Chua Chee Huan. Singapore: Oral History Department, 1992. ISEAS, NLB, NTUNIE, NUS.

669. A. Ghani Hamid (Abdul Ghani Hamid). "Malay Musician". In *Vanishing Trades of Singapore*, edited by Lo-Ang Siew Ghim and Chua Chee Huan. Singapore: Oral History Department, 1992. ISEAS, NLB, NTUNIE, NUS.

670. Abdul Shariff Aboo Kassim. "Vulnerability of Malays in the Workforce". *Karyawan: Professionals for the Community* 10, issue 1 (July 2009): 26–29. ISEAS, NLB, NTUNIE, NUS.

671. Abdullah Tarmugi. "Young Malay Professionals Key to the Future". *Speeches* 25, no. 3 (May–June 2001): 72–80. ISEAS, NLB, NTU, NTUNIE.

672. Aboo Bakar Aliar. "Malay School Leavers in Singapore". Academic exercise, Department of Social Work and Social Administration, University of Singapore, 1969. 95 pp. NTUNIE, NUS.

673. Aljunied, Sharifah Zahra. "Ethnic Distribution of Employment in Singapore: The Malays". Academic exercise, Department of Economics and Statistics, University of Singapore, 1980. 102 pp. NUS.

674. Burdon, T.W. "The Fishing Methods of Singapore". *JMBRAS* 27, pt. 2 (June 1954): 5–76. ISEAS, NLB, NTUNIE, NUS.

675. Chiew Seen Kong. "Ethnicity, Economic Development and Occupational Change in Singapore, 1957–1980". *Akademika* 30 (January 1987): 73–89. ISEAS, NTUNIE, NUS.

676. Faizah Rahmat. "Crossing the Low-Wage Barrier: Issues in Promoting Sustained Employability". *MENDAKI Policy Digest* (2007): 51–62. ISEAS, NTUNIE, NUS.

677. Faizah Rahmat. "Experiencing the Tough Times — Employability Beyond Employment". *MENDAKI Policy Digest* (2008): 27–36. ISEAS, NLB, NTUNIE, NUS.

678. Halimah Yaacob. "Wake-up Call for the Malay Workforce". *Karyawan: Professionals for the Community* 4 (January–April 1998): 4–6. ISEAS, NLB, NTUNIE, NUS.

679. Hashim Pendek. "Malay Fishermen of Singapore". Academic exercise, Department of Social Studies, University of Singapore, 1964. 233 pp. NUS.

680. Kobayashi, Yasuko. "Mocking without Mockery: Singaporean Malays and Indonesian Domestic Workers". *Review of Indonesian and Malaysian Affairs* 38, no. 1 (2004): 99–122. ISEAS, NLB, NTUNIE, NUS.

681. Lee K.M., William. "The Economic Marginality of Ethnic Minorities: An Analysis of Ethnic Income Inequality in Singapore". *Asian Ethnicity* 5, issue 1 (February 2004): 27–41. NLB.

682. Lee Kiat Jin. "Chinese and Malays in Singapore: Incomes, Education and Employment, 1954–1995". In *Race, Ethnicity, and the State in Malaysia and Singapore*, edited by Lian Kwen Fee. Boston: Brill Leiden, 2006. ISEAS, NLB, NTUNIE, NUS.

683. *List of Advanced Practice Nurses, Registered Nurses and Registered Nurses (Psychiatric): Supplement to the Republic of Singapore Government Gazette.* Singapore: Singapore National Printer, 1985–. NLB, NUS.

684. *List of Registered Midwives: Supplement to the Republic of Singapore Government Gazette.* Singapore: Singapore National Printer, 1985–. NLB, NUS.

685. *List of Professional Engineers: Supplement to the Republic of Singapore Government Gazette.* Singapore: Singapore National Printer, 1984–. NLB, NUS.

686. *Modern Challenges Facing Working Muslim Women: A Forum.* Organized by Ba'alwi Mosque, Singapore, 1999. 32 pp. NUS.

687. Muhammad Yusuf Zabidin. "The Malaysian Seaman and His Family". Academic exercise, University of Malaya, Singapore, 1962. 71 pp. NUS.

688. Nachatar Singh Sandhu. "The 'Jaga-kreta' Boy: A Study of the Jaga Kreta System in Singapore". Academic exercise, Department of Social Studies, University of Malaya, Singapore, 1959. 132 pp. NUS.

689. Othman Haron Eusofe. *Malay Participation in the Labour Market: Challenges & Opportunities*. Seminar Papers, no. 16. Singapore: Department of Malay Studies, National University of Singapore, 1995. 17 pp. ISEAS, NLB, NUS.

690. Quek Pei Huan, Vivian. "The Myth of Sports as an Equalizer of Society: The Case of Malay Football Players in the S-League". Academic exercise, Department of Sociology, National University of Singapore, 2008. 68 pp. NUS.

691. Rafiz Mohyi Hapipi. "Surfing the Tide: Negotiating Social Challenges". *MENDAKI Policy Digest* (2006): 30–50. ISEAS, NLB, NTUNIE, NUS.

692. *Register of Practitioners (Architects): Supplement to the Republic of Singapore Government Gazette*. Singapore: Singapore National Printer, 1996–. NLB, NUS.

693. *Report on the Labour Force Survey of Singapore*. Singapore: Ministry of Labour, 1973–. ISEAS, NLB, NTUNIE, NUS.

694. Saw Swee-Hock. "Labour Force". In *The Population of Singapore*. Singapore: Institute of Southeast Asian Studies, 2012. ISEAS, NLB, NTUNIE, NUS.

695. Siglap Community Centre. Youth Group. *A Report on the Fishermen of Siglap*. Edited by Chou Loke Ming. Singapore: Siglap Community Centre, 1977. 50 pp. ISEAS, NLB, NUS.

696. *Singapore Yearbook of Labour Statistics*. Singapore: Research and Statistics Department, Ministry of Labour, 1977–. ISEAS, NLB, NTUNIE, NUS.

697. *Study on Malay/Muslim Workers in Singapore: Issues of Training and Re-training*. Singapore: Association of Muslim Professionals, 1998. 128 pp. NLB.

698. Suriati Supani. "Harnessing Trendsetters amidst Globalisation". *MENDAKI Policy Digest* (2006): 51–82. ISEAS, NLB, NTUNIE, NUS.

699. Tham Seong Chee. "Chorak2 Pekerjaan dalam Masharakat Melayu: Suatu Kajian terhadap Sifat2 dan Masa'alah2-nya dari Segi2 Sejarah dan Budaya dengan Merojok kapada Masharakat Tionghoa di-Malaya dan Singapura = Occupational Patterns in Malay Society: An Historical and Cultural Enquiry into Their Nature and Problems". PhD dissertation, Department of Malay Studies, University of Singapore, 1975. 2 vols. ISEAS, NUS.

700. Wang Chang-Vun, David. "The Malay Taxi-Drivers in Singapore". Academic exercise, Department of Social Work and Social Administration, University of Singapore, 1969. 102 pp. NUS.

701. Wong Thian Yow, Ernest. "The Economics of Malaysian Labour in the Harbour Launch Industry, Clifford Pier-Telok Ayer Basin, Singapore, 1958". Academic exercise, Department of Economics, University of Malaya, Singapore, 1959. 57 pp. NUS.

702. Woo Kwok Fai, Louis. "Equalizing Education and Earning among Ethnic and Socio-economic Groups in Singapore". PhD dissertation, Stanford University, 1983. 275 pp. ISEAS, NTUNIE, NUS.

703. Yeo Yong Boon, George. "Attracting Malay/Muslim Talent". *Speeches* 14, no. 6 (November/December 1990): 82–84. ISEAS, NLB, NTUNIE, NUS.

Business, Commerce and Industry

704. *25th Anniversary Publication: DPMS.* Singapore: Dewan Perniagaan Melayu Singapura, 1981. 168 pp. NLB, NUS.

705. Abdul Hamid Abdullah. "Economic Dynamism: How Far Have We Achieved?" *Karyawan: Professionals for the Community* 3 (June 1997): 8–9. ISEAS, NLB, NTUNIE, NUS.

706. *Berita DPMS.* Singapore: Dewan Perniagaan Melayu Singapura, 1978–. NLB, NUS.

707. Dana, Leo-Paul. "Chapter 14 Singapore". In *Asian Models of Entrepreneurship from the Indian Union to the Japanese Archipelago: Context, Policy and Practice.* Singapore: World Scientific, 2014. ISEAS, NLB, NTU, NUS.

708. Dewan Perniagaan dan Perusahaan Melayu Singapura. *Annual Report.* Singapore: Dewan Perniagaan dan Perusahaan Melayu Singapura [19—]–. NLB.

709. Dewan Perniagaan Melayu Singapura. *Annual Report*. Singapore: DPMS, [19—]-. NUS.

710. Dewan Perniagaan Melayu Singapura. *Trade, Investment & Tourism: Perkampungan Melayu* Singapore: Singapore Malay Chamber of Commerce, 1985. 105 pp. NUS.

711. *Dewaniaga: Buletin Dewan Perniagaan Melayu Singapura*. Singapore: DPMS, 1982-.

712. *Dewaniaga = Trade News*. Singapore: Dewan Perniagaan Melayu Singapura, 1990-. NLB.

713. *Fokus: Muslim Consumer Directory*. Singapore: Wolfe International, [2004]-. NLB.

714. "The Enterprising Alsagoffs of Singapore: Men of Property". In *Singapore Days of Old: A Special Commemorative History of Singapore Published on the 10th Anniversary of Singapore Tatler*. Hong Kong: Illustrated Magazine Publishing Co. Ltd., 1992. ISEAS, NLB, NTUNIE, NUS.

715. Fazilah Abdul Aziz. "The Malay Food Business: A Reflection on the Singapore Malays". Research exercise, Department of Malay Studies, National University of Singapore, 1996. 41 pp. NUS.

716. Freitag, Ulrike. "From Golden Youth in Arabia to Business Leaders in Singapore: Instructions of a Hadrami Patriarch". In *Southeast Asia and the Middle East: Islam, Movement, and the Longue Durée*, edited by Eric Tagliacozzo. Singapore: NUS Press, 2009. ISEAS, NLB, NTUNIE, NUS.

717. Gibson-Hill, Carl Alexander. "The Boats of Local Origin Employed in the Malayan Fishing Industry". *JMBRAS* 27, pt. 2 (1954): 145–74. ISEAS, NLB, NTUNIE, NUS.

718. Gibson-Hill, Carl Alexander. "The Fishing Boats Operated from Singapore Island". *JMBRAS* 23, pt. 3 (1950): 148–70. ISEAS, NLB, NTUNIE, NUS.

719. Green, Anthony. "Hadhramis, Shipping and the Hajj: The View from Singapore". In *Hadhrami Arabs Across the Indian Ocean: Contributions to Southeast Asian Economy and Society*, edited by

Syed Farid Alatas. Singapore: National Library Board, 2010. ISEAS, NLB, NUS.

720. Halimah Rahmat. "A Study of the Social, Educational and Economic Background of Successful Malay Businessmen". Research exercise, Department of Malay Studies, National University of Singapore, 1991. 38 pp. NUS.

721. *International Halal Trade Directory.* Singapore: Enorea Mediarep & Marketing, 2004–. NLB.

722. Jalil Haron. "Penyertaan Masyarakat Melayu dalam Perdagangan/ Perniagaan". Paper presented at a forum organized by Majlis Pusat Pertubuhan-Pertubuhan Budaya Melayu Singapura on 29 January [198-?]. 6 pp. NLB.

723. "KEMAS: Pengisytiharan". In *Trade, Investment of Tourism: Perkampungan Melayu.* Singapore: Singapore Malay Chamber of Commerce, 1985. NLB, NUS.

724. Khoo Chooi Ling. "Malay Business in Singapore". Research exercise, Department of Malay Studies, National University of Singapore, 1996. 36 pp. NUS.

725. Lee Poh Neo, Christina. "A Study of Geylang Serai Market". Academic exercise, Department of Geography, National University of Singapore, 1986. 102 pp. NUS.

726. Lim, Kevin and Cheryl-Ann Low. "Maritime Trade and Piracy in Singapore and the Malay Archipelago before the Nineteenth Century". *History Journal* 1993/94: 16–20. NLB.

727. Mattar Yasser. "Arab Ethnic Enterprises in Colonial Singapore: Market Entry and Exit Mechanisms 1819–1965". *Asia Pacific Viewpoint* 45, no. 2 (August 2004): 165–79. ISEAS, NLB, NTUNIE.

728. Muhamad Azman Atan. "Sejarah dan Pembangunan Dewan Perniagaan Melayu Singapura". Academic exercise, Department of Malay Studies, National University of Singapore, 1994. 57 pp. NUS.

729. *Muslim Business and Consumer Directory of Singapore.* Singapore: Nusa Media, [199-]–. NLB.

730. *Muslim Trade.* Singapore: Nusantara Publication, 1973–. NUS.

731. Noraisah Omar. "Problems and Prospect of Entering Business among Singapore Malays". Research exercise, Department of Malay Studies, National University of Singapore, 1996. 45 pp. NUS.

732. Osman-Gani, Ahad M. and Joo-Seng Tan. "Influence of Culture on Negotiation Styles of Asian Managers: An Empirical Study of Major Cultural/Ethnic Groups in Singapore". *Thunderbird International Business Review* 44, no. 6 (2002): 819–39. NUS.

733. *Perayaan Jubli Emas 50, Syarikat Kerjasama Serbaguna Guru-Guru Melayu Singapura, 7 September 1931–1981*. Singapore: Syarikat Kerjasama Serbaguna Guru-Guru Melayu Singapura, 1981. 67 pp. NUS.

734. Robert, Crispina. "Miss Match". *Her World* (May 2007): 100–2. NLB.

735. Rozlinda Abdul Rahim. "Malay's Perception of Business". Research exercise, Department of Malay Studies, National University of Singapore, 1991. 41 pp NUS.

736. Rozylawati Rohani. "The Regionalisation of Malay-Muslim Businesses in Singapore". Research exercise, Department of Malay Studies, National University of Singapore. 1996. 50 pp. NUS.

737. Sarbene Jantan. "Obstacles to the Rise of the Malay Entrepreneurial Class: The Case of Singapore". Academic exercise, Department of Southeast Asian Studies Programme, National University of Singapore, 1995. 65 pp. NUS.

738. Seah Yien Chiong. "Ethnicity and Entrepreneurship in Singapore". Academic exercise, Department of Economics & Statistics, National University of Singapore, 1992. 68 pp. NUS.

739. *Senarai Anggota Biasa DPMS = SMCC Ordinary Members List*. Singapore: Dewan Perniagaan Melayu Singapura, 1990–. NLB.

740. Serjeant, Robert Bertram. "The Hadrami Network". In *Asian Merchants and Businessmen in the Indian Ocean and the China Sea*, edited by Denys Lombard and Jean Aubin. New Delhi; New York: Oxford University Press, 2000. ISEAS, NUS.

741. Shahrir Ariff. "They Really Mean Business: The Making of Malay Entrepreneurs". *Singapore Business* 11 (February 1987): 21–27. ISEAS, NLB, NTUNIE, NUS

742. Shaikh Yaseer Idris Mattar. "The Socioeconomics of Arab Ethnic Entrepreneurship in Singapore: The Muslim Ummah: Challenges, Directions and Reflections". *The Fount Journal*, no. 1 (2000): 95–116. ISEAS, NUS.

743. *Singapore and Malayan Directory*. Singapore: Fraser and Neave, 1922–40. 18 vols. Title varies. NLB, NUS.

744. *The Singapore and Malayan Directory for Containing Directories of the Straits Settlements, Perak, Selangor, Negri Sembilan, Pahang, Kedah, Perlis, Kelantan, Trengganu, Johore, Siam, Labuan, Brunei, British North Borneo, Sarawak, Sumatra (East Coast)*. Singapore: Printers Ltd., 1881–1940. 28 vols. ISEAS (1937), NUS.

745. *Singapore and Straits Directory*. Singapore: Mission Press, 1880–1921. 36 vols. Title and publisher varies. ISEAS (1914–15), NLB, NUS.

746. *Singapore Directory for the Straits Settlements*. Singapore: Straits Times Office, 1878–79. 2 vols. NLB, NUS.

747. *Singapore Halal Directory 2012/2013*. Singapore: Marshall Cavendish for Majlis Ugama Islam Singapura, 2012. 344 pp. NLB, NTUNIE, NUS.

748. *The Singapore Muslim Business Directory*. Singapore: Man's Grafik & Advertising, 1993–. NLB.

749. *Singapore Muslim Consumer Guide*. Singapore: SSA Media, 1998. 214 pp. ISEAS, NLB.

750. *Singapore Muslim Trade & Business Directory*. Singapore: SSA Media, 1997. 277 pp. ISEAS, NLB, NUS.

751. Stephens, Harold. "Down River Singapore with the Bugis Traders". *Asia Magazine* 21 (12 September 1982): 14–18. NLB, NUS.

752. Sullivan, Margaret. *Can Survive La: Cottage Industries in High Rise Singapore*. Singapore: Graham Brash Singapore, 1985. 255 pp. ISEAS, NLB, NTUNIE, NUS.

753. Talib, Ameen Ali. "Can Malay/Muslims be Successful Entrepreneurs?" *Karyawan: Professionals for the Community* 3 (June 1997): 4–7. ISEAS, NLB, NTUNIE, NUS.

754. Tham Chee Seong. "Culture and Management Teaching: The Case of Malay Culture". *Journal of Management Education* 16, no. 4 (1992): 61–71. NTUNIE (online), NUS.

755. *Times Business Directory of Singapore*. Singapore: Times Periodicals, 1984–. ISEAS, NLB, NTUNIE, NUS.

756. Tyabji, Amina. "Minority Muslim Business in Singapore". In *Islam and the Economic Development of Southeast Asia: The Muslim Private Sector in Southeast Asia*, edited by Mohamed Ariff. Singapore: Social Issues in Southeast Asia, Institute of Southeast Asian Studies, 1991. ISEAS, NLB, NTUNIE, NUS.

757. *Upacara Perasmian Pejabat Baru DPMS pada 28 Syaaban 1408H di Anson Road #24-07 International Plaza Singapore 0207 = Official Opening of SMCC New Office on 16 April 1988*. Singapore: DPMS, 1988. 91 pp. NLB, NUS.

758. Zakaria Buang. "Enterprising Malays". *Mirror* 24, no. 23 (December 1988): 1–3. ISEAS, NLB, NUS.

759. Zalina Kassim. "Change on a Malay Small-holding in Singapore: A Case Study". Academic exercise, University of Singapore, 1968. Microform. NUS.

760. Zuraidah Ibrahim. "The New Breed of Malay Entrepreneurs". *Singapore* (September 1992): 8–13. NLB, NUS.

Finance

761. Che Raenahani Che Mustafa. "Amanah Saham Mendaki: Kajian Terhadap Asal-usul, Matlamat dan Perkembangannya". Academic exercise, Department of Malay Studies, National University of Singapore, 1994. 58 pp. NUS.

762. Fazida A. Razak and Jamari Mokhtar. "Riba: Responses of the Muslim World and Singapore Muslims". *Fajar Islam* 1, no. 1 (1988): 45–58. ISEAS, NLB, NUS.

763. Goh, Wallace. "Investing ala Shari'ah". *Fundsupermart* 40 (2007): 26–27. NLB.

764. Hu, Richard. "Window of Opportunities for Islamic Financing". *Karyawan: Professionals for the Community* 3 (June 1997): 10–11, 18. ISEAS, NLB, NTUNIE, NUS.

765.   "ICPAS CPE Offers CIMA Certificates in Islamic Finance". *CPA Singapore* 2, no. 9 (September 2011): 21. NLB, NUS.

766.   Islamic Banking Summit. "Papers presented at the Islamic Banking Summit 2006: 'Responding to the Challenges of Globalization'", held in Singapore, 3–4 October 2006.

767.   Lau Pau. "Tax Legislation and Issues in Islamic Finance". In *Theory and Practice of Islamic Finance*, edited by Saw Swee-Hock and Karyn Wong. Singapore: Saw Centre for Financial Studies, 2008. 152 pp. NLB, NUS.

768.   Maysami, Rami Cooper. "Is Islamic Insurance a Viable Alternative? Evidence from Singapore". *Asia Financial Planning Journal* 7, no. 4 (July 2006): 28–31. NLB, NUS.

769.   Mohd Azhar bin Khalid. "Investments Risks vs Returns: What to Expect?" *Karyawan: Professionals for the Community* 3 (June 1997): 12–13. ISEAS, NLB, NTUNIE, NUS.

770.   Mohd. Jakfar Embek. "Initial Thoughts on Islamic Banking & Finance and Corporate Social Responsibilities (CSR)". *Jurnal Dakwah* 2 (December 2011): 14–27. NLB.

771.   Mohd. Nizam Ismail. "Are We Ambitious Enough?" *Karyawan: Professionals for the Community* 9, issue 2 (January 2009): 9–10. ISEAS, NLB, NTUNIE, NUS.

772.   Muhammad Rizal Alias. "'Playing Snowmonth': Malay ROSCAs in Singapore". Academic exercise, Department of Sociology, National University of Singapore, 2012. 64 pp. NUS.

773.   *Seminar Institusi Kewangan Islam, 2hb Oktober 1988, Auditorium Pusat Islam Singapura.* Anjuran Majlis Ugama Islam Singapura dengan kerjasama Haiah Dakwah Pusat. Singapore: MUIS, 1988. 30 pp. NUS.

774.   Tay Ee Hong, Alvin. "A Study on How the Malays/Muslims Use Their CPF Withdrawals". Research exercise, Department of Malay Studies, National University of Singapore, 1995. 54 pp. NUS.

775.   Tyabji, Amina. "The Management of Muslim Fund in Singapore". In *The Islamic Voluntary Sector in Southeast Asia: Islam and Economic Development of Southeast Asia*, edited by Mohamed Arif. Singapore: Social Issues in Southeast Asia, Institute of Southeast Asian Studies, 1991. ISEAS, NLB, NTUNIE, NUS.

Economic Policy and Conditions

776. Aljunied, Sharifah Zahra. "A General Outlook of Malay Participation in the Singapore Economy". *Sedar* (1981): 49–65. ISEAS, NLB, NUS. Also published in: *Inspiration: Madrasah Al-Maarif Al-Islamiah 50th Anniversary and Official Opening Ceremony, 15 March 1987*. Singapore: Madrasah Al-Maarif Al-Islamiah, 1987. NLB, NUS.

777. *Antara Dua Dekad*. Penerbit Eksekutif dan Pengarah Kreatif, Sujimy Mohd. Singapore: Screenbox, MediaCorp TV Suria, 2002. 4 videocassettes (VHS). 120 min. NLB.

778. Azhari Zahri. "Beberapa Masalah Ekonomi-Sosial dalam Masyarakat Melayu Singapura". *Beriga* 4, no. 1 (1970): 28–33. NLB, NUS.

779. Beaulie, Peter Dennis. "Singapore: A Case Study of Communalism and Economic Development". PhD dissertation, University of Washington, 1975. Ann Arbor, Mich.: University Microfilms International, 1976. 340 pp. ISEAS, NUS.

780. Buchanan, Iain. *Singapore in Southeast Asia: An Economic and Political Appraisal*. London: Bell, 1972. 336 pp. ISEAS, NLB, NTU, NTUNIE, NUS.

781. Chee, Stephen. "Malaysia and Singapore: The Political Economy of Multiracial Development". *Asian Survey* 14, no. 2 (1974): 183–91. ISEAS, NLB, NTU, NTUNIE, NUS.

782. *Economic & Social Statistics, Singapore, 1960–1982*. Singapore: Department of Statistics, 1983. 270 pp. ISEAS, NLB, NTUNIE, NUS.

783. Fong P.E. "The Economic Status of Malay Muslims in Singapore". *Journal of Institute of Muslim Minority Affairs* 3, no. 2 (1981): 148–61. ISEAS, NUS.

784. Hashim Ali. "Malays as a Minority: Problems to Economic Integration". Academic exercise, Department of Sociology, University of Singapore, 1976. 105 pp. ISEAS, NUS.

785. Jenkins, David and V.G. Kulkarni. "Joining the Mainstream: Things are Looking Up for Singapore's Malay Community". *Far Eastern Economic Review* 124, no. 26 (28 June 1984): 26–32. ISEAS, NLB, NTUNIE, NUS.

786.   Johann Johari. "Dollars & Sense: Economic & Financial Literacy amidst Global Shopping Gallery". *MENDAKI Policy Digest* (2007): 83–92. ISEAS, NTUNIE, NUS.

787.   Julina Khusaini. *Melayu@2000*. Singapore: MediaCorp TV12 Singapore, 2000. 3 videodiscs. 150 min. NLB.

788.   *Knowledge-Based Economy = Ekonomi Berteras llmu*. Singapore: Publicity and Community Relations Committee, Malay/Muslim KBE Convention, 2000. 1 computer optical disc. NLB.

789.   Kongres Ekonomi Masyarakat Melayu-Islam Singapura (1985: Singapura). *KEMAS, Dewan Persidangan Singapura, 13-15hb September 1985*. Anjuran Dewan Perniagaan Melayu Singapura, Majlis Pusat Pertubuhan-Pertubuhan Budaya Melayu Singapura, [dan] Syarikat Kerjasama Serbaguna Guru-Guru Melayu Singapura. Singapore: Jawatankuasa Penerbitan KEMAS, 1985. 242 pp. ISEAS, NLB, NUS.

790.   Lee Hsien Loong. "Balancing Economic and Social Development of the Malay Community". *Speeches* 24, no. 5 (September–October 2000): 28–32. ISEAS, NLB, NTUNIE.

791.   Lee Hsien Loong. "Malay/Muslims Must Prepare for Knowledge-Based Economy". *Speeches* 23, no. 4 (July–August 1999): 17–22. ISEAS, NLB, NTU, NTUNIE.

792.   Lee W.K. "The Poor in Singapore: Issues and Options". *Journal of Contemporary Asia* 31, no. 1 (2001): 57–70. ISEAS, NTUNIE, NUS.

793.   Maarof Salleh. "Winning Solutions in the IT Race". In *Jendela Kata: Kumpulan Ucapan Muis Siri ke-3*. Singapore: Majlis Ugama Islam Singapura, 2000. ISEAS, NLB, NTUNIE.

794.   Malik, M.M. "Western Intellectual Insights for Muslim Policy Makers on Religion-Based Economy". *International Journal of Social Science and Humanity* 5, no. 10 (2015): 879. NUS.

795.   Mastura Manap. "Impediments to Malay Mobility in Singapore — A Political Economy Approach". *MENDAKI Policy Digest* (2008): 109–21. ISEAS, NLB, NTU, NTUNIE, NUS.

796.   Moorthy, Md. Rashid K.S. "Economic Composition of the Malay Population in Singapore, 1980". Academic exercise, Department of Geography, National University of Singapore, 1990. 114 pp. NUS.

797. Pang Eng Fong. "The Economic Status of Malay Muslims in Singapore". *Jamiyah Bulletin* 1, no. 3 (1982): 4–9. NLB, NUS.

798. Pang Eng Fong. "Growth, Inequality and Race in Singapore". In *Singapore: Society in Transition*, edited by Riaz Hassan. Kuala Lumpur: Oxford University Press, 1976. ISEAS, NLB, NTUNIE, NUS. Also published under the same title: *International Labour Review* 3 (January 1975): 15–38. NLB, NTUNIE, NUS.

799. *Progress of the Malay Community in Singapore since 1980*. Singapore: Ministry of Community Development, Youth and Sports, [2007?]. 26 pp. NLB, NTUNIE, NUS. An update of: *Progress of the Malay Community in Singapore since 1990*. Singapore: Ministry of Information and the Arts, 2001. 60 pp. ISEAS, NLB, NTUNIE, NUS.

800. Rao, V.V. Bhanoji and M.K. Ramakrishnan. *Income Inequality in Singapore: Impact of Economic Growth and Structural Change, 1966–1975*. Singapore: Singapore University Press, 1980. 161 pp. ISEAS, NLB, NTUNIE, NUS.

801. Ramthan Hussain. "Back to School in KBE". *Karyawan: Professionals for the Community* 5 (January–April 1999): 10–11. ISEAS, NLB, NTUNIE, NUS.

802. "Seminar Penyertaan Masyarakat Melayu dalam 25 Tahun Pembangunan Nasional Singapura: Pencapaian dan Cabaran pada Abad ke-21". Anjuran Majlis Pusat di Maktab Rendah Victoria, Marine Vista, Singapura, 29 and 30 September 1984. 1 vol. (various foliations). ISEAS, NLB, NUS.

803. "Social Action till Year 2005: Facing Current Challenges, Emerging Trends & Social Impact of the Knowledge-based Economy: A Community Seminar". Organized by the Association of Muslim Professionals, 2005. 1 vol. (various foliations). NLB.

EDUCATION

- *General Works*
- *Policy and Curriculum Planning*
- *Malays/Muslims and Education*
- *Malay-Medium Education*
- *Islamic Education*
- *Technical, Pre-School and Special Education*
- *Students, Aid and Scholarship*
- *Academic Performance and Achievement*

General Works

804. Alhadad, Sharifah Hana. "Greater Flexibility in Secondary Schools: The Challenge for a Level Playing Field". In *MENDAKI Policy Digest* (2013): 59–67. NLB, NTUNIE.

805. Chen Ai Yen and Koay Siew Luan. *Transforming Teaching, Inspiring Learning: 60 Years of Teacher Education in Singapore, 1950-2010.* Singapore: National Institute of Education, 2010. 232 pp. ISEAS, NLB, NTUNIE, NUS

806. *Education in Singapore.* Singapore: Educational Publications Bureau, 1969–94. ISEAS, NTU, NTUNIE, NUS.

807. *Educational Systems of the Chief Crown Colonies and Possessions of the British Empire, Including Reports on the Training of Native Races. Part 3, Federated Malay States, Hong Kong. Straits Settlements, Fiji, Falkland Islands.* Special Reports on Educational Subjects (Great Britian, Board of Education), vol. 14. London: Dawsons of PallMall, 1968. 371 pp. NLB, NUS.

808. Gopinathan S. (Gopinathan Saravanan). "Towards a National System of Education in Singapore, 1945–1970: With Special Reference to the Media of Instruction in School". MEd dissertation, School of Education, University of Singapore, 1972. 153 pp. NTUNIE, NUS.

809. Gopinathan S. (Gopinathan Saravanan). *Towards a National System of Education in Singapore. 1945-1973.* Singapore: Oxford University Press, 1974. 178 pp. ISEAS, NLB, NTUNIE, NUS.

810. Ho Seng Ong. *Education for Unity in Malaya: An Evaluation of the Education System of Malaya with Special Reference to the Need for Unity in Its Plural Society.* Penang: Malayan Teacher's Union, 1952. 209 pp. ISEAS, NTUNIE, NUS

811. Hussin Mutalib. "Islamization of the Social Sciences: The Singapore Experience". Paper presented at the International Conference on Islam in ASEAN's Institutions of Higher Learning II, organized by Universiti Kebangsaan Malaysia, 1990. 20 pp. NUS.

812. *Ilmu.* Singapore: Abdullah Musa for Lembaga Biasiswa Kenangan Maulud, 198_-. NLB.

813. Jumari Naiyan. "Need for a Strong Foundation". *Karyawan: Professionals for the Community* 2 (October 1995): 5–7. ISEAS, NLB, NTUNIE, NUS.

814. Lee Yock Suan. "A Need for Life-Long Learning". *Karyawan: Professionals for the Community* (February 1996): 10–11, 18. ISEAS, NLB, NTUNIE, NUS.

815. Mason, Frederic. *The Schools of Malaya*. Singapore: Donald Moore, 1959. 39 pp. ISEAS, NLB, NTUNIE, NUS.

816. Nagle, J.S. *The Educational Needs of the Straits Settlements and Federated Malay States*. Baltimore: John Hopkins University, 1928. 194 pp. NLB, NTUNIE, NUS.

817. Ng L.T., Andrew. "Education and Ethnic Problems in Singapore 1959–1969". Dip. Ed. dissertation, University of Keele, 1971. 57 pp. NUS.

818. Quah, Stella R. "Education and Social Class in Singapore". In *Social Class in Singapore*, edited by Stella R. Quah et al. Singapore: Times Academic Press, Centre for Advanced Studies, National University of Singapore, 1991. ISEAS, NLB, NTUNIE, NUS.

819. Singapore. Commission of Inquiry into Education. *Commission of Inquiry into Education, Singapore: Final Report*. Chairman, Lim Tay Boh. Singapore: Commission of Inquiry into Education, 1964. 162 pp. ISEAS, NTUNIE.

820. Singapore. Ministry of Education. *Ten-year Programme: Data and Interim Proposals*. Singapore: Ministry of Education, 1949. 113 pp. NTUNIE, NUS.

821. Tan, Charlene. "Deep Culture Matters: Multiracialism in Singapore Schools". *International Journal of Educational Reform* 21, no. 1 (2012): 24–38. NTUNIE, NUS.

822. Tan Keng Yam, Tony. "Education: Its Quality Can be Improved". *Speeches* 14, no. 4 (July/August 1990): 37–43. ISEAS, NLB, NTUNIE, NUS.

823. Tan Yap Kwang, Chow Hong Kheng, and Christine Goh, eds. *Examinations in Singapore: Change and Continuity (1891–2007)*. Singapore: World Scientific for Singapore Examinations and Assessment Board, 2008. 147 pp. ISEAS, NLB, NTU, NTUNIE, NUS.

824.   Thiyagarajan Mannarlingam. "Access to Higher Education: A Case Study of National University of Singapore". Academic exercise, Department of Sociology, National University of Singapore, 1989. 71 pp. NTUNIE, NUS.

825.   Wong Hoy Kee, Francis and Gwee Yee Hean. *Official Reports on Education: The Straits Settlements and the Federated Malay States, 1870–1939.* Singapore: Pan Pacific Book Distributors, 1980. 164 pp. ISEAS, NLB, NTUNIE, NUS.

826.   Wong Hoy Kee, Francis and Gwee Yee Hean. *Perspectives: The Development of Education in Malaysia and Singapore.* Kuala Lumpur: Heinemann, 1972. 177 pp. ISEAS, NLB, NTUNIE, NUS.

827.   Wong, Ruth. *Educational Innovation in Singapore.* Paris: UNESCO Press, 1974. 82 pp. ISEAS, NLB, NTUNIE, NUS.

Policy and Curriculum Planning

828.   Barr, Michael D. "Racialised Education in Singapore". *Educational Research for Policy and Practice* 5, no. 1 (2006): 15–31. NTUNIE, NUS.

829.   Bell, David Scott. "Unity in Diversity: Education and Political Integration in an Ethnically Pluralistic Society". PhD dissertation, Indiana University, 1972. Ann Arbor, Mich.: University Microfilms International, 1975. 653 pp. ISEAS, NLB, NTUNIE, NUS.

830.   Chin Yean Lin, Alice. "The 'Lows' under the Primary Streaming System in Singapore". Academic exercise, Department of Sociology, National University of Singapore, 1994. 67 pp. NUS.

831.   *Educational Policy in the Colony of Singapore: Ten Years Programme.* Singapore: Govt. Printer, 1948. 50 pp. NLB, NTUNIE.

832.   Ee Tiang Hong. "Education in Malaysia and Singapore: A Comparative Study of Racial and Cultural Factors as Determinants of Educational Policy, 1945–1970". PhD dissertation, University of Western Australia, 1985. 216 pp. NTUNIE, NUS.

833.   Fadilah Isnin, comp. *Pembelajaran Bahasa Melalui Puisi.* Ketua Projek, Fadilah Isnin. Singapore: Pusat Bahasa Melayu Singapura, Bahagian

Perancangan dan Pembangunan Kurikulum, Kementerian Pendidikan Singapura, 2013. 146 pp. NLB.

834.   Fadilah Isnin, comp. *Penerapan Budaya dalam Pembelajaran Bahasa.* Ketua Projek, Fadilah Isnin. Singapore: Pusat Bahasa Melayu Singapura, Bahagian Perancangan dan Pembangunan Kurikulum, Kementerian Pendidikan, 2014. 112 pp. NLB.

835.   Gopinathan Saravanan. "Language and Values in Education". In *Education and the Nation State: The Selected Works of S. Gopinathan.* New York, NY: Routledge, 2013. ISEAS, NLB, NTU, NTUNIE, NUS.

836.   Hough, G.C. "Notes on the Educational Policy of Sir Stamford Raffles". *JMBRAS* 11, pt. 2 (December 1933): 166–70. ISEAS, NLB, NTUNIE, NUS.

837.   Juve, Richard G. "Education as an Integrating Force in Singapore: A Multi-Cultural Society". PhD dissertation, Rutgers University, 1975. Ann Arbor, Mich.: University Microfilms International, 1986. 452 pp. ISEAS, NLB, NTUNIE, NUS.

838.   Ka-Im Chionh, Karen. "Multilingual and Multicultural Attitudes: Considerations for the Curriculum in Singapore". MA dissertation, Department of English Language & Literature, National University of Singapore, 1988. 123 pp. NUS.

839.   Khartini Khalid et al. *Goh Chok Tong, Portrait of a Leader: A Tribute from the Malay/Muslim Community of Singapore.* Editor, Saat A. Rahman. Singapore: Tribute to Mr Goh Chok Tong Organising Committee, 2005. 117 pp. NLB, NTUNIE.

840.   Loo Shaw Chang. "A Chronology of Developments in Bilingual Education in Singapore Schools 1951–1977". In *Studies in Bilingual Education,* edited by R. Lord and B.K. T'sou. Hong Kong: Language Centre, University of Hong Kong, 1976. ISEAS, NLB, NTUNIE, NUS.

841.   Mardiana Abu Bakar. "30 Years of Streaming — Are We Still Giving Some Students Half a Loaf?" *MENDAKI Policy Digest* (2008): 123–38. ISEAS, NTUNIE, NUS.

842.   Pairah Satariman. "Kurikulum Bahasa Melayu Peringkat Sekolah Menengah di Singapura: Satu Penilaian Terhadap Pembentukan dan

Pelaksanaannya". MA dissertation, Department of Malay Studies, National University of Singapore, 2006. 269 pp. NUS.

843. Siti Khadijah Setyo. "A General Scan for Education Policy". In *MENDAKI Policy Digest* (2013): 83–94. NLB.

844. Siti Nur Ida Mohd. Ali. "A Review of Singapore's Education Policy Changes and Their Impact on the Malay/Muslim Community". *MENDAKI Policy Digest* (2012): 19–35. NLB, NTUNIE.

845. Stevenson, Rex. *Cultivators and Administrators: British Educational Policy towards the Malays, 1875–1906*. Kuala Lumpur: Oxford University Press, 1975. 240 pp. ISEAS, NLB, NTUNIE, NUS.

846. *Sukatan Pelajaran Bahasa Melayu: Sekolah Rendah 2015*. Singapore: Curriculum Planning and Development Division, Ministry of Education, 2014. 94 pp. NLB.

847. Tajul Arif Mohd Yusof. "Pendidikan Berteraskan Kebolehan (Ability-driven Education): Reformasi dalam Pengajaran Bahasa Melayu". Paper presented at a Persidangan Antarabangsa Bahasa, Sastera dan Kebudayaan Melayu ke 2, anjuran Jabatan Bahasa dan Kebudayaan Melayu, Kumpulan Akademik Bahasa dan Kebudayaan Asia, Institut Pendidikan Nasional, Universiti Teknologi Nanyang, Singapura, 1–3 September 2002. 19 pp. ISEAS, NLB.

848. Wilson, Harold (Edmond). "Educational Policies in a Changing Society: Singapore, 1918–1959". PhD dissertation, University of British Columbia, 1978. 410 pp. ISEAS, NTUNIE, NUS.

849. Wilson, Harold E. (Edmond). *Social Engineering in Singapore: Educational Policies and Social Change, 1819–1972*. Singapore: Singapore University Press, 1978. 300 pp. ISEAS, NLB, NTU, NTUNIE, NUS.

850. Wong Mei Kwong. "The Bilingual Policy in the Singapore Schools". Academic exercise, Department of Political Science, University of Singapore, 1978. 58 pp. ISEAS, NTUNIE, NUS.

851. Zahoor Ahmad. "Educational Policy & Administration in Singapore". *Intisari* 3, no. 3 (1969): 84–94. ISEAS, NLB, NUS.

Malays/Muslims and Education

852. Ahmad Mattar. "Pendidikan Masyarakat Melayu Sebelum dan dalam Tahun Lapan-Puluhan". *Analisa* (1981): 31–34. NLB, NUS.

853. Ahmad Mattar. "The Singapore Malays: Their Education and Role in National Development". In *People's Action Party 1954–1979: Petir 25th Anniversary Issue*. Singapore: Central Executive Committee, PAP, 1979. ISEAS, NLB, NTU, NTUNIE, NUS.

854. Ahmad Mattar. "Tertiary Fees for Malay Students". *Petir: Organ of the People's Action Party* (August 1990): 46–48. ISEAS, NLB, NTUNIE, NUS.

855. Awang Had Salleh. "Malay Teacher Training in British Malaya, 1878–1941: A General Survey". Academic exercise, Faculty of Education, University of Malaya, 1967. 229 pp. NTUNIE, NUS.

856. Azhar Ibrahim Alwee. "Orientalisme dalam Pengajian Melayu". Paper presented at a Persidangan Antarabangsa Bahasa, Sastera dan Kebudayaan Melayu ke 2, anjuran Jabatan Bahasa dan Kebudayaan Melayu, Kumpulan Akademik Bahasa dan Kebudayaan Asia, Institut Pendidikan Nasional, Universiti Teknologi Nanyang, Singapura, 1–3 September 2002. 19 pp. ISEAS, NLB.

857. *Bakti*. Singapore: KGMS, 1977–. ISEAS, NLB, NUS. Continues *Berita KGMS*. Singapore: KGMS, 1973–76. ISEAS, NLB, NUS.

858. Banafie, Siti Jamaliah J. "Singapore Malay Teacher's Union Complex (Geylang Serai)". Academic exercise, National University of Singapore, 1988. 1 vol. NUS.

859. Chao Syh Kwang. "Some Aspects of Nation-building in Singapore with Special Reference to Education". MSocSc dissertation, Institute of Social Studies (Netherlands), 1971. 99 pp. NUS.

860. Chow Yaw Huah. *Sang Nila Utama Secondary School*. Singapore: National Library Board Singapore, 2011. Available at <http://infopedia. nl.sg/articles/SIP_1107_2011-03-24.html>.

861. "Enrichment Programme Session with the Top 10%". Organized by Yayasan MENDAKI, 25 May 1991. NLB.

862. Fadzli Baharom Adzahar. "'Taking the Gravel Road': Educational Aspirations of Working Class Malay Youths". Academic exercise, Department of Sociology, National University of Singapore, 2009. 67 pp. NUS.

863. Fong Ho Kheorg and Phyllis Chew. *An Evaluation and Investigation of Yayasan MENDAKI Tutorial Programme in English and Mathematics at Primary 6 Level*. Singapore: Institute of Education, 1988. 1 vol. NTUNIE, NUS.

864. "The Future of Malay School Leavers". *Intisari* 3, no. 3 (1969): 25–27. ISEAS, NLB, NUS.

865. Ghadessy, Mohsen. "Some Guidelines for Classroom Activities: MENDAKI Tuition Classes". *Guidelines = A Periodical for Classroom Language Teachers* 7, no. 1 (June 1985): 85–92. NUS.

866. Gillis, Kay. "The Malay Educational Council". Paper presented at a Symposium on Path Not Taken: Political Pluralism in Postwar Singapore, jointly sponsored by the Centre for Social Change Research at the Queensland University of Technology and the Asia Research Institute at the National University of Singapore held in Singapore on 14–15 July 2005. ISEAS.

867. Goh Chok Tong. "Total Effort: Raise Malay Community's Performance [Speech Delivered at Opening Ceremony of Singapore Malay-Muslim Development Congress, Singapore Conference Hall, May 1989]". *Speeches* 13, no. 3 (May/June 1989): 8–17. ISEAS, NLB, NTU, NTUNIE, NUS.

868. *Harapan*. Singapore: Yayasan MENDAKI, 1993–. NLB.

869. Hussin Mutalib. "Education and Singapore Muslims: An Overview of the Issues, Parameters and Prospects". *Fajar Islam* 2, no. 2 (1989): 1–18. ISEAS, NLB, NUS.

870. Isa Hassan. "Modernization: Education and the Malay Community". Academic exercise, Department of Sociology, University of Singapore, 1977. 34 pp. ISEAS, NUS.

871. *KGMS 60 Tahun (1947–2007)*. Singapore: Kesatuan Guru-Guru Melayu Singapura, 2007. 1 vol. (unpaged). NUS.

872. *KGMS, 1947–1972*. Singapore: Kesatuan Guru-Guru Melayu Singapura, 1972. 1 vol. (unpaged). ISEAS, NLB, NUS.

873.   *Kongres Pendidikan Anak-Anak Islam, 28–30 Mei 1982, Singapura.* Singapore: MENDAKI, 1982. 126 pp. ISEAS, NLB, NUS.

874.   Kursiah A. Latif. "Reasons for Malay/Muslim Parents' Preference towards Private Tuition". Research exercise, Department of Malay Studies, National University of Singapore, 1996. 40 pp. NUS.

875.   Lee Kuan Yew. "Education: The Key to Progress". *Speeches* 14, no. 5 (September/October 1990): 1–2. ISEAS, NLB, NTUNIE, NUS.

876.   Lee Kuan Yew. "MENDAKI's Task is to Raise Education of all Malays". *Speeches* 5, no. 12 (June 1982): 5–25. ISEAS, NLB, NTUNIE, NUS.

877.   Lek Yik Yang, Leonard. "Mendaki Weekend Tuition Scheme: An Analysis of Its Progress made in Malay Education". Research exercise, Department of Malay Studies, National University of Singapore, 1996. 69 pp. NUS.

878.   Liaw Yock Fang. "Malay Studies and National Development". Paper presented at a Seminar on Research Programs in Singapore, organized by Nanyang University in cooperation with the University of Singapore and other institutions in Singapore, 6–7 August 1970. 6 pp. ISEAS, NLB, NUS.

879.   Lily Zubaidah Rahim. "Understanding the Malay Educational Marginality". In *The Singapore Dilemma: The Political and Educational Marginality of the Malay Community.* Kuala Lumpur: Oxford University Press, 1998. 302 pp. ISEAS, NLB, NTUNIE, NUS.

880.   "Malay Education, Analysis and Recommendations". *Intisari* 3, no. 3 (1969): 35–50. ISEAS, NLB, NUS.

881.   Mansor Haji Sukaimi. "Kurun 21: Persiapan untuk Anak-Anak". *Karyawan: Professionals for the Community* (July 1996): 8–9, 12. ISEAS, NLB, NTUNIE, NUS.

882.   *Maths @home: Learning Kit for Parents.* Singapore: Association of Muslim Professionals, [2005?]. 121 pp. NLB.

883.   *Mendaki: Panduan untuk Ibu Bapa dan Waris mengenai Pembelajaran dan Pelajaran Anak-anak Islam.* Singapore: Sekretariat Mendaki, 1982. 8 pp. NLB.

884.   *Milestones in the Education System and Its Implications on the Malay/ Muslim Community.* Singapore: Yayasan MENDAKI, 2004. 21 pp. NTUNIE.

885.   *Pendidikan Bangsa Melayu: Majalah Qalam, Bilangan 88, November 1957.* 105 pp. Kuala Lumpur: Klasika Media-Akademi Jawi Malaysia dengan kerjasama Center for Integrated Area Studies (CIAS), Kyoto University, 2014. NLB.

886.   Phua Swee Liang. "Ability-factors and Familial Psychological Circumstances: Chinese and Malays of Singapore". PhD dissertation, University of Alberta, 1976. 3 microfiches. ISEAS, NTUNIE.

887.   Raffles, Thomas Stamford, Sir, 1781–1826. *Minute by Sir T.S. Raffles on the Establishment of a Malay College at Singapore.* [S.l.: s.n.], 1819. 24 pp. NLB.

888.   *Report on: The Study on the Academic Aspirations and Retraining Needs of Malay/Muslim ITE Graduates.* Singapore: Yayasan MENDAKI, 1998. 22 pp. NTUNIE.

889.   "Seminar Menghadapi Cabaran-cabaran Pendidikan Dalam Tahun-Tahun Delapan Puluhan: Kertas Kerja-Kertas Kerja". Anjuran Kesatuan Guru-Guru Melayu Singapura, Singapura, 1978. 77 pp. ISEAS, NLB.

890.   Shaharuddin Maaruf. "The Deeper Roots of Educational Problems". *Karyawan: Professionals for the Community* 2 (February 1996): 6–7. ISEAS, NLB, NTUNIE, NUS.

891.   Sharifah Maisharah Mohamed. "Improving the Education of the Malays: Time for a Change". *Karyawan: Professionals for the Community* 9, issue 1 (July 2008): 10–12. ISEAS, NLB, NTUNIE, NUS.

892.   Sharom Ahmat. "Singapore Malays: Education and National Development". *Suara Universiti* 2, no. 1 (1970): 41–56. ISEAS, NUS.

893.   Sidek Saniff. *Education and Singapore Malay Society: Prospects and Challenges.* Seminar Papers, no. 4. Singapore: Department of Malay Studies, National University of Singapore, 1992. 15 pp. ISEAS, NTUNIE, NUS.

894.   Sidek Saniff. "Encourage the Pursuit of Knowledge". *Speeches* 15, no. 1 (January/February 1991): 52–61. ISEAS, NLB, NTUNIE, NUS.

895. Sidek Saniff. "Pendidikan Melayu dan Perkembangannya". *Titian Ilmu* 2 (April 1991): 4–5. NLB, NTUNIE, NUS.

896. Siti Hajar Esa. "Racializing Empowerment: Disjunction between the Rhetorics and Realities of Malay Academic Upliftment Efforts". Academic exercise, Department of Sociology, National University of Singapore, 2009. 67 pp. NUS.

897. Siti Suraya Bohari. "Home Support for Education". Research exercise, Department of Malay Studies, National University of Singapore, 1993. 54 pp. NUS.

898. Sitiurika Ahmad. "Embracing Education without Borders". *MENDAKI Policy Digest* (2006): 5–29. ISEAS, NTUNIE, NUS.

899. *Suara MENDAKI.* Singapore: Yayasan MENDAKI, 1984–. NLB, NUS.

900. Tan, Diana. "The MENDAKI Tertiary Fee Scheme". *Mirror* 26, no. 14 (July 1990): 4–6. NLB, NUS.

901. Tan Keng Yam, Tony. "A Good Education is the Best Legacy: [Speech at the MUIS Bursaries Presentation Ceremony, September 1981]". *Speeches* 5, no. 4 (October 1981): 67–70. ISEAS, NLB. NTUNIE, NUS.

902. Tengku Sri Indra Ismail. "Education and the Malays, 1945–1965". In *Malays/Muslims in Singapore: Selected Readings in History, 1819–1965*, edited by Khoo Kay Kim, Elinah Abdullah and Wan Meng Hao. Subang Jaya, Selangor: Pelanduk Publications in cooperation with Centre for Research on Islamic and Malay Affairs, 2006. ISEAS, NLB, NTUNIE, NUS.

903. Tengku Sri Indra Ismail. "Malay Education in Singapore, 1959–1972". Academic exercise, Department of History, University of Singapore, 1976. 71 pp. NTUNIE, NUS.

904. Tham Seong Chee. "A Cultural Logic versus Development Imperatives: A Perspective on Education among Singapore Malays". *Fajar Islam* 2 (1989): 37–50. ISEAS, NLB, NUS.

905. Tham Seong Chee. "Education, Society and Economic Mobility among the Malays". *Suara Universiti* 2, no. 1 (January 1971): 33–40. ISEAS, NUS.

906.   *Vision, Strategic Thrusts and Recommendations for KBE Convention, 14 November 1999.* Singapore: KBE Convention Steering Committee, 1999. 15 pp. ISEAS.

907.   Wan Hussin Zoohri. "Education and the Malay Community". *Commentary* 8, no. 182 (1989): 86–93. ISEAS, NLB, NTUNIE, NUS.

908.   Yaacob Ibrahim. "What are Schools for?" *Karyawan: Professionals for the Community* 2 (February 1996): 8–9. ISEAS, NLB, NTUNIE, NUS.

909.   Yang Razali Kassim. "Education and the Malays in Singapore (1954–1979): The Position, Perceptions and Response of a Minority Community". Academic exercise, Department of Political Science, National University of Singapore, 1979. 158 pp. NUS.

910.   Yatiman Yusof. "Beberapa Pandangan dan Pendapat mengenai Sistem Pelajaran Nasional, Chadangan KGMS 1971". *Analisa* (1970/71): 60–73. ISEAS, NLB, NUS.

911.   Zahoor Ahmad. "Malay Education in Singapore". In *150 Years of Education in Singapore* edited by T.R. Doraisamy. Singapore: TTC Publications Board, Teachers Training College, 1969. ISEAS, NLB, NTUNIE, NUS.

912.   Zahoor Ahmad. "Policies and Politics in Malay Education in Singapore 1951–1965, with Special Reference to the Development of the Secondary School System". MEd dissertation, School of Education, University of Singapore, 1969. 282 pp. NLB, NTUNIE, NUS.

913.   Zubaidah Ariffin. "A Study of Home Support for Education among Malay Families Nature, Types and Problems". Research exercise, Department of Malay Studies, National University of Singapore, 1991. 59 pp. NUS.

Malay-Medium Education

914.   Abdul Aziz Mohammed Nor. "The Higher Forms in the Malay School". Academic exercise, Department of Social Studies, University of Singapore, 1962. 71 pp. NTUNIE, NUS.

915.   Aminah Ahmad Jalaludin. "The Malay-Medium School Girl and Her Social Setting". Academic exercise, Department of Social Work and Social Administration, University of Singapore, 1970. 130 pp. NUS.

916.   Anis Sabirin. "What Do Malay Teachers Read: A Study of 17 Teachers from 2 Malay Schools". Academic exercise, University of Malaya, Singapore, 1959. 41 pp. NUS.

917.   Gordon, Shirley. "Malay Education: Analysis and Recommendations". *Intisari* 3, no. 3 (1969): 32–50. ISEAS, NLB, NUS.

918.   Hadijah Rahmat. "Pelajaran Melayu (1) Sebelum Merdeka". *Mekar* (October 1980): 14–15. NLB, NUS.

919.   Hadijah Rahmat. "Pelajaran Melayu (2) Sesudah Merdeka". *Mekar* (November 1980): 18–19. NLB, NUS.

920.   Hafiza Talib. *Sekolahku Tinggal Kenangan*. Singapore: Hafiza Talib, 2015. 261 pp. NLB.

921.   Kamsiah Abdullah. *Benih Budiman: Suatu Analisis Sosio-Sejarah Persekolahan Melayu di Singapura*. Tanjong Malim, Perak: Penerbit Universiti Pendidikan Sultan Idris, 2007. 261 pp. ISEAS, NLB, NUS.

922.   Kamsiah Abdullah. "Penyaluran Budaya Sekolah Melayu: Satu Proses Mencapai Kesempurnaan". In *Ke arah Keseimbangan Insan: Persidangan Antarabangsa Bahasa, Sastera dan Budaya Melayu I: Pascasidang*, vol. 2, edited by Kamsiah Abdullah et al. Singapore: Jabatan Bahasa dan Kebudayaan Melayu, Institut Pendidikan Nasional, Universiti Teknologi Nanyang, 2002. ISEAS, NLB, NTUNIE, NUS.
       (Originally presented at a Persidangan Antarabangsa Bahasa, Sastera dan Budaya Melayu: Ke arah Keseimbangsan Insan, anjuran Institut Pendidikan Nasional, Universiti Teknologi Nanyang, York Hotel, Singapore, 17–18 Julai 1998).

923.   Kamsiah Abdullah. "Sekolah Menengah Melayu di Singapura". *JMBRAS* 72, pt. 1 (2000): 29–41. ISEAS, NLB, NTUNIE, NUS.

924.   Liaw Yock Fang. "The Economic Value of Malay Education". *Intisari* 3, no. 3 (1968): 29–31. ISEAS, NLB, NTUNIE, NUS.

925.   Lim Peng Han. "An Analysis of Factors Affecting the Development of Malay Secondary Schools and Malay Secondary School Libraries within the Multilingual School System during Colonial and Post Colonial Rule in Singapore, 1819–1985". PhD dissertation, Loughborough University, 2012. 293 pp. ISEAS, NUS.

926.   Mahmud Ahmad. "Malay Schools in Singapore". *Intisari* 3, no. 3 (1969): 21–23. ISEAS, NLB, NUS.

927.   Mohd. Hashim Abdul Hamid. "Science, Technology and Post Secondary Education in Malay Medium". *Intisari* 3, no. 3 (1969): 74–75. ISEAS, NLB, NUS.

928.   Mokhtar Abdullah. "The Value of Malay Education in Singapore". *Intisari* 3, no. 3 (1969): 13–19. ISEAS, NLB, NTUNIE, NUS.

929.   *Pameran Kemajuan Pelajaran Aliran Melayu: Chenderamata.* Singapore: Kementrian Pelajaran, 1966. 1 vol. NLB.

930.   "Seminar on Malay Education". *Intisari* 3, no. 3 (1969): 60–72. ISEAS, NLB, NUS.

931.   "Seminar Pendidikan Melayu: Kertas Kerja". Anjuran Kesatuan Guru-Guru Melayu Singapura [dan] Lembaga Tetap Kongres, Universiti Singapura, 13hb–15hb Januari 1968. 1 vol. (various foliations). NUS.

932.   Sharom Ahmat. "University Education in Singapore: The Dilemma of the Malay-Medium Educated". In *Development of Higher Education in Southeast Asia: Problems and Issues,* edited by Yip Yat Hoong. Singapore: Regional Institute of Higher Education and Development, 1973. ISEAS, NLB, NTUNIE, NUS.

933.   Wazir, Johan Karim. "A Sudy of Under and Over Achievers in Malay Medium Secondary Schools in Singapore". Academic exercise, University of Singapore, 1970. 112 pp. NUS.

934.   "Wither Malay Education?" *Intisari* 3, no. 3 (1969): 7–94. ISEAS, NLB, NUS.

Islamic Education

935.   *50 Golden Jubilee Anniversary, 1958–2008, Madrasah Wak Tanjong Al Islamiah.* Singapore: Madrasah Wak Tanjong Al Islamiah, 2008. 57 pp. NLB, NUS.

936.   Abdul Samad Junied. *Perkembangan Pendidikan Islam di Singapura: Satu Kajian Kes Madrasah Aljunied Al-Islamiyah, 1970–1990.* Singapore AFIA Media International, 1999.

937.   Abdullah Othman. "The Role of Madrasah Education in Singapore: A Study on the Philosophy and Practice of Madrasah Education in a Secular State and Plural Society". MA dissertation, International Islamic University Malaysia, 2007. 99 pp.

938.   Abu Bakar Hashim. "The Madrasah in Singapore: Past, Present and Future". *Fajar Islam* 2 (1989): 27–36. ISEAS, NLB, NUS.

939.   Afiza Hashim and Lai Ah Eng. "Case Study of a Madrasah: Madrasah Maarif". In *Secularism and Spirituality: Seeking Integrated Knowledge and Success in Madrasah Education in Singapore*, edited by Noor Aisha Abdul Rahman and Lai Ah Eng. Singapore: Marshall Cavendish Academic, 2006. ISEAS, NLB, NTU, NTUNIE, NUS.

940.   Ahmad Fahmi Yusoff. "The Nature and Role of Current Day Madrasahs in Singapore". Research exercise, Department of Malay Studies, National University of Singapore, 1991. 75 pp. NUS.

941.   Ahmad Ibrahim. "Islamic Education in Singapore". *Muslim World League Magazine* 3, no. 11 (1967): 4–20. NLB, NUS.

942.   Ahmad Qadri Mohamed Sidek. "Pendidikan Islam di Singapura: Satu Analisa Kritikal". *Jurnal Dakwah* 1, no. 1 (December 2010): 69–88. NLB.

943.   Ahmad Sonhadji Mohamad. "Pendidikan Islam di Singapura". *Maharajan ke 60* (1987): 70. NLB.

944.   *Alaf Millennium Madrasah Al-Maarif Charity Dinner 2002.* Singapore: [s.n.], 2002. NLB.

945.   Alatas, Syed Farid. "Knowledge and Education in Islam". In *Secularism and Spirituality: Seeking Integrated Knowledge and Success in Madrasah Education in Singapore*, edited by Noor Aisha Abdul Rahman and Lai Ah Eng. Singapore: Institute of Policy Studies; Marshall Cavendish Academic, 2006. ISEAS, NLB, NTU, NTUNIE, NUS.

946.   Alatas, Syed Farid. "Pendidikan Madrasah di Singapura". In *Pendidikan Islam di Asia Tenggara dan Asia Selatan*, edited by S. Yunanto et al. Jakarta: RIDEP Institute-Friedrich Ebert Stiftung, 2005. NLB.

947.   Aljuffri, Syed Abdillah Ahmad. "Sejarah Madrasah Aljunied". In *Madrasah Aljunied: A Tradition of Excellence: A Commemorative Magazine to Inaugurate the Official Opening of the New Building, 21 April 2000/16 Muharram 1421H*: 21. NLB.

948. Aljunied, Farah Mahamood. "Integrated and Holistic Madrasah Education Curriculum: The Singapore Madrasah Model". Paper presented at a Conference on Madrasah Education, Singapore, 15–16 March 2013. 19 pp.

949. Aljunied, Farah Mahamood. "Madrasah with a View". *Warita Kita* 136 (November/December 2001): 16–17. ISEAS, NLB, NUS.

950. Aljunied, Syed Ahmad Omar. *Al Hidayah: Magazine of Madrasah Aljunied 1970*. Singapore: Lembaga Majallah Madrasah al-Junied al-Islamiah, 1970. 80 pp. NUS.

951. Aljunied, Syed Muhd Khairudin and Dayang Istiaisyah Hussin. "Estranged from the Ideal Past: Historical Evolution of Madrassahs in Singapore". *Journal of Muslim Minority Affairs* 25, no. 2 (2005): 249–60. NTUNIE, NUS.

952. "Al-Saqqaf School of Singapore: A Pioneering Venture in the Island". *The Muslim World League Journal* 10, no. 1 (November 1982): 49–53. NUS.

953. *Assirat: Ulang Tahun Ketujuh Puluh 1912M–1982M Madrasah Alsagoff Al-Arabiah, December 1982*. Singapore: Madrasah Alsagoff Al-Arabiah, 1982. 88 pp.

954. Azhar Ibrahim Alwee. "An Evaluation of Madrasah Education, Perspectives and Lessons from the Experiences of Some Muslim Societies". In *Secularism and Spirituality: Seeking Integrated Knowledge and Success in Madrasah Education in Singapore*, edited by Noor Aisha Abdul Rahman and Lai Ah Eng. Singapore: Institute of Policy Studies; Marshall Cavendish Academic, 2006. ISEAS, NLB, NTU, NTUNIE, NUS.

955. Bazita Abu Bakar. *Hubungan Gaya Pembelajaran dengan Pencapaian Akademik: Tinjauan di Tiga Buah Madrasah Sepenuh Masa di Singapura*. Johor: Universiti Teknologi Malaysia, 2006.

956. *Berita Perdaus*. Singapore: Persatuan Pelajar-Pelajar Agama Dewasa Singapura, 1966–. NUS.

957. "Bringing Madrasah Education to a Higher Level". *Warita Kita* 137 (January/February 2002): 8–9. ISEAS, NLB, NUS.

958. Chee Min Fui. "The Historical Evolution of Madrasah Education in Singapore". In *Secularism and Spirituality: Seeking Integrated Knowledge*

and Success in Madrasah Education in Singapore, edited by Noor Aisha Abdul Rahman and Lai Ah Eng. Singapore: Institute of Policy Studies; Marshall Cavendish Academic, 2006. ISEAS, NLB, NTU, NTUNIE, NUS.

959. Chee Min Fui. "The History of Madrasah Education in Singapore". MA dissertation, National University of Singapore, 2000. NUS.

960. Chew Ghim Lian, Phyllis. "Literacy Wars: Children Education and Weekend Madrasahs in Singapore". In Religious Pluralism, State and Society in Asia, edited by Chiara Formichi. Abingdon, Oxon: New York: Routledge, 2014. NLB, NTU.

961. Dayang Istiaisyah Hussain. "School Efficiency and Nation Building in Singapore: Analysis of Discourses on Madrasah and Why Madrasah Stand Out from National Schools". MA dissertation, National University of Singapore, 2003. NUS.

962. Dirgahayu Alsagoff: Alsagoff Alumni, Gala Dinner 2012, Saturday, 29 December 2012, Fairmont Hotel. Singapore: Madrasah Alsagoff Al-Arabiah, 2012. 30 pp.

963. Hussain Suradi. "Pendidekan dan Pengajaran Islam di Singapura". In Report of the Seminar on Islamic Education in Singapore. Singapore: Muslim Society, University of Singapore, 1966. NUS.

964. Hussin Mutalib. "Islamic Education in Singapore: Present Trends and Challenges for the Future". Journal of Muslim Minority Affairs 16, no. 2 (1996): 233–39. ISEAS, NTUNIE, NUS.

965. Inspiration: Madrasah Al-Maarif Al-Islamiah 50th Anniversary and Official Opening Ceremony, 15th March 1987. Singapore: Madrasah Al-Maarif Al-Islamiah, 1987. 144 pp. NLB, NUS.

966. Intan Azura Mokhtar. "Madrasahs in Singapore: Bridging between Their Roles and Resources". Journal of Muslim Minority Affairs 3, no. 1 (March 2010): 111–25. ISEAS, NTUNIE, NUS.

967. Kamaruzaman Afandi. "Eyes on Tomorrow: Challenges for the 21st Century Asatizah". Nadi 2, no. 6 (June 2006): 2–6. NLB, NUS.

968. Mahdi Mahyudin, Azeemah Mustafa, and Yang Razali Kassim. "Whither Our Madrasahs?" Karyawan: Professionals for the Community 9, issue 1 (July 2008): 22–24. ISEAS, NLB, NTUNIE, NUS.

969.   *Mahrajan ke 60: Madrasah Aijunied AI-Islamiyah, 1927–1987.* Singapore: Madrasah Aljunied Al-Islamiyah, 1987. 119 pp. NLB.

970.   Majlis Ugama Islam Singapura. *National Madrasah Education System.* Singapore: Majlis Ugama Islam Singapura, 1998.

971.   Majlis Ugama Islam Singapura. Islamic Education Strategic Unit. *Singapore Islamic Education System: Conceptual Framework.* Singapore: Islamic Religious Council of Singapore, 2004. 1 CD-ROM. ISEAS.

972.   "Management Committee of Madrasah Al-Maarif". In *Inspiration: Madrasah Al-Maarif Al-Islamiah 50th Anniversary and Official Opening Ceremony, 15 March 1987.* Singapore: Madrasah Al-Maarif Al-Islamiah, 1987. NLB, NUS.

973.   Mansor Haji Sukaimi, ed. *Koleksi Kertas MENDAKI = A Collection of MENDAKI Papers.* Singapore: MENDAKI, 1982. 263 pp. ISEAS, NLB, NUS.

974.   "Menyingkap Sejarah Madrasah: Dua Fungsi Utama Hasilkan Ramai 'Insanul Kamil'". In *Malam Amal Madrasah Al-Junied, 31 Mei 1996.* Singapore: [s.n.], 1996. NLB.

975.   Mohammad Abdul Halim Mohammad Noor. "Peranan Madrasah di Singapura dalam Dakwah Selepas Kemerdekaan dan Masalahnya". MUsuluddin dissertation, Jabatan Dakwah dan Pembangunan Insan, Akademi Pengajian Islam, Universiti Malaya, 2008. 131 pp. NUS.

976.   Mohd Dzulfiqhar Mohd. "The Future Challenges of Madrasahs in Singapore". *Karyawan: Professionals for the Community* 3 (September–November 1997): 20–21. ISEAS, NLB, NTUNIE, NUS.

977.   Muhammad Haniff Hassan. "Pendidikan Islam di Singapura". Paper presented at a Seminar Islam di Pusat-Pusat Pengajian Tinggi ASEAN = 3rd Seminar on Islam in ASEAN Institution of Higher Learning. Anjuran bersama Fakulti Pengajian Islam, UKM dan Kerajaan Negeri Melaka, 5–7 November 2002. NLB.

978.   Muhammad Nasir, ed. "Alsagoff School in Singapore". *The Muslim World League Journal* 10, no. 1 (1982–83): 49–53. NLB, NUS.

979.   Muhd. Haikal Harun, Muhd. Hasanul Arifin Zawawi, and Zuraimi Musa. "A Critical Analysis on the Problems of Religious Education in Singapore and Its Implications upon Society". In *Issues Facing the*

Malay/Muslim Community in Singapore. Singapore: Lembaga Biasiswa Kenangan Maulud, 2010. NLB.

980.   Mukhlis Abu Bakar. "Between State Interests and Citizen Rights: Whither the Madrasah?" In *Secularism and Spirituality: Seeking Integrated Knowledge and Success in Madrasah Education in Singapore*, edited by Noor Aisha Abdul Rahman and Lai Ah Eng. Singapore: Institute of Policy Studies; Marshall Cavendish Academic, 2006. ISEAS, NLB, NTU, NTUNIE, NUS.

981.   Mukhlis Abu Bakar. *Islamic Religious Schools in Singapore: Recent Trends and Issues*. Seminar Paper, no. 26. Singapore: Department of Malay Studies, National University of Singapore, 1999. 21 pp. ISEAS, NLB, NUS.

982.   Noor Aisha Abdul Rahman. "The Aims of Madrasah Education in Singapore". In *Secularism and Spirituality: Seeking Integrated Knowledge and Success in Madrasah Education in Singapore*, edited by Noor Aisha Abdul Rahman and Lai Ah Eng. Singapore: Institute of Policy Studies; Marshall Cavendish Academic, 2006. ISEAS, NLB, NTU, NTUNIE, NUS.

983.   Noor Aisha Abdul Rahman and Lai Ah Eng, eds. *Secularism and Spirituality: Seeking Integrated Knowledge and Success in Madrasah Education in Singapore*. Singapore: Institute of Policy Studies; Marshall Cavendish Academic, 2006. 191 pp. ISEAS, NLB, NTU, NTUNIE, NUS.

984.   Nurhaizatul Jamila Jamil and Valerie Chew. *Madrasah Education*. Singapore: National Library Board, 2010. Available at <http://infopedia.nl.sg/articles/SIP_1661_2010-04-07.html>.

985.   Ooi Giok Ling and Chee Min Fui. "They Play Soccer Too!-Madrasah Education in Multicultural Singapore". *Asia Pacific Journal of Education* 27, no. 1 (2007): 73–84. NTUNIE, NUS.

986.   *Our Heritage, Our Pride: Celebrating Beyond 100 Years of Formal Islamic Education*. Singapore: Madrasah Alsagoff Al-Arabiah, 2010. 48 pp.

987.   "Pendidikan Madrasah". *Warita* 123 (September–October 1999): 2–4. ISEAS, NLB, NUS.

988.   "Perayaan Jubli Emas Sekolah Ugama Aljunied (1927–1977): Cenderamata". Singapore: Madrasah Aljunied, 1977. 1 vol. NLB.

989. Rajmah Taib. "Madrasah al-Rahmah al-Islamiah: An Islamic School at Bedok". Academic exercise, National University of Singapore, 1989. 229 pp. NUS.

990. Ridhwan Mohd Basor. "State and Society: State's Management and Malay/Minorities' Response in the Madrasah Issue". Paper presented at a Graduates Seminar on Nation-building in the Malay World, held at The Shaw Foundation Building, AS7 Auditorium, National University of Singapore, 28–29 October 2009. ISEAS, NUS.

991. "Religious or Public Education? The Madrasah Dilemma". In *Muslims in Singapore: Piety, Politics and Policies*, by Kamaludeen Mohamed Nasir, Alexius A. Pereira and Bryan S. Turner. London; New York, NY: Routledge, 2010 ISEAS, NLB, NUS.

992. Roslinda Sahamad. "Facing Up to the Challenge: Madrasahs of Modern Singapore". Academic exercise, Department of Malay Studies, National University of Singapore, 1995. 58 pp. NUS.

993. Rozhan Kuntom. "A General Survey of Muslim Religious Schools in Malaya". Academic exercise, Department of Malay Studies, University of Malaya, Singapore, 1957. 75 pp. NUS.

994. Saeda Buang. "Pendidikan Islam di Singapura: Lingkaran Falsafah, Wawasan dan Matlamat". Paper presented at a Persidangan Antarabangsa Bahasa, Sastera dan Kebudayaan Melayu ke 2, anjuran Jabatan Bahasa dan Kebudayaan Melayu, Kumpulan Akademik Bahasa dan Kebudayaan Asia, Institut Pendidikan Nasional, Universiti Teknologi Nanyang, Singapura, 1–3 September 2002. 23 pp. ISEAS, NLB.

995. Saeda Buang. "Religious Education as Focus of Curriculum: A Brief Inquiry into Madrasah Curriculum in Singapore". In *Religious Diversity in Singapore*, edited by Lai Ah Eng. Singapore: Institute of Southeast Asian Studies, 2008. ISEAS, NLB, NTUNIE, NUS.

996. Samuel, Dhoraisingam S. "Madrasahs (Arabic Schools): Al-Junied and Alsagoff Al Islamiah". In *Singapore's Heritage through Places of Historical Interest*. Singapore: Dhoraisingam S. Samuel, 2010. ISEAS, NLB, NTUNIE NUS.

997. "Secebis Sejarah Perkembangan Madrasah Aljunied Al-Islamiah". In *Malam Amal Madrasah Al-Junied, 31 Mei 1996*. Singapore: [s.n.], 1996. NLB.

998. *Sekolah Ugama Radin Mas.* Singapore: Sekolah Ugama Radin Mas, 1984. 47 pp. NLB.

999. *Seminar on Islamic Education in Singapore, University of Singapore, 17–19 September, 1966: Report.* Singapore: University of Singapore Muslim Society, 1966. 127 pp. ISEAS, NLB, NTUNIE, NUS.

1000. "Shared Vision Towards a Madrasah of Excellence". *Warita Kita* 138 (March/April 2002): 3–5. ISEAS, NLB, NUS.

1001. Sharifah Salwah Ahmad. "Quest for Quality: Asatizahs in Madrasahs". Research exercise, Department of Malay Studies, National University of Singapore, 1996. 39 pp. NUS.

1002. Shifa Mohd Ariff. "Shades of Green: A Study of a Singapore Madrasah in Southeast Asian Perspective". Academic exercise, Department of Southeast Asian Studies Programme, National University of Singapore, 2002–3. 80 pp. ISEAS, NUS.

1003. Siddique, Sharon and Yang Razali Kassim. "Muslim Society, Higher Education and Development: The Case of Singapore". In *Muslim Society, Higher Education and Development in Southeast Asia,* edited by Sharom Ahmat and Sharon Siddique. Singapore: Institute of Southeast Asian Studies, 1987. ISEAS, NLB, NTUNIE, NUS.

1004. *Singapore Malay Minority Heritage under Threat.* New York: Singapore Rights Watch, 2000. ISEAS.

1005. Siti Masyitah A. Rahman, ed. *Al-Istiqamah: 60th Anniversary Commemorative Magazine of Madrasah Al-Maarif Singapore, 1997.* Singapore: Madrasah Al-Maarif, 1997. 67 pp. NLB.

1006. Siti Nur 'Alaniah Abdul Wahid. "State & Madrasah Education: The Case of Singapore". MA dissertation, Pengajian Islam, Universiti Islam Negeri Syarif Hidayatullah, Jakarta, 2011.

1007. "Statistics on Private Education Institutions, 2013". In *Education Statistics Digest 2014.* Singapore: Ministry of Education, 2014. NLB.

1008. Tan, Charlene. "Maximising the Overlapping Area: Multiculturalism and a Muslim Identity for Madrasahs in Singapore". *Journal of Beliefs & Values* 30, no. 1 (2009): 41–48. NTUNIE, NUS.

1009. Tan, Charlene and Dewi Abbas. "Madrasahs and the State: Which Worldview?" In *Education in Singapore: Taking Stock, Looking Forward,* edited by Jason Tan. Singapore: Pearson Education South Asia Pte. Ltd., 2012. NLB, NTU.

1010. Tan Tay Keong. "Knowledge Has Many Colours, the Public Policy Management of Madrasah Education". In *Secularism and Spirituality: Seeking Integrated Knowledge and Success in Madrasah Education in Singapore*, edited by Noor Aisha Abdul Rahman and Lai Ah Eng. Singapore: Institute of Policy Studies; Marshall Cavendish Academic, 2006. ISEAS, NLB, NTU, NTUNIE, NUS.

1011. Tan, Charlene and Hairon Salleh. "Reforming Madrasa Curriculum in an Era of Globalization The Singapore Case". In *Reforms in Islamic Education: International Perspectives*, edited by Charlene Tan. London; New York: Bloomsbury Academic, 2014. NLB.

1012. Tuminah Sapawi. "Madrasah Aljunied: The Tradition of Excellence Forging into the Future". In *Madrasah Aljunied: Tradition of Excellence: A Commemorative Magazine to Inaugurate the Official Opening of the New Building, 21 April 2000/16 Muharram 1421H.*

1013. Yaacob Elias. "Sistem Pendidekan Islam di Singapura Hari Ini". In *Report of the Seminar on Islamic Education in Singapore*. Singapore: University of Singapore Muslim Society, 1966. NUS.

1014. Yang Razali Kassim. "Remodelling the Madrasah in Singapore: Past, Present and Future". *Karyawan: Professionals for the Community* 9, issue 1 (July 2008): 25–27. ISEAS, NLB, NTUNIE, NUS.

1015. Yang Razali Kassim and Winda Guntor. "Flashback — the Madrasah Issue in 1990: Restructuring the Madrasah System". *Karyawan: Professionals for the Community* 9, issue 1 (July 2008): 28–30. ISEAS, NLB, NTUNIE, NUS.

1016. Zahoor Ahmad. "Growth of Islamic Education in Singapore". *Muslim World League Magazine* 3, no. 11 (1967): 37–46. NLB, NUS.

1017. Zainah Alias. "The Goals of Madrasah Educational System in Singapore: Obstacles and Recommendation". Academic exercise, Department of Sociology, National University of Singapore, 1998. 116 pp. NTUNIE, NUS.

1018. Zainul Abidin Rasheed "Islamic Education in Singapore". *Fajar Islam* 2 (1989): 19–26. ISEAS, NLB, NUS.

1019. Zubaidah Ghani and Fauziah Soeratman. "The Madrasah System in Singapore: A Brief Survey". *Sedar* (1977): 44–50. ISEAS, NLB, NUS.

Technical, Pre-School and Special Education

1020. Abdul Razak Chanbasha. "Helping the Slow Learners". *Karyawan: Professionals for the Community* 2 (February 1996): 12–13. ISEAS, NLB, NTUNIE, NUS.

1021. Chong, T. "Vocational Education in Singapore: Meritocracy and Hidden Narratives". *Discourse: Studies in the Cultural Politics of Education* 35, no. 5 (2014): 637–48. NUS.

1022. Fatimah Haron. "A Study into the Effects of Kindergarten Education on the Malay Child". Academic exercise, Department of Sociology, University of Singapore, 1971. 111 pp. NUS.

1023. Julinah Sulaiman. "Illumination through Education: ITE as a Gateway to Higher Education". *MENDAKI Policy Digest* (2007): 33–49. ISEAS, NTUNIE, NUS.

1024. Kamsiah Abdullah. "Inculcation of Islamic Values in Muslim Pre-school Education in Singapore". *Fajar Islam* 1, no. 1 (1988): 59–68. ISEAS, NLB, NUS.

1025. Siti Khadijah Setyo. "'Melentur Buluh Biarlah dari Rebungnya': Elevating the Malay/Muslim Community through Early Childhood Education". In *MENDAKI Policy Digest* (2012): 13–25. NLB.

1026. Suriati Abdolah. "The Pre-school Needs of Young Malay/Muslim Parents". Research exercise, Department of Malay Studies, National University of Singapore, 1996. 30 pp. NUS.

Students, Aid and Scholarship

1027. Ahmad S. Said. "Exploratory Survey of Aspirations of Some Malay Pre-University Students". *Educator* 1 (May/August 1970): 35–36. NTUNIE.

1028. *Buku Cenderamata Sempena Tawaran Dermasiswa MUIS-LBKM*. Singapore: LBKM, 1975–. NLB, NUS.

1029.   Cheong Choy Leng. "Student Religious Identity and Choice of Faculty in the National University of Singapore: A Comparative Study". Academic exercise, National University of Singapore, 1987. 60 pp. NUS.

1030.   Gunn, G.T. and Shirley Gordon. "Malay Secondary School Students: Malaya & Singapore". *Intisari* 3, no. 3 (1969): 52–72. ISEAS, NLB, NUS.

1031.   Kamsiah Abdullah. *The Critical Thinking and Reading Abilities of Singaporean Malay Students*. Edited by Rogayah Hj. A. Razak. Kuala Lumpur: Academy of Malay Studies, University of Malaya, 2003. 226 pp. ISEAS, NTUNIE.

1032.   Kang, Trivina. "Schools and Post-secondary Aspirations among Female Chinese, Malay and Indian Normal Stream Students". In *Beyond Rituals and Riots: Ethnic Pluralism and Social Cohesion in Singapore*, edited by Lai Ah Eng. Singapore: Eastern Universities Press, 2004. ISEAS, NLB, NTUNIE, NUS.

1033.   Lembaga Biasiswa Kenangan Maulud. *Review Paper on "L.B.K.M. Status and New Directions"*. Singapore: LBKM, 1977. 14 pp. ISEAS.

1034.   Lembaga Biasiswa Kenangan Maulud. Sidang Agung (ke 7: 1976: Singapura). *Sidang Agung Perwakilan yang ke Tujuh Lembaga Biasiswa Kenangan Maulud, Ahad 28hb Mac di Dewan Peringatan Victoria = Seventh Annual Delegates Conference, P.M.B.M. Scholarship Fund Board, Sunday, 28th March, 1976 at the Victoria Memorial Hall*. Singapore: LBKM, 1976. 104 pp. NLB, NUS.

1035.   Lembaga Biasiswa Kenangan Maulud, Sidang Agung (ke 17: 1998: Singapura). *Sidang Agung Perwakilan ke-17 Lembaga Biasiswa Kenangan Maulud, Ahad 28 Jun 1998*. Singapore: LBKM, 1982. 60 pp. NLB.

1036.   Najmah Sidik. "Study of the NUS Malay Undergraduates and Their Expectations for Themselves and for the Malay Community". Research exercise, Department of Malay Studies, National University of Singapore, 1996. 29 pp. NUS.

1037.   Nazri Othman. "The Malay Undergraduates of NUS: A Study of Their Perceptions and Values on Education, Work, Religion, Malay Values and Modernization". Research exercise, Department of Malay Studies, National University of Singapore, 1993. 54 pp. NUS.

1038. Pereira, Sara. "A Study of the Lembaga Biasiswa Kenangan Maulud's Contribution to Malay Education in Singapore". Research exercise, Department of Malay Studies, National University of Singapore, 1996. 1 vol. (various pagings). NTUNIE (microfilm), NUS.

1039. Puah Kia Kiang. "The Use of Time among Selected Malay Tertiary Students in Their Daily Activities". Research exercise, Department of Malay Studies, National University of Singapore, 1991. 28 pp. NUS.

1040. Rina Haideati Misri. "Pelajar Wanita Melayu di Institusi Pengajian Tinggi: Peranan dan Jangkaan Mereka". Research exercise, Department of Malay Studies, National University of Singapore, 1996. 30 pp. NUS.

1041. Saat A. Rahman et al. *Menyemai Kecemerlangan: Empat Dekad Pencapaian LBKM 1965–2005 = Nurturing Excellence: Four Decades of Achievements PMBM Scholarship Fund Board 1965–2005*. Singapore: Lembaga Biasiswa Kenangan Maulud, 2005. 168 pp. ISEAS, NLB.

1042. Singapore Dawoodi Bohra Muslim Association. *Souvenir Magazine in Aid of Scholarship Fund, 1973*. Singapore: Singapore Dawoodi Bohra Muslim Association, 1973. 139 pp. NUS.

1043. *Suara*. Singapore: Persekutuan Bahasa Melayu Universiti Singapura, 1967. NLB, NUS.

1044. *Suara Mahasiswa*. Singapore: Persatuan Bahasa Melayu, Universiti National Singapura, 1982–. NLB, NUS.

1045. Tan (Eng Thye), Jason and Ho Boon Tiong. "Study on Malay/Muslim Polytechnic and GCE 'A' Level Students: Aspirations and Factors Affecting the Choices in Their Academic Paths: Final Report to the Yayasan Mendaki Board of Directors". 1999. 15 pp. NTUNIE.

1046. Tan (Eng Thye), Jason and Ho Wah Kam. "'A' Levels or a Polytechnic Diploma? Malay Students' Choices of Post-secondary Options". In *Challenges Facing the Singapore Education System Today*, edited by Jason Tan, S. Gopinathan, and Ho Wah Kam. Singapore: Prentice Hall, 2001. ISEAS, NLB, NTUNIE, NUS.

1047. Yow Sook Yin. "Reading Preferences of Malay Undergraduates in the National University of Singapore". Research exercise, Department of Malay Studies, National University of Singapore, 1994. 48 pp. NUS.

Academic Performance and Achievement

1048.   Abdul Aziz Mohamed Yusof. "Academic Motivation, Perception of Parental Press and the Academic Achievement of Malay Pupils". MA dissertation, National University of Singapore, 1990. 216 pp. NTUNIE, NUS.

1049.   Abdullah Tarmugi. "Closing Malay's Performance Gap". *Speeches* 25, no. 2 (March/April 2001): 77– 80. ISEAS, NLB, NTUNIE, NUS.

1050.   Abdullah Tarmugi. "Mendaki Programmes: Boost to Educational Performance". *Speeches* 19, no. 1 (January–February 1995): 89–91. ISEAS, NLB, NTUNIE, NUS.

1051.   Ahmad Mattar. "Malays Today Well Educated". *Petir: Organ of the People's Action Party* 8 (February 1981): 22–23. ISEAS, NLB, NTUNIE, NUS. Also published in Malay under the title: "Orang-Orang Melayu Sekarang Terpelajar". *Petir: Organ of the People's Action Party* 4 (March 1981): 31–33. ISEAS, NLB, NTUNIE, NUS.

1052.   Chin Chain Yu. *Understanding Malay Academic Underachievement in Singapore: A Deconstructivist Approach to Study Malay Academic Underachievement through Looking at Language.* Saarbrucken, Germany: LAP Lambert Academic Pub. GmbH & Co., 2011. 60 pp. NLB, NTUNIE.

1053.   Fadzli Baharom Adzahar, Allan Lee, and Christopher Naranjan Selvaraj. "Bridging the 'Gravel Road': Towards the Effective Utilization of Mentorship Programs in Lifting Malay Educational Aspirations". In *Issues Facing the Malay/Muslim Community in Singapore: A Collection of Essays Submitted by University Students in Conjunction with the Socialive! Challenge 2010 organised by PMBM Scholarship Fund Board (LBKM) & Berita Harian*. Singapore: LBKM, 2010. NLB.

1054.   Goh Chok Tong. "The Malay Community Has Progressed but Has Potential to Do Better". *Speeches* 14, no. 2 (May/April 1990): 9–12. ISEAS, NLB, NTU, NTUNIE, NUS.

1055.   Goh Chok Tong. "The Malays in Singapore: Progress and Challenges". *Speeches* 19, no. 5 (1995): 19–25. ISEAS, NLB, NTU, NTUNIE, NUS.

1056.   Goh Chok Tong. "MENDAKI Marks a Decade of Progress". *Speeches* 16, no. 6 (November/December 1992): 8–13. ISEAS, NLB, NTU, NTUNIE, NUS.

1057. Haffidz A. Hamid et al. *Factors Affecting Malay-Muslim Pupils' Performance in Education*. Occasional Paper Series, no. 1–95. Singapore: Association of Muslim Professionals, 1995. 39 pp. ISEAS, NLB, NTUNIE. Originally presented at a seminar organized by AMP at the Royal Holiday Inn, Crown Plaza Hotel, Singapore, 10 December 1994. 25 pp. NUS.

1058. Julinah Sulaiman. "Beyond the School Gate — Bringing Learning Opportunities Home". *MENDAKI Policy Digest* (2008): 45–56. ISEAS, NTUNIE, NUS.

1059. Kamsiah Abdullah. "Adakah Murid-Murid Melayu Secara Tabii Lemah dalam Matematik?" Paper presented at a Persidangan Antarabangsa Bahasa, Sastera dan Kebudayaan Melayu ke 2, anjuran Jabatan Bahasa dan Kebudayaan Melayu, Kumpulan Akademik Bahasa dan Kebudayaan Asia, Institut Pendidikan Nasional, Universiti Teknologi Nanyang, Singapura, 1–3 September 2002. 20 pp. ISEAS, NLB.

1060. Mohamed Irwan Mohamed Taib. "Malay Students between Aspirations and Expectations: An Interview with Dr Trivina Kang". *Karyawan: Professionals for the Community* 9, issue 1 (July 2008): 16–17. ISEAS, NLB, NTUNIE, NUS.

1061. Mohammad Noorfarhan Sulaiman, Mirshasha Mohamed Taib, and Nur Hamizah Rosidin. "The Malay Mathematical Problem: The Downward Trend of Passes in PSLE Mathematics among Malay Students". In *Issues Facing the Malay/Muslims Community in Singapore*. Singapore: Lembaga Biasiswa Kenangan Maulud, 2010. NLB.

1062. Mohd Alami Musa. "Building on Our Strengths". *Karyawan: Professionals for the Community* (February 1996): 4–5. ISEAS, NLB, NTUNIE, NUS.

1063. Ng Kai Li, Glanies. "Identification of Racial Identity Profiles and Linkages among Racial Identity, Educational Beliefs, and Academic Achievement amongst Singapore Chinese and Malays". Academic exercise, Department of Psychology, National University of Singapore, 2011. 92 pp. NUS.

1064. "Percentage of P1 Cohort Admitted to Post-Secondary Education Institutions by Ethnic Group". In *Education Statistics Digest 2014*. Singapore: Ministry of Education, 2014. NLB. (Percentage from 2003 to 2012).

1065.   "Percentage of Pupils who Passed PSLE by Ethnic Group". In *Education Statistics Digest 2014*. Singapore: Ministry of Education, 2014. NLB. (Percentage from 2003 to 2012).

1066.   "Percentage of Pupils with at Least 3 'A'/'H2' Passes & Pass in GP/K&I by Ethnic Group". In *Education Statistics Digest 2014*. Singapore: Ministry of Education, 2014. NLB. (Percentage from 2003 to 2012).

1067.   "Percentage of Pupils with at Least 5 'O' Level Passes by Ethnic Group". In *Education Statistics Digest 2014*. Singapore: Ministry of Education, 2014. NLB. (Percentage from 2003 to 2012).

1068.   Ramthan Hussain. "Helping the One Left Behind: Face to Face with Imran Mohamed". *Karyawan: Professionals for the Community* (December 1994): 16–17. ISEAS, NLB, NTUNIE, NUS.

1069.   Samsiah Sanip. "Educational Performance and Socialization in Malay Families: An Exploratory Study". Academic exercise, Department of Sociology, National University of Singapore, 1986. 82 pp. NUS.

1070.   Sha'ari Tadin. "A Sociological Study of Performance and Motivation of School Children in an Integrated Secondary School". MSocSc dissertation, Department of Sociology, National University of Singapore, 1983. 168 pp ISEAS, NTUNIE, NUS.

1071.   Sha'ari Tadin. "Why Malays Succeed: A Case Study". Paper presented at a seminar organized by the Institute of Southeast Asian Studies, Singapore, 1990. 29 pp. ISEAS.

1072.   Sidek Saniff. "Taking Stock of Malay Students' Performance". *Speeches* 16, no. 3 (May/June 1992): 68–84. ISEAS, NLB, NTUNIE, NUS.

1073.   Sidek Saniff. "Upgrading the Educational Performance of Malay/Muslim Pupils". *Fajar Islam* 2 (1989): 51–70. ISEAS, NLB, NUS.

1074.   Tan, C. (Charlene). "Narrowing the Gap: The Educational Achievements of the Malay Community in Singapore". *Intercultural Education* 18, no. 1 (2007): 53–64. NTUNIE, NUS.

1075.   Tan Eng Thye, Jason. "Educational Underachievement of the Malay Minority in Singapore, 1981–1992: Problems and Policies". MEd dissertation, University of Hong Kong, 1993. 148 pp.

1076.   Tan Eng Thye, Jason. "Improving Malay Educational Achievement in Singapore: Problems and Policies". *Asia Pacific Journal of Education* 17, no. 1 (1997): 41–57. NLB, NTUNIE, NUS.

1077.   Tan Eng Thye, Jason. "Joint Government-Malay Community Efforts to Improve Malay Educational Achievement in Singapore". *Comparative Education* 31, no. 3 (November 1995): 339–53. NTUNIE, NUS.

1078.   Tan Jin Aun, Peter. "Attributional Analysis of Malay and Chinese Academic Achievement". Academic exercise, Department of Social Work and Psychology, National University of Singapore, 1992. 55 pp. NUS.

1079.   Tan Keng Yam, Tony. "Differences in Educational Achievement: A Cause for Concern". *Speeches* 14, no. 6 (November/December 1990): 34–61. ISEAS, NLB, NTUNIE, NUS.

1080.   Tan Keng Yam, Tony. "Time to Nurture Top Malay Students: [Speech at the Berita Harian Achiever of the Year Award, 7 August 2001]". *Speeches* 4 (July–August 2001): 40–44. ISEAS, NLB, NTUNIE, NUS.

1081.   Tan Leng Nee and Naznee Jumabhoy. "The Achievement, Motivation, Aspirations and Occupational Interests of Singapore Malay and Chinese Students in Integrated Schools". Academic exercise, Department of Sociology, University of Singapore, 1971. 120 pp. NUS.

1082.   Yeo Geok Lee. "Profile of the Malay-Streamed Undergraduate with Special Emphasis on Educational Attainment". Academic exercise, Department of Sociology, University of Singapore, 1980. 152 pp. NUS.

ETHNOLOGY

- *Ethnicity, Ethnic Groups and Relations*
- *Malays and Muslims*
- *Indonesians*
- *Arabs*
- *Chinese and Indian Muslims*

Ethnicity, Ethnic Groups and Relations

1083. Alfian Sa'at. "The Racist's Apology". *Focas: Forum on Contemporary Art & Society* 4 (2002): 385–93. ISEAS, NLB, NTUNIE, NUS. Available at <http://alfian.diaryland.com/apology.html>.

1084. Cheong Seet Ee, Candy. 'Managing Ethnicity in Singapore". Academic exercise, Department of Political Science, National University of Singapore, 2011. 47 pp. NUS.

1085. Chew Sock Foon. "Ethnicity and Nationality in Singapore". PhD dissertation, University of Maryland, 1982. Ann Arbor, Mich.: University Microfilms International, 1984. 295 pp. ISEAS, NTUNIE, NUS. Published under the same title: Athens, Ohio: Ohio University, Center for International Studies, 1987. 229 pp. ISEAS, NLB, NTUNIE, NUS.

1086. Chiew Seen Kong. "Ethnicity and National Integration: The Evolution of a Multi-ethnic Society". In *Singapore: Development Policies and Trends*, edited by Peter S.J. Chen. Singapore: Oxford University Press, 1983. ISEAS, NLB, NTU, NTUNIE, NUS.

1087. Chiew Seen Kong. "Ethnicity, the Media and National Identity: The Singapore Experience". *Mirror* 25, no. 14 (July 1989): 12–14. ISEAS, NLB, NUS.

1088. Chiew Seen Kong. "National Identity, Ethnicity and National Issues". In *In Search of Singapore's National Values*, edited by Jon S.T. Quah. Singapore: Institute of Policy Studies, 1990. ISEAS, NLB, NTU, NTUNIE, NUS.

1089. Chiew Seen Kong. "Relations between the Principal Ethnic Groups of Malaysia and Singapore". *Southeast Asian Journal of Sociology* 1, no. 1 (May 1968): 63–78. ISEAS, NLB, NUS.

1090. Chiew Seen Kong. "Singaporean National Identity". MSocSci dissertation, Department of Sociology, University of Singapore, 1971. 227 pp. ISEAS, NUS.

1091. Chiew Seen Kong and Tan Ern Ser. *The Singaporean: Ethnicity, National Identity and Citizenship: Singapore Identity and Citizenship*. Singapore: Institute of Policy Studies, 1990. 1 vol. (various pagings). NTUNIE, NUS.

1092. Chin, Yolanda and Norman Vasu. *The Ties that Bind and Blind: A Report on Inter-Racial and Inter-Religious Relations in Singapore*. Singapore: Centre of Excellence for National Security, S. Rajaratnam School of International Studies, Nanyang Technological University, 2012. 30 pp. NTUNIE, NUS. Previous ed. published: 2007. 38 pp. ISEAS, NLB, NTUNIE, NUS.

1093. Clammer, John. "Ethnicity & the Classification of Social Difference in Plural Societies: A Perspective from Singapore". *Journal of Asian African Studies* 20, no. 3/4 (1985): 141–55. NLB, NTUNIE, NUS.

1094. Clammer, John. *Ethnographic Survey of Singapore: A Final Report*. Singapore: Department of Sociology, National University of Singapore, 1977. 20 pp. ISEAS, NUS.

1095. Clammer, John. "The Institutionalization of Ethnicity: The Culture of Ethnicity in Singapore". *Ethnic and Racial Studies* 5, no. 2 (1982): 127–39. NUS.

1096. Forum "Ethnicity and Singaporean Singapore". Organized by the National University of Singapore, held at Guild House on 14 June 1990. 1 vol. (various foliations). NUS.

1097. Goh Chok Tong. "Give and Take Needed in Multi-Racial Society: [Dialogue with Young Malay-Muslim Professionals organised by MENDAKI Club, 2 February 2002]". *Speeches* 26, no. 1 (January–February 2002): 5–12. ISEAS, NLB, NTU, NTUNIE.

1098. Hodder, B.W. "Racial Groupings in Singapore". *Malayan Journal of Tropical Geography* 1 (October 1953): 25–36. ISEAS, NLB, NTUNIE, NUS.

1099. Hussin Mutalib. "Singapore's Ethnic Relations' Scorecard". *Journal of Developing Societies* 28, no. 1 (March 2012): 31–55. ISEAS, NTUNIE, NUS.

1100. *Journeys: Rediscovering the Malay Legacy*. Singapore: SMU, 2006. 136 pp. NLB.

1101. Khoo Cheng Eng, Roland. "Management of Ethnic Relations in Singapore: Change in 1986?" Academic exercise, National University of Singapore, 1987. 71 pp. NUS.

1102. Lai Ah Eng. *Meanings of Multiethnicity: A Case Study of Ethnicity and Ethnic Relations in Singapore.* Kuala Lumpur; New York: Oxford University Press, 1995. 233 pp. ISEAS, NLB, NTUNIE, NUS.

1103. Lee Joo Cheng, Lillian. "Growth of a Multiracial Society in Nineteenth Century Singapore: A Socio-economic Study". Academic exercise, National University of Singapore, 1982. 103 pp. NUS.

1104. Lee Kiat Jin. "The State and the Management of Ethnic Relations in Singapore". Academic exercise, Department of Sociology, National University of Singapore, 1991. 56 pp. NUS.

1105. Leifer, Michael. "Communal Violence in Singapore". *Asian Survey* 4, no. 10 (1964): 1115–21. ISEAS, NLB, NTU, NTUNIE, NUS.

1106. Lian Kwee Fee. "Race and Racialization in Malaysia and Singapore". In *Race, Ethnicity, and the State in Malaysia and Singapore*, edited by Lian Kwen Fee. Boston: Brill Leiden, 2006. ISEAS, NLB, NTUNIE, NUS.

1107. Lim Chai Yean, Peggy. "Ethnic Strategies in Singapore Politics". Academic exercise, Department of Political Science, National University of Singapore, 1990. 100 pp. NUS.

1108. Lim Len Neo. "The Development of Racial Perception and Communal Attitudes among Children Attending the Chinese, English and Malay Media of an Integrated Primary School". Academic exercise, Department of Sociology, University of Singapore, 1971. 60 pp. NTUNIE, NUS.

1109. Mathews, Mathew. "The State and Implication of Our Differences: Insights from the IPS Survey on Race, Religion and Language". In *Singapore Perspectives 2014: Differences.* Singapore: LKY School of Public Policy, NUS; World Scientific, 2014. NLB.

1110. Muhammad Ruzaini Naim Azman. "Emotional Journeys Through Uncharted Waters: Mobility Experience and Friendship Formation". Academic exercise, Department of Sociology, National University of Singapore, 2014. 99 pp. NUS.

1111. Neville, Warwick. "Singapore Ethnic Diversity and Its Implications". *Annals of the Association of American Geographers* 56, no. 2 (June 1966): 236–53. NTUNIE, NUS.

1112.   Ragayah Eusoff. *The Merican Clan: A Story of Courage and Destiny.* Singapore: Times Books, 1997. 216 pp. ISEAS, NLB, NUS.

1113.   Sin C.H. "The Politics of Ethnic Integration in Singapore: Malay 'Regrouping' as an Ideological Construct". *International Journal of Urban and Regional Research* 27, no. 2 (2003): 527–44. NUS.

1114.   *Some Aspects of Sino-Malay Social Relationship in Singapore.* Hong Kong: University of Hong Kong Jubilee Congress, 1962. 14 pp. NLB.

1115.   Sun Tsai-Wei. "The Ethnic Triangle: State, Majority and Minority in Indonesia, Malaysia and Singapore". PhD dissertation, National University of Singapore, 2010. NUS.

1116.   Ward, C. and M. Hewstone. "Ethnicity, Language and Intergroup Relation in Malaysia and Singapore: A Social Psychological Analysis". *Journal of Multi-Cultural and Multi-Lingual Development* 6, no. 3/4 (1985): 271–96. NLB, NTUNIE, NUS.

1117.   Wee, Ann E. "Chinese-Malay Relationships: The Conflict of Social Values in a Plural Society". In *Symposium on Economic and Social Problems of the Far East*, edited by E.P. Szczepanix. Hong Kong: Hong Kong University Press, 1962. NUS.

1118.   Wu Y.H., David. "Ethnic Relations and Ethnicity in a City-State: Singapore". In *Ethnicity and Interpersonal Interaction: A Cross-cultural Study*, edited by David Y.H. Wu. Singapore: Maruzen Asia, 1982. ISEAS, NLB, NTU, NTUNIE, NUS.

1119.   Yeo Yong Boon, George. "Strengthening a Multi-racial Society: Understanding Each Other with Wider Perspectives: [Speech at the Opening of Asian Civilisations Museum's (ACM) Second Temporary Exhibition — "Harmony of Letters: Islamic Calligraphy from the Tareq Rajab Museum", Singapore, 28 Nov 97]". *Speeches (Singapore)* 21, no. 6 (November/December 1997): 60–63. ISEAS, NLB, NTU, NTUNIE.

1120.   Yong Mun Cheong. "Some Thoughts on Modernization and Race Relations in the Political History of Singapore". In *Asian Traditions and Modernization: Perspectives from Singapore*, edited by Yong Mun Cheong. Singapore: Times Academic Press, 1992. 288 pp. ISEAS, NTU, NTUNIE, NUS. Second edition: Singapore: Eastern University Press, 2004. 252 pp. NLB.

Malays and Muslims

1121. A. Samad Ismail (Abdul Samad Ismail). "Melayu versus Arab". *Dewan Budaya* 14, no. 9 (September 1992): 20–21. ISEAS, NLB, NTUNIE, NUS.

1122. Alatas, Syed Hussein. *The Myth of the Lazy Native: A Study of the Image of the Malays, Filipinos and Javanese from the 16th to the 20th Century and Its Function in the Ideology of Colonial Capitalism.* London; New York: Routledge, 2010. 267 pp. NLB, NTUNIE, NUS. Previous ed. published: London: F. Cass, 1977. 267 pp. ISEAS. Translated into Malay under the title: *Mitos Peribumi Malas.* Kuala Lumpur: Dewan Bahasa dan Pustaka, 2009. 280 pp. NLB.

1123. Aljunied, Syed Muhd Khairudin. "British Discourses and Malay Identity in Colonial Singapore". *Indonesia and the Malay World* 37, no. 107 (2009): 1–21. ISEAS, NLB, NTUNIE, NUS.

1124. Aljunied, Syed Muhd Khairudin. "Ethnic Resurgence, Minority Communities, and State Policies in a Network Society: The Dynamics of Malay Identity Formation in Postcolonial Singapore". *Identities: Global Studies in Culture and Power* 17, nos. 2 & 3 (2010): 304–26. NUS.

1125. Aljunied, Syed Muhd Khairudin. "Making Sense of an Evolving Identity: A Survey of Studies on Identity and Identity Formation among Malay-Muslims in Singapore". *Journal of Muslim Minority Affairs* 26, no. 12 (December 2006): 371–82. ISEAS, NTUNIE, NUS.

1126. Aljunied, Syed Muhd Khairudin. "Malay Identity in Postcolonial Singapore". In *Melayu: The Politics, Poetics and Paradoxes of Malayness*, edited by Maznah Mohamad and Syed Muhd Khairudin Aljunied. Singapore: NUS Press, 2011. 370 pp. ISEAS, NLB, NTU, NTUNIE, NUS.

1127. Almashur, Shariffa Salmah Syed Alwee. "Malay Perceptions of Themselves as a Minority in Multi-Racial Society with Special Reference to a Selection of Malay Professionals". Research exercise, Department of Malay Studies, National University of Singapore, 1993. 48 pp. NUS.

1128. Azhar Ibrahim Alwee. *Narrating Presence: Awakening from Culture Amnesia.* Singapore: The Malay Heritage Foundation and Select Publishing, 2014. 116 pp. ISEAS, NLB, NTUNIE, NUS.

1129. Azmoon Ahmad. "A Community at a Crossroads: The Perspective of a Community Leader". In *Singapore 2065: Leading Insights on Economy and Environment from 50 Singapore Icons and Beyond*, edited by Euston Quah. Singapore; New Jersey: World Scientific Publishing, 2015. ISEAS, NLB, NTU, NTUNIE, NUS.

1130. Barnard, Timothy P. *Contesting Malayness: Malay Identity Across Boundaries*. Singapore: Singapore University Press, 2004. 318 pp. ISEAS, NLB, NTUNIE, NUS.

1131. Barr, Michael D. and Jevon Low. "Assimilation as Multiracialism: The Case of Singapore's Malays". *Asian Ethnicity* 6, no. 3 (October 2005): 161–82. NLB, NTUNIE, NUS.

1132. Bunnell, Tim. "Post-maritime Transnationalization: Malay Seafarers in Liverpool." *Global Networks* 7, no. 4 (2007): 412–429. NTUNIE, NUS.

1133. Bunnell, Tim. "Routes of Identity: Malay Liverpool and the Limits of Transnationalism". *Pacific Affairs* 83, no. 3 (September 2010): 459–79. ISEAS, NLB, NTU, NTUNIE, NUS.
("This paper situates migration experiences in broader 'routes of identity'. In the case of Malay ex-seamen in Liverpool, UK, all of whom are now in their seventies or eighties, this has meant tracing life geographies extending back well over half a century).

1134. Firus Abdullah. "Dilema Melayu Singapura". *Dewan Masyarakat* 25, no. 2 (February 1987): 22–24. NLB.

1135. Gibson-Hill, Carl Alexander. "The Orang Laut of Singapore River and the Sampan Panjang". *JMBRAS* 25, pt. 1 (1952): 161–74. ISEAS, NLB, NTUNIE, NUS.

1136. Hanna, Willard A. *The Malays' Singapore*. Southeast Asia Series, vol. 14, nos. 2–6 (1966). 5 parts. ISEAS, NUS.

1137. Hidayah Amin, ed. *The Pursuit of Knowledge: Stories that Inspire and Empower*. Singapore: Centre for Research on Islamic and Malay Affairs for Lembaga Biasiswa Kenangan Maulud, 2015. 94 pp. NLB.

1138. Hong Sze Ern, Jonas. "Being a Malay Christian: Negotiating Malayness in Singapore". Academic exercise, Department of Sociology, National University of Singapore, 2011. 52 pp. NUS.

1139.   Hussain Haikal and Atiku Garba Yahaya. "Muslims in Singapore: The Colonial Legacy and the Making of Minority". *Journal of Muslim Minority Affairs* 17, no. 1 (April 1997): 83–88. ISEAS, NTUNIE, NUS.

1140.   Hussin Mutalib. "Dilemmas of a Minority Community in a Secular, Modern City-State: The Case of Singapore Muslims". *The Fount Journal* 1 (2000): 65. ISEAS, NLB, NUS.

1141.   Hussin Mutalib. *Singapore Malays: Being Ethnic Minority and Muslim in a Global City-state*. New York: Routledge, 2014. 204 pp. ISEAS, NLB, NTU, NTUNIE, NUS. Also published in Malay under the title: *Melayu Singapura: Sebagai Kaum Minoriti dan Muslim dalam Sebuah Negara Global*. Singapore: NUS Press; Kuala Lumpur: Strategic Information and Research Development Centre, 2015. 302 pp. NLB, NTUNIE, NUS.

1142.   Hussin Mutalib. "Singapore Muslims: The Quest for Identity in a Modern City-State". *Journal of Muslim Minority Affairs* 25, no. 1 (April 2005): 53–72. ISEAS, NTUNIE, NUS.

1143.   Imran Hashim. "Changing Nature of Malay Identity". *Karyawan: Professionals for the Community* 6, issue 1 (November 2005): 16–17. ISEAS, NLB, NTUNIE, NUS.

1144.   Imran Tajudeen. "State Constructs of Ethnicity in the Reinvention of Malay–Indonesian Heritage in Singapore". *Traditional Dwellings and Settlements Review* 18, no. 2 (2007): 7–27. NTUNIE, NUS.

1145.   Iskander Mydin. "The Ethnic Cauldron: Tracing Malay Identities". *BeMuse* (October–December 2008): 48–53. NLB, NUS.

1146.   Kahn, Joel S. *Other Malays: Nationalism and Cosmopolitanism in the Modern Malay World*. Asian Studies Association of Australia Southeast Asia publication. Singapore: Singapore University Press, 2006. 228 pp. ISEAS, NLB, NTU, NTUNIE, NUS.
(The author challenges the kampung version of Malayness, arguing that it ignores the immigration of Malays from outside the peninsula to participate in trade and commercial agriculture, the substantial Malay population in towns and cities (including Singapore), and the reformist Muslims who argued for a common bond in Islam).

1147. Lee Kwee Eng. "Maintenance of Group Identity: The Case of the Malays in Singapore". Academic exercise, Department of Sociology, National University of Singapore, 1982. 121 pp. NUS.

1148. Lian Kwen Fee. "The Construction of Malay Identity Across Nations: Malaysia, Singapore and Indonesia". *Bijdragen tot de Taal-, Land- en Volkenkunde* 157, no. 4 (2001): 861–79. ISEAS, NLB, NTUNIE, NUS.

1149. Logan, J.R. "The Orang Biduanda Kallang of the River Pulai in Johore". *Journal of the Indian Archipelago and Eastern Asia* 1, no. 1 (1847): 299–302. ISEAS, NLB, NUS.

1150. Logan, J.R. "The Orang Sletar of the Rivers and Creeks of the Old Strait and Estuary of the Johor". *Journal of the Indian Archipelago and Eastern Asia* 1, no. 1 (1847): 302–4. ISEAS, NLB, NUS.

1151. Marranci, Gabriele. "Integration, Minorities and the Rhetoric of Civilization: The Case of British Pakistani Muslims in the UK and Malay Muslims in Singapore". *Ethnic and Racial Studies* 34, no. 5 (2011): 814–32. ISEAS, NLB, NUS.

1152. Maznah Mohamad. "Singapore Malays: Being Ethnic Minority and Muslim in a Global City-State". *Pacific Affairs* 87, no. 2 (June 2014): 385–87. ISEAS, NLB.

1153. "Melayu Singapura". In *Ensiklopedia Sejarah dan Kebudayaan Melayu*, vol. 3, pp. 1513–16. Kuala Lumpur: Dewan Bahasa dan Pustaka, 1998. NLB, NTUNIE, NUS.

1154. Muhammad Hafiz B. Roslee. "The New Malay: Class Habitus and Symbolic Struggle Over Malayness in Singapore". Academic exercise, Department of Sociology, National University of Singapore, 2008. 47 pp. NUS.

1155. *Muslims in Singapore: A Photographic Portrait*. Singapore: Published for Muslim Religious Council of Singapore by MPH Magazines, 1984. 111 pp. ISEAS, NLB, NTUNIE, NUS.

1156. Noraslinda Muhamad Zuber. "Singapore Malay Identity: A Study of Dominant Perceptions of Islam in Post-Independence Singapore". PhD dissertation, Department of Malay Studies, National University of Singapore, 2010. NUS.

1157. Norhazlina Md Yusof. "Caught in the Middle: Apostasy and the Politics of Identity Construction amongst the Malays in Singapore". Academic exercise, Department of Sociology, National University of Singapore, 2001. 79 pp. NUS.

1158. Nurhidayahti Mohammad Miharja. "On Orientalist Terms: Malays in Singapore and Textbook Prescriptions". *Studies in Ethnicity and Nationalism* 14, no. 3 (2014): 436–51. ISEAS, NUS.

1159. Nurliza Yusof. "Being Malay in Singapore: Perceptions and Articulations of Identity". Academic exercise, Department of Sociology, National University of Singapore, 1986. 87 pp. NUS.

1160. Ong Beng Ann, Sherman. *Di Mana Bumi Dipijak = The Ground I Stand*. Singapore: S. Ong, 2002. 1 videocassette (Digital Betacam). 24 min. NUS.
      ("About an elderly Malay woman who was born in Malaysia but raised in Singapore...Her revelatory confessions gave us an insight into the life of a minority in Singapore's 'heartland'").

1161. Phang Fong May. "Mutual Images: Factors Contributing to the Mutual Stereotypes of the Chinese and Malays in Singapore Today". Academic exercise, Department of Sociology, National University of Singapore, 1986. 46 pp. NUS.

1162. "A Question of Identity". *Asiaweek* 18, no. 31 (July 1992): 44–45. ISEAS, NLB, NTUNIE, NUS.

1163. Rahil Ismail and B.J. Shaw. "Singapore's Malay-Muslim Minority: Social Identification in a Post-'9/11' World". *Asian Ethnicity* 7, no. 1 (2006): 37–51. NTUNIE, NUS.

1164. Reid, Anthony. "Understanding Melayu (Malay) as a Source of Diverse Modern Identities". *Journal of Southeast Asian Studies* 32, no. 3 (October 2001): 295–313. ISEAS, NLB, NTU, NTUNIE, NUS.

1165. Ridley, H.N. 'The Orang Laut of Singapore". *JSBRAS* 41 (1904): 129–30. ISEAS, NLB, NUS.

1166. Sharifah Mohamed. *Kenapa Saya Menulis*. Singapore: Sharifah Mohamed, 2015. 183 pp. NLB.

1167. Siddique, Sharon. "Muslim Minorities". *Assyahid* 1, no. 1 (1983): 125–30. ISEAS, NLB, NUS.

1168. Sidek Saniff. *Paradigma Melayu Singapura*. Singapore: Taman Bacaan Pemuda Pemudi Melayu Singapura, 2010. 299 pp. ISEAS, NLB, NTU, NTUNIE.

1169. Sopher, David E., ed. *The Sea Nomads: A Study of the Maritime Boat People of Southeast Asia*. Singapore: National Museum, 1977. 444 pp. NLB.

1170. Stimpfl, Joseph Richard. "Growing Up Malay in Singapore". In *Race, Ethnicity, and the State in Malaysia and Singapore*, edited by Lian Kwee Fee. Boston: Brill Leiden, 2006. ISEAS, NLB, NTUNIE, NUS. Also published under the same title in: *Southeast Asian Journal of Social Science* 25, no. 2 (1997): 117–38. ISEAS, NTUNIE.

1171. Stimpfl, Joseph Richard. "Who Shall We Be? Constructing Malay Identity in a Singapore Secondary School". PhD dissertation, University of Pittsburg, 1990. Ann Arbor, Mich.: University Microfilms International, 1991. 243 pp. NTUNIE, NUS.

1172. Suriani Suratman. "The Malays of Clementi: An Ethnography of Flat Dwellers in Singapore". MA dissertation, Monash University, 1986. 328 pp. ISEAS, NUS.

1173. Suriani Suratman. *Problematic Singapore Malays: Sustaining a Portrayal*. Occasional Paper Series, no. 2. Singapore: Leftwrite Center in collaboration with the Reading Group Singapore, 2010. 20 pp. ISEAS. Also published under the same title as: Seminar Papers, no. 36. Singapore: Department of Malay Studies, National University of Singapore, 2005. 1 vol. (unpaged). NLB, NUS.

1174. Tan, Charlene. "(Re)imagining the Muslim Identity in Singapore". *Studies in Ethnicity and Nationalism* 8, issue 1 (April 2008): 31–41. ISEAS, NTUNIE, NUS.

1175. Tham Seong Chee. *Defining "Malay"*. Seminar Papers, no. 6. Singapore: Department of Malay Studies, National University of Singapore, 1993. 18 pp. ISEAS, NLB, NUS.

1176. Thomson, J.T. "Remarks on the Sletar and Sabimba Tribes". *Journal of Indian Archipelago and Eastern Asia* 1 (1847): 341–52. ISEAS, NLB, NUS.

1177. Wan Abdul Rahman Ahmad. "The Island Malays: Study of a Group of Malays in an Island of Singapore: Their Life, Customs, Beliefs and the Degree to Which They Communicate with Other Places to Meet Their Various Needs". Academic exercise, Department of Social Studies, University of Malaya, Singapore, 1961. 88 pp. NUS.

1178. "Workshop on Redefining Identity: Malay Ethnicity and the State". Organized by the Institute of Southeast Asian Studies, Singapore, 21 December 1988. 257 pp. ISEAS.

1179. Yusuf Sulaiman. "Reflections on the Singapore Muslim Identity". *Karyawan: Professionals for the Community* 9, issue 2 (January 2009): 2–4. ISEAS, NLB, NTUNIE, NUS.

1180. Zainul Abidin Rasheed. "Muslims in Multi-Racial Singapore: New Dynamics in Nation Building". In *Jendela Kata: Pesan & Ucapan 1993–1997*. Singapore: Majlis Ugama Islam Singapura, 1998. ISEAS, NLB, NTUNIE, NUS.

1181. Zulkifli Baharudin. "The Challenges Within". *Karyawan: Professionals for the Community* 5 (January–April 1999): 8–9. ISEAS, NLB, NTUNIE, NUS.

Indonesians

1182. Abdul Aziz Johari. "The Javanese People in Singapore". Academic exercise, Department of Social Studies, University of Malaya, Singapore, 1962. 106 pp. NUS.

1183. Abdullah Malim Baginda. "The Boyanese of Singapore: A Study of One of the Indonesian Minority Groups in Singapore". Academic exercise, University of Malaya, Singapore, 1959. 113 pp. NUS.

1184. Abdullah Malim Baginda. "Our Baweanese People". In *Intisari* 2, no. 4 (1964): 15–71. ISEAS, NLB, NUS.

1185. Ahmad Haji Tahir. *Shair Saudara Bawean*. Singapore: Malaya Press, 1930. 49 pp. London: Reprographic Section, Reference Service Division, British Library. Microfilm. NLB.

1186. "Boyanese". In *Singapore: The Encyclopedia*. Edited by T.T.B. Koh, T. Auger, J. Yap, and Ng W.C. Singapore: Editions Didier Millet in association with the National Heritage Board, 2006. ISEAS, NLB, NTUNIE, NUS.

1187. Chew, Daniel. "A Baweanese Pondok at Everton Road". In *Tanjong Pagar: Singapore's Cradle of Development*. Singapore: Tanjong Pagar Citizen's Consultative Committee, 1989. NLB.

1188. Chew Oon Ai, Joy. "The Bataks in Singapore: A Study of Group Cohesion and Assimilation". M.SocSci Dissertation, Department of Sociology, University of Singapore, 1978. 194 pp. ISEAS, NUS.

1189. Chia Hwee Hwee. "A Story of the Javanese and Boyanese in Singapore". Academic exercise, National University of Singapore, 1993. NUS.

1190. Davison, Julian. "Over the Bounding Main". *Expat* (March 2005): 82–92. NLB, NUS.

1191. Dewi Indrawati, Sukiyah, and Lukman Solihin. *Menjadi Boyan: Strategi Adaptasi Keturunan Bawean Singapura*. Jakarta: Direktorat Tradisi. Direktorat Jenderal Nilai Budaya, Seni dan Film, Kementrian Kebudayaan dan Pariwisata, 2011. 79 pp. ISEAS, NLB.

1192. "Historic Sites: Pondok Peranakan Gelam Club". *Treasures of Time* (April–May 2002): 11–13. NLB, NTUNIE.

1193. Imran Tajudeen. "State Constructs of Ethnicity in the Reinvention of Malay-Indonesian Heritage in Singapore". *Traditional Dwellings and Settlements Review* 18, no. 2 (2007): 7–27. NTUNIE, NUS.

1194. Julina Khusairi. "The Baweanese and the Javanese in Singapore: A Comparative Analysis of Integration in a Plural Society". Academic exercise, National University of Singapore, 1989. 83 pp. NUS.

1195. Mansor Haji Fadzal. "My Baweanese People". *Intisari* 2, no. 4 (1964): 11–14. ISEAS, NLB, NUS.

1196. Mariam Mohamed Ali. "Ethnic Hinterland: Contested Spaces between Nations and Ethnicities in the Lives of Baweanese Labor Migrants". PhD dissertation, Harvard University, 1996. Ann Arbor, Mich.: University Microfilms International, 1997. 466 pp. NUS.

1197. Norhafizah Madbi. "Exploring Bawean Identity/ies in Singapore". Academic exercise, National University of Singapore, 2011. 89 pp. NUS.

1198.   "Our People from Bawean". *Citizen* 7, no. 18 (16 September 1978): 3, 5–7. NLB.

1199.   Putten, Jan van der. "A Malay of Bugis Ancestry: Haji Ibrahim's Strategies of Survival". *Journal of Southeast Asian Studies* 32, no. 3 (October 2001): 343–54. ISEAS, NLB, NTU, NTUNIE, NUS.

1200.   Rizwana Begum. "More Bawean Here than in Bawean". *Singapore* (May–June 1999): 22. NLB, NUS.

1201.   Samuel, Dhoraisingam S. "Baweanese Pondok". In *Singapore's Heritage: Through Places of Historical Interest*. Singapore: Elixir Consultancy Service, 1991. ISEAS, NLB, NTUNIE, NUS.

1202.   Shamsul Bahrin, Tunku. "The Growth and Distribution of the Indonesian Population in Malaya". *Bijdragen tot de taal land- en volkenkunde* 123 (1967): 267–86. ISEAS, NLB, NTUNIE, NUS.

1203.   Shamsul Bahrin, Tunku. "The Indonesians in Malaya: A Study of the Pattern of Migration to Malaya". MA dissertation, University of Sheffield, 1964. 1 microfilm reel. ISEAS, NUS.

1204.   Sundusia Rosdi, comp. *Masyarakat Bawean Singapura: La-A-Obĕ*. Singapore: Persatuan Bawean Singapura, 2015. 250 pp. NLB.

1205.   Sundusia Rosd.. "Shair Saudara Boyan: Menyingkap Sejarah Masyarakat Bawean". *BiblioAsia* (January 2011): 19–26. NLB, NTUNIE, NUS.

1206.   Vredenbregt, Jacob. *Bawean dan Islam*. Seri INIS, jilid 8. Penerjemah, A.B. Lapian. Jakarta: INIS, 1990. 214 pp. ISEAS, NLB, NUS.

1207.   Vredenbregt, Jacob. "Bawean Migration: Some Preliminary Notes". *Bijdragen Tot de Taal - Land- en Volkenkunde* 120 (1964): 109–37. ISEAS, NTUNIE, NUS.

Arabs

1208.   A. Samad Ismail (Abdul Samad Ismail). "Melayu versus Arab". *Dewan Budaya* 14, no. 9 (September 1992): 20–21. ISEAS, NLB, NTUNIE, NUS.

1209.   Abdul Halim Abdul Karim. "Ethnic Networking: Whither the Arabs?" *Al-Mahjar: A Publication of the Arab Association of Singapore* 2, no. 1 (1997): 13–15. NLB, NUS.

1210. Alatas, Syed Farid et al. "Hadhrami Identity and the Future of Arabs in Singapore". *Al-Mahjar: A Publication of the Arab Association of Singapore* 1, no. 1 (1996): 2–3. NLB, NUS. Available at <http://www.alwehdah.org/almahjarfiles/mahjar1a.pdf>.

1211. Alatas, Syed Farid. "Hadhrami Diaspora". *Al-Mahjar: A Publication of the Arab Association of Singapore* 1, no. 1 (1996): 9–10. NLB, NUS.

1212. Aljufri, Syed Abdillah. "Renungan". In *Al-Wehdah Al- Arabiah Celebrates 40th Anniversary = Al-Wehdah Al-Arabiah Menyambut Ulang Tahun ke-40*. Singapore: Al-Wehdah Al-Arabiah, 1986. NLB, NUS.

1213. Aljunied, Syed Muhd Khairudin. "Hadhramis within Malay Activism: The Role of Al-Saqqaf(s) in the Post-War Singapore". In *The Hadhrami Diaspora in Southeast Asia: Identity Maintenance or Assimilation?*, edited by Ibrahim Abushouk Ahmed and Hassan Ahmed. Leiden: Boston: Brlll, 2009. ISEAS, NLB, NTUNIE, NUS.

1214. Aljunied, Syed Muhd Khairudin. "The Role of Hadramis in Post-Second World War Singapore: A Reinterpretation". *Immigrants & Minorities* 25, no. 2 (2007): 163–83. NUS.

1215. Alsagoff, A.M. (Syed Mohsen). "The Arabs of Singapore". *Genuine Islam* 6, no. 2 (1941): 73–75. ISEAS, NUS.

1216. Alsagoff, Hussein Agil. "The Singapore Arabs in Transition". In *Al-Wehdah Al-Arabiah Celebrates 40th Anniversary = Al-Wehdah Al-Arabiah Menyambut Ulang Tahun ke-40*. Singapore: Al-Wehdah Al-Arabiah, 1986. NLB, NUS.

1217. *Al-Wehdah Al-Arabiah Celebrates 40th Anniversary = Al-Wehdah Al-Arabiah Menyambut Ulang Tahun ke-40*. Singapore: Al-Wehdah Al-Arabiah, 1986. 80 pp. NLB, NUS.

1218. *Al-Wehdah Al-Arabiah Menyambut Ulang Tahunnya yang ke 38: Sempena Pelancaran Pungutan "Dana Pembangunannya", Menuju ke Masa Hadapan yang Jaya dan Maju*. Singapore: Al-Wehdah Al-Arabiah, 1985. 116 pp. NLB.

1219. Arai, Kazuhiro. "The History of Hadhrami Migration to Southeast Asia: The Case of the Al-'Attas Family". In *Population Movement Beyond the Middle East: Migration, Diaspora, and Network*, edited by

Akira Usuki, Omar Farouk Bajunid, and Tomoko Yamagish. Osaka, Japan: Japan Center for Area Studies, National Museum of Ethnology, 2005. NLB.

1220. Arai, Kazuhiro. "The Role of the Family Connection in the Migration of Hadhrami Sada: A Case of the Al-'Attas Family". In *Hadhrami Arabs Across the Indian Ocean: Contributions to Southeast Asian Economy and Society,* edited by Syed Farid Alatas. Singapore: National Library Board, 2010. ISEAS, NLB, NUS.

1221. Farouk Bajunid. "The Arabs in Southeast Asia: A Preliminary Overview". *Hiroshima Journal of International Studies* (1996): 21–38. Available at <http://harp.lib hiroshima-ucjp/handle/harp/758>.

1222. "Grand Old Lady Meets the Dame at Birthday Bash". *Al-Mahjar: A Publication of the Arab Association of Singapore* 2, no. 2 (1997): 2. NLB, NUS.

1223. Harasha Kalid Bafana. "The Arab Identity: Dilemma or Non-Issue?" *Al-Mahjar: A Publication of the Arab Association of Singapore* 1, no. 1 (1996): 5. NLB, NUS.

1224. Harasha Kalid Bafana. "The Singapore Hadrami Arab Identity". Academic exercise, Department of Sociology, National University of Singapore, 1996. 62 pp. NUS.

1225. Heikel Khalid Bafana. "The Singapore Arabs of Today". *Al-Mahjar: A Publication of the Arab Association of Singapore* 2, no. 1 (1997): 12–13. NLB, NUS.

1226. Lee Hsien Loong. "Honouring the Contributions of Our Smaller Communities [Speech Delivered at the Arab Association's 46th Anniversary Dinner, 8 November 1992]". *Speeches (Singapore)* 16 (November–December 1992): 75–79. ISEAS, NLB, NTU, NTUNIE. Available at <http://stars.nhb.gov.sg/stars/tmp/lhl19921108s.pdf>.

1227. Lim Lu Sia. "The Arabs of Singapore: A Sociographic Study of Their Place in the Muslim and Malay World of Singapore". Academic exercise, Department of Sociology, National University of Singapore, 1987. 90 pp. ISEAS, NUS.

1228. Mohammad Redzuan Othman. "The Origins and Contributions of Early Arabs in Malaya". In *Southeast Asia and the Middle East: Islam,*

Movement, and the Longue Duree, edited by Eric Tagliacozzo. Singapore: NUS Press, 2009. ISEAS, NLB, NTUNIE, NUS.

1229. Morley, J.A.E. "The Arabs and the Eastern Trade". *JMBRAS* 22, no. 1 (1949): 143–76. ISEAS, NLB, NTUNIE, NUS.

1230. Nargis Mohamad Talib. "Arab Women in Singapore: Ethnic Consciousness and Boundary Maintenance". Academic exercise, Department of Sociology, National University of Singapore, 2000. 59 pp. NUS.

1231. Nurfadzilah Yahaya. "Tea and Company: Interaction between the Arab Elite and the British in Cosmopolitan Singapore". In *The Hadhrami Diaspora in Southeast Asia: Identity Maintenance or Assimilation?,* edited by Ibrahim Abushouk Ahmed and Hassan Ahmed Ibrahim. Leiden; Boston: Brill, 2009. ISEAS, NLB, NTUNIE, NUS.

1232. Nurzan Muhammad Wahie. "The Arabs in Singapore". Academic exercise, Department of Social Studies, University of Malaya, 1960. 72 pp. NUS.

1233. Omar Farouk Bajunid. "The Arabs and the Nation-State in Southeast Asia — Part 1". *Al-Mahjar: A Publication of the Arab Association of Singapore* 2, no. 1 (1997): 4–6. NLB, NUS.

1234. Omar Farouk Bajunid. "The Arabs and the Nation-State in Southeast Asia — Part 2, Aspects of the Arabs Presence". *Al-Mahjar: A Publication of the Arab Association of Singapore* 2, no. 2 (1997): 7–9. NLB, NUS.

1235. Omar Farouk Bajunid. "The Arabs and the Nation-State in Southeast Asia — Part 3". *Al-Mahjar: A Publication of the Arab Association of Singapore* 3, no. 1 (1998): 12–13. NLB, NUS.

1236. Omar Farouk Bajunid. "The Arabs and the Nation-State in Southeast Asia — Part 4, The Role of the Arabs in the New Nation States". *Al-Mahjar: A Publication of the Arab Association of Singapore* 3, no. 2 (1998): 9–11. NLB, NUS.

1237. "One Hundred Twenty Arab Family Clans in Singapore". *Al-Mahjar: A Publication of the Arab Association of Singapore* 3, no. 2 (1998): 5. NLB, NUS.

1238. "The Pioneering Aljunieds: Philanthropic Calls". In *Singapore Days of Old: A Special Commemorative History of Singapore Published on the 10th Anniversary of Singapore Tatler*. Hong Kong: Illustrated Magazine Publishing Co. Ltd., 1992. NLB, NTUNIE, NUS.

1239. Riddell, Peter G. "Arab Migrants and Islamization in the Malay World During the Colonial Period". *Indonesia and the Malay World* 29, no. 84 (2001): 113–28. ISEAS, NLB, NTUNIE, NUS.

1240. Southern Cross "The A. Belkoff Murder Mystery". In *Tales of Malaya*. Penang: Criterion Press, 1908. NLB.

1241. Suryahti Abdul Latiff. "Where are the Arabs?" *Singapore* (March–April 1995): 25. NLB, NUS.

1242. Talib, Ameen Ali. "Hadramis in Singapore". *Journal of Muslim Minority Affairs* 17, no. 1 (1997): 89–96. ISEAS, NTUNIE, NUS.

1243. Talib, Ameen Ali, Helmi Talib, and Khaled Talib. *Arabs in Singapore: A Vision for the Future*. Singapore: [s.n.], 1992. 10 pp. NUS.

Chinese and Indian Muslims

1244. Farish A. Noor (Farish Ahmad Noor). "Belonging, Yet Distinct: The Fate of the Indian Muslims in Malaysia and Singapore". In *Diaspora: The Story of the South Asian Muslim Diaspora in Southeast Asia Today*. Kuala Lumpur: Malaysian Social Research Institute, 2013. ISEAS, NLB, NTU.

1245. Farish A. Noor (Farish Ahmad Noor). "Muslim Brotherhood above the Empire: The Khilafat Movement in India and Its Impact on Indian Muslims in British Malaya and Singapore". In *Diaspora: the Story of the South Asian Muslim Diaspora in Southeast Asia Today*. Kuala Lumpur: Malaysian Social Research Institute, 2013. ISEAS, NLB, NTU.

1246. Ibrahim, Bibijan. "The Dawoodi Bohra Muslims: Ethnic Boundary Maintenance, with Special Focus on Marriage". Academic exercise, Department of Sociology, University of Singapore, 1977. 77 pp. NUS.

1247. Mani, A. "Aspects of Identity and Change among Tamil Muslims in Singapore". *Journal of Institute of Muslim Minority Affairs* 13, no. 2 (July 1992): 337–57. NUS.

1248. Shankar, Ravi A. *Tamil Muslims in Tamil Nadu, Malaysia and Singapore: Historical Identity, Problems of Adjustment, and Change in the Twentieth Century*. Kuala Lumpur: A. Jayanath, 2001. 147 pp. ISEAS, NUS.

1249. Singh, Anil Sona. "Neither 'Malay' nor 'Indian': The Racial State and the Tamil Muslim Dilemma in Singapore". Academic exercise, Department of Sociology, National University of Singapore, 2007. 54 pp. NUS.

1250. Syed Muhammad Baquir Md. Ibrahim. "The Tamil Muslim Community in Singapore". Academic exercise, Department of Social Work, University of Singapore, 1974. 121 pp. ISEAS, NUS.

1251. Tan Huism. "Chinese Muslims in Singapore: The Negotiation of Identity". Academic exercise, Department of Sociology, National University of Singapore, 1989. 43 pp. NUS.

1252. Yeo Yong Boon, George. "Unity in Diversity". *Speeches* 16, no. 4 (July–August 1992): 105–8. ISEAS, NLB, NTU, NTUNIE.

HEALTH

- *Public Health*
- *Health Conditions*
- *Diseases and Illnesses*

Public Health

1253. Campbell, J. Argyll. "Diet, Nutrition and Excretion of the Asiatic Races in Singapore". *JMBRAS* 76 (1917): 57–65; 79 (1918): 107–12. ISEAS, NLB, NUS.

1254. Foo L.L. et al. "Breastfeeding Prevalence and Practices among Singaporean Chinese, Malay and Indian Mothers". *Health Promotion International* 20, no. 3 (2005): 229–37. NTUNIE, NUS.

1255. Giam, Y.C. et al. "Drug Eruptions from Phenylbutazone in Jamu". *Annals of the Academy of Medicine, Singapore* 15, no. 1 (1986): 118–21. NLB, NTUNIE, NUS.

1256. Hairudin Harun. *Medicine and Imperialism: A Study of the British Colonial Medical Establishment, Health Policy and Medical Research in the Malay Peninsula, 1786–1918*. London: University of London Library, 1990. 6 microfiches. NLB, NUS.

1257. Jumari Naiyan. "Suatu Pilihan Peribadi". *Karyawan: Professionals for the Community* (August 1994): 15–16. ISEAS, NLB, NTUNIE, NUS.

1258. Lim, Leslie, ed. *Kampong Amber: Community Health Survey, 1979*. Singapore: National University of Singapore, 1983. 3 microfiches. NUS.

1259. Mohan, T.C. 'A Study of the P Blood Group System in the Singapore Population". *Singapore Medical Journal* 30, no. 4 (1989): 372–75. NLB, NUS.

1260. Muir, C.S. "Demography and Age-Sex Distribution of the Autopsy Populations of Multiracial Singapore". *Singapore Medical Journal* 5, no. 2 (1964): 96–104. NLB, NUS.

1261. *National Health Survey 2010, Singapore*. Singapore: Epidemiology and Disease Control Division, Ministry of Health, 2011. 187 pp. ISEAS, NTUNIE, NUS.

1262. Noorul Fatha. "'Health is Wealth': A Call to Action". *MENDAKI Policy Digest* (2013): 75–79. NLB.

1263. Noriza Mustapa and Lee Geok Yian. "Pilot Testing the Malay Version of the EORTC Questionnaire". *Singapore Nursing Journal* 34, no. 2 (April/June 2007): 16–20. NLB, NUS.

1264. Ratnam, K.V. "Efficacy of Health Education Programme on Awareness of AIDS among Transsexuals". *Singapore Medical Journal* 31, no. 1 (1990): 33–37. NLB, NUS.

1265. Tan, Nalla. "Intake of Foods Containing Proteins of High Biological Value in Families of Low Income Groups in Singapore". *Singapore Medical Journal* 11, no. 2 (1970): 130–37. NLB, NUS.

1266. Viegas, O.A. et al. "Ethnicity and Obstetric Performance in Singapore". *Journal of Biosocial Science* 27, no. 2 (1995): 151–62. NUS.

1267. Zuraimi Mohd Dahlan. "Socioeconomic Factors and Health". *Karyawan: Professionals for the Community* 10, issue 1 (July 2009): 11–12. ISEAS, NLB, NTUNIE, NUS.

Health Conditions

1268. Bhuiyan, Z.A., B.A. Zilfalil, and R.C.M. Hennekam. "A Malay Boy with the Cornelia de Lange Syndrome: Clinical and Molecular Findings". *Singapore Medical Journal* 47, no. 8 (August 2006): 724–27. NLB, NUS.

1269. Blake, N.M. et al. "The Distribution of Red Cell Enzyme Groups among Chinese and Malays in Singapore". *Singapore Medical Journal* 14, no. 1 (1973): 2–8. NLB, NUS.

1270. Chan M.F. et al. "Reducing Depression among Community-Dwelling Older Adults Using Life-story Review: A Pilot Study". *Geriatric Nursing* 35, no. 2 (2014): 105–10. NUS.

1271. Charumathi Sabanayagam et al. "The Association between Socioeconomic Status and Overweight/Obesity in a Malay Population in Singapore". *Asia-Pacific Journal of Public Health* 21, no. 4 (October 2009): 487–96. NUS.

1272. Chia S.E. "Pulmonary Function in Healthy Chinese, Malay and Indian Adults in Singapore". *Annals of the Academy of Medicine, Singapore* 22, no. 6 (November 1993): 878–84. NLB, NTUNIE, NUS.

1273. Chia S.E. and S.Y. Hoe. "Ventilatory Function in Malay Female Workers in Singapore". *Annals of the Academy of Medicine, Singapore* 17, no. 3 (1988): 443–46. NLB, NTUNIE, NUS.

1274. Chong Siow Ann et al. "The Prevalence and Impact of Major Depressive Disorder among Chinese, Malays and Indians in an Asian Multi-Racial Population". *Journal of Affective Disorders* 138, nos. 1–2 (2012): 128–36. NUS.

1275. Duncan, M.T. et al. "Ventilatory Function in Malay Muslims During Normal Activity and the Ramadan Fast". *Singapore Medical Journal* 31, no. 6 (1990): 543–47. NUS.

1276. Emmanuel, S.C., A.J. Chen, and A. Phe. "Cigarette Smoking in Singapore". *Singapore Medical Journal* 29, no. 2 (1988): 119–24. NLB, NUS.

1277. Emmanuel, S.C., C.K. Ho, and A.J. Chen. "Cigarette Smoking among School Children in Singapore. Part 1, Smoking Prevalence". *Singapore Medical Journal* 31, no. 3 (1990): 211–16. NLB, NUS.

1278. Farhan Ali and Hidayah Amin. "The Forgotten Infant: Pre-Natal Health and the Future of the Community". *Karyawan: Professionals for the Community* 9, issue 1 (July 2008): 3–5. ISEAS, NLB, NTUNIE, NUS. Also published in Malay under the title: "Kesihatan Pre-Natal dan Masa Depan Masyarakat Melayu/Islam". *Karyawan* 9, issue 1 (July 2008): 6–8. ISEAS, NLB, NTUNIE, NUS.

1279. *Haj Medical Guide Book*. Singapore: Majlis Ugama Islam Singapura, 1990. 29 pp. NLB.

1280. Hughes, Kenneth et al. "Obesity and Body Mass Indices in Chinese, Malays and Indians in Singapore". *Annals of the Academy of Medicine, Singapore* 19, no. 3 (1990): 333–38. NLB, NTUNIE, NUS.

1281. Hughes, Kenneth, et al. "Physical Activity in Chinese, Malays and Indians in Singapore". *Annals of the Academy of Medicine, Singapore* 19, no. 3 (1990): 326–29. NLB, NTUNIE, NUS.

1282. Husain, R., Cheah S.H. and M.T. Duncan. "Cardiovascular Reactivity in Malay Moslems during Ramadan". *Singapore Medical Journal* 37, no. 4 (August 1996): 393–401. NLB, NUS.

1283. Jamilah Yusop. *Berat Mata Memandang*. Singapore: Jamilah Yusop, 2015. 67 pp. NLB.

1284. Jazlan Joosoph et al. "A Survey of Fasting during Pregnancy". *Singapore Medical Journal* 45, no. 12 (December 2004): 583–86. NLB, NUS.

1285. Koh Yan Tong, Catherina J. Goenadi, and Srinivasan Sanjay. "Ramadan and Eye Drops: Attitudes and Practices of Malay Muslims in Singapore". *Annals of the Academy of Medicine, Singapore* 42 no. 11 (November 2013): 613–14. NTUNIE.

1286. Lamoureux, Ecosse L. et al. "Vision Impairment, Ocular Conditions, and Vision-specific Function: The Singapore Malay Eye Study". *Opthalmology* 115, issue 11 (November 2008): 1973–81. NUS.

1287. Lamoreux, Ecosse L. et al. "Visual Impairment, Causes of Vision Loss, and Falls: The Singapore Malay Eye Study". *Investigative Opthalmology & Visual Science* 49, no. 2 (2008): 528–33. NTUNIE, NUS.

1288. Lee H.P. "Patterns of Smoking among Singaporeans". *Annals of the Academy of Medicine, Singapore* 18, no. 3 (1989): 286–91. NLB, NTUNIE, NUS.

1289. Lee H.P. et al. "An Epidemiological Survey of Blood Pressures in Singapore". *Journal of Chronic Disease* 30 (1977): 793–802. NUS.

1290. Lee H.P. et al. "Smoking in a Local Community in Singapore". *Singapore Medical Journal* 20, no. 2 (1979): 323–29. NLB, NUS.

1291. Minaguchi, K. et al. "Salivary Proline-Rich Protein Polymo-Phisms in Chinese, Malays and Indians in Singapore". *Human Heredity* 40, no. 2 (1990): 89–98. NUS.

1292. Mohd Suhaimi Ismail. "Health and Wellness: New Challenges in the Malay/Muslim Community". *Karyawan: Professionals for the Community* 10, issue 1 (July 2009): 5–7. ISEAS, NLB, NTUNIE, NUS.

1293. Muhd Ridzwan Rahmat. "The Fat Tsunami". *Karyawan: Professionals for the Community* 10, issue 1 (July 2009): 18–19. ISEAS, NLB, NTUNIE, NUS.

1294. Phoon W.O. et al. "Health Problems of the Older Age Groups in the Community". *Annals of the Academy of Medicine, Singapore* 5, no. 2 (1976): 169–74. NLB, NTUNIE, NUS.

1295. Picco, Louisa et al. "Smoking and Nicotine Dependence in Singapore: Findings from a Cross-Sectional Epidemiological Study". *Annals of the Academy of Medicine, Singapore* 41, no. 8 (2012): 325–34. NTUNIE, NUS.

1296. Saha, N. and B. Banerjee. "Erythrocyte G-6-PD Deficiency among Chinese and Malays of Singapore". *Tropical and Geographical Medicine* 23, no. 2 (1971): 141–44. NLB, NUS.

1297. Saha, N. and B. Banerjee "Xga Blood Groups in Chinese, Malays and Indians in Singapore". *Vox sanguinis* 24 (1973): 542–44. NUS.

1298. Saha, N. and Y.W. Ong. "Distribution of Haptoglobins in Different Dialect Groups of Chinese, Malays and Indians in Singapore". *Annals of the Academy of Medicine, Singapore* 13, no. 3 (1984): 498–501. NLB, NTUNIE, NUS.

1299. Soh Keng Chuan, Ee Heok Kua, and Tze Pin Ng. "Somatic and Non-affective Symptoms of Old Age Depression: Ethnic Differences among Chinese, Indians and Malays". *International Journal of Geriatric Psychiatry* 24, no. 7 (2009): 723–30. NTUNIE, NUS.

1300. Tan K.L. "Transcutaneous Bilirubinometry in Chinese and Malay Neonates". *Annals of the Academy of Medicine, Singapore* 14, no. 4 (1985): 591–94. NLB, NTUNIE. NUS.

1301. Tian Ho-Heng et al. "Effects of Fasting during Ramadan Month on Cognitive Function in Muslim Athletes". *Asian Journal of Sports Medicine* 2, no. 3 (2011): 145–53. NTUNIE, NUS.

1302. Ting A. et al. "The Distribution of HL-A Leukocyte Antigens in Singapore, Chinese, Malays and Indians". *Tissue Antigens* 1, no. 6 (1971): 258–64. NTUNIE, NUS.

1303. Wang D.Y. and K. Shanmugaratnam. "The Plasma Levels of Dehydroepiandrosterone Sulphate, and Rosterone Sulphate, Cortisol and Transcortin in Chinese, Indian and Malay Males". *Singapore Medical Journal* 10, no. 1 (1969): 18–23. NLB, NUS.

1304. Wong Mee Lian et al. "Concerns over Participation in Genetic Research among Malay-Muslims, Chinese and Indians in Singapore: A Focus Group Study". *Community Genetics* 7, no. 1 (2004): 44–54. NUS.

1305. Wong P.C.N. "A Comparative Epidemiologic Study of Fractures among Indian, Malay and Swedish Children". *Medical Journal of Malaya: The Official Organ of the Malaya Branch of the British Medical Association* 20, no. 2 (December 1965): 132–35. NLB, NUS.

1306. Wong P.C.N. "eMoral Neck Fractures among the Major Racial Groups in Singapore: Incidence Patterns Compared with Non-Asian Communities. No.11". *Singapore Medical Journal* 5, no. 4 (1964): 150–57. NLB, NUS.

1307. Yohanna Abdullah and Radiah Salim. *Shattered: We Heal,* edited by Noorunnisa d/o PK Ibrahim Kutty. Singapore: Club HEAL, 2014. 108 pp. NLB.

1308. Zee K.O. and P.K. Chew. "Ventilatory Function in Normal Industrial Malay Workers in Singapore". *Singapore Medical Journal* 17, no. 4 (1976): 242–47. NLB, NUS.

Diseases and Illnesses

1309. Ali, A.B. et al. "BRCA1 Disease-Associated Haplotypes in Singapore Malay Women with Early-Onset Breast/Ovarian Cancer". *Breast Cancer Research and Treatment* 104, issue 3 (September 2007): 351–53. NTUNIE, NUS.

1310. Cheah J.S., B.Y. Tan, and A.F. Wong. "The Prevalence and Causes of Glycosuria in 28,765 Young Men in the Population in Singapore". *Singapore Medical Journal* 12, no. 6 (1971): 314–18. NLB, NUS.

1311. Cheah J.S., J.A. Tambyah, and N.R. Mitra. "Prevalence and Causes of Glycosuria among the Ethnic Groups in Singapore". *Singapore Medical Journal* 13, no. 6 (1972): 273–79. NLB, NUS.

1312. Cheah J.S., J.A. Tambyah, and N.R. Mitra. "Prevalence of Diabetes Mellitus among the Ethnic Groups in Singapore". *Tropical & Geographical Medicine* 27 (1975): 14–16. NUS.

1313. Chia K.S., H.P. Lee, and J. Lee. "Incidence of Primary Liver Cancer in Singapore, 1968–1982". *Annals of the Academy of Medicine, Singapore* 18, no. 3 (1989): 313–16. NLB, NTUNIE, NUS.

1314. Chong Y.H., Alan and H.P. Lee. "Pyloric Stenosis in the Ethnic Groups of Singapore". *Singapore Medical Journal* 17, no. 3 (1976): 181–83. NLB, NUS.

1315. Desowitz, R.S., V. Zaman, and W.K. Ng. "The Incidence of Intestinal Parasites in Various Communities of Singapore Island". *Singapore Medical Journal* 2, no. 3 (1961): 91–93. NLB, NUS.

1316. Foong W.P., Athena et al. "Rationale and Methodology for a Population-Based Study of Eye Diseases in Malay People: The Singapore Malay Eye Study (SiMES)". *Ophthalmic Epidemiology* 14, no. 1 (2007): 25–35. NTUNIE, NUS.

1317. Fung Wye Poh et al. "Idiopathic Ulcerative Colitis in Malays". *Annals of the Academy of Medicine, Singapore* 4, no. 2 (1975): 186–89. NLB, NTUNIE, NUS.

1318. Gao, X.L. et al. "Dental Caries Prevalence and Distribution among Preschoolers in Singapore". *Community Dental Health* 26, no. 1 (2009): 12–17. NUS.

1319. Goh, C.R. et al. "Measuring Quality of Life in Different Cultures: Translation of the Functional Living Index for Cancer (FLIC) into Chinese and Malay in Singapore". *Annals of the Academy of Medicine, Singapore* 25, no. 3 (May 1996): 323–34. NLB, NTUNIE, NUS.

1320. Hong Ching Ye et al. "Ethnic Differences among Chinese, Malay and Indian Patients with Type 2 Diabetes Mellitus in Singapore". *Singapore Medical Journal* 45, no. 4 (April 2004): 154–60. NLB, NUS.

1321. Hughes, K. et al. "Cardiovascular Disease in Chinese, Malays and Indians in Singapore. I, Differences in Mortality". *Journal of Epidemiology and Community Health* 44, no. 1 (1990): 24–28. NTUNIE, NUS.

1322. Hughes, Kenneth et al. "Cardiovascular Disease in Chinese, Malays and Indians in Singapore. II, Differences in Risk Factor Levels". *Journal of Epidemiology and Community Health* 44, no. 1 (1990): 29–35. NTUNIE, NUS.

1323. Hughes, Kenneth. *The Epidemiology of Cardiovascular Diseases in the Ethnic Groups of Singapore.* Tokyo: SEAMIC/IMFJ, 1993. 211 pp. NUS.

1324. Hughes, Kenneth et al. "Ischaemic Heart Disease and Its Risk Factors in Singapore in Comparison with the Other Countries". *Annals of the Academy of Medicine, Singapore* 18, no. 3 (1989): 245–49. NLB, NTUNIE, NUS.

1325. Hughes, Kenneth. "Mortality from Cardiovascular Disease in Chinese, Malays and Indians in Singapore in Comparison with England and Wales, USA and Japan". *Annals of the Academy of Medicine, Singapore* 18, no. 6 (1989): 642–45. NLB, NTUNIE, NUS.

1326. Hughes, Kenneth et al. "Risk Factors for Ischaemic Heart Disease in Ethnic Groups of Singapore". In *Proceedings of the International Epidemiological Association Xth Scientific Meeting*. Vancouver: University of British Columbia, 1984.

1327. Kan S.P. and J.S. Cheah. "Prevalence and Intensity of Helminthic Infections in Adults among the Ethnic Groups in Singapore". *Singapore Medical Journal* 11, no. 4 (1970): 283–86. NLB, NUS.

1328. Kang J.Y. "The Influence of Sex, Race and Dialect on Peptic Ulcer and Non-ulcer Dyspepsia in Singapore". *Annals of the Academy of Medicine, Singapore* 12, no. 4 (1983): 527–31. NLB, NTUNIE, NUS.

1329. Kang J.Y. "Mortality from Peptic Ulcer in Singapore, 1938–1980". *Singapore Medical Journal* 24, no. 6 (1983): 333–36. NLB, NUS.

1330. Kang J.Y. et al. "Racial Differences in Peptic Ulcer Frequency in Singapore". *Digestive Diseases and Sciences* 31, suppl. (1986): 825–28. NUS.

1331. Kua E.H. "Dementia in Elderly Malays: Preliminary Findings of a Community Survey". *Singapore Medical Journal* 34, no. 1 (1993): 26–28. NUS.

1332. Lee H.P. and K.C. Lun. "Standardised Mortality Ratios for Some Cancer Sites among the Main Ethnic and Chinese Dialect Groups in Singapore, 1970". *Singapore Medical Journal* 23, no. 2 (1982): 85–89. NLB, NUS.

1333. Lee H.P., J. Lee, and K. Shanmugaratnam. "Trends and Ethnic Variation in Incidence and Mortality from Cancers of the Colon and Rectum in Singapore, 1968 to 1982". *Annals of the Academy of Medicine, Singapore* 16, no. 3 (1987): 397–401. NLB, NTUNIE, NUS.

1334. Lee H.P., N.E. Day, and K. Shanmugaratnam. *Trends in Cancer Incidence in Singapore, 1968–1982*. Lyon: International Agency for Research on Cancer, 1988. 153 pp. NLB, NUS.

1335. Lee R. et al. "Impact of Race on Morbidity and Mortality in Patients with Congestive Heart Failure: A Study of the Multiracial Population in Singapore". *International Journal of Cardiology* 134, no. 3 (2009): 422–25. NUS (online).

1336. Lee Y.S. "Adenomas, Metaplastic Polyps and Other Lesions of the Large Bowel: An Autopsy Survey". *Annals of the Academy of Medicine, Singapore* 16, no. 3 (1987): 412–20. NLB, NTUNIE, NUS.

1337. Lee Y.S. "Subsite Distribution of Large Bowel Cancers among the Ethnic and Dialect Groups in Singapore". *Annals of the Academy of Medicine, Singapore* 15, no. 1 (1986): 57–61. NLB, NTUNIE, NUS.

1338. Lim P. and O.T. Khoo. "New Diabetics in Singapore". *Singapore Medical Journal* 12, no. 6 (1971): 319–22. NLB, NUS.

1339. Muir, C.S. "Coronary Heart Disease in Seven Racial Groups in Singapore". *British Heart Journal* 22, no. 1 (1960): 45–53. NLB, NUS.

1340. Oon C.J. et al. "Epidemiology of Viral Hepatitis B in Singapore". In *Viral Hepatitis and Liver Disease*, edited by G.N. Vyas, J.L. Dienstag, and J.H. Hoofnagle. Orlando, Fla.: Grune & Stratton, 1984. NUS.

1341. "Peranan Masyarakat Melayu/Islam dalam Menangani HIV/AIDs (HIV/AIDs and the Malay/Community)". *The Act* 35 (2007): 30–31. NLB.

1342. Radiah Salim. "Zulm and Chronic Illnesses". *Karyawan: Professionals for the Community* 10, issue 1 (July 2009): 20–22. ISEAS, NLB, NTUNIE, NUS.

1343. Rosman, M. (Mohamad) et al. "Review of Key Findings from the Singapore Malay Eye Study (SiMES-1)". *Singapore Medical Journal* 53, no. 2 (2012): 82–87. NUS.

1344. Rosman, M. (Mohamad) et al. "Singapore Malay Eye Study: Rationale and Methodology of 6-year Follow-up Study (SiMES-2)". *Clinical & Experimental Ophthalmology* 40, no. 6 (2012): 557–68. NTUNIE, NUS.

1345. Saha, N. "Biochemical Characteristics of Glucose-6-Phosphate Dehydrogenase Variants among the Malays of Singapore with Report of a New Non-deficient (Gd Singapore) and Three Deficient Variants". *Jinrui idengaku Zasshi* 36, no. 4 (December 1991): 307–12. NUS.

1346. Shankar A. et al. "Association Between Body Mass Index and Chronic Kidney Disease in Men and Women: Population-based Study of Malay

Adults in Singapore". *Nephrology Dialysis Transplantation* 23, no. 6 (2008): 1910–18. NUS.

1347.   Shanmugaratnam K. "Cancer in Singapore: Ethnic and Dialect Group Variations in Cancer Incidence". *Singapore Medical Journal* 14, no. 2 (1973): 69–81. NLB, NUS.

1348.   Shanmugaratnam K., H.P. Lee, and N.E. Day. *Cancer Incidence in Singapore 1968–1977*. Lyon: International Agency for Research in Cancer, 1983. 171 pp. NUS.

1349.   Shen S.Y. et al. "The Prevalence and Types of Glaucoma in Malay People: The Singapore Malay Eye Study". *Investigative Ophthalmology & Visual Science* 49, no. 9 (2008): 3846–51. NTUNIE, NUS.

1350.   Sng Jen Hwei. "BRCA1 c.2845insA is Founder Mutation in Singaporean Malay Women with Early Onset Breast/Ovarian Cancer". *Annals of the Academy of Medicine, Singapore* 32, no. 5, suppl. (September 2003): 53–55. NLB, NTUNIE, NUS.

1351.   Tan L.C.S. et al. "Incidence of Parkinson's Disease in Singapore". *Parkinsonism & Related Disorders* 13, no. 1 (2007): 40–43. NUS.

1352.   *Trends in Chronic Kidney Failure in Singapore 2010–2011*. Singapore Renal Registry report no. 9. Singapore: Health Promotion Board, 2014. 145 pp. NLB, NUS.

1353.   *Trends in Stroke in Singapore, 2005–2012*. Singapore Stroke Registry Report no. 3. Singapore: Health Promotion Board, 2014. 46 pp. NLB, NUS.

1354.   Verkooijen, Helena M. et al. "Multiparity and the Risk of Premenopausal Breast Cancer: Different Effects Across Ethnic Groups in Singapore". *Breast Cancer Research and Treatment* 113, no. 3 (2009): 553–58. NTUNIE, NUS.

1355.   Wang H. Seow and Lee Hin Peng. "Trends in Cancer Incidence among Singapore Malays: A Low-risk Population". *Annals of the Academy of Medicine, Singapore* 33, no. 1 (January 2004): 57–62. NLB, NTUNIE, NUS.

1356.   Wong Tien Yin et al. "Prevalence and Causes of Low Vision and Blindness in an Urban Malay Population: The Singapore Malay Eye Study". *Archives of Ophthalmology* 126, no. 8 (2008): 1091–99. NUS.

HISTORY

- *General Works*
- *Early History and Malay Kingdoms (before 1819)*
- *Colonialism and Pre-Independence Period (1819–1965)*
- *Post Independence Period (after 1965)*

General Works

1357. Alatas, Syed Hussein, Khoo Kay Kim, and Kwa Chong Guan. *Malays/ Muslims and the History of Singapore*. Occasional Paper Series, nos. 1–98. Singapore: Centre for Research on Islamic & Malay Affairs, 1998. 61 pp. ISEAS, NTUNIE, NUS, NLB.

1358. Barnard, Timothy P. and Syed Muhd Khairudin Aljunied. "Temasek, Singapura & Singapore: From Ancient to Colonial Port". In *Malay Heritage of Singapore*, edited by Aileen T. Lau and Bernhard Platzdasch. Singapore: Suntree Media in association with Malay Heritage Foundation, 2010. ISEAS, NLB, NTUNIE, NUS.

1359. Gan, Mary. "Walk on By". *City Streets* 2 (August 1990): 36–40. ISEAS, NLB, NUS.

1360. Kamaludeen Mohamed Nasir and Syed Muhd Khairudin Aljunied. *Muslims as Minorities: History and Social Realities of Muslims in Singapore*. Bangi: Universiti Kebangsaan Malaysia, 2009. 129 pp. ISEAS, NLB, NTU, NUS.

1361. Kamsiah Abdullah et al. *Malay Heritage of Singapore*. Edited by Aileen T. Lau and Bernhard Platzdasch. Singapore: Suntree Media in association with Malay Heritage Foundation, 2010. 236 pp. ISEAS, NLB, NTUNIE, NUS.

1362. Lee, Edwin. "Singapore: Lessons from History in National Development". In *Malaysia and Singapore: Problem and Prospects*, edited by Azizah Kassim and Lau Teik Soon. Singapore: Singapore Institute of International Affairs, 1991. ISEAS, NLB, NTUNIE, NUS.

1363. Lyons, Lenore and Michele Ford. "Singapore First: Challenging the Concept of Transnational Malay Masculinity". In *Reframing Singapore: Memory, Identity, Trans-Regionalism*, edited by Derek Heng and Syed Muhd. Khairudin Aljunied. Amsterdam: Amsterdam University Press, 2009. 318 pp. ISEAS, NLB, NUS.

1364. Miksic, John N. "Beyond the Grave: Excavations North of the Keramat Iskandar Shah 1988". *Heritage* 10 (1988): 34–56. NLB, NUS.

Early History and Malay Kingdoms (before 1819)

1365. Agus Salim. *Kesah Raja2 Melayu Singapura*. Kuala Lumpur: Dewan Bahasa dan Pustaka, 1969. 100 pp. NLB, NUS.

1366. Ali Aziz. *Kerajaan Melayu Singapura Lama*. Kuala Lumpur: Pustaka Antara, 1965. 104 pp. ISEAS, NLB, NTUNIE, NUS.

1367. Andaya, Leonard Y. "The Kingdom of Johor, 1641–1728: A Study of Economic and Political Developments in the Straits of Malacca". PhD dissertation, Cornell University, Ithaca, 1971. 452 pp. ISEAS, NLB, NUS.

1368. Azhar Ibrahim Alwee. "Singapura dalam Sastera Sejarah Melayu". Research exercise, Department of Malay Studies, National University of Singapore, 1996. 38 pp. NUS.

1369. Badriyah Haji Salleh. "Syair as a Historical Source: The Syair Tantangan Singapura, a 19th Century Text". In *New Perspective and Research on Malaysian History: Essays on Malaysian Historiography*. Kuala Lumpur: The MBRAS, 2007. NLB.

1370. Badriyah Haji Salleh. *Warkah Al-Ikhlas 1818–1821*. Kuala Lumpur: Dewan Bahasa dan Pustaka, 1999. 270 pp. ISEAS, NLB, NUS.

1371. Calless, Brian E. "The Ancient History of Singapore". *Journal of Southeast Asian History* 10 (1969): 1–11. ISEAS, NLB, NUS.

1372. Hussin Mutalib. "Colonialism and the Fall of Malay Sultanates and States in Southeast Asia". Paper presented at the International Conference on Malay Sultanates in Nusantara. Organized by Universiti Brunei Darussalam, Brunei, 1994. 33 pp.

1373. Linehan, W. "The Kings of 14th Century Singapore". *JMBRAS* 20, pt. 2 (1947): 117–26. ISEAS, NLB, NTUNIE, NUS.

1374. Low, Cheryl-Ann. "A Brief History of the Malay Kingdom of Singapore". *History Journal* (1993/94): 6–13. NLB.

1375. Muhammad Haji Salleh. *Syair Tantangan Singapura Abad Kesembilan Belas*. Kuala Lumpur: Dewan Bahasa dan Pustaka, 1994. 127 pp. NLB.

1376. Suzana Tun Hj Othman. *Institusi Bendahara: Permata Melayu yang Hilang*. Kuala Lumpur: Pustaka BSM Enterprise, 2002. 195 pp. NLB.

1377. Wheatley, Paul. "John Crawfurd's Description of the Ruins of Ancient Singapore". In *The Golden Khersonese: Studies in the Historical Geography of the Malay Peninsula before A.D. 1500*. Kuala Lumpur: University of Malaya Press, 1980. ISEAS, NLB, NTUNIE, NUS.

1378. Winstedt, R.O. "Abdul-Jalil, Sultan of Johore (1699–1719), Abdul-Jamal, Temenggong (Ca. 1750) and Raffles Founding of Singapore". *JMBRAS* 11, pt. 2 (1933): 161–65. ISEAS, NLB, NTUNIE, NUS.

1379. Winstedt, R.O. "Tumasik or Old Singapore". *JMBRAS* 12, pt. 1 (1934): 31–36. ISEAS, NLB, NTUNIE, NUS.

Colonialism and Pre-Independence Period (1819–1965)

1380. Abdullah, Munshi. "The Early History of Singapore". *Inter-Ocean: A Dutch East Indian Magazine Covering Malaysia and Australasia* 8, no. 12 (December 1927) 717–18. NLB.

1381. Abdullah, Munshi. "First British Occupation of the Island of Singapore: Excerpt from the Hikayat Abdullah". *Asiatic Review* 34 (1938): 137–39. NLB.

1382. Abdullah, Munshi. *The Hikayat Abdullah*. An annotated translation by A.H. Hill. Kuala Lumpur: Oxford University Press, 1970. 353 pp. ISEAS, NLB, NUS.

1383. Abdullah, Munshi. *Karya Lengkap Abdullah bin Abdul Kadir Munsyi*. Edited by Amin Sweeney. Jakarta: Kepustakaan Populer Gramedia; Paris: École française d'Extrême-Orient, 2005–8. 3 vols. NLB, NTUNIE, NUS.

1384. Abdullah Ali. "Raffles and Singapore". Academic exercise, Raffles College, Singapore, 1949. 94 pp. NUS.

1385. Abdullah Ayub. "The Johor Succession Controversy, 1850–1878". Academic exercise, Department of History, University of Malaya, Singapore, 1953. 50 pp. NUS.

1386. Abdullah Zakaria Ghazali. "Persaingan di Antara Keluarga Sultan dengan Keluarga Temenggung di Johor 1835–1885". PhD dissertation, Universiti Malaya, 1984. 387 pp. NUS.

1387. Alatas, Syed Hussein. *Thomas Stamford Raffles, 1781–1825, Schemer or Reformer?* London: Angus and Robertson, 1971. 65 pp. ISEAS, NLB, NTUNIE, NUS.

1388. Aljunied, Syed Muhd Khairudin. *Colonialism, Violence and Muslims in Southeast Asia: The Maria Hertogh Controversy and Its Aftermath.* New York, NY: Routledge, 2009. 185 pp. ISEAS, NLB, NTU, NTUNIE, NUS.

1389. Aljunied, Syed Muhd Khairudin. "Rethinking Riots in Colonial South East Asia: The Case of the Maria Hertogh Controversy in Singapore, 1950–54". *South East Asia Research* 18, no. 1 (March 2010): 105–31. ISEAS, NTUNIE.

1390. Barnard, Timothy P. and Jan van der Putten. "'Art for Society': Language, Literature and Film in the Singaporean Malay Community". Paper presented at Symposium on Paths Not Taken: Political Pluralism in Postwar Singapore, jointly sponsored by the Centre for Social Change Research at the Queensland University of Technology and the Asia Research Institute at the National University of Singapore held in Singapore on 14–15 July 2005. ISEAS, NUS.

1391. Barnard, Timothy P. and Syed Muhd Khairudin Aljunied. "A Century of Hope, Experiment & Change". In *Malay Heritage of Singapore*, edited by Aileen T. Lau and Bernhard Platzdasch. Singapore: Suntree Media in association with Malay Heritage Foundation, 2010. ISEAS, NLB, NTUNIE, NUS.

1392. Buckley, Charles Burton. *An Anecdotal History of Old Times in Singapore … from the Foundation of the Settlement under the Honourable the East India Company on February 6th 1918, to the Transfer to the Colonial Office as Part of the Colonial Possessions of the Crown on April 1st 1867.* New ed. Singapore: Oxford University Press, 1984. 790 pp. ISEAS, NLB, NTUNIE, NUS.

1393. Buyong Adil. *Sejarah Singapura: Rujukan Khas Mengenai Peristiwa-Peristiwa Sebelum Tahun 1824.* Kuala Lumpur: Dewan Bahasa dan Pustaka, 1972. 134 pp. ISEAS, NLB, NUS.

1394. Carroll, Diana. "The Hikayat Abdullah: Discourse of Dissent". *JMBRAS* 72, pt. 2 (1999): 92–129. ISEAS, NLB, NTUNIE, NUS.

1395.   Clutterbuck, Richard L. *Conflict and Violence in Singapore and Malaysia 1945–1983*. Singapore: Graham Brash, 1985. 412 pp. ISEAS, NLB, NTU, NTUNIE, NUS.

1396.   Clutlerbuck, Richard L. *Riot and Revolution in Singapore and Malaya, 1945–1963*. London: Faber and Faber, 1973. 321 pp. ISEAS, NLB, NTUNIE, NUS.

1397.   Cody, Mary Kilcline. "Mis-Fits in the Text: The Singapore Riots of 1950". BA (Hons) dissertation, Australian National University, 2001. 121 pp. ISEAS.

1398.   Falconer, John. *A Vision of the Past: A History of Early Photography in Singapore and Malaya: The Photographs of G.R. Lambert and Co., 1880–1910*. Singapore: Times Editions, 1987. 192 pp. ISEAS, NLB, NTUNIE, NUS.

1399.   Farish A. Noor (Farish Ahmad Noor). *From Empire to the War on Terror: The 1915 Indian Sepoy Mutiny in Singapore as a Case Study of the Impact of Profiling of Religious and Ethnic Minorities*. RSIS Working Paper, no. 206. Singapore: S. Rajaratnam School of International Studies, Nanyang Technological University, 2010. 26 pp. ISEAS, NLB, NTU, NTUNIE, NUS.

1400.   Farish A. Noor (Farish Ahmad Noor). "From Loyal Subject to Mistrust Other: The 1915 Singapore Sepoy Mutiny and Its Impact on Indian Muslims in British Malaya and Singapore". In *Diaspora: The Story of the South Asian Muslim Diaspora in Southeast Asia Today*. Kuala Lumpur: Malaysian Social Research Institute, 2013. ISEAS, NLB, NTU.

1401.   Fatini Yaacob. *Natrah (1937–2009) @ Nadra @Huberdina Maria Hertogh @ Bertha: Cinta, Rusuhan, Air Mata*. Skudai, Johor: Universiti Teknologi Malaysia, 2010. 474 pp. NLB, NUS. Also published in English under the title: *Natrah: In the Name of Love*. Translated by Maryam Abdullah, Zurhaida Mohd. Ismail, and Flora Emilia Abdullah. Skudai, Johor: Universiti Teknologi Malaysia, Institut Terjemahan Negara Malaysia, 2011. 397 pp. NLB, NTU.

1402.   Foo Kim Leng. "1964 Singapore Riots". Academic exercise, Department of History, National University of Singapore, 1981. 117 pp. NUS.

1403. Hadijah Rahmat. *Antara Dua Kota: Menjejaki Kesan-kesan Peninggalan Sejarah Munsyi Abdullah di Melaka dan Singapura.* Singapore: Regional Training and Pub. Centre, 1999. 291 pp. ISEAS, NLB, NTUNIE, NUS.

1404. Harper, R.W.E. and Harry Miller. *Singapore Mutiny.* Singapore: Oxford University Press, 1984. 254 pp. ISEAS, NLB, NTUNIE, NUS.

1405. Haughton, H.T. "Landing of Raffles in Singapore by an Eye-Witness". *JSBRAS* 10 (1882): 285–86. ISEAS, NLB, NUS.

1406. Hughes, Tom Eames. *Tangled Worlds: The Story of Maria Hertogh.* Singapore: Institute of Southeast Asian Studies, 1980. 64 pp. ISEAS, NLB, NTUNIE, NUS.

1407. Ibnu Ahmad al-Kurauwi. *Namaku Bukan Maria.* Batu Caves, Selangor: PTS Litera Utama, 2011. 410 pp. NUS.

1408. Jesudason, Rosemary Shanta. "The Causes and Significance of the Hertogh Riots". Academic exercise, Department of History, University of Singapore, 1969. 63 pp. NUS.

1409. Khoo K.K. (Kay Kim). "Malay Society, 1874–1920s". *Journal of Southeast Asian Studies* 5, no. 2 (1974): 179–98. ISEAS, NLB, NTUNIE, NUS.

1410. Khoo Kay Kim, Elinah Abdullah, and Wan Meng Hao, eds. *Malays/ Muslims in Singapore: Selected Readings in History, 1819–1965.* Subang Jaya, Selangor: Pelanduk Publications in cooperation with Centre for Research on Islamic and Malay Affairs, Singapore, 2006. 395 pp. ISEAS, NLB, NTUNIE, NUS.

1411. Kuwajima, Sho. *First World War and Asia: Indian Mutiny in Singapore (1915).* Osaka: S. Kuwajima, 1988. 154 pp. ISEAS.

1412. Kwa Chong Guan. "Why Did Tengku Hussein Sign the 1819 Treaty with Stamford Raffles". In *Malays/Muslims in Singapore: Selected Readings in History 1819–1965*, edited by Khoo Kay Kim, Elinah Abdullah, and Wan Meng Hao. Subang Jaya, Selangor: Pelanduk Publications in cooperation with Centre for Research on Islamic and Malay Affairs, Singapore, 2006. ISEAS, NLB, NTUNIE, NUS.

1413. Kwok, Edmund. "The Impact of British Rule on the Position of Traditional Malay Rulers in Singapore". *Journal of the History Society* (1989/90): 5–7. NLB, NUS.

1414. Lee Ah Chai. "Singapore under the Japanese, 1942–45". Academic exercise, Department of History, University of Malaya, Singapore, 1956. 63 pp. NUS.

1415. Lee Kuan Yew. *The Battle for Merger*. Singapore: National Archives of Singapore; Straits Times Press, 2014. 207 pp. ISEAS, NLB.

1416. Lim Choon Hoon. "The Battle of Pasir Panjang Revisited". *Pointer: Journal of the Singapore Armed Forces* 28, no. 1 (January/March 2002): 6–20. ISEAS, NLB, NTU, NUS.

1417. Loh Kah Seng. "Kampong, Fire, Nation: Towards a Social History of Postwar Singapore". *Journal of Southeast Asian Studies* 40, no. 3 (October 2009): 613–43. ISEAS, NLB, NTUNIE, NUS.

1418. Maideen, Haja. *The Nadra Tragedy: The Maria Hertogh Controversy*. Subang Jaya: Pelanduk Publications, 2000. 386 pp. ISEAS, NLB, NTUNIE, NUS. Also published in Malay under the title: *Tragedi Nadra: Kontroversi Maria Hertogh*. Petaling Jaya: IBS Buku, 1989. 329 pp. NUS.

1419. Makepeace, Walter, Gilbert E. Brooke, and Roland St. J. Braddel, eds. *One Hundred Years of Singapore, Being Some Account of the Capital of the Straits Settlement from Its Foundation by Sir Stamford Raffles on the 6th February 1819 to the 6th February 1919*. London: J. Murray, 1921. 12 vols. ISEAS, NTUNIE, NUS.

1420. "Malay Amoks and Piracies: What Can We Do to Abolish Them?" *The Journal of the Indian Archipelago and Eastern Asia* 3, no. 33 (1849): 463–67. ISEAS, NLB, NUS.

1421. Merican, Muhammad Ansari. "The Maria Hertogh Riots, 1950 = Rusuhan Nadra, 1950". Academic exercise, Department of History, University of Singapore, 1974. 95 pp. NUS.

1422. Moore, Donald and Joanna Moore. *The First 150 Years of Singapore*. Singapore: Donald Moore Press Ltd., 1969. 731 pp. ISEAS, NLB, NTUNIE, NUS.

1423. Mosbergen, Rudolf William. "The Sepoy Rebellion: A History of the Singapore Mutiny, 1915". Academic exercise, Department of History, University of Malaya, Singapore, 1954. 71 pp. NUS.

1424.   Netto, Leslie. *Maria: Based on a True Story*. Singapore: Derby Publishers, 1996. 105 pp. ISEAS, NLB, NTUNIE.

1425.   Nordin Hussin. "Malay Press and Malay Politics: The Hertogh Riots in Singapore". *Asia Europe Journal* 3, no. 4 (2005): 561–75. ISEAS, NLB, NTU, NUS.

1426.   Nordin Hussin. *The Moslem Riots of 11 December 1950 in Singapore*. Bangi: Universiti Kebangsaan Malaysia, 1988. 131 pp. ISEAS.

1427.   Nur Azha Putra and Yang Razali Kassim. "Modernisation and Social Change: Rethinking History of the Malay/Muslim Community (1819–1930s)". *Karyawan: Professionals for the Community* 7, no. 1 (November 2006): 20–23. ISEAS, NLB, NTUNIE, NUS.

1428.   Ong Ai Choo. "The Sepoy Mutiny in Singapore, 1915". Academic exercise, Department of History, University of Singapore, 1974. 39 pp. NUS.

1429.   Onraet, R. "The Singapore Riots of December 1950". *British Malaya* (September 1951): 328–30. NLB, NUS.

1430.   Raffles, Thomas Stamford, Sir. "The Founding of Singapore". *JSBRAS* 2 (1878/79): 175–82. ISEAS, NLB, NUS.

1431.   Read, W.H. "The Landing of Raffles at Singapore". *JSBRAS* 12 (1883): 282–83. ISEAS, NLB, NUS.

1432.   "Riots in Singapore and the Reunion of the Hertogh Family". *Illustrated London News* 217 (23 December 1950): 1027. NLB, NUS.

1433.   Sheppard, Mubin, ed. *150th Anniversary of the Founding of Singapore*. Singapore: Malaysian Branch of the Royal Asiatic Society, 1973. 317 pp. ISEAS, NLB, NTUNIE, NUS.

1434.   "Singapore Riots which Arose Out of the Case of Maria Hertogh". *Illustrated London News* 217 (16 December 1950): 989. NLB, NUS.

1435.   Singapore. Singapore Riots Inquiry Commission. *Report of the Singapore Riots Inquiry Commission, 1951*. Singapore: Government Printing Office, 1951. 98 pp. ISEAS, NLB, NTUNIE, NUS.

1436.   Stockwell, A.J. "Imperial Security and Moslem Militancy, with Special Reference to the Hertogh Riots in Singapore (Dec 1950)". *Journal of Southeast Asian Studies* 17, no. 2 (1986): 322–35. ISEAS, NLB, NTUNIE, NUS.

1437. Manogaran Suppiah. "Telok Blangah: Cradle of Modern Johor, 1800–1895". Academic exercise. Department of History, National University of Singapore, 1988. 109 pp. NUS.

1438. Manogaran Suppiah. "The Temenggongs of Telok Blangah: The Progenitor of Modern Johor". In *Malays/Muslims in Singapore: Selected Readings in History 1819-1965*, edited by Khoo Kay Kim, Elinah Abdullah, and Wan Meng Hao. Subang Jaya, Selangor: Pelanduk Publications in cooperation with Centre for Research on Islamic and Malay Affairs, Singapore, 2006. ISEAS, NLB, NTUNIE, NUS.

1439. Swettenham, F.A. "Malay Problem, 1926". *British Malaya* 1, no. 1 (May 1926): 7–14. NLB, NUS.

1440. Tan Li-Jen and Shabbir Hussain Mustafa, eds. *Camping and Tramping: Through the Colonial Archive: The Museum in Malaya*. Singapore: NUS Museum, 2011. 133 pp. NUS.

1441. Tarling, Nicholas. "The Singapore Mutiny, 1915". *JMBRAS* 55, pt. 2 (1982): 26–59. ISEAS, NLB, NTUNIE, NUS.

1442. Tate, D.J.M., comp. *Straits Affairs: The Malay World and Singapore: Being Glimpses of the Straits Settlements and the Malay Peninsula in the Nineteenth Century as Seen Through the Illustrated London News and Other Contemporary Sources*. Hong Kong: John Nicholson Ltd., 1989. 130 pp. ISEAS, NLB, NTUNIE, NUS.

1443. Teo Eng Liang. *Malay Encounter During Benjamin Peach Keasberry's Time in Singapore, 1835 to 1875*. Singapore: Trinity Theological College, 2009. 330 pp. ISEAS, NLB, NUS.

1444. Tiwary, Ram Awadh. "Raffles at Singapore". Academic exercise, Department of History, University of Malaya, Singapore, 1959. 104 pp. NUS.

1445. Tregonning, K.G. "Singapore: 1819-1926". In *The British in Malaya: The First Forty Years, 1786-1826*. Tucson: University of Arizona Press, 1965. ISEAS, NLB, NUS.

1446. Trocki, C.A. (Carl A.). *Prince of Pirates: The Temenggongs and the Development of Johor and Singapore, 1784-1885*. Singapore: Singapore University Press, 2007. 246 pp. ISEAS, NLB, NTUNIE, NUS.

1447. Trocki, C.A. (Carl A.) "The Temenggongs of Johor, 1784-1885". PhD dissertation, Cornell University, 1975. 387 pp. NUS. Published under the same title: Ann Arbor, Mich.: University Microfilms, 1975. 387 pp. ISEAS, NUS.

1448.   Turnbull, C.M. *A History of Singapore, 1819–1988.* Singapore: Oxford University Press, 1989. 388 pp. ISEAS, NLB, NTUNIE, NUS.

1449.   Wake, C.H. "Raffles and the Rajas: The Founding of Singapore in Malayan and British Colonial History". *JMBRAS* 48, no. 1 (1975): 47–73. ISEAS, NLB, NTUNIE, NUS.

1450.   Winstedt, R.O. "The Founder of Singapore". *JSBRAS* 82 (1920): 127. ISEAS, NLB, NUS.

1451.   Wright, A. (Arnold) and H.A. Cartwright, eds. *Twentieth Century Impressions of British Malaya: Its History, People, Commerce, Industries, and Resources.* London: Lloyd's Greater Britain Pub., 1908. ISEAS, NLB, NTUNIE, NUS.

1452.   Wu Jialin, Christina. "Under the Skin: Colonial-Local Anxieties of the Domestic Realm in the Maria Hertogh Controversy". Academic exercise, Department of History, National University of Singapore, 2009. 62 pp. ISEAS.

1453.   Yong Mun Cheong. *The Indonesian Revolution and the Singapore Connection: 1945–1949.* Singapore: Singapore University Press, 2003. 210 pp. NLB, NUS. Also published under the same title: Leiden: KITLV Press, 2003. 210 pp. ISEAS, NLB, NUS.

1454.   Zakaria Mohammad Ali. "The Reign of Abu Bakar of Johor, 1862–1895". Academic exercise, Department of History, University of Malaya, Singapore, 1954. 52 pp. NUS.

Post-Independence Period (after 1965)

1455.   Ashfaq Hussein. "The Post Separation Effect on the Malays and Their Response". *Journal of the Historical Society* (July 1970): 67–72. ISEAS, NLB, NTU, NUS.

1456.   Green, Anthony. *Continuing the Legacy: 30 Years of the Mosque Building Fund in Singapore.* Singapore: Majlis Ugama Islam Singapura, 2007. 136 pp. NLB, NUS.

1457. Hussain Haikal and Atiku Garba Yahaya. "Muslims in Singapore: The Colonial Legacy and the Making of Minority". *Journal of Muslim Minority Affairs* 17, no. 1 (April 1997): 83–88. ISEAS, NTUNIE, NUS.

1458. Hussin Mutalib "Masyarakat Melayu Singapura Sejak Dua Dekad Lalu". *Jurnal Pengajian Melayu* 7 (1997): 104–16. NLB, NUS.

1459. Muhamad Azman Atan. "Sejarah dan Pembangunan Dewan Perniagaan Melayu Singapura". Academic exercise, Department of Malay Studies, National University of Singapore, 1994. 57 pp. NUS.

1460. Noraslinda Muhamad Zuber. "Singapore Malay Identity: A Study of Dominant Perceptions of Islam in Post-Independence Singapore". PhD dissertation, Department of Malay Studies, National University of Singapore, 2010. NUS.

1461. Zainul Abidin Rasheed. "Muslims in Multi-Racial Singapore: New Dynamics in Nation Building". *Jendela Kata: Pesan & Ucapan* (1993–97): 11–22. Singapore: Majlis Ugama Islam Singapura, 1998. ISEAS, NLB, NTUNIE, NUS.

JOURNALISM, MASS MEDIA AND PUBLISHING

- *Journalism*
- *Mass Media*
- *Publishing*

Journalism

1462. Azrina Md. Zain. "Saya Tidak Berdendam". *Dewan Masyarakat* 43, no. 11 (November 2005): 24–25. NLB, NTUNIE, NUS.

1463. Ghazali Ismail. *Tempat Jatoh Lagi di-Kenang.* Singapore: Penerbitan Riwayat, 1968. 105 pp. ISEAS, NLB, NUS.

1464. Ghazali Ismail. *Warta dan Wartawan.* Singapore: Malaya Publishing House, 1969. 73 pp. ISEAS, NLB, NUS.

1465. Ghazali Ismail. *Wartawan dalam Sa-ribu Suasana.* Kuala Lumpur: Utusan Melayu, 1967. 233 pp. ISEAS, NLB, NTUNIE, NUS.

1466. Ishak Haji Muhammad. *Pengalaman Pak Sako Tiga Tahun di Singapura.* Petaling Jaya: Pustaka Budaya Agency, 1975. 61 pp. ISEAS, NLB, NUS.

1467. Jeniri Amir. "Perjuangan Getir Wartawan Melayu". *Dewan Masyarakat* 43, no. 11 (November 2005): 11–14. ISEAS, NLB, NTUNIE, NUS.

1468. Persatuan Wartawan Melayu Singapura. *Temasha Wartawan, 14th May '72.* Singapore: Persatuan Wartawan Melayu Singapura, 1972. 1 vol. (unpaged). NUS.

1469. Roff, William R. "The Ins and Outs of Hadhrami Journalism in Malaya, 1900–1941: Assimilation or Identity Maintenance?" In *The Hadhrami Diaspora in Southeast Asia: Identity Maintenance or Assimilation?*, edited by Ibrahim Abushouk Ahmed and Hassan Ahmed Ibrahim. Leiden; Boston: Brill, 2009. ISEAS, NLB, NTUNIE, NUS.

1470. Za'aba. "Malay Journalism in Malaya". *JMBRAS* 19, pt. 2 (October 1941): 244–50. ISEAS, NLB, NTUNIE, NUS. Also published in Malay under the title: "Kewartawanan Melayu di Malaya". *Dewan Budaya* 6, no. 8 (August 1984): 42–45. NLB, NTUNIE, NUS.

Mass Media

1471. A.M. Iskandar Ahmad. *Persuratkhabaran Melayu. 1876–1968.* Kuala Lumpur: Dewan Bahasa dan Pustaka, 1980. 221 pp. NLB, NUS. Previous ed. published: Kuala Lumpur: Dewan Bahasa dan Pustaka, 1973. 190 pp. ISEAS, NLB, NUS.

1472.   Abdul Jalil Haji Anuar. "Majalah Melayu di Singapura". *Pelita Bahasa: ke Arah Kesempurnaan Bahasa* 3, no. 8 (Ogos 1991): 38–39. NLB, NUS.

1473.   Abu Bakar Hamzah. "Al-Imam: Its Role in Malay Society, 1906–1908". MPhiI dissertation, University of Kent, 1981. 320 pp. NUS. Also published under the same title: Kuala Lumpur: Pustaka Antara, 1991. 253 pp. ISEAS, NLB, NUS.

1474.   Ahmat Adam. *Sejarah dan Bibliografi Akhbar dan Majalah Melayu Abad Kesembilan Belas.* Bangi, Selangor: Penerbit Universiti Kebangsaan Malaysia, 1992. 168 pp. ISEAS, NLB, NTUNIE, NUS.

1475.   Alfian Sa'at. "Theorising Aksi Mat Yoyo: On the Children's TV Show Aksi Mat Yoyo and 'That Things with Malays and Cats'". *Focas: Forum on Contemporary Art & Society* 6 (2007): 202–9. ISEAS, NLB, NTUNIE, NUS.

1476.   Ang Mui Sing. "Language and Television Broadcasting in Singapore: Policy and Practice". Academic exercise, Department of English Language & Literature, National University of Singapore, 1985. 59 pp. NUS.

1477.   Anuar Othman. "Ketandusan Majalah Kanak-Kanak Berbahasa Melayu di Singapura". *Singapore Book World* 17, no. 2 (1987): 35–36. ISEAS, NLB, NTUNIE, NUS.

1478.   *Di Sebalik Jendela Utusan: Suara Keramat.* Kuala Lumpur: Utusan Melayu (Malaysia), 1989. 180 pp. ISEAS, NLB, NUS.

1479.   Emmanuel, Mark. "Viewspapers: The Malay Press of the 1930s". *Journal of Southeast Asian Studies* 41, issue 1 (February 2010): 1–20. ISEAS, NLB, NTU, NTUNIE, NUS.

1480.   Faridah Hassan. "Sikap Mahasiswa-Mahasiswa Melayu Universiti Nasional Singapura terhadap Rancangan-rancangan Radio Melayu Perbadanan Penyiaran Singapura (SBC) = The Attitudes of Malay NUS Undergraduates towards Malay Radio Programmes of SBC". Research exercise, Department of Malay Studies, National University of Singapore, 1993. 54 pp. NUS.

1481.   "Jawi Peranakan". In *Ensiklopedia Sejarah dan Kebudayaan Melayu*, vol. 2, pp. 1032–33. Kuala Lumpur: Dewan Bahasa dan Pustaka, 1995. NLB, NTUNIE, NUS.

1482. Kartini Saparudin. "A Self More Refined: Representations of Women in Malay Magazines of the 1950s". Academic exercise, Department of History, National University of Singapore, 2002. 77 pp. NUS.

1483. Kartini Saparudin. "A History More Refined Malay Women's and Men's Magazines of the 1950s in Singapore and Malaya". *BiblioAsia* 4, no. 4 (January 2009): 25–30. NLB, NTUNIE, NUS.

1484. "Kencana". In *Ensiklopedia Sejarah dan Kebudayaan Melayu*, vol. 2, p. 1148. Kuala Lumpur: Dewan Bahasa dan Pustaka, 1995. NLB, NTUNIE, NUS.

1485. Kwek, Ivan. "Malayness as Mindset: When Television Producers Imagine Audiences as Malay". In *Melayu: The Politics, Poetics and Paradoxes of Malayness*, edited by Maznah Mohamad and Syed Muhd. Khairudin Aljunied. Singapore: NUS Press, 2011. 370 pp. ISEAS, NTU, NTUNIE, NUS.

1486. "Lembaga Malaya". In *Ensiklopedia Sejarah dan Kebudayaan Melayu*, vol. 2, pp. 1348–49. Kuala Lumpur: Dewan Bahasa dan Pustaka, 1995. NLB, NTUNIE, NUS.

1487. Muhammad Shahril Shaik Abdullah. "The Impact of New Media on Social Activism". *MENDAKI Policy Digest* (2008): 67–77. ISEAS, NTUNIE, NUS.

1488. Nik Ahmad Hassan. "The Early Phase of the Malay Vernacular Press, 1876–1906". *JMBRAS* 36, pt. 1 (1963): 37–78. ISEAS, NLB, NTUNIE, NUS.

1489. Nik Ahmad Hassan. "The Malay Vernacular Press". Academic exercise, Department of History, University of Malaya, Singapore, 1988. 50 pp. NUS.

1490. "Qalam". In *Ensiklopedia Sejarah dan Kebudayaan Melayu*, vol. 4, p. 2063. Kuala Lumpur: Dewan Bahasa dan Pustaka, 1999. NLB, NTUNIE, NUS.

1491. Ruhaizah Osman. "Tinjauan mengenai Pandangan Mahasiswa/Siswi Melayu Universiti Nasional Singapura (NUS) terhadap Rancangan-Rancangan Melayu yang Disiarkan Menerusi Televisyen oleh Perbadanan Penyiaran Singapura (SBC)". Research exercise, Department of Malay Studies, National University of Singapore, 1994. 60 pp. NUS.

1492. Rusdin Yaakub and Abdul Malik Haji Abdullah, comps. *Cenderamata Genap 25 Tahun Utusan Melayu Akhbar Kebangsaan Melayu yang Dipunyai dan Diusahakan oleh Bangsa Melayu, 29 Mei 1939-29 Mei 1964*. Kuala Lumpur: Utusan Melayu Press, 1964. 272 pp. ISEAS, NLB.

1493. "Sekata". In *Ensiklopedia Sejarah dan Kebudayaan Melayu*, vol. 4, p. 2159. Kuala Lumpur: Dewan Bahasa dan Pustaka, 1999. NLB, NTUNIE, NUS.

1494. "Sekola Melayu". In *Ensiklopedia Sejarah dan Kebudayaan Melayu*, vol. 4, p. 2162. Kuala Lumpur: Dewan Bahasa dan Pustaka, 1999. NLB, NTUNIE, NUS.

1495. Sundusia Rosdi. "Lembaran Akhbar Silam: Jawi Peranakkan, 1876–1895". *BiblioAsia* 4, no. 4 (January 2009): 36–42. NLB, NTUNIE, NUS.

1496. Tan Yew Soon and Soh Yew Peng. *The Development of Singapore's Modern Media Industry*. Singapore: Times Academic Press, 1994. 263 pp. ISEAS, NLB, NTUNIE, NUS.

1497. "Utusan Melayu". In *Ensiklopedia Sejarah dan Kebudayaan Melayu*, vol. 4, p. 2563. Kuala Lumpur: Dewan Bahasa dan Pustaka, 1999. NLB, NTUNIE, NUS.

1498. "Utusan Melayu Filem & Sports". In *Ensiklopedia Sejarah dan Kebudayaan Melayu*, vol. 4, pp. 2562–63. Kuala Lumpur: Dewan Bahasa dan Pustaka, 1999. NLB, NTUNIE, NUS.

1499. *Utusan Melayu 10 Tahun*. Singapore: Utusan Melayu, 1949. 267 pp. ISEAS, NLB.

1500. *Utusan Melayu 25 Tahun*. Kuala Lumpur: Utusan Melayu Press Limited, 1964. 277 pp. ISEAS, NLB.

1501. "Warta Ahad". In *Ensiklopedia Sejarah dan Kebudayaan Melayu*, vol. 4, p. 2588. Kuala Lumpur: Dewan Bahasa dan Pustaka, 1999. NLB, NTUNIE, NUS.

1502. "Warta Jenaka". In *Ensiklopedia Sejarah dan Kebudayaan Melayu*, vol. 4, p. 2588. Kuala Lumpur: Dewan Bahasa dan Pustaka, 1999. NLB, NTUNIE, NUS.

1503. "Warta Malaya". In *Ensiklopedia Sejarah dan Kebudayaan Melayu*, vol. 4, p. 2589. Kuala Lumpur: Dewan Bahasa dan Pustaka, 1999. NLB, NTUNIE, NUS.

1504. Zahairin Abdul Rahman. "Utusan Melayu: Origin and History, 1939–1959". Academic exercise. Department of History, National University of Singapore, 1987. 88 pp. NUS.

1505. Zahairin Abdul Rahman. "The Voice of the Rakyat: Utusan Melayu from Inception to 1959". In *Malays/Muslims in Singapore: Selected Readings in History 1819–1965*, edited by Khoo Kay Kim, Elinah Abdullah, and Wan Meng Hao. Subang Jaya, Selangor: Pelanduk Publications in cooperation with Centre for Research on Islamic and Malay Affairs, Singapore, 2006. ISEAS, NLB, NTUNIE, NUS.

1506. Zainul Abidin Rasheed. "Akhbar Melayu di Singapura: Sumbangan dan Cabaran". *Titian Ilmu* 2 (April 1991): 44–47. NLB, NUS.

1507. Zainuddin Maidin. *Di Depan Api di Belakang Duri: Kisah Sejarah Utusan Melayu*. Cheras, Kuala Lumpur: Utusan Publications, 2013. 512 pp. NLB.

1508. Zakiah Hanum. "Jawi Peranakan". *Dewan Budaya* 21, no. 2 (19 February 1999): 46. ISEAS, NLB, NTUNIE, NUS.

1509. Zulkipli Mahmud. *Warta Malaya: Penyambung Lidah Bangsa Melayu, 1930–1941*. Bangi: Jabatan Sejarah, Universiti Kebangsaan Malaysia, 1979. 142 pp. NLB.

Publishing

1510. A. Wahab Hamzah and Hadijah Mohd. Sani. "Singapura: Pusat Kegiatan Intelektual Melayu". In *Pameran Percetakan Awal dalam Bahasa Melayu, 4 Jun–9 Jun 1990, Balai Budaya, Dewan Bahasa dan Pustaka*. Kuala Lumpur: Dewan Bahasa dan Pustaka, 1990. NUS.

1511. Abdul Aziz Hussain. "Penerbitan Buku2 dan Majalah2 Melayu di Singapura di antara Bulan September 1945 dengan Bulan September 1958". Academic exercise, Universiti Malaya Singapura, 1959. Microform. NUS.

1512. Ang, Bernice, Siti Hazariah Abu Bakar, and Noorashikin Zulkifli. "Writing to Print: The Shifting Roles of Malay Scribes in the

19th Century". *BiblioAsia* 9, no. 1 (January–April 2013): 40–43. NLB, NTUNIE, NUS.

1513.   Birch, E.W. "The Vernacular Press in the Straits". *JSBRAS* 4 (1879): 51–55. ISEAS, NLB, NUS.

1514.   Byrd, Cecil K. *Books in Singapore: A Survey of Publishing, Printing, Bookselling, and Library Activity in the Republic of Singapore.* Singapore: Chopmen Enterprise, 1970. 161 pp. ISEAS, NLB, NTUNIE, NUS.

1515.   Byrd, Cecil K. *Early Printing in the Straits Settlements, 1806–1858.* Singapore: National Library, 1970. 53 pp. ISEAS, NLB, NTUNIE, NUS.

1516.   *Directory of Members.* Singapore: Singapore Book Publishers Association, [1978]–2009. ISEAS, NLB, NUS.

1517.   Hashimah Johari. "Early Book Publishing in Malay by Malay Publishers in Singapore and the Malay Peninsular until 1929". MA dissertation, University of London, 1988. 138 pp. NUS.

1518.   Hashimah Johari. "Early Book Publishing in the Malay Language". In *The Need to Read: Essays in Honour of Hedwig Anuar,* edited by S. Gopinathan and Valerie Barth. Singapore: Festivals of Book Singapore, 1989. ISEAS, NLB, NTUNIE, NUS.

1519.   Ibrahim Ismail. "Early Malay Printing in the Straits Settlements by Missionaries of the London Missionary Society". MA dissertation, University College, London, 1980. 98 pp. ISEAS, NLB.

1520.   Ibrahim Ismail. "The Printing of Munshi Abdullah's Edition of the Sejarah Melayu in Singapore". *Kekal Abadi* 5, no. 3 (1986): 13–19. ISEAS, NLB, NUS.

1521.   Kanayson A. "The Newspapers of Singapore 1824–1894". *Journal of South Seas Society* (1973): 159–68. NUS.

1522.   Lee Geok Boi. *Pages from Yesteryear: A Look at the Printed Works of Singapore, 1819–1957.* Singapore: Singapore Heritage Society, 1989. 43 pp. ISEAS, NLB, NTUNIE, NUS.

1523.   Lim Peng Han. "Singapore an Emerging Centre of 19th Century Malay School Book Printing and Publishing in the Straits Settlements, 1819–1899". *BiblioAsia* 4, no. 4 (January 2009): 4–11. NLB, NTUNIE, NUS.

1524. Mazelan Anuar. "Penerbitan Buku Melayu di Singapura, 2001–2010". *BiblioAsia* 7, no. 1 (April 2011): 28–31. NLB, NTUNIE, NUS.

1525. Md. Sidin Ahmad Ishak. *Penerbitan & Percetakan Buku Melayu, 1807–1960*. Kuala Lumpur: Dewan Bahasa dan Pustaka, 1998. 466 pp. NLB, NUS.

1526. Proudfoot, Ian. "A Formative Period in Malay Book Publishing". *JMBRAS* 59, no. 2 (1986): 101–32. ISEAS, NLB, NUS.

1527. Proudfoot, Ian. "A Nineteenth-Century Malay Bookseller's Catalogue". *Kekal Abadi* 6, no. 4 (December 1987): 1–11. ISEAS, NLB, NUS.

1528. *Publishing in Singapore. Country Report & Directory of Members*. Singapore: Singapore Book Publishers Association, 2011. 136 pp. ISEAS, NLB, NUS.

1529. Pustaka Nasional. In *Ensiklopedia Sejarah dan Kebudayaan Melayu*, vol. 3, pp. 1815–16. Kuala Lumpur: Dewan Bahasa dan Pustaka, 1998. NLB, NTUNIE, NUS

1530. Teh-Gallop, Annabel. "Early Malay Printing". *JMBRAS* 3, pt. 1 (1990): 85–124. ISEAS, NLB, NTUNIE, NUS.

LANGUAGE

- *Language Policy and Usage*
- *Bilingualism and Multilingualism*
- *Malay Language*

Language Policy and Usage

1531. Afrendas, Evangelos A. and Eddie C.Y. Kuo, eds. *Language and Society in Singapore*. Singapore: Singapore University Press, 1980. 300 pp. ISEAS, NLB, NTUNIE, NUS.

1532. Chan Heng Chee. "Language and Culture in a Multi-Ethnic Society: A Singapore Strategy". *Ilmu Masyarakat* 5 (1984): 62–70. ISEAS, NUS.

1533. Gopinathan Saravanan. "Singapore's Language Policies: Strategies for a Plural Society". In *Southeast Asian Affairs 1979*, edited by Leo Suryadinata. Singapore Institute of Southeast Asian Studies, 1979. ISEAS, NLB, NTUNIE, NUS.

1534. Kuo C.Y., Eddie. "Language in the Family Domain in Singapore: An Analysis of the 1980 Census Statistics". *Singapore Journal of Education* 8, no. 1 (1985): 27–39. NLB, NTUNIE, NUS.

1535. Kuo C.Y., Eddie. "Languages in the Singapore Social Context". In *Papers on Southeast Asian Language*, edited by Teodoro A. Llamzon. Singapore: Singapore University Press for SEAMEO Regional Language Centre, 1979. ISEAS, NLB, NTUNIE, NUS.

1536. Kuo C.Y., Eddie. "Language, Nationhood and Communication Planning: The Case of a Multilingual Society". *Southeast Asia Journal of Social Science* 4, no. 2 (1976): 31–42. ISEAS, NLB, NUS.

1537. Kuo C.Y., Eddie. "Language Status and Literacy Trend in a Multilingual Society: Singapore". *RELC Journal* 5, no. 1 (1974): 1–15. ISEAS, NLB, NTUNIE, NUS.

1538. Kuo C.Y., Eddie. *A Sociolinguistic Profile of Singapore*. Singapore: Published for the Department of Sociology, University of Singapore by Chopmen Enterprises, 1976. 17 pp. ISEAS, NLB, NTUNIE, NUS. Also published under the same title in: *Singapore: Society in Transition*, edited by Riaz Hassan. Kuala Lumpur: Oxford University Press, 1976. ISEAS, NLB, NTUNIE, NUS.

1539. Lee Hsien Loong. "The Importance of Language in Daily Life". *Speeches* 14, no. 2 (March/April 1990): 33–35. ISEAS, NLB, NTUNIE, NUS.

1540. Leong Sin May. "Studies of Language in the Straits Settlements and the Malay States, 1875–1919". Academic exercise, Department of English Language & Literature, National University of Singapore, 1983. 67 pp. NUS.

1541. Low Kee Cheok and Mary Tay Wan-Joo. "The Language and Sociolinguistic Situation in Singapore". In *Report of the Regional Workshop on the Feasibility of a Sociolinguistic Survey of Southeast Asia 1973*. Singapore: RELC, 1973. NLB, NTUNIE, NUS.

1542. *Memoranda Angkatan Sasterawan '50*. Petaling Jaya: Fajar Bakti, 1987. 209 pp. NUS. Previous ed. published under the title: *Memoranda: Kumpulan Tulisan Angkatan Sasterawan '50 dengan Lampiran Rumusan Kongres Bahasa dan Persuratan Melayu Ketiga*. Kuala Lumpur: Oxford University Press, 1962. 281 pp. NLB, NUS.

1543. Mohamed Pitchay Gani Mohamed Abdul Aziz, ed. *Mangkin Kreativiti Bangsa dalam Bahasa*. Singapore: Angkatan Sasterawan '50, 2004. 36 pp. NLB, NTUNIE, NUS.

1544. Ng Chye Len, Katherine. "Newspaper: A Case Study in Language Policy and Mass Media in Singapore". Academic exercise, Department of English Language & Literature, National University of Singapore, 1986. 40 pp. NUS.

1545. Platt, John. "Social Class, Ethnicity and Language Choice: Language Use in Major Shopping Areas in Singapore". *Southeast Asian Journal of Social Science* 13, no. 1 (1985): 61–81. ISEAS, NLB, NTUNIE, NUS.

1546. Roksana Bibi Abdullah. "Sub-Ethnic Languages in Singapore: Issues on Maintenance and Shift". Paper presented at Kongres IX Bahasa Indonesia, organized by Pusat Bahasa, Jakarta, 28 Oktober–1 November 2008. 35 pp.

1547. Vaish, Vinity. "Mother Tongues, English, and Religion in Singapore". *World Englishes* 27, nos. 3–4 (2008): 450–64. NTUNIE, NUS.

Bilingualism and Multilingualism

1548. Bokhorst-Heng, Wendy D. et al. "English Language Ownership among Singaporean Malays: Going Beyond the NS/NNS Dichotomy". *World Englishes* 26, no. 4 (2007): 424–45. NTUNIE, NUS.

1549. Bokhorst-Heng, Wendy D. and Imelda Santos Caleon. "The Language Attitudes of Bilingual Youth in Multilingual Singapore". *Journal of Multilingual and Multicultural Development* 30, no. 3 (2009): 235–51. NTUNIE, NUS.

1550. Chong Loong Jin, Euiv_n and Mark F. Seilhamer. "Young People, Malay and English in Multilingual Singapore". *World Englishes* 33, issue 3 (September 2014) NUS.

1551. Johari Mohamed Rais. "The Social and Personal Correlates of English Language Achievement of Malay Pupils in Singapore". MEd dissertation, National University of Singapore, 1989. 154 pp. NTUNIE, NUS.

1552. Kuo C.Y., Eddie. "Some Macro-Sociological Issues in Multilingual Societies". In *Studies in Bilingual Education*, edited by R. Lord and B.K. T'sou. Hong Kong: Language Centre, University of Hong Kong, 1976. ISEAS, NLB, NTUNIE, NUS.

1553. Lee Chen. "A Study of Code-Switching and Borrowing in Bilingual Children in Singapore". MA dissertation, Department of English Language & Literature, National University of Singapore, 1991. 198 pp. + 1 video cassette (120 min.). NUS.

1554. Norwita Mohamed Ariff. "The Communicative Competence of a Bilingual Child". Academic exercise, Department of English Language & Literature, National University of Singapore, 1988. 70 pp. + 1 sound cassette. NUS.

1555. Rita Zamzamah Nazeer. "The Complexities Beneath the Perfect Picture: A Postmodern Perspective of Three Malay-Muslim Bilingual Children's Home Practices". Academic exercise, National Institute of Education, Nanyang Technological University, 2004. NTUNIE. Available at <http://hdl.handle.net/10497/2233>.

1556. Saravanan, Vanithamani. "Bilingual Chinese, Malay and Tamil Children's Language Choices in a Multi-lingual Society". *Early Child Development and Care* 152, no. 1 (1999): 43–54. NTUNIE, NUS.

1557. Segeram, S.C. "Attitudes & Attained Proficiency in ESL: A Sociolinguistic Study of Native Speakers of Malays in Singapore". MA dissertation, Department of English Language & Literature, National University of Singapore, 1986. 98 pp. NUS.

1558. Seong T.B. and L.B. Soon. "Challenges Confronting Translators in Multilingual and Multi-ethnic Singapore". *Babel* 47, no. 1 (2001): 22–34. NTUNIE, NUS.

1559. Sng Keow Hong. "Some Phonetic Properties Which May Distinguish Tamil, Chinese and Malay Speakers of English in Singapore from Each Other". Academic exercise, Department of English Language & Literature, National University of Singapore, 1987. 38 pp. + 1 sound cassette (21 min.). NUS.

Malay Language

1560. Ab. Razak Ab. Karim. *Bicara Bahasa: Panduan Mudah & Sistematik Tatabahasa Bahasa Melayu.* Singapore: Kesatuan Guru-Guru Melayu Singapura, 2015. 244 pp. NLB.

1561. Abbas Mohd Shariff. "Institut Perkembangan Kurikulum: Buku-Buku Teks dan Peralatan Mengajar dalam Bahasa Melayu dalam Dekad 80-an". *Sekata* 8, no. 2 (December 1990): 15–22. ISEAS, NLB, NTUNIE, NUS.

1562. Abbas Mohd Shariff. "Pengaruh Bahasa Arab dalam Bahasa Melayu". *Sekata* 5, no. 1 (December 1988): 20–33. NLB, NTUNIE, NUS.

1563. *Analisa: Jurnal Persatuan Bahasa Melayu, Universiti Kebangsaan Singapura.* Singapore: Persatuan Bahasa Melayu, Universiti Kebangsaan Singapura, 1981–. NLB. Continues *Analisa.* Singapore: Persekutuan Bahasa Melayu Universiti Singapura, [197–]–1980. ISEAS, NLB, NUS.

1564. *Bahasa.* Singapore: Persekutuan Bahasa Melayu Universiti Malaya, 1957–68. NUS.

1565. *Bahasa Jiwa Bangsa: 25 Rencana Pilihan Haji Muhammad Ariff Ahmad.* Singapore: Berita Harian, 1990. 97 pp. NLB.

1566. *Bahasa dan Jati Diri Melayu.* Singapore: Pusat Bahasa Melayu Singapura, Unit Bahasa Melayu, Cawangan Bahasa Ibunda, Bahagian Perancangan dan Pembangunan Kurikulum, Kementerian Pendidikan Singapura, 2013. 315 pp. NLB.

1567. Bibi Jan Mohd Ayyub. "Language Issues in the Malay Community". In *Language, Society and Education in Singapore: Issues and Trends,* edited by S. Gopinathan et al. Singapore: Times Academic Press, 1994. ISEAS, NLB, NTUNIE, NUS.

1568. Chia Leeann. *Conversational Malay for the Healthcare Profession*. Singapore: The Inksmith Pte. Ltd., 2012. 98 pp. NLB.

1569. Dennys, Nicholas Belfield. *A Handbook of Malay Colloquial as Spoken in Singapore: Being a Series of Introductory Lessons for Domestic and Business Purpose*. Singapore: Mission Press, 1878. 204 pp. NLB, NUS.

1570. Goh Chok Tong. "The Role of Malay Language and Culture in a Multiracial Society". *Speeches* 12, no. 4 (July/August 1988): 27–30. ISEAS, NLB, NTUNIE, NUS.

1571. Hadijah Rahmat. "Bahasa Melayu di Singapura: Cabaran dan Masa Depan". In *Citra Murni Insan dalam Dunia Pendidikan: Sebuah Feskrip untuk Abbas Mohammad Shariff*, edited by Hadijah Rahmat, Mana Sikana, and Kartini Anwar. Singapore: Institut Pendidikan Nasional Singapura, Universiti Teknologi Nanyang, 2011. NLB, NTUNIE.

1572. Hafiz Husain. "Cabaran-cabaran dalam Pengajaran dan Pembelajaran Bahasa Melayu di Sekolah". *Bakti* 2, no. 9 (1981): 4–5, 8. NLB, NTUNIE, NUS. Also published under the same title in: *Analisa* (1980/81): 48–53. ISEAS, NLB, NUS.

1573. Hajar Abdul Rahim. "Analisis Sosio-Kognitif terhadap Penggunaan Leksis Bahasa Melayu dalam Bahasa Inggeris Standard di Malaysia dan di Singapura". In *Bahasa: Memeluk Akar Menyuluh ke Langit*, edited by Paitoon M. Chaiyanara. Singapore: Jabatan Bahasa dan Budaya Melayu, Institut Pendidikan National, Universiti Teknologi Nanyang, 2006. ISEAS, NLB, NTUNIE.

1574. Harun A. Ghani. "Bahasa di Kalangan Penagih Dadah". *Sekata* 8, no. 2 (December 1990): 5–14. ISEAS, NLB, NTUNIE, NUS.

1575. *Huraian Sukatan Pelajaran Bahasa Melayu 2008: Darjah 1 hingga Darjah 4*. Singapore: Curriculum Planning and Development Division, Ministry of Education, 2007. 109 pp. NLB.

1576. Hussin Mutalib. "The Role of Malay Language and Culture in Singapore (*in Malay*)". Paper presented at Singapore Lecture in conjunction with the annual "Singapore Malay Language Month and Literary Awards" ceremony, Orchard Hotel, Singapore, 17 July 1999.

1577. Idros Samsudin. "Lembaga Bahasa Melayu dan ASAS 50". *Dewan Sastera* 18, no. 4 (April 1988): 78–79. NLB, NTUNIE, NUS.

1578. Juffri Supaat and Nazeerah Gopaul, eds. *Aksara: Menjejaki Tulisan Melayu = The Passage of Malay Scripts*. Penterjemah, Azizah Zakaria. Singapore: National Library Board, 2009. 269 pp. NLB, NTUNIE.

1579. *Kajian Pengajaran: Perancangan dan Pelaksanaan*. Singapore: Pusat Bahasa Melayu Singapura, Bahagian Perancangan dan Pembangunan Kurikulum, Kementerian Pendidikan Singapura, 2012. 269 pp. NLB.

1580. Kamsiah Abdullah. "Attitudes and Motivation of Malay Students in Secondary Schools in Singapore Towards the Learning of English and Malay". *Singapore Journal of Education* 7, no. 1 (1985): 45–55. ISEAS, NLB, NTUNIE, NUS.

1581. Kamsiah Abdullah. *Pendidikan Bahasa Melayu di Singapura*. Kuala Lumpur: Dewan Bahasa dan Pustaka, 2010. 431 pp. NLB, NTUNIE, NUS.

1582. Kamsiah Abdullah. *Rangkai Penelitian Bahasa dan Pemikiran*. Singapore: Majlis Bahasa Melayu Singapura dan Deezed Consult, 2002. NLB, NTUNIE.

1583. Kamsiah Abdullah. "Sikap dan Motivasi Penuntut Melayu di Sekolah Menengah Singapura terhadap Bahasa Melayu dan Bahasa Inggeris". MEd dissertation, Universiti Malaya, 1984. 246 pp. NUS.

1584. Kamsiah Abdullah. "Sikap dan Motivasi Sebagai Pemboleh Ubah dalam Pembelajaran Bahasa". *Dewan Bahasa* 31, no. 12 (December 1987): 903–18. NLB, NUS.

1585. Kamsiah Abdullah. *Sikap, Penguasaan dan Penggunaan Bahasa Melayu di Singapura*. Singapore: Angkatan Sasterawan 50, 2000. 236 pp. NLB, NTUNIE, NUS.

1586. Kamsiah Abdullah and Gloria R. Poedjosoedarmo. "The Influence of English on the Writing in Malay of Malay Singaporean Students". *Jurnal Pengajian Melayu* 11 (2001): 126–40. NLB.

1587. Kamsiah Abdullah and Hadijah Rahmat. *Functional Objectives in Language Learning: Malay Language: A Report on Phase II of the Project*. Singapore: Institute of Education, 1990. 108 pp. NTUNIE.

1588. *Kongres Bahasa Kebangsaan: Kertaskerja*. Anjuran Lembaga Tetap Kongres. Singapore: Yayasan Asia, 1966. 208 pp. NLB, NTUNIE.

1589. *Kurikulum Berasaskan Sekolah: Inovasi dalam Pengajaran dan Pembelajaran.* Singapore: Pusat Bahasa Melayu Singapura, Bahagian Perancangan dan Pembangunan Kurikulum, Kementerian Pendidikan Singapura, 2012 252 pp. NLB.

1590. *Kurikulum Berasaskan Sekolah: Sekolah Rendah dan Menengah: Panduan Guru* Singapore: Unit Bahasa Melayu and Pusat Bahasa Melayu, Cawangan Bahasa Ibunda, Bahagian Perancangan dan Pembangunan Kurikulum, Kementerian Pendidikan Singapura, 2010. 49 pp. NLB.

1591. Liaw Yock Fang. "Malay Language and Literature in Singapore". In *Singapore Studies*, edited by Basant K. Kapur. Singapore: Singapore University Press, 1986. ISEAS, NLB, NTUNIE, NUS.

1592. Masuri S.N. "Masa Depan Bahasa dan Sastera Melayu di Singapura". *Dewan Sastera* 11, no. 3 (March 1981): 24–28. NLB, NTUNIE, NUS.

1593. Masuri S.N. and Salmiah Ismail. "Kami Mampu Mendaulatkan Bahasa dan Sastera Melayu Singapura". *Dewan Sastera* 17, no. 4 (April 1987): 20–24. NLB, NTUNIE, NUS.

1594. Maxwell, W.E. "Malay Words of Portuguese Origins". *JSBRAS* 3, no. 16 (December 1885): 64–70. ISEAS, NLB, NUS.

1595. *Menyemai Bahasa Menuai Budi: Seminar Bahasa Melayu 2014.* Singapore: Pusat Bahasa Melayu Singapura, Unit Bahasa Melayu, Cawangan Bahasa Ibunda, Bahagian Perancangan dan Pembangunan Kurikulum, Kementerian Pendidikan Singapura, 2014. 419 pp. NLB.

1596. Mohamed Pitchay Gani Mohamed Abdul Aziz. *Legasi Bahasa Melayu.* Singapore: ASAS 50 Press, 2009. 199 pp. NLB, NTUNIE, NUS.

1597. Mohamed Pitchay Gani Mohamed Abdul Aziz. *Melayu Singapura dalam Kritikan: Isu Bahasa dan Bangsa.* Singapore: Angkatan Sasterawan 50, 2002. 184 pp. NLB, NTUNIE, NUS.

1598. Mohamed Pitchay Gani Mohamed Abdul Aziz and Muhammad Jailani Abu Talib, eds *Bahasa Sumber Intelektual Peribumi.* Singapore: Angkatan Sasterawan 50, 2009. 158 pp. NLB, NTUNIE, NUS.

1599. Mohd. Maidin Packer Mohamad. "ML1 for Primary Students". *Petir: Organ of the People's Action Party* (January 1989): 37. ISEAS, NLB,

NTUNIE, NUS. Also published in Malay under the title: "Perlukah ML1 untuk Murid-murid Sekolah Rendah?" *Petir: Organ of the People's Action Party* (January 1989): 53–55. ISEAS, NLB, NTUNIE, NUS.

1600. Mohd. Salleh Daud. "Problems and Prospects in Malay Language (ML2) Teaching". Paper presented at a seminar on the Role of Educational Materials in Singapore Schools, organized by Singapore Book Publishers Association, March 1973. 3 pp. NLB, NTUNIE, NUS.

1601. Mohd. Taib Osman. "The Language of the Editorials in Malay Vernacular Newspapers up to 1941: A Study in the Development of Malay Language in Meeting New Needs". Academic exercise, Department of Malay Studies, University of Malaya, Singapore, 1958. 88 pp. NUS. Published under the same title: Kuala Lumpur: Dewan Bahasa dan Pustaka, 1966. 88 pp. ISEAS, NLB, NUS.

1602. Muhammad Ariff Ahmad. "Masalah-masalah Pengajaran Bahasa Melayu sebagai Bahasa Kedua". *Singapore Journal of Education* 2, no. 1 (1979): 61–68. ISEAS, NLB, NTUNIE, NUS.

1603. Muhammad Ariff Ahmad. "Penglibatan Guru dan Masyarakat dalam Meningkatkan Penggunaan Bahasa Melayu yang Betul". *Sekata* 5, no. 3 (December 1988): 3–10. ISEAS, NLB, NTUNIE, NUS.

1604. Mukhlis Abu Bakar. "Cerita dan Identiti dalam Percakapan". *Dewan Bahasa* 43, no. 10 (October 1999): 937–43. NLB.

1605. Nor Azah Abdul Aziz. "Language Use Patterns in the Three-Tier Malay Family". Research exercise, Department of Malay Studies, National University of Singapore, 1992. 51 pp. NUS.

1606. Norafidah Tajuddin. "Penilaian Terhadap Penutur Bahasa Standard dan Dialek Jawa Singapura". *Jurnal Dewan Bahasa* 36, no. 5 (May 1992): 408–20. NLB, NTUNIE, NUS.

1607. Nurulazmi Manan. "Perbandingan Morfologi Bahasa Melayu dan Bahasa Bawean". MEd dissertation, National Institute of Education, Nanyang Technological University, 2013.

1608. Paitoon M. Chaiyanara et al., ed. *Bahasa: Memeluk Akar Menyuluh ke Langit*. Singapore: Jabatan Bahasa dan Budaya Melayu, Institut Pendidikan National, Universiti Teknologi Nanyang, 2006. 489 pp. ISEAS, NTUNIE, NLB.

1609. Pakir, Anne. "The Future of Baba Malay: Peranakan Plays as Cultural Record". *Singa* 19 (December 1989): 75–83. ISEAS, NLB, NTUNIE, NUS.

1610. Pereira, Valerie Jane. "Reading & Spelling in a Shallow Orthography: Malay". Academic exercise, Department of Social Work and Psychology, National University of Singapore, 1992. 112 pp. NUS.

1611. "Persidangan Antarabangsa Bahasa, Sastera dan Budaya Melayu: Ke arah Keseimbangan Insan". Anjuran Institut Pendidikan Nasional, Universiti Teknologi Nanyang, York Hotel, Singapore, 17–18 Julai 1998. 2 vols. (various foliations). NLB, NUS.

1612. Pijnappel, J. "On the Roots in the Malay Language". *JSBRAS* 16 (December 1885): 251–63. ISEAS, NLB.

1613. Rahmad Buang. "Dilemma Guru-Guru Bahasa Kedua Melayu". *Bakti* 2 (1981): 2. NLB, NTUNIE, NUS.

1614. Rizwana Abdul Azeez. "Creating a Modern Singapore Muslim Community: A Tale of Language Dissonances". ISEAS Working Papers no. 2 (2014). Singapore: Institute of Southeast Asian Studies, 2014. 18 pp. ISEAS, NUS. Available at <http://www.iseas.edu.sg/documents/publication/ISEAS_Working%20Paper_%20No%202.pdf>.

1615. Roksana Bibi Abdullah. *Bahasa Melayu di Singapura: Pengalihan dan Pengekalan = Malay Language in Singapore*. Singapore: DeeZed Consult, 2003. 323 pp. NLB.

1616. Roksana Bibi Abdullah. "Fitur-Fitur Bahasa Melayu di Singapura". In *Bahasa Melayu Bahasa Dunia-Persidangan Internasional*. Johor Baharu, Johor: Universiti Pendidikan Sultan Idris, 2009.

1617. Roksana Bibi Abdullah. "Inter influencing of Language Between Chinese and Malay Communities". In *Malay Studies International Conference*, edited by Awang Sariyan. Beijing: Beijing Foreign Studies University, 2008.

1618. Roksana Bibi Abdullah. *Pengajaran dan Pembelajaran Bahasa Melayu sebagai Bahasa Ketiga (Program Khas) = Teaching and Learning of Malay as a Third Language (Special Programme)*. In *Regional Malay Language Pedagogy Convention*. Seremban: Ministry of Education, Malaysia, 2009.

1619.   Roksana Bibi Abdullah. "Pengalihan Bahasa di Kalangan Masyarakat
        Bawean di Singapura: Sebab dan Akibat". In *Bahasa: Memeluk Akar
        Menyuluh ke Langit*, edited by Paitoon M. Chaiyanara. Singapore: Jabatan
        Bahasa dan Budaya Melayu, Institut Pendidikan National, Universiti
        Teknologi Nanyang, 2006. ISEAS, NLB, NTUNIE.

1620.   Roksana Bibi Abdullah. "Penggunaan Bahasa di Kalangan Generasi
        Ketiga di Singapura: Satu Analisa Sebab dan Akibat". Paper presented
        at a Persidangan Antarabangsa Bahasa, Sastera dan Kebudayaan
        Melayu ke 2, anjuran Jabatan Bahasa dan Kebudayaan Melayu, Kumpulan
        Akademik Bahasa dan Kebudayaan Asia, Institut Pendidikan Nasional,
        Universiti Teknologi Nanyang, Singapura, 1–3 September 2002. 23 pp.
        ISEAS, NLB.

1621.   Roksana Bibi Abdullah. "Penggunaan Bahasa Melayu di Singapura: Satu
        Kajian Kes di Geylang, Singapura". Academic exercise, Fakulti Sains
        Kemasyarakatan dan Kemanusiaan, Universiti Kebangsaan Malaysia,
        1989. 193 pp. NUS. Also published under the same title in: *Sekata 8*,
        no. 1 (June 1990): 31–39. ISEAS, NLB, NTUNIE, NUS.

1622.   Roksana Bibi Abdullah. "Perkembangan Bahasa Melayu di Singapura
        Sejak Tahun 1959". *Titian Ilmu* 2 (April 1991): 16–26. NLB, NTUNIE,
        NUS.

1623.   Rusydiah Abdul Razak. "A Study of Colloquial Malay — Nya and Punya".
        Academic exercise, Department of English Language & Literature,
        National University of Singapore, 2014. NUS.

1624.   S. Markasan (Suratman Markasan). "Bahasa dan Kesusasteraan Melayu
        Singapura di Persimpangan". *Dewan Bahasa* 32, no. 6 (January 1988):
        423–85. NLB, NUS.

1625.   S. Markasan (Suratman Markasan). "Penggunaan dan Perkembangan
        Bahasa dan Sastera Melayu di Singapura". *Analisa* (1981): 40–47. NLB,
        NUS.

1626.   S. Markasan (Suratman Markasan). "Peranan Angkatan Sasterawan 50
        dalam Pembinaan dan Pengembangan Bahasa dan Sastera Melayu di
        Singapura". Kertas kerja yang dibentang dalam Pertemuan Sasterawan
        Nusantara, anjuran bersama Dewan Bahasa dan Pustaka & Gabungan
        Persatuan Penulis Nasional, Kuala Lumpur, 5 dan 6 Disember 1981.
        NUS.

1627. S. Markasan (Suratman Markasan). "Peranan Sastera Melayu dalam Pembinaan dan Penyatuan Bahasa Melayu: Satu Tinjauan Ringkas". *Sekata* 4, no. 1 (December 1989): 40–43. ISEAS, NLB, NTUNIE, NUS.

1628. S. Markasan (Suratman Markasan). "Perlukah Kita Mempunyai Bahasa Melayu Baku dar. Bilakah Bahasa Melayu Harus Menjadi Bahasa Baku?" *Sekata* 4, no. 1 (December 1987): 5–15. NLB, NTUNIE, NUS.

1629. Salmiah Ismail. "Liaw Yock Fang: Saya Optimis dengan Perkembangan Bahasa Melayu di Singapura". *Dewan Sastera* 15, no. 8 (August 1985): 19–21. NLB, NTUNIE, NUS.

1630. Selamat Omar. "Bahasa Melayu dalam Sistem Pendidikan Dwibahasa: Identiti dan Permasalahannya: Pengalaman Singapura". Paper presented at a Pertemuan Guru-Guru Nusantara ke-5, anjuran KGMS, Singapura, 24–25 November 1989. NLB, NTUNIE, NUS.

1631. Seminar Bahasa Melayu (2012: Singapura). *Kecekapan Berbahasa dan Penghayatan Nilai Pendidikan Abad ke 21*. Singapore: Pusat Bahasa Melayu Singapura, Bahagian Perancangan dan Pembangunan Kurikulum, Kementerian Pendidikan Singapura, 2012. 420 pp. NLB.

1632. "Seminar dan Pameran Pengajaran Bahasa Melayu di Sekolah Rendah". Anjuran bersama Unit Bahasa Melayu Bahagian Sekolah, Kementerian Pelajaran dengan Jawatankuasa Pusat Guru-Guru Bahasa Melayu Sekolah Rendah, Singapura, 9–10 September 1985. 1 vol. (various foliations). NUS.

1633. Seminar Pengajaran Bahasa Melayu (1982: Singapura). *Ke Arah Pengajaran dan Pembelajaran Bahasa Melayu yang Lebih Berkesan, di Institut Pendidikan pada Hari Sabtu 24 April '82*. Singapore: Kesatuan Guru-guru Melayu Singapura, 1982. 1 vol. (various foliations). NLB, NUS.

1634. Seminar Pengajaran Bahasa Melayu Sebagai Bahasa Kedua di Sekolah-sekolah Menengah (1974: Singapura). *Rumusan-Rumusan (dan Kertaskerja) Seminar Pengajaran Bahasa Kedua di Sekolah-Sekolah Menengah*. Anjuran Yunit Bahasa dan Kesusasteraan Melayu. Kementerian Pelajaran Singapura. Singapore: Kementerian Pelajaran, 1974. 1 vol. (various foliations). NLB, NUS.

1635. "Seminar Sebutan Baku, Hotel Mandarin, Singapura". Anjuran Majlis Bahasa Melayu Singapura & Persatuan Guru-Guru Agama Singapura, Ahad, 22 Ogos 1993. 44 pp. NLB.

1636. "Seminar Sebutan Baku Bahasa Melayu". Anjuran Jawatankuasa Bahasa Melayu Kementerian Pelajaran Singapura dengan kerjasama Jawatankuasa Pusat Guru-Guru Bahasa Melayu (Sekolah Rendah), Pusat Islam Singapura, 8–10 September 1992. 1 vol. (various foliations). NLB, NUS.

1637. Sidek Saniff. *Peranan dan Penggunaan Bahasa di Singapura*. Kuala Lumpur: Persatuan Linguistik Malaysia, 1994. 42 pp. ISEAS, NLB.

1638. *Sukatan Pelajaran Bahasa Melayu Sekolah Menengah 2011*. Singapore: Curriculum Planning & Development Division, 2011. 84 pp. NLB, NTUNIE. Available at <http://www.moe.gov.sg/education/syllabuses/mother-tongue-languages/files/malay-secondary-2011.pdf>.

1639. Supki Haji Sidek. "Satu Ujian Pencapaian Kefahaman Membaca dalam Bahasa Melayu bagi Murid Melayu Singapura di Peringkat Sijil Am Pelajaran (Peringkat Biasa)". MEd dissertation, Fakulti Pendidikan, Universiti Malaya, 1984. 194 pp. NUS.

1640. Syed Husin Ali. "Pertubuhan2 Bahasa dan Sastera Melayu (di Singapura) Selepas Perang Dunia II (khasnya ASAS 50)". Academic exercise, Department of Malay Studies, University of Malaya, Singapore, 1959. 67 pp. Published under the same title in: *Bahasa* 2, no. 2 (March 1960): 1–6. NLB, NUS.

1641. Tham Seong Chee. "The Malay Language in Singapore". In *Papers on Southeast Asian Languages,* edited by Teodoro A. Llamzon. Singapore: Singapore University Press, 1979. ISEAS, NLB, NTUNIE, NUS.

1642. Tham Seong Chee. "Trends in the Development of the Malay Language with Some Reference to Singapore". *Review of Southeast Asian Studies* 8 (December 1978): 25–33. ISEAS, NLB, NUS.

LAW

- *General Works*
- *Legal Status of Muslims*
- *Administration of Muslim Law Act (AMLA)*
- *Family Law*
- *Syariah Law and Syariah Court*

General Works

1643. Ahmad Ibrahim. *Developments in the Marriage Laws in Singapore since 1959.* Singapore: Malayan Law Journal, 1979. 70 pp. ISEAS, NLB, NUS.

1644. Ahmad Ibrahim. *Towards a History of Law in Malaysia and Singapore.* Kuala Lumpur: Dewan Bahasa dan Pustaka, 1995. 152 pp. NLB, NUS. Previous ed. published under the same title: Singapore: Stamford College Press, 1970. 86 pp. ISEAS. Also published in Malay under the title: *Mendekati Sejarah Undang-Undang di Malaysia dan Singapura.* Penterjemah, Muhammad Bukhari Abd. Hamid. Kuala Lumpur: Dewan Bahasa dan Pustaka, 1995. 158 pp. ISEAS, NLB, NTUNIE, NUS.

1645. *Al-Mizan: Balancing the Scales of Justice.* Singapore: Association of Muslim Lawyers, 2013–. NLB.

1646. Hickling, R.H. "Language, Law and Singapore". In *Malayan Law Review, 1992.* Singapore: Institute of Policy Studies, 1992. NLB.

1647. *The Law Society of Singapore Directory.* Singapore: Law Society, 1990–. NLB, NUS.

1648. *List of Advocates and Solicitors in Alphabetical Order.* Singapore: Law Society of Singapore, 1979–89. NLB, NUS.

1649. Reddy, A. Balasubramaniam and Chandrasegar Chidambaran. "Marriage of the Muslim Women and the Women's Charter". *Law Times* (1977): 17–20. NLB, NUS.

1650. *Reprint of the Constitution of the Republic of Singapore: Incorporating All Amendments in Force on 20th March 1992.* Singapore: Attorney-General, 1992. 117 pp. ISEAS, NLB, NTUNIE, NUS.

1651. S.K.D. "Alsagoff Case". *Malayan Law Journal* 24, no. 11 (1958): lxvii–xii. NLB, NTUNIE, NUS.

1652. *Sultan Hussain Ordinance. Chapter 382.* Singapore: Government Printer, 2000. 3 pp. NUS.

Legal Status of Muslims

1653. A. Samad Ismail (Abdul Samad Ismail). "Majulah Singapura". *Dewan Budaya* 13, no 11 (November 1991): 7–11. ISEAS, NLB, NTUNIE, NUS.

1654.   Ahmad Ibrahim. "Legal Position of Muslims in Singapore". *World Muslim League Magazine* 1, no. 1 (1963): 37–50; 1, no. 2 (1963): 30–39; 1, no. 3 (1964): 51–57; 1, no. 4 (1964): 45–53; 1, no. 6 (1964): 11–12. NLB, NUS.

1655.   Ahmad Ibrahim. *The Legal Status of Muslims in Singapore*. Singapore: Malayan Law Journal, 1965. 75 pp. ISEAS, NLB, NUS. Also published under the title: "The Legal Status of the Muslims in Singapore". *World Muslim League Magazine* 1, no. 5 (1964): 42–52. NLB, NUS.

1656.   Ahmad Ibrahim. *Muslims in Singapore*. Singapore: [s.n., 1965?]. 19 pp. NLB.

1657.   Mir-Hosseini, Ziba. *The Construction of Gender in Islamic Legal Thought and Strategies for Reform*. MUIS Occasional Papers Series, paper no. 8. Singapore: Majlis Ugama Islam Singapura, 2009. 25 pp. ISEAS, NLB.

1658.   Singapore. Legislative Assembly. Select Committee on the Administration of Muslim Law Bill. *Report of the Select Committee on the Administration of Muslim Law Bill*. Singapore: Printed by Lee Kim Heng, Acting Government Printer, 1961. 26 pp. NUS.

1659.   Singapore. Legislative Assembly. Select Committee on the Muslims (Amendment) Bill. *Official Report*. Singapore: Government Printer, 1960. 12 pp. NUS.

1660.   Singapore. Legislative Assembly. Select Committee on the Muslims (Amendment) Bill. *Report of the Select Committee on the Muslims (Amendment) Bill*. Papers, L.A. 14 of 1960. Singapore: Government Printer, 1960. 1 vol. (various pagings). NLB, NUS.

1661.   Singapore. Legislative Assembly. Select Committee on the Muslims Bill. *Official Report, Tuesday, 26th February, 1957, Official Report, Tuesday, 5th March, 1957*. Singapore: Government Printer, 1957. 24 pp. NUS.

1662.   Singapore. Legislative Assembly. Select Committee on the Muslims Bill. *Report*. Singapore: Government Printer, 1957. 1 vol. (various pagings). NUS.

1663.   Singapore. Select Committee on the Administration of Muslim Law (Amendment) Bill. *Report of the Select Committee on the Administration of Muslim Law (Amendment) Bill (Bill no. 18/98)*. Singapore: Printed for the Government of Singapore by the Government Printers, 1999. NUS.

1664. Thio Su Mien. "Fundamental and Minority Rights in the Singapore Constitution". *Students Union Annual* (1965/66): 59–62. ISEAS, NLB, NUS.

1665. Wee, Ann. "Muslim Women and the Law: A Case Study". *Social Dimension* 2 (1989): 10–11. NLB, NTUNIE, NUS.

Administration of Muslim Law Act (AMLA)

1666. *Administration of Muslim Law Act. Chapter 3*. Rev. ed. 2009. Singapore: Printed by the Government Printer, 2009. 83 pp. NUS. Previous ed.: Rev. ed. 1985. Singapore: Law Revision Commission, 1986. 55 pp. ISEAS, NLB, NTUNIE, NUS.

1667. *Administration of Muslim Law Act. Chapter 3, Administration of Muslim Law (Fitrah) Rules*. Subsidiary Legislation, S 175/85. Rev. ed. 1990. Singapore: Printed by the Government Printer, 1992. 6 pp. ISEAS, NLB, NTUNIE, NUS

1668. *Administration of Muslim Law Act. Chapter 3, Administration of Muslim Law (Mosque Building and MENDAKI Fund) Rules*. Subsidiary Legislation, S248/84. Rev. ed. 1990. Singapore: Printed by the Government Printer, 1992. 5 pp. ISEAS, NLB, NTUNIE, NUS.

1669. *Administration of Muslim Law Act. Chapter 3, Muslim Converts Rules*. Subsidiary Legislation, S80/75. Rev. ed. 1990. Singapore: Printed by the Government Printer, 1992. 2 pp. ISEAS, NLB, NTUNIE, NUS.

1670. *Administration of Muslim Law Act. Chapter 3, Muslim Marriage and Divorce Rules*. Subsidiary Legislation, S165/68. Rev. ed. 1990. Singapore: Printed by the Government Printer, 1992. 32 pp. ISEAS, NLB, NTUNIE, NUS.

1671. "Administration of Muslim Law in Singapore". *Malayan Law Journal* 2 (November 1968): xlvi. NLB, NUS.

1672. Aljunied, Syed Muhd Khairudin. "AMLA, Mosque and Madrasahs in Contemporary Singapore". *Karyawan: Professionals for the Community* 9, issue 2 (January 2009): 11–13. ISEAS, NLB, NTUNIE, NUS.

1673. Kalthom Muhammad Isa. "Muslim Women in the Context of Modern Society: A Case Study of the Administration of Muslim Law Act (AMLA)

Singapore". Academic exercise, MA dissertation, Interdisciplinary Islamic Studies, Syarif Hidayatullah State Islamic University, Jakarta, 2011. 61 pp.

1674. Mohd Nizam Ismail. "Are We Ambitious Enough?" *Karyawan: Professionals for the Community* 9, issue 2 (January 2009): 9–10. ISEAS, NLB, NTUNIE, NUS.

1675. Raihan Ismail. "AMLA and the Problem of Dysfunctional Families". *Karyawan: Professionals for the Community* 9, issue 2 (January 2009): 18–20. ISEAS, NLB, NTUNIE, NUS.

1676. *Rang Undang-Undang Pentadbiran Hukum Islam, 1960.* Singapore: Di-chetak oleh Pemangku Penchetak Kerajaan, 1961. 35 pp. ISEAS, NLB.

1677. Sadali Rasban. *Critical Analysis of AMLA in Estate Matters.* Singapore: HTHT Advisory Services, Pustaka Nasional, 2010. 74 pp. NLB, NUS.

1678. Sallim Jasman. "Undang-Undang Pentadbiran Islam dan Mahkamah Syariah di Singapura". In *Pembangunan Undang-Undang di Rantau ASEAN*, disunting oleh Abdul Monir Yaacob dan Suzalie Mohamad. Kuala Lumpur: Institut Kefahaman Islam, Malaysia, 2002. ISEAS, NLB, NUS.

1679. Selvam, Arfat. "AMLA and the Changing Economic Landscape". *Karyawan: Professionals for the Community* 9, issue 2 (January 2009): 14–15. ISEAS, NLB, NTUNIE, NUS.

1680. Siraj, Mehrun. "The Singapore Administration of Muslim Law Act, 1966". *World Muslim League Magazine* 3, no. 11 (1967): 21–46. NLB, NUS.

1681. Suhana Dupree. "Undang-undang Pentadbiran Islam di Singapura: Satu Tinjauan Ringkas". Academic exercise, Universiti Malaya, 1988.

1682. Yang Razali Kassim. "AMLA: Time for Sweeping Change?" *Karyawan: Professionals for the Community* 9, issue 2 (January 2009): 6–8. ISEAS, NLB, NTUNIE, NUS.

1683. Zaleha Ahmad. "Minor Marriage: How will the AMLA Amendments Help?" *Karyawan: Professionals for the Community* 9, issue 2 (January 2009): 24–26. ISEAS, NLB, NTUNIE, NUS.

Family Law

1684. Ahmad Ibrahim (1916–99). *Family Law in Malaysia and Singapore.* Singapore: Malayan Law Journal, 1984. 359 pp. NLB, NUS. First published: Singapore: Malayan Law Journal, 1978. 313 pp. ISEAS, NTUNIE, NUS.

1685. Ahmad Ibrahim. *The Status of Muslim Women in Family Law in Malaysia, Singapore and Brunei.* Singapore: Malayan Law Journal, 1965. 121 pp. ISEAS, NLB, NUS.

1686. Halijah Mohamad. "Muslim Personal Law in Singapore and Issues Affecting Women". In *Religious Activism and Women's Development in Southeast Asia.* Singapore: Association of Muslim Professionals, 2011. NLB, NUS.

1687. McBride, John Douglas. *Law in the Pluralistic State: Malay and Chinese Family Law in the Pluralistic State of Singapore.* PhD dissertation, Southern Illinois University, 1971 Ann Arbor, Mich.: University Microfilms, 1971. 1 microfilm reel. ISEAS, NLB, NUS.

1688. Mohd. Siraj. "Status of Muslim Woman [and] Family Law in Singapore". *Intisari* 2, no. 2 (1964): 9–17. NLB, NUS.

1689. Noor Aisha Abdul Rahman. "Convention on the Elimination of Discrimination Against Women and the Prospect of Development of Muslim Personal Law in Singapore". *Journal of Muslim Minority Affairs* 34, no. 1 (March 2014) 45–65. ISEAS, NTUNIE, NUS.

1690. Noor Aisha Abdul Rahman. "Muslim Personal Law within Singapore Legal System History, Prospects and Challenges". *Journal of Muslim Minority Affairs* 29, no. 1 (March 2009): 109–26. ISEAS, NTUNIE, NUS.

1691. Salbiah Ahmad. "The Administration of Muslim Family Law in Singapore". LLM dissertation, Kulliyyah of Laws, International Islamic University Malaysia, 1989. 515 pp. NUS.

1692. Siraj, Mehrun. "Recent Changes in the Administration of Muslim Family Law in Malaysia and Singapore". *International and Comparative Law Quarterly* 7 (1968): 221–32. NTUNIE, NUS.

1693. Siraj, Mehrun. "The Status of Muslim Women in the Family Law in Singapore". *World Muslim League Magazine* 1, no. 2 (1963): 40–52. NLB,

NUS. Also published under the same title in: *Intisari* 2, no. 2 (1964): 9–17. ISEAS, NLB, NUS.

1694.   Wee, Kenneth. "The Family and the Law in Singapore". In *The Contemporary Family in Singapore: Structure and Change*, edited by Eddie C.Y. Kuo and Aline Wong. Singapore: Singapore University Press, 1976. ISEAS, NLB, NTUNIE, NUS.

Syariah Law and Syariah Court

1695.   A. Rahman Saleh. "Changes to the Powers of the Syariah Court". *Singapore Law Gazette* (June 1999): 20–21. NLB, NUS.

1696.   Abri, Khalid. *Khutbah Nikah.* Singapore: Alharamain, 1981. 75 pp. NUS.

1697.   Ahmad Ibrahim. *Islamic Law in Malaya.* Singapore: Malaysian Sociological Research Institute, 1965. 444 pp. ISEAS, NLB, NTUNIE, NUS.

1698.   Ahmad Ibrahim. "Muslim Marriage and Divorce in Singapore". *Malayan Law Journal* 28, no. 2 (1962): i–xviii. NUS.

1699.   Ahmad Ibrahim. "The Muslims in Malaysia and Singapore: The Laws of Matrimonial Property". In *Family Law in Asia and Africa*, edited by J.N.D. Anderson. London: Allen & Unwin, 1968. ISEAS, NUS.

1700.   Ahmad Nizam Abbas. "The Islamic Legal System in Singapore". *Pacific Rim Law & Policy Journal* 21, no. 1 (2012): 163–87. NTUNIE, NUS.

1701.   Aidil Zulkifli. "The Fate of Fatwa in Singapore". *Karyawan: Professionals for the Community* 10, issue 1 (July 2009): 3–4. ISEAS, NLB, NTUNIE, NUS.

1702.   Bartholomew, Geoffrey Wilson. "The Application of Sharia in Singapore". *American Journal of Comparative Law* 13 (1964): 385–413. NUS.

1703.   Bartholomew, Geoffrey Wilson. "The Jurisdiction of the Shariah Court in Singapore". *Sedar* 2 (1969/70): 31–41. ISEAS, NLB, NUS.

1704.   *Buku Panduan Pernikahan dan Perceraian Singapura.* Singapore: Mahkamah Singapura dengan kerjasama Pejabat Pernikahan Orang-Orang Islam Singapura dan Persatuan Ulama dan Guru-guru Agama Islam Singapura, 2006. 167 pp.

1705.   Chua Boon Lan. "Muslim Law of Marriage (Syed Abdullah Al-Shatiri v. Shariffa Salmah)". *Malaya Law Review* 1, no. 2 (1959): 362–64. ISEAS, NLB, NUS.

1706.   "Divorces and Annulments by Ethnic Group of Couple". In *Yearbook of Statistics, Singapore, 2015*, p. 41. Singapore: Department of Statistics, 2015. ISEAS, NLB, NTU, NTUNIE, NUS. Available at <http://www. singstat.gov.sg/docs/default-source/default-document-library/publications/ publications_and_papers/reference/yearbook_2015/yos2015.pdf>. (Statistics for 2008–14 from Syariah Court and Registry of Muslim Marriages).

1707.   "Divorces under the Administration of Muslim Law Act by Age Group and Sex of Divorcees, 1980–2014". In *Statistics on Marriages and Divorces, Singapore, 2014*, pp. 84–85. Singapore: Department of Statistics, 2015. NLB. Available at <http://www.singstat.gov.sg/docs/ default-source/default-document-library/publications/publications_and_ papers/marriages_and_divorces/smd2014.pdf>.

1708.   "Divorces under the Administration of Muslim Law Act by Duration of Marriage, 1980–2014". In *Statistics on Marriages and Divorces, Singapore, 2014*, p. 86. Singapore: Department of Statistics, 2015. NLB. Available at <http://www.singstat.gov.sg/docs/default-source/default-document-library/ publications/publications_and_papers/marriages_and_divorces/smd2014. pdf>.

1709.   Djamour, Judith. *The Muslim Matrimonial Court in Singapore*. London: Oxford University Press, 1966. 189 pp. ISEAS, NLB, NTUNIE, NUS.

1710.   Enon Mansor, Fatimah Eunos, and Osman Sidek. *Tranquil Hearts: A Guide to Marriage*. Singapore: Majlis Ugama Islam Singapura, The Muslim Converts' Association of Singapore, 1998. 270 pp. ISEAS, NLB.

1711.   Habibi, Syed Ahmad Moinuddin. "Islamic Divorce as a Socio-Legal Institution". PhD dissertation, Faculty of Law, University of Singapore, 1970. 267 pp. NUS.

1712.   Hairani Saban Hardjoe. "Hukum Faraid and the Application of AMLA as 'The Statutory Adjunct of Muslim Law in Singapore': Legal Reflection on the Case of Mohamed Ismail Bin Ibrahim v Mohd Taha Bin Ibrahim". *The Singapore Law Gazette* (October 2006): 25–26, 28–35. NLB, NUS.

1713.   Hairani Saban Hardjoe. "'Letter of Wishes' and Consent in the Muslim Estate — Validation Process". *The Singapore Law Gazette* (June 2007): 18–24. NLB, NUS.

1714.   Halijah Mohamad. "Tackling of the Problem of Early Marriages and Divorce". *Karyawan: Professionals for the Community* 9, issue 2 (January 2009): 21–23. ISEAS, NLB, NTUNIE, NUS.

1715.   Hooker, M.B. (Michael Barry). "Problems in Malay Law: A Comment on (Zainoon V. Mohamed Zain [1981] 2 MLJ III)". *Malayan Law Journal* 1 (April 1982): xcvii–ix. NLB, NTUNIE, NUS.

1716.   Hooker, M.B. (Michael Barry). "Qadi Jurisdiction in Contemporary Malaysia and Singapore". In *Public Law in Contemporary Malaysia*, edited by Wu Min Aun. Petaling Jaya: Longman, 1999. ISEAS, NLB, NUS.

1717.   Hooker, M.B. (Michael Barry). "The Straits Settlements and Singapore". In *Islamic Law in South-East Asia*. Singapore: Oxford University Press, 1984. ISEAS, NLB, NUS.

1718.   "Inter-Ethnic Divorces under the Administration of Muslim Law Act by Age Group of Male and Female Divorcees, 2014". In *Statistics on Marriages and Divorces, Singapore, 2014*, p. 89. Singapore: Department of Statistics, 2015. NLB. Available at <http://www.singstat.gov.sg/docs/default-source/default-document-library/publications/publications_and_papers/marriages_and_divorces/smd2014.pdf>.

1719.   "Inter-Ethnic Divorces under the Administration of Muslim Law Act by Ethnic Group of Male and Female Divorcees, 2014". In *Statistics on Marriages and Divorces, Singapore, 2014*, p. 89. Singapore: Department of Statistics, 2015. NLB. Available at <http://www.singstat.gov.sg/docs/default-source/default-document-library/publications/publications_and_papers/marriages_and_divorces/smd2014.pdf>.

1720.   Kassim, Murgiana. "Problems of Polygamy and Divorce in Singapore". *Law Times* 2, no. 2 (1966): 13–14. NLB, NUS.

1721.   Majlis Ugama Islam Singapura. Jawatankuasa Fatwa. *Kumpulan Fatwa 1*. Singapore: Majlis Ugama Islam Singapura, 1987. 40 pp. NLB, NUS.

1722.   Majlis Ugama Islam Singapura. Jawatankuasa Fatwa. *Kumpulan Fatwa 2*. Singapore: Majlis Ugama Islam Singapura, 1991. 41 pp. NLB, NUS.

1723. Majlis Ugama Islam Singapura. Jawatankuasa Fatwa. *Kumpulan Fatwa 3.* Singapore: Majlis Ugama Islam Singapura, 1998. 41 pp. NLB.

1724. Marlena Samsan. "Hak-Hak Wanita Selepas Perceraian Menurut Mazhab Shafi'i". *Jurnal Dakwah* 2 (2011): 52–108. NLB.

1725. Mohamed Fatris Bakaram. "Theories of Iftā' in Islamic Law with Special Reference to the Shāfi'ī School of Law and Their Application in Contemporary Singapore". PhD dissertation, University of Birmingham, 2010.

1726. Muhammad Haniff Hassan and Sharifah Thuraiya Su'ad Ahmad Alhabshi. "The Training, Appointment, and Supervision of Islamic Judges in Singapore". *Pacific Rim Law & Policy Journal* 21, no. 1 (2012): 189–214. NTUNIE, NUS.

1727. Muhammad Muzammil Muhammad. *The Shariah Court and Its Shortcomings in the Administration of Muslim Law in Singapore.* [S.1.: s.n., 198–?]. 10 pp. NUS.

1728. "Muslim Marriage and Divorce in Singapore". *World Muslim League Magazine* 3, no. 9 (1966): 18–26; 3, no. 10 (1966): 4–14. NLB, NUS.

1729. Nik Hasyila Nik Ibrahim "The Training, Appointment, and Supervision of Islamic Lawyers in Singapore". *Pacific Rim Law & Policy Journal* 21, no. 1 (2012): 215–22. NTUNIE, NUS.

1730. Noor Aisha Abdul Rahman. "The Syariah Court and the Administration of the Muslim Law on Divorce in Singapore". PhD dissertation, National University of Singapore, 2000. 387 pp. NUS.

1731. Noor Aisha Abdul Rahman. "Traditionalism and Its Impact on the Administration of Justice: The Case of the Syariah Court of Singapore". *Inter-Asia Cultural Studies* 5, no. 3 (December 2004): 415–32. NTUNIE, NUS.

1732. Noor Mohamed Marican. "Islamic Law in a Secular Society". Paper presented at a Regional Islamic Convention, arranged by the Islamic Centre, Jamiyah Singapore, 24–27 April 1986. 44 pp. ISEAS, NUS.

1733. Pasuni Maulan. "Education and Training of Shariah Judges and Lawyers in Singapore". Paper presented at a 5th SEASA Conference, Singapore: the Education and Training of Shariah Judges and Lawyers. Organized by Majlis Ugama Islam Singapura and held at the

Auditorium, Islamic Centre, Singapore, February 26–28, 1988/Rejab 8–10, 1408. 23 pp. ISEAS, NLB, NTUNIE. Also published under the same title in: *Fajar Islam* 1, no. 1 (1988): 33–44. ISEAS, NLB, NUS.

1734. "Recognition of Muslim Law in the Straits Settlements". *Malayan Law Journal* 11 (1942): i–ii; 12 (1946): lxxxvii–iii. NLB, NTUNIE, NUS.

1735. Sadali Rasban. *Baitulmal Dalam Sistem Fara'id: Renungan & Semakan Semula*. Singapore: HTHT Advisory Services Pte. Ltd., 2015. 191 pp. NLB.

1736. Sadali Rasban. *Dying Intestate*. Singapore: HTHT Advisory Services, 2012. 49 pp. NLB.

1737. Sadali Rasban. *Hibah al Ruqba & Joint Tenancy in Shari'ah Law*. Singapore: HTHT Advisory Services, Pustaka Nasional, 2010. 139 pp. NLB, NUS. Also published in Malay under the title: *Hibah al Ruqba dan Pemilikan Bersama (Joint Tenancy) dalam Hukum Syariah*. Singapore: HTHT Advisory Services, 2010. 160 pp. NLB, NUS.

1738. Sadali Rasban. *Isu-Isu Harta Pusaka*. Singapore: HTHT Advisory Services, 2012. 52 pp. NLB, NUS.

1739. Sadali Rasban. *Joint Tenancy — The Shariah Perspectives*. Singapore: HTHT Advisory Services, 2010. 27 pp. NLB.

1740. Sadali Rasban. "Muslims and Financial Planning". *Karyawan: Professionals for the Community* 9, issue 2 (January 2009): 16–17. ISEAS, NLB, NTUNIE, NUS.

1741. Sadali Rasban. *Nuzriah*. Singapore: HTHT Advisory Services, 2012. 62 pp. NLB.

1742. Sadali Rasban and Ismail Mohd. @ Abu Hassan. *Estate Planning for Muslims*. Singapore: HTHT Advisory Services, 2010. 222 pp. NLB. Previous ed. published under the same title: Singapore: HTHT Advisory Services Pte. Ltd., 2004. 191 pp. NUS.

1743. Sadali Rasban and Ismail Mohd. @ Abu Hassan. *Muslim Law in Wealth and Estate Transfer*. Singapore: HTHT Advisory Services, 2010. 162 pp. NUS.

1744. Sadali Rasban and Ismail Mohd. @ Abu Hassan. *Nazar (Vow) & Hibah (Gift)*. Singapore: HTHT Advisory Services, Pustaka Nasional, 2010. 117 pp. NLB, NUS.

1745.   "Seminar on Marriage and Divorce in Islam & the Civil Law". Jointly organized by the Muslim Converts' Association of Singapore & the Young Women Muslim Association at Plaza Hotel, 31 August–1 September 1985. 1 vol. (various foliations). NUS.

1746.   Shamsiah Abdul Karim. "Contemporary Shari'a Compliance Structuring for the Development and Management of Waqf Assets in Singapore". *Kyoto Bulletin of Islamic Area Studies* (March 2010): 4–64.

1747.   "Shariah Court, Singapore". *Malayan Law Journal* 24 (December 1958): lxxv. NLB, NTUNIE, NUS.

1748.   Shunmugam, Priscilla Twu-Jyen. "British Malaya 1786–1942: The Influence of Colonialism on Malay Law". Assignment (LLB dissertation), Faculty of Law, National University of Singapore, 2006. 86 pp. NUS.

1749.   Singapore. Syariah Cour:. *Singapore Syariah Appeals Reports*. Singapore: Academy Pub., 2012. 5 vol. + 1 suppl. NLB, NUS.

1750.   Siraj, Mehrun. "Ancillary Orders on Muslim Divorce: The Practice of the Shariah Court in Singapore". *Malaya Law Review* 8, no. 1 (1966): 86–94. NLB, NUS.

1751.   Siraj, Mehrun. "Conciliation Procedures in Divorce Proceedings". *Malaya Law Review* 7 (1965): 314–25. NLB, NUS.

1752.   Siraj, Mehrun. "The Control of Polygamy". *Malaya Law Review* 6 (1964): 378–405. NLB, NUS.

1753.   Siraj, Mehrun. "Effective Administration (of the Shariah Court) & Social Change". *Intisari* 2, no. 2 (1964): 19–22. ISEAS, NLB, NUS.

1754.   Siraj, Mehrun. "Enticement of Minor and the Validity of Her Marriage Under Muslim Law". *Malaya Law Review* 5, no. 2 (1963): 392–97. NLB, NUS.

1755.   Siraj, Mehrun. "The Shariah Court of Singapore and Its Control of the Divorce Rate". *Malaya Law Review* 5, no. 1 (1963): 148–59. NLB, NUS.

1756.   Siraj, Mehrun. "The Shariah Court, Singapore". *World Muslim League Magazine* 1, no. 1 (1953): 31–36. NLB, NUS.

1757.   Suhaimi Mustar. "Fatwa". *Nadi* 1 (June 2005): 22. NLB, NUS.

1758. Suhaimi Salleh. *Isu-isu Wasiat, Faraid & Harta Pusaka di Singapura.* Singapore: Barakah Capital Planners, 2012. 240 pp. NLB.

1759. Suraya Mohamed Suppien. "The Syariah Court of Singapore: A Study of Its Role as an Institution in the Muslim Community". Research exercise, Department of Malay Studies, National University of Singapore, 1993. 60 pp. NUS.

1760. Tan Su Tiak and Edmund Leow. "The Islamic Regime for Succession and Inheritance – A Quick Introduction". *Singapore Law Gazette* (March 2004): 28–29. NLB, NUS.

1761. Taylor, E.N. "Mohammedan Divorce by Khula". *JMBRAS* 21, pt. 2 (September 1948): 3–39. ISEAS, NLB, NTUNIE, NUS.

LITERATURE

- *General Works*
- *Folklore, Classical and Children's Literature*
- *Malay Literature*

General Works

1762. A. Rahman Hanafiah (Abdul Rahman Hanafiah) (Mana Sikana), and Anuar Othman. *Jatuh ke Laut Menjadi Pulau: Pemikiran Sastera Malaysia & Singapura*. Singapore: Anuar Othman & Associates Media Enterprise, 2003. 451 pp. NLB, NTUNIE.

1763. *Dialog Selatan 1 (1:1992 Johor Bahru)*. Kuala Lumpur: Dewan Bahasa dan Pustaka, 1995. 200 pp. ISEAS, NLB, NUS.

1764. *Dialog Selatan III Singapura-Johor-Riau (3:2000)*. Singapore: ASAS 50, 2000. 1 vol. (various pagings). NLB.

1765. Hadijah Rahmat, ed. *Yang Terukir: Bahasa dan Persuratan Melayu Sempena 50 Tahun Kemerdekaan Singapura*. Singapore: Majlis Bahasa Melayu Singapura, 2015. 252 pp. NLB.

1766. Kong, Lily. "Environmental Cognition: The Malay World in Colonial Fiction". Academic exercise, Department of Geography, National University of Singapore, 1985. 101 pp. NUS.

1767. Liaw Yock Fang. "Singapore Literature". In *Encyclopedia of World Literature in the 20th Century*, edited by Leonard Klein. New York: Frederick Ungar Publishing Co., 1984. NLB, NTUNIE, NUS.

1768. *Pertemuan Kedua: Antologi Cerpen Penulis-penulis Singapura-Johor-Riau*. Diselenggarakan oleh Suratman Markasan. Kuala Lumpur: Dewan Bahasa dan Pustaka, 1995. 366 pp. NLB, NUS.

1769. Tan Ee Sze. "Markers of Regional & Ethnic Identity in Dialogue in Singaporean Fiction". Academic exercise, Department of English Language & Literature, National University of Singapore, 1987. 52 pp. NUS.

1770. Thurairasasingam, Constance. "A Historical Survey of Western Perceptions of Asian Characters in Adult Fiction Set in Malaya and Singapore". B.A. (Hons) dissertation, Monash University, 1985. 84 pp. NLB.

1771. Zawiyah Yahya. "Portrayal of the Malay in Novels in English by Malaysian and Singapore Writers". *Sari* 4, no. 1 (January 1986): 81–87. ISEAS, NLB, NTUNIE, NUS. Also published in Malay under the title: "Watak Melayu Dalam Novel Inggeris Tempatan". *Dewan Sastera* 19, no. 11 (November 1989): 90–96. NLB, NTUNIE, NUS.

Folklore, Classical and Children's Literature

1772. Azhar Ibrahim Alwee. "Singapura dalam Sastera Sejarah Melayu". Research exercise, Department of Malay Studies, National University of Singapore, 1996. 38 pp. NUS.

1773. Braginskii, V.I. *The System of Classical Malay Literature*. Working Papers 11. Leiden: KITLV Press, 1993. 131 pp. ISEAS, NLB, NTUNIE, NUS.

1774. Djamal Tukimin. *Pantun dalam Sejarah Perkembangan Pemikiran Melayu di Singapura Moden: Kajian & Himpunan*. Bangi: Institut Alam dan Tamadun Melayu, 2011. 517 pp. NLB.

1775. Hadijah Rahmat. *In Search of Modernity: A Study of the Concepts of Literature, Authorship and Notions of Self in "Traditional" Malay Literature*. Kuala Lumpur: Academy of Malay Studies, University of Malaya, 2001. 399 pp. ISEAS, NLB, NTUNIE, NUS.

1776. Hadijah Rahmat. *Peranan dan Perkembangan Sastera Kanak-kanak*. Kuala Lumpur: Dewan Bahasa dan Pustaka, 2006. 209 pp. NTUNIE.

1777. Hadijah Rahmat. "Suatu Kajian Mengenai Perkembangan Sastera Kanak-Kanak dalam Bahasa Melayu". *Singapore Book World* 21 (1990/91): 37–48. NLB, NUS.

1778. Hidayah Amin. *The Mango Tree*. Illustrated by Idris Ali. Singapore: Helang Books, 2013. 32 pp. NLB.

1779. Liaw Yock Fang. *Sejarah Kesusastraan Melayu Klasik*. Jakarta: Yayasan Pustaka Obor Indonesia, 2011. 633 pp. NLB. Also published in Indonesian under the same title: Jakarta: Erlangga, 1991–93. 2 vols. ISEAS, NLB. Previous ed. published under the same title: Singapore: Pustaka Nasional, 1975. 355 pp. NTUNIE, NUS. Also published in English under the title: *A History of Classical Malay Literature*. Translators, Razif Bahari and Harry Aveling. Singapore: Institute of Southeast Asian Studies, 2013. 505 pp. ISEAS, NLB, NTUNIE, NUS.

1780. Ma, Mimira Min. "A Comparative Study of Stories Known to Malay and Chinese Children in Singapore at the Present Time". Research exercise, Department of Social Studies, University of Malaya, Singapore 1959. 152 pp.

1781. Tol, Roger. "The Persistent Misinterpretation of the Swordfish Attack on Singapore". *Indonesia and the Malay World* 35, no. 102 (July 2007): 247–52. ISEAS, NLB, NTUNIE.

Malay Literature

1782. A.M. Thani, ed *Esei Sastera ASAS 50*. Kuala Lumpur: Dewan Bahasa dan Pustaka, 1981. 216 pp. ISEAS, NLB, NTUNIE, NUS.

1783. A. Rahman Hanafiah (Abdul Rahman Hanafiah) (Mana Sikana). *Sastera Singapura dan Malaysia di Era Pascamoden*. Singapore: Persama Enterprise, 2003. 580 pp. NLB, NTUNIE.

1784. A. Rahman Hanafiah (Abdul Rahman Hanafiah) (Mana Sikana). "Sastera Singapura Mutakhir: Satu Pengamatan Awal". Paper presented at a Persidangan Antarabangsa Bahasa, Sastera dan Kebudayaan Melayu ke 2, anjuran Jabatan Bahasa dan Kebudayaan Melayu, Kumpulan Akademik Bahasa dan Kebudayaan Asia, Institut Pendidikan Nasional, Universiti Teknologi Nanyang, Singapura, 1–3 September 2002. 25 pp. ISEAS, NLB.

1785. A. Rahman Hanafiah (Abdul Rahman Hanafiah) (Mana Sikana). *Teori dan kritikan sastera Malaysia dan Singapura*. [Malaysia]: Pustaka Karya, 2005. 316 pp. NLB, NTUNIE.

1786. A. Wahab Ali. "Kesusasteraan Melayu Tahun-Tahun Enampuluhan". *Dewan Sastera* 3, no. 10 (October 1973): 43–47; 3, no. 11 (November 1973): 56–60. NLB, NTUNIE, NUS.

1787. Abdul Hamid Ahmad. "Cerpen-Cerpen Melayu dalam Pemerintahan Jepun". *Mastika* 29, no. 2 (February 1969): 46–50. ISEAS, NUS.

1788. Ahmad Mashadi. "Kajian Tema-Tema Sajak-Sajak Melayu Singapura yang diterbitkan di Berita Minggu dari Januari 1989 hingga Oktober 1990". Academic exercise, Department of Malay Studies, National University of Singapore, 1991. 63 pp. NUS.

1789. Aliman Hassan. *Sekadar Pengisi Ruang: Bicara Peribahasa, Pantun Pusaka dan Puisi Semasa tentang Kisah dan Telatah Manusia*. Singapura ASAS 50, 1993. 330 pp. ISEAS, NLB, NUS.

1790. *Anugerah Persuratan 2003: Kumpulan Karya dan Ulasan Juri*. Penyelenggara Mohamed Pitchay Gani Mohamed Abdul Aziz. Singapore: Majlis Bahasa Melayu Singapura, 2003. 285 pp. NLB, NTUNIE, NUS.

1791. *Anugerah Persuratan 2005: Kumpulan Karya & Ulasan Juri.* Penyelenggara Mohamed Pitchay Gani Mohamed Abdul Aziz. Singapore: Majlis Bahasa Melayu Singapura, 2005. 277 pp. NLB, NTUNIE, NUS.

1792. *Anugerah Persuratan 2011: Kumpulan Karya & Ulasan Juri.* Penyelaras Siti Hafizah Ismail. Edited by Abdullah Othman, Azhar Ibrahim Alwee, and Juffri Supa'at. Singapore: Darul Andalus dengan kerjasama Majlis Bahasa Melayu Singapura, 2013. 205 pp. NLB.

1793. Arena Wati, comp. *Cerpen Zaman Jepun: Satu Kajian.* Kuala Lumpur: Pustaka Antara, 1980. 205 pp. NLB, NUS.

1794. Aveling, Harry. *Contemporary Literary Theory and the Study of Malay Literature.* Seminar Papers, no. 10. Singapore: Department of Malay Studies, NUS, [1993?]. 31 pp. ISEAS, NLB, NTUNIE.

1795. Azhar Ibrahim Alwee. "In the Pursuit of Spirituality: Notion of the Pious in Contemporary Singapore Malay Literature". *The Arts* 13 (April/May 2004): 21–25. NLB.

1796. Azhar Ibrahim Alwee. "Suratman Markasan: Malay Literature and Social Memory". *BiblioAsia* 10, no. 1 (April–June 2014): 28–33. NLB.

1797. Azizah Juma'at. "Kesusasteraan Melayu Singapura: Perkembangan dan Kesinambungan". Research exercise, Department of Malay Studies, National University of Singapore, 1996. 52 pp. NUS.

1798. Banks, David J. *From Class to Culture: Social Conscience in Malay Novels since Independence.* New Haven, Conn.: Yale University Southeast Asia Studies, 1987. 200 pp. ISEAS, NLB, NTUNIE, NUS.

1799. Bengkel "ASAS 50 dan Sastera Melayu Moden" (1980: Kuala Lumpur). *Warisan ASAS 50: Kumpulan Kertas Kerja, Ceramah dan Bengkel Asas 50 dan Sastera Melayu Moden.* Kuala Lumpur: Dewan Bahasa dan Pustaka, 1981. 87 pp. NLB, NTUNIE, NUS.

1800. Djamal Tukimin and ASAS '50. *Sejarah Tidak Pernah Luka Kita yang Berduka: Landskap Sastera Melayu Singapura Pasca Angkatan 50.* Singapore: Pustaka Nasional Pte. Ltd., 2008. 329 pp. NLB, NTUNIE, NUS.

1801. Hadijah Rahmat. *Sastera & Manusia Melayu Baru: Kumpulan Esei & Wawancara.* Singapore: Persatuan Wartawan Melayu Singapura, 1998. 333 pp. NLB, NTUNIE.

1802. Hadijah Rahmat. "Singapura dan Persuratan Baru". In *Aksara: Menjejaki Tulisan Melayu*, edited by Juffri Supaat and Nazeerah Gopaul. Singapore: National Library Board, 2009. NLB, NTUNIE.

1803. Hadijah Rahmat, Dewani Abbas, and Azhar Ibrahim Alwee, eds. *Citra Minda: Antologi Esei*. Singapore: Majlis Bahasa Melayu Singapura, 2003. 285 pp. NLB, NTUNIE.

1804. Hashim Awang. "Tulisan Tentang Cerpen Melayu Selepas Perang: Satu Kritikal Survey". *Dewan Bahasa* 13, no. 8 (August 1969): 351–65. NLB, NUS.

1805. Isa Kamari. *Potret Puisi Melayu Singapura*. Singapore: The Malay Heritage Foundation and Select Publishing, 2014. 392 pp. NLB, NUS, NTUNIE.

1806. Ismail Hussein. *Pengarang-Pengarang Melayu di-Singapura Selepas Perang Dunia II (1945–1958)*. Singapore: Jabatan Pengajian Melayu Universiti Malaya, 1959. 55 pp. NLB.

1807. Ismail Hussein. "Singapura Sebagai Pusat Kesusasteraan Melayu Selepas Perang". *Dewan Bahasa* 3, no. 1 (November 1959): 539–56. NLB, NUS.

1808. Koster, G.L. "A Voyage to Freedom: Imagining the Portuguese in Harun Aminurrashid's Historical Novel Panglima Awang". *Indonesia and the Malay World* 37, no. 109 (November 2009): 375–96. ISEAS, NLB, NTUNIE, NUS.

1809. Li Chuan Siu. *Ikhtisar Sejarah Kesusasteraan Melayu Baru, 1830–1945*. Kuala Lumpur: Pustaka Antara, 1966. 246 pp. ISEAS, NLB, NUS.

1810. Li Chuan Siu. *Ikhtisar Sejarah Pergerakan dan Kesusasteraan Melayu Modern 1945-1965*. Kuala Lumpur: Penerbitan Pustaka Antara, 1967. 552 pp. NLB, NTUNIE, NUS.

1811. Liaw Yock Fang. "Minority Literature among the Ethnic Malays". *Solidarity* 101 (1984): 33–36. ISEAS, NUS.

1812. Lie T.S. "A Bird's-Eye View of the Development of Modern Malay Literature (1921–1941)". *Review of Indonesian and Malayan Affairs* 2, no. 2 (April–June 1968): 11–27; 2, no. 3 (July–September 1968): 1–5. ISEAS, NLB.

1813.   Malayan Writers' Conference (1ˢᵗ: 1962: Singapore). *Report of Malayan Writers' Conference, Singapore, 16th–18th March 1962*. Singapore: Dewan Bahasa dan Kebudayaan Kebangsaan, 1962. 207 pp. ISEAS, NTUNIE, NUS. Also published in Malay under the title: *Penyata Mushawarah Penulis-Penulis Malaya di Singapura*. Singapore: Dewan Bahasa dan Kebudayaan Kebangsaan, 1963. 262 pp. NLB, NUS.

1814.   Masuri S.N. *Dalam Merenung Dalam: Kumpulan Esei & Kritikan 1977–2005*. Editor, Mohamed Pitchay Gani Bin Mohamed Abdul Aziz. Singapore: Angkatan Sasterawan '50, 2006. 245 pp. NLB, NTUNIE, NUS.

1815.   Masuri S.N. "The Development of Malay Fiction in Singapore". In *Fictions of Singapore*, edited by Edwin Thumboo. [S.1.]: ASEAN Committee on Culture and Information, 1990. ISEAS, NLB, NTUNIE, NUS.

1816.   Masuri S.N. *Penulis dengan Ketukangannya*. Seminar Papers, no. 1/2. Singapore: Department of Malay Studies, National University of Singapore, 1991. 9 pp. ISEAS, NLB, NUS.

1817.   Mohamed Pitchay Gani Mohamed Abdul Aziz. "Psikologi Melayu Singapura dalam Karya Kreatif". In *Di Bawah Langit Tanah Pertiwi: Koleksi Cerpen dan Sajak Sempena Ulang Tahun Republik Singapura Ke 50*. Singapore: Angkatan Sasterawan '50, 2015. NLB.

1818.   Mohamed Pitchay Gani Mohamed Abdul Aziz, ed. *Dari Gerhana ke Puncak Purnama: Warna Suasana Kesusasteraan Melayu Pasca 1965*. Singapore: Angkatan Sasterawan '50, 2011. 25 pp. NLB, NTUNIE, NUS.

1819.   Mohamed Pitchay Gani Mohamed Abdul Aziz, ed. *Pertemuan Sasterawan Nusantara XII: Sastera Melayu Warisan Jati Diri dan Jagat*. Singapore: Angkatan Sasterawan '50, National Library Board, 2003. 400 pp. NLB, NTUNIE, NUS.

1820.   Mohd. Aidil Subhan Mohd. Sulor. "Cerpen Remaja Melayu Singapura: Satu Pengamatan Stilistik". Paper presented at a Persidangan Antarabangsa Bahasa, Sastera dan Kebudayaan Melayu ke 2, anjuran Jabatan Bahasa dan Kebudayaan Melayu, Kumpulan Akademik Bahasa dan Kebudayaan Asia, Institut Pendidikan Nasional, Universiti Teknologi Nanyang, Singapura, 1–3 September 2002. 15 pp. ISEAS, NLB.

1821.   Mohd. Thani Ahmad. "Penghasilan Cerpen-Cerpen Melayu dalam Tahun-Tahun 60-an". *Devan Sastera* (February 1974): 57–60; (March 1974): 55–60. NLB, NTUNIE, NUS.

1822.   Muhammad Arif Ahmad and Mohd Raman Daud. "Literary Pursuits, Pantuns & Folklore". In *Malay Heritage of Singapore*, edited by Aileen T. Lau and Bernhard Platzdasch. Singapore: Suntree Media in association with Malay Heritage Foundation, 2010. ISEAS, NLB, NTUNIE, NUS.

1823.   Mukhlis Abu Bakar and Hadijah Rahmat, eds. *Seminar Masuri S. N.: Kumpulan Kertas Kerja.* Singapore: Jabatan Bahasa dan Kebudayaan Melayu, Kumpulan Akademik Bahasa dan Kebudayaan Asia, Institut Pendidikan Nasional, Universiti Teknologi Nanyang, 2008. 401 pp. NLB, NTUNIE.

1824.   Mushawarah Penulis-Penulis Malaya (1962: Singapura). *Pembukaan Rasmi oleh Paduka Yang Mulia Yang di-Pertuan Negara, Singapura, Inche Yusuf bin Ishak pada Hari Juma'at 16hb March 1962, di Panggong Victoria.* Di selenggarakan oleh Dewan Bahasa dan Pustaka, Kuala Lumpur. Singapore: Dewan Bahasa dan Kebudayaan Kebangsaan, 1962. 1 vol. NLB.

1825.   Noor S.I. (Ismail Haji Omar). *Sastera Melayu Singapura: Penulis dan Ketukangannya: Satu Pengalaman.* Seminar Papers, no. 1/2. Singapore: Department of Malay Studies, National University of Singapore, 1990. 13 pp. ISEAS, NLB, NUS.

1826.   Othman Puteh. *Cerpen Melayu Selepas Perang Dunia Kedua: Satu Analisa tentang Pemikiran dan Struktur.* Kuala Lumpur: Dewan Bahasa dan Pustaka, 1983. 264 pp. NLB, NTUNIE, NUS.

1827.   Perkampungan Sastra (1973: Singapura). Angkatan Sasterawan '50 Menganjurkan Perkampungan Sastra '73, Sabtu 4hb-Ahad 5hb Ogos 1973 di Khemah Percutian Tanah Merah. Singapore: Angkatan Sasterawan '50, 1973. 100 pp. ISEAS, NLB, NUS.

1828.   Rasiah Halil. "Post-War Malay Novelists: An Analysis of Their Awareness and Approach to Societal Problems". MA dissertation, Department of Malay Studies, University of Singapore, 1985. 177 pp. NUS.

1829.   S. Markasan (Suratman Markasan). "Cerpen Melayu Singapura Mutakhir: Ke Mana Arahnya?" Kertas kerja yang dibentang dalam Pertemuan Penulis Singapura, 9–10 Ogos 1981. NUS.

1830. S. Markasan (Suratman Markasan). "Cerpen Melayu Singapura Mutakhir Mencari Warna". Kertas kerja yang dibentang di Simposium Sastra Tumasik-Lingga (Singapura–Riau), 10 September 1985, Pekan Baru. NUS. Also published under the same title in: *Dewan Sastera* 16, no. 3 (March 1986): 57–62. NLB, NTUNIE, NUS.

1831. S. Markasan (Suratman Markasan). "Contemporary Singapore Malay Literature as Seen Through Two Streams of Social Critique". *Malay Literature* 4, no. 1 (1991): 1–11. NLB.

1832. S. Markasan (Suratman Markasan). "Kedudukan Sastera Melayu Singapura Mutakhir". Kertas Kerja yang dibentang dalam Pertemuan Sasterawan Nusantara IV, Negara Brunei Darussalam, 9–12 Disember 1985. NUS.

1833. S. Markasan (Suratman Markasan). *Kembali ke Akar Melayu, Kembali ke Akar Islam. Jilid 3, Kumpulan Kertas Kerja 1986–2012.* Editor, Nooraman Tukisan. Singapore: Darul Andalus, 2013. 2052 pp. NLB.

1834. S. Markasan (Suratman Markasan). *Kembali ke Akar Melayu, Kembali ke Akar Islam. Jilid 4, Kumpulan Ucapan & Temu Ramah 1987–2012.* Editor, Nooraman Tukisan. Singapore: Darul Andalus, 2013. 905 pp. NLB.

1835. S. Markasan (Suratman Markasan). "Kesusasteraan Melayu di Singapura Dulu dan Masa Depan". Kertas kerja yang dibentang dalam Persidangan Penulis-Penulis ASEAN, Kuala Lumpur, 1–3 Disember 1977. 33 pp. ISEAS, NTUNIE, NUS.

1836. S. Markasan (Suratman Markasan). "Kritik Sastra di Singapura". Kertas kerja yang dibentang dalam Temu Kritikus dan Sastrawan, Jakarta, anjuran bersama Ditjen Kebudayaan DEPDIKBUD, dan Dewan Kesenian Jakarta, 12–16 Disember 1984. NUS.

1837. S. Markasan (Suratman Markasan). "Puisi Melayu Singapura dalam Gelombang Tiga Zaman". *Dewan Sastera* 20, no. 1 (January 1990): 41–47. NLB, NTUNIE, NUS.

1838. S. Markasan (Suratman Markasan). "Sastera Melayu dalam Masyarakat Singapura". Kertas kerja yang dibentang dalam Pertemuan Sasterawan Nusantara, Jakarta, 11–14 Disember 1979. NUS. Also published under the same title in: *Singapore Book World* 14 (1983): 27–32. ISEAS, NLB, NTUNIE, NUS.

1839. S. Markasan (Suratman Markasan). "Sastera Melayu Singapura Mutakhir dalam Dua Jalur Kritik Sosial". Kerta kerja yang dibentang di Hari Sastera, di Pulau Pinang, 28 November–1 Disember 1985. 12 pp. ISEAS.

1840. *Sasterawan.* Singapore: Angkatan Sasterawan '50 dengan kerjasama Island Society, 1971–. ISEAS, NLB, NUS.

1841. *Sedekad Hadiah Sastera, 1973–83.* Singapore: Majlis Pusat Pertubuhan-Pertubuhan Budaya Melayu Singapura, 1983. 20 pp. NLB, NUS.

1842. Shamsul Amri Baharudin. "Ilmu Kolonial Raffles: Pengasas Ilmu". *Dewan Budaya* (July 2005): 42–44. ISEAS, NLB, NTUNIE, NUS.

1843. Tan Chin Kwang. "Latar Belakang Intelektuel Penulis2 Cherpen Melayu Sa-lepas Perang Dunia Kedua (1946–1970)". MA dissertation, Department of Malay Studies, University of Singapore. 1972. 266 pp. NUS.

1844. Tan Chin Kwang. "Post-War Malay Fiction and Its Critics and Scholars: A Study in the Problems of Intellectualism and Literary Development". PhD dissertation, Department of Malay Studies, University of Singapore, 1978. 376 pp. NUS.

1845. Tham Seong Chee. "Literary Response and the Social Process: An Analysis of Cultural and Political Beliefs Among Malay Writers". In *Essays on Literature and Society in Southeast Asia: Political and Sociological Interpretation*, edited by Tham Seong Chee. Singapore: Singapore University Press, 1981. ISEAS, NLB, NTU, NTUNIE, NUS. Also published under the same title in: *Southeast Asian Journal of Social Science* 3, no. 1 (1975): 85–106. ISEAS, NLB, NTU, NTUNIE, NUS.

1846. Tham Seong Chee. "Modernization and Value Perception among Malay Writers". *Commentary* 2, no. 1 (1976): 36–47. ISEAS, NLB, NTUNIE, NUS.

1847. Winstedt, R.O. "A History of Malay Literature". *JMBRAS* 17, pt. 3 (1939): 1–243. ISEAS, NLB, NTUNIE, NUS.

1848. Yazid Hussein et al., comps. *Pragmatik Sastera dalam Falsafah Pragmatisme.* Singapore: Unit Bahasa Melayu, Maktab Rendah Pioneer, 2013. 95 pp. NLB.

1849. Za'aba. "Modern Development: A History of Malay Literature". *JMBRAS* 18, pt. 3 (1940): 142–62. ISEAS, NLB, NTUNIE, NUS.

POLITICS

- *Politics and Government*
- *Leadership*
- *Political Participation*
- *National Integration*
- *Defence and Security*
- *Internationalization and International Relations*

Politics and Government

1850. Abdul Halim Kader. *Malay Muslim Singaporeans: Where Do We Stand?* Singapore: Taman Bacaan Pemuda Pemudi Melayu Singapura, 2012. 254 pp. ISEAS, NLB, NTUNIE, NUS.

1851. Abdul Latiff Sahan. "Political Attitudes of the Malays: 1945–1953". Academic exercise, Department of History, University of Malaya, Singapore, 1959. 93 pp. NUS.

1852. Adibah Amin. "Singapura dan Manusia Tiga Dimensi". *Dewan Masyarakat* 26, no. 3 (March 1988): 30–31. ISEAS, NLB, NTUNIE, NUS.

1853. Ahmad Mattar. "All Singaporeans Share a Common Loyalty". *Speeches* 4, no. 9 (1981): 49–50. ISEAS, NLB, NTUNIE, NUS.

1854. Alfian Sa'at. "Political Integration and the Singapore Malay Community". *Focas: Forum on Contemporary Art & Society* 4 (2002): 385–93. ISEAS, NLB, NTUNIE, NUS.

1855. Aljunied, Syed Muhd Khairudin. "Hadhramis within Malay Activism: The Role of Al-Saqqaf(s) in the Post-War Singapore". In *The Hadhrami Diaspora in Southeast Asia: Identity Maintenance or Assimilation?*, edited by Ibrahim Abushouk Ahmed and Hassan Ahmed. Leiden: Boston: Brlll, 2009. ISEAS, NLB, NTUNIE, NUS.

1856. Aljunied, Syed Haroon Mohamed. "Social Background and Representation in the Higher Civil Service in Malaysia and Singapore". MEc dissertation, Universiti Malaya, 1974. 266 pp. NUS.

1857. Bedlington, Stanley. "Political Integration and the Singapore Malay Community". *Journal of the Historical Society* (1971): 47–54. ISEAS, NLB, NTU, NUS.

1858. Bedlington, Stanley. "The Singapore Malay Community: The Politics of State Integration". PhD dissertation, Cornell University, New York, 1974. 538 pp. ISEAS, NTUNIE, NUS.

1859. "Bringing the Races Together". *Asiaweek* 17, no. 32 (9 August 1991): 22–23. ISEAS, NLB, NTUNIE, NUS.

1860. Brown, David. "Ethnicity and Corporatism in Singapore". In *The State and Ethnic Politics in Southeast Asia*. London: Routledge, 1994. ISEAS, NLB, NTU, NTUNIE, NUS.

1861. Busch, Peter Alan. *Legitimacy and Ethnicity: A Case Study of Singapore.* Lexington, Mass.: Lexington Books, 1974. 157 pp. ISEAS, NLB, NTUNIE, NUS.

1862. Busch, Peter Alan. "Political Unity & Ethnic Diversity: A Case Study of Singapore". PhD dissertation, Yale University, 1972. Ann Arbor, Mich.: University Microfilms International, 1974. 438 pp. ISEAS, NTUNIE, NUS.

1863. Chan Heng Chee. *Singapore: The Politics of Survival, 1965–1967.* Singapore: Oxford University Press, 1971. 65 pp. ISEAS, NLB, NTU, NTUNIE, NUS.

1864. Chang Chak Yin. "Political Violence in Malaysia and Singapore". MA dissertation, University of Western Ontario, 1971. London: Central Microfilm Unit, Public Archives of Canada, 1971. 1 microfilm reel. NUS.

1865. Chua Beng Huat. "Singapore 1990: Celebrating the End of an Era". In *Southeast Asian Affairs 1991*, edited by Sharon Siddique and Ng Chee Yuen. Singapore: Institute of Southeast Asian Studies, 1991. ISEAS, NLB, NTU, NTUNIE, NUS.

1866. Clammer, John. "Minorities and Minority Policy in Singapore". *Southeast Asian Journal of Social Science* 16, no. 2 (1988): 96–110. ISEAS, NLB, NTU, NTUNIE, NUS.

1867. Goh Chok Tong. "Role of Malay Community Organisations in Nation-Building: [Speech at the Majlis Pusat 30th Anniversary Dinner, 30 Oct 99]". *Speeches* 23, no. 5 (September–October 1999): 1–6. ISEAS, NLB, NTU, NTUNIE, NUS.

1868. Hang Tuah Arshad. *Ilmu Politik Melayu.* Singapore: D. Moore, 1966. 204 pp. ISEAS, NLB, NUS.

1869. Hussin Mutalib. "Authoritarian Democracy and the Minority Muslim Polity in Singapore". In *Islam and Politics in Southeast Asia*, edited by Johan Saravanamuttu. London; New York: Routledge, 2010. ISEAS, NTU.

1870. Hussin Mutalib. "Dilemmas of a Minority Community in a Secular, Modern City-State: The Case of Singapore Muslims". *The Fount Journal* 1 (2000): 65. ISEAS, NLB, NUS.

1871. Hussin Mutalib. *Singapore's Elected Presidency and the Quest for Regime Dominance.* Singapore: Department of Political Science, National University of Singapore, 1994. 51 pp. ISEAS, NUS.

1872. Hussin Mutalib. *Singapore Malays: Being Ethnic Minority and Muslim in a Global City-state*. New York: Routledge, 2014. 204 pp. ISEAS, NLB, NTU, NTUNIE, NUS. Also published in Malay under the title: *Melayu Singapura: Sebagai Kaum Minoriti dan Muslim dalam Sebuah Negara Global*. Singapore: NUS Press; Kuala Lumpur: Strategic Information and Research Development Centre, 2015. 302 pp. NLB, NTUNIE, NUS.

1873. Hussin Mutalib. "The Singapore Minority Dilemma: Between Malay Persistence and State Resistance". *Asian Survey* 51, no. 6 (2011): 1156–71. ISEAS, NLB, NTU, NTUNIE, NUS.

1874. Ismail Pantek. "PM Melayu di Singapura?" *Karyawan: Professionals for the Community* 9, issue 2 (January 2009): 32–33. ISEAS, NLB, NTUNIE, NUS.

1875. Kamaludeen Mohamed Nasir, Alexius A. Pereira, and Bryan S. Turner. *Muslims in Singapore: Piety, Politics and Policies*. London; New York, NY: Routledge, 2010. 128 pp. ISEAS, NLB, NTU, NTUNIE, NUS.

1876. Law Kam-Yee. "Civic Disobedience of Malay Muslims in Post-September 11th Singapore". *Development* suppl. 46, no. 1 (March 2003): 107–11. ISEAS, NTUNIE, NUS.

1877. Lau Teik Soon. *Majority-Minority Situation in Singapore*. Singapore: Department of Political Science, University of Singapore, 1974. 18 pp. ISEAS, NLB, NUS.

1878. Lily Zubaidah Rahim. "A New Dawn in PAP-Malay Relations?" In *Impressions of the Goh Chok Tong Years in Singapore*, edited by Bridget Welsh et al. Singapore: NUS Press in collaboration between Lee Kuan Yew School of Public Policy, National University of Singapore and Institute of Policy Studies, 2009. ISEAS, NLB, NTU, NUS.

1879. Lily Zubaidah Rahim. "Political Representation of Malay Interests". In *The Singapore Dilemma: The Political and Educational Marginality of the Malay Community*. Kuala Lumpur: Oxford University Press, 1998. ISEAS, NLB, NTU, NTUNIE, NUS.

1880. Lily Zubaidah Rahim. *The Singapore Dilemma: The Political and Educational Marginality of the Malay Community*. New York: Oxford University Press, 1998. 380 pp. ISEAS, NLB, NTU, NTUNIE, NUS. Also published in Malay under the title: *Dilema Singapura: Peminggiran*

Politik dan Pelajaran Masyarakat Melayu. Penterjemah, Yunus Ali. Kuala Lumpur: Institut Terjemahan Negara Malaysia Berhad, 2004. 380 pp. NTUNIE, NUS.

1881. Milner, A.C. *Kerajaan: Malay Political Culture on the Eve of Colonial Rule.* Tucson, Ariz.: Published for the Association for Asian Studies by the University of Arizona Press, 1982. 178 pp. ISEAS, NLB, NTU, NTUNIE.

1882. Ong Chit Chung. "The 1959 Singapore General Elections". Academic exercise, Department of History, University of Singapore, 1973. 99 pp. NUS. A condensed version published in: *Journal of Southeast Asia Studies* 6, no. 1 (1975): 61–86. ISEAS, NLB, NTUNIE, NUS.

1883. Roff, William R. *Origins of Malay Nationalism.* Kuala Lumpur: University of Malaya Press, 1994. 303 pp. ISEAS, NLB, NTUNIE, NUS. First published: New Haven: Yale University Press, 1967. 297 pp. ISEAS, NLB, NTU, NTUNIE.

1884. Soenarno Radin. "Malay Nationalism, 1896–1941". *Journal of Southeast Asian History* 1, no. 1 (March 1960): 1–33. ISEAS, NLB, NTU, NUS.

1885. Soenarno, Radin. "Nasionalisma Melayu hingga T.M. 1948". *Bahasa* 2, no. 1 (March 1959): 38–53. NLB, NTUNIE, NUS.

1886. Soenarno, Radin. "The Political Attitudes of the Malays before 1945". Academic exercise, University of Malaya, Singapore, 1959. 59 pp. NUS.

1887. Tantow, David. "Politics of Heritage in Singapore". *Indonesia and the Malay World* 40, no. 118 (November 2012): 332–53. NLB.

1888. Yang Razali Kassim. "Winning Over the Malay Community: The Politics of Engagement". In *Impressions of the Goh Chok Tong Years in Singapore*, edited by Bridget Welsh et al. Singapore: NUS Press in collaboration between Lee Kuan Yew School of Public Policy, National University of Singapore and Institute of Policy Studies, 2009. ISEAS, NLB, NTU, NUS.

1889. Yusuf Ngah. "Malay Nationalism, 1945–1957". MA dissertation, University of Otago, 1967. 1 microfilm reel (312 pp.). ISEAS, NLB, NUS.

Leadership

1890. Abdullah Tarmugi. "The Challenge for the Malay Leadership". *Petir: Organ of the People's Action Party* (May 1986): 18. ISEAS, NLB, NTUNIE, NUS.

1891. Bambang Sugeng Kajairi. "The New Generation of Leaders in Singapore". Academic exercise, Department of Political Science, National University of Singapore, 1989. 112 pp. NUS.

1892. Goh Chok Tong. "Towards More Malay Leaders in All Fields: [Speech Delivered at the Singapore Malay Chamber of Commerce Hari Raya Adilfitri '88 Dinner Function and Malay Muslim Businessman of the Year Award, Westin Stamford, My 28 '88]". *Speeches* 12, no. 3 (May–June 1988): 12–15; 12, no. 4 (July/August 1988): 27–30. ISEAS, NLB, NTU, NTUNIE, NUS.

1893. Hussin Mutalib. "On Leaders and Leadership: Malays, Muslims and Mainstream Singapore Society". Paper presented at Seminar on Malay-Muslim Leadership in Singapore, organized by Central Council of Malay Cultural Organisations, Plaza Hotel, Singapore, 1988.

1894. Hussin Mutalib. "The Quest for Leadership Legitimacy among Singapore Malays". *Asian Journal of Political Science* 20, no. 1 (2012): 70–85. ISEAS, NTU, NTUNIE, NUS.

1895. Ismail Kassim. "Problems of Elite Cohesion: A Perspective from a Minority Community". MSocSci dissertation, Department of Political Science, University of Singapore, 1973. 192 pp. NUS. Published under the same title: Singapore: Singapore University Press, 1974. 146 pp. ISEAS, NLB, NTU, NTUNIE, NUS.

1896. Kamaludeen Mohamed Nasir. "The Muslim Power Elites in Singapore". MA dissertation, National University of Singapore. 108 pp. NUS.

1897. Lee Kuan Yew. "Gradual Integration or Separate Collective Leadership". *Speeches* 25, no. 2 (March–April 2001): 15–21. ISEAS, NLB, NTU, NTUNIE, NUS.

1898. Lee Kuan Yew. "Politics and Religion Should Best be Kept Separate". *Speeches* 12, no. 6 (November/December 1988): 10–13. ISEAS, NLB, NTU, NTUNIE, NUS.

1899. Lily Zubaidah Rahim. "Minimizing the Political Resources of the Malay Community". In *The Singapore Dilemma: The Political and Educational Marginality of the Malay Community*. Kuala Lumpur: Oxford University Press, 1998. ISEAS, NLB, NTU, NTUNIE, NUS.

1900. Sukmawati Haji Sirat. "Trends in Malay Political Leadership: The People's Action Party's Malay Political Leaders and the Integration of the Singapore Malays". PhD dissertation, University of South Carolina, 1996. 334 pp. ISEAS, NUS.

1901. "Why Team MPs?" *Petir: Organ of the People's Action Party* (December 1987): 3, 8. ISEAS, NLB, NTUNIE, NUS.

1902. Yang Razali Kassim. "Obama: What He Means for Singapore?" *Karyawan: Professionals for the Community* 9, issue 2 (January 2009): 27–29. ISEAS, NLB, NTUNIE, NUS.

1903. Yang Razali Kassim. "Politics, Leadership & Organisations: The Next Five Years". *Karyawan: Professionals for the Community* 2 (October 1995): 8–9. ISEAS, NLB, NTUNIE, NUS.

Political Participation

1904. A. Rahim Ishak. "Why Malays are Solidly with the PAP". *Petir: Organ of the People's Action Party* 6 (September 1980): 56–59. ISEAS, NLB, NTUNIE, NUS. Also published in Malay under the title: "Mengapa Orang Melayu Berdiri Teguh dengan PAP". *Petir: Organ of the People's Action Party* 3 (December 1980): 30–32. ISEAS, NLB, NTUNIE, NUS.

1905. Chan Heng Chee. "Political Parties". In *Government and Politics in Singapore*, edited by Jon S.T. Quah, Chan Heng Chee, and Seah Chee Meow. Singapore: Oxford University Press, 1987. ISEAS, NLB, NTU, NTUNIE, NUS.

1906. Cheng Cheang Wing. "Electoral Reform for Multi-racial Representation: A Study of the GRC System in Singapore". Academic exercise, Department of Political Science, National University of Singapore, 1989. 116 pp. NUS.

1907.   Cohen, Mervin. "The Political Culture of the Malays". Research exercise, Department of Malay Studies, National University of Singapore, 1991. 61 pp. NUS.

1908.   Daud Yusoff. "The Political Consciousness of Malay Tertiary Students". Research exercise, Department of Malay Studies, National University of Singapore, 1994. 68 pp. NUS.

1909.   Elinah Abdullah. "Malay Political Activities in Singapore, 1945–59". Academic exercise, Department of History, National University of Singapore, 1992. 108 pp. NUS. Published under the title: "The Political Activities of the Singapore Malays, 1910–1942". In *Malays/Muslims in Singapore: Selected Readings in History 1819–1965*, edited by Khoo Kay Kim, Elinah Abdullah, and Wan Meng Hao. Subang Jaya, Selangor: Pelanduk Publications in cooperation with Centre for Research on Islamic and Malay Affairs, Singapore, 2006. ISEAS, NLB, NTUNIE, NUS.

1910.   Goh Chok Tong. "A Minority Right: Ensuring Multi-Racial Representation in the Singapore Parliament". *The Parliamentarian: Journal of the Parliaments of the Commonwealth* 70 (January 1989): 6–11. NTUNIE, NUS.

1911.   Goh Chok Tong. "The Role of the Malay Affairs Bureau". *Petir: Organ of the People's Action Party* (July 1990): 49. ISEAS, NLB, NTUNIE, NUS.

1912.   "GRC Hearings: Significant Shift in Positions". *Petir: Organ of the People's Action Party* (March 1988): 4–7. ISEAS, NLB, NTUNIE, NUS.

1913.   Harun A. Ghani. "GRC dengan Masyarakat Islam Singapura". *Petir: Organ of the People's Action Party* (February 1988): 21. ISEAS, NLB, NTUNIE, NUS.

1914.   Hussin Mutalib. "Singapore's 1991 General Election". In *Southeast Asian Affairs 1992*, edited by Dajit Singh. Singapore: Institute of Southeast Asian Studies, 1992. ISEAS, NLB, NTU, NTUNIE, NUS.

1915.   Hussin Mutalib. "Domestic Politics". In *Singapore: Year in Review, 1991*, edited by Lee Tsao Yuan. Singapore: Institute of Policy Studies, 1992. ISEAS, NLB, NTU, NUS.

1916. Hussin Mutalib. "Singapore's December 1992 By-Elections: Interpreting the Results and the Signals". *Round Table: Commonwealth Journal of International Affairs* 326 (1993): 159–68. NUS.

1917. "Kesatuan Melayu Singapura (KMS)". In *Ensiklopedia Sejarah dan Kebudayaan Melayu*, vol. 2, p. 1186. Kuala Lumpur: Dewan Bahasa dan Pustaka, 1994. NLB, NTUNIE, NUS.

1918. Kutty, M.G. "SMNO Shakes Off Communal Image". *Malaysian Business* (16 December 1984): 8. ISEAS, NLB, NUS.

1919. Lee, Michelle. "Malay-Muslims Should be More Pro-active in Community and Nation". *Petir: Organ of the People's Action Party* (January/February 2002): 24. ISEAS, NLB, NUS.

1920. Lily Zubaidah Rahim. "Winning and Losing Malay Support: The Capricious Course of PAP-Malay Community Relations, 1950s and 1960s". Paper presented to a Symposium on Path Not Taken: Political Pluralism in Postwar Singapore, jointly sponsored by the Centre for Social Change Research at the Queensland University of Technology and the Asia Research Institute at the National University of Singapore held in Singapore on 14–15 July 2005. ISEAS.

1921. Lim Phek Noi, Maria. "Political Consciousness of Young Professionals in Singapore". Academic exercise, Department of Sociology, National University of Singapore, 1992. 72 pp. NUS.

1922. Maarof Salleh. "Masyarakat Islam Singapura dan Pendekatan kepada Persoalan-Persoalan Nasional". *Analisa* (1981): 5–11. NLB, NUS.

1923. MacDougall, John Arthur. "Shared Burdens: A Study of Communal Discrimination by the Political Parties of Malaysia and Singapore". PhD dissertation, Harvard University, 1968. 390 pp. ISEAS, NUS.

1924. "Malay Activists Pledge Loyalty to Nation". *Petir: Organ of the People's Action Party* (April 1987): 7. ISEAS, NLB, NTUNIE, NUS. Also published in Malay under the title: "Para Aktivis Melayu Berikrar Taat Setia kepada Negara". *Petir: Organ of the People's Action Party* (April 1987): 37. ISEAS, NLB, NTUNIE, NUS.

1925. "Malays in the Hot Seats". *Asiaweek* 17, no. 32 (9 August 1991): 23. ISEAS, NLB, NTUNIE, NUS.

1926. Mohd. Azhar Terimo. "UMNO and Malay Political Activities in Singapore, 1959–1965". Academic exercise, Department of History, National University of Singapore, 1998. 57 pp. NUS. Published under the title: "From Self-Government to Independence: UMNO and Malay Politics in Singapore, 1959–1965". In *Malays/Muslims in Singapore: Selected Readings in History 1819–1965*, edited by Khoo Kay Kim, Elinah Abdullah, and Wan Meng Hao. Subang Jaya, Selangor: Pelanduk Publications in cooperation with Centre for Research on Islamic and Malay Affairs, Singapore, 2006. ISEAS, NLB, NTUNIE, NUS.

1927. Mohamad Maidin. "Why Malays Support the PAP". *Petir: Organ of the People's Action Party* (July/August 2006): 42–43. NLB, NTUNIE, NUS.

1928. "Mr Goh is Eager to Woo the Professional Malays". *Country Report: Singapore* 4 (1990): 10. ISEAS, NLB, NUS.

1929. People's Action Party (Singapore). *Chenderamata Pameran Ulang Tahun ke-15 Petir = P.A.P. 15th Anniversary Exhibition Souvenir*. Singapore: P.A.P. 15th Anniversary Exhibition Sub-Committee, 1969. 36 pp. NLB.

1930. Rustam A. Sani. "The Origin of the Malay Left: An Analysis of the Social Roots". MA dissertation, University of Kent, Canterbury, 1975. 103 pp. ISEAS, NUS.

1931. Schoppert, Peter. "The Younger Generation and Singapore Politics". MSocSc dissertation, Department of Political Science, National University of Singapore 1987. 245 pp. NUS.

1932. Sinanovic, Ermin. *Singapore's Malay Muslim Community: A Moral Voice? Comparative Perspectives on Integration in a Global Age*. Occasional Paper Series, no. 1-2013. Singapore: Centre for Research on Islamic and Malay Affairs, 2013. 34 pp. NLB.

1933. Singam, Constance et al. *The Future of Civil Society in Singapore*. Occasional Paper Series, no. 4-97. Singapore: Association of Muslim Professionals, 1997. 43 pp. ISEAS, NLB, NTUNIE, NUS.

1934. Stockwell, A.J. *British Policy and Malay Politics during the Malayan Union Experiment 1945–1948*. Kuala Lumpur: Printed for the Council of the Malaysian Branch of the Royal Asiatic Society by Arts Printing Works, 1979. 206 pp. ISEAS, NTU, NTUNIE, NUS.

1935.   *Suara P.K.M.S.* Singapore: Pertubuhan Kebangsaan Melayu Singapura, 1972–. NLB, NUS.

1936.   "Tribute to PM Lee Kuan Yew by Malay Activists". *Petir: Organ of the People's Action Party* (July 1990): 45. ISEAS, NLB, NTUNIE, NUS. Also published in Malay under the title: "Penghargaan Para Aktivis Melayu buat Perdana Menteri Encik Lee Kuan Yew". *Petir: Organ of the People's Action Party* (July 1990): 51. ISEAS, NLB, NTUNIE, NUS.

1937.   *Utusan = Message.* Singapore: Pertubuhan Kebangsaan Melayu Singapura, 1981–88. NUS.

1938.   *Utusan PKMS = PKMS Message.* Singapore: Pertubuhan Kebangsaan Melayu Singapura, 1983–. NLB, NUS.

1939.   "Why Sharifah is such an Activist". *Petir: Organ of the People's Action Party* (January 1989): 42–43. ISEAS, NLB, NTUNIE, NUS.

1940.   Zakaria Buang. "Playing Vital Role". *Mirror* 25, no. 15 (August 1989): 5–7. ISEAS, NLB, NUS.

National Integration

1941.   Ahmad Mattar. "The Future of Multiracialism in Singapore". *Petir: Organ of the People's Action Party* (April 1987): 3–7. ISEAS, NLB, NTUNIE, NUS. Also published in Malay under the title: "Masa Depan Konsep Berbilang Bangsa di Singapura". *Petir: Organ of the People's Action Party* (April 1987): 32–36. ISEAS, NLB, NTUNIE, NUS.

1942.   Betts, Russell Henry. "Multiracialism, Meritocracy and the Malays of Singapore". PhD dissertation, Massachusetts Institute of Technology, 1976. Ann Arbor, Mich.: University Microfilms International, 1977. 372 pp. ISEAS, NLB, NUS.

1943.   Chua Beng Huat. "Multiculturalism in Singapore: An Instrument of Social Control". *Race & Class* 44, no. 3 (2003): 58–77. NTUNIE, NUS.

1944.   Chua Beng Huat and Kwok Kian Woon. "Social Pluralism in Singapore". In *The Politics of Multiculturalism: Pluralism and Citizenship in Malaysia, Singapore and Indonesia,* edited by Robert W. Hefner. Honolulu: University of Hawaii, 2001. ISEAS, NTU, NTUNIE, NUS.

1945. Goh Chok Tong. "Building a Multi-Racial Nation through Integration: [Speech at the Second National Convention of Singapore Malay/Muslim Professionals, 5 Nov 2000]". *Speeches* 24, no. 6 (November 2000): 13–21. ISEAS, NLB, NTU, NTUNIE.

1946. Goh Chok Tong. "Role of Malay Community Organisations in Nation-building: [Speech at the Majlis Pusat 30th Anniversary Dinner, 30 Oct 99]". *Speeches* 23, no. 5 (September–October 1999): 1–6. ISEAS, NLB, NTU, NTUNIE, NUS.

1947. Hussin Mutalib. "In Quest of a Singapore National Identity: The Triumphs and Trials of Government Policies". In *Imaging Singapore*, edited by Ban Kah Choon, Ann Pakir, and Tong Chee Kiong. Singapore: Times Academic Press, 1992. ISEAS, NLB, NTU, NTUNIE, NUS.

1948. Hussin Mutalib. "Nation-Building and National Identity in Singapore: Old Problems, New Challenges". Fourth Malaysia–Singapore Forum, University of Malaya, Kuala Lumpur, December 1994. 31 pp.

1949. Leung Wun Yin, Felicia. "The Merits of Meritocracy: Meanings and Implications for Singapore". Academic exercise, Department of Political Science, National University of Singapore, 1987. 65 pp. NUS.

1950. Low Zoey. "Frustrations. Acquiescence and Belonging: Negotiating the Discourses of Multiracialist and Meritocracy as a Singaporean Malay". Academic exercise, Department of Sociology, National University of Singapore, 2013. 54 pp. NUS.

1951. Siddique, Sharon. "Corporate Pluralism: Singapore Inc. and the Association of Muslim Professionals". In *The Politics and Multiculturalism: Pluralism and Citizenship in Malaysia, Singapore and Indonesia*, edited by Robert W. Hefner. Honolulu: University of Hawaii, 2001. NTUNIE, NUS.

1952. Tan Khee Giap. "Rejuvenated Singapore, Renewed Social Contract, Getting the Correct Politics and Community Priority: Implications for Malay/Muslim Singaporeans". In *MENDAKI Policy Digest* (2013): 69–73. NLB.

1953. "TV Forum: We Do Have a National Identity". *Petir: Organ of the People's Action Party* 6 (September 1980): 40–43. ISEAS, NLB, NTUNIE, NUS.

Defence and Security

1954. Abu Yazid Abidin. "Sejarah Kepahlawanan Askar Melayu". *Dewan Masyarakat* 2, no. 3 (March 1964): 6–9. NLB, NUS.

1955. "Askar Melayu Mara! Mara! Mara!" *Dewan Masyarakat* 21, no. 2 (February 1983): 5–9. NLB, NTUNIE, NUS.

1956. Bedlington, Stanley Sanders. "Ethnicity and the Armed Forces in Singapore". In *Ethnicity and the Military in Asia*, edited by DeWitt C. Ellinwood and Cynthia H. Enloe. New Brunswick, N.J.: Transaction Books, 1981. ISEAS, NUS.

1957. "Debating as a Matter of Race: Singapore". *Asiaweek* 13, no. 17 (April 1987): 18–21. ISEAS, NLB, NTUNIE, NUS.

1958. Dol Ramli. "History of the Malay Regiment, 1933–1942". *JMBRAS* 28, pt. 1 (July 1965): 199–243. ISEAS, NLB, NTUNIE, NUS.

1959. "Heat over the Malay Question: Controversies". *Asiaweek* 13, no. 13 (5 April 1987): 12. ISEAS, NLB, NTUNIE, NUS.

1960. Holloway, Nigel. "Double-Edged Sword: The Government Speaks Out on Defence and the Role of Malays". *Far Eastern Economic Review* 136 (2 April 1987): 30–31. ISEAS, NLB, NTU, NTUNIE, NUS.

1961. Jones, Alan. "Internal Security in British Malaya, 1895–1942". PhD dissertation, Yale University, 1970. Ann Arbor, Mich.: University Microfilms International, 1971. ISEAS, NLB, NUS.

1962. "Malays in SAF: Don't Meddle in Our Affairs, Foreign Politicians Told". *Petir: Organ of the People's Action Party* (April 1987): 9–12. ISEAS, NLB, NTUNIE, NUS.

1963. "Posing a Question of Loyalty: Singapore". *Asiaweek* 13, no. 12 (March 1987): 33. ISEAS, NLB, NTUNIE, NUS.

1964. Puteri Roslina Abdul Wahid. "Orang Melayu Dalam 'British Army': Pengalaman Peribadi Baharuddin bin Ishak". *Malaysia Dari Segi Sejarah* 13 (1984): 91–101. NLB, NUS.

1965. Roach, Kent. "National Security, Multiculturalism and Muslim Minorities". *Singapore Journal of Legal Studies* (2006): 405–38. NTU, NTUNIE, NUS. Available at <http://law.nus.edu.sg/sjls/articles/SJLS-Dec-2006-405.pdf>. (Case studies of Muslims in Canada and Singapore).

1966. Sheppard, Mubin C. "The Malay Regiment at War". *British Malaya* 21, no. 2 (June 1946): 22–23. NLB, NUS.

1967. Sheppard, M.C. (Mubin C.). "The Malay Soldier". *The Straits Times Annual* (1939): 26–35. NLB, NTUNIE, NUS.

1968. Tan, Kenneth Paul. "Crisis, Self-Reflection, and Rebirth in Singapore's National Life Cycle". In *Southeast Asian Affairs 2003*, edited by Daljit Singh and Chin Kin Wah. Singapore: Institute of Southeast Asian Studies, 2003. ISEAS, NLB, NTU, NTUNIE.

1969. Tan T.H., Andrew. "Singapore's Approach to Homeland Security". In *Southeast Asian Affairs 2005*, edited by Chin Kin Wah and Daljit Singh. Singapore: Institute of Southeast Asian Studies, 2005. ISEAS, NTU, NTUNIE, NUS.

1970. Taylour, Richard "Training Malays to Guard Their Own Coasts: Naval Volunteers in the Straits Settlements". *The Straits Times Annual* (1937): 86–88. NLB, NTUNIE, NUS.

1971. Walsh, Sean P. "The Roar of the Lion City: Ethnicity, Gender, and Culture in the Singapore Armed Forces". *Armed Forces & Society* 33, no. 2 (2007): 265–85. NTUNIE, NUS.

1972. Wan Meng Hao. "Malay Soldiering in Singapoe, 1910–1942". In *Malays/Muslims in Singapore: Selected Readings in History 1819–1965*, edited by Khoo Kay Kim, Elinah Abdullah, and Wan Meng Hao. Subang Jaya, Selangor: Pelanduk Publications in cooperation with Centre for Research on Islamic and Malay Affairs, Singapore, 2006. ISEAS, NLB, NTUNIE, NUS.

Internationalization and International Relations

1973. "Herzog's Visit in Perpective: Focus". *Mirror* 23, no. 1 (January 1987): 8–9. ISEAS, NLB, NUS.

1974. Holloway, Nigel. "The Buck Stops There: Lee Kuan Yew Says He Did Not Know About the Herzog Visit". *Far Eastern Economic Review* 134 (25 December 1986): 20. ISEAS, NLB, NTU, NTUNIE, NUS.

1975. Holloway, Nigel. "The Loyalty Factor: Malays Debate Reaction to Herzog Visit and Lee's Comment". *Far Eastern Economic Review* 135 (19 February 1987): 42–43. ISEAS, NLB, NTU, NTUNIE, NUS.

1976. Khoo Kia Hui, Serena. "The 'Herzog Affair' and Its Impact on Intra-ASEAN Political Relations". Academic exercise, Department of Political Science, National University of Singapore, 1987. 89 pp. NUS.

1977. Koh, Gillian and Ooi Giok Ling. "Singapore: A Home, A Nation?" In *Southeast Asian Affairs 2002*, edited by Daljit Singh and Anthony L. Smith. Singapore: Institute of Southeast Asian Affairs, 2002. ISEAS, NTU, NTUNIE.

1978. Lily Zubaidah Rahim. *Singapore in the Malay World: Building and Breaching Regional Bridges*. London, New York: Routledge, 2009. 230 pp. ISEAS, NLB, NTU, NTUNIE, NUS.

1979. "Malaysia Strongly Protest Against Herzog's Visit to Singapore". *Islamic Herald* 10, no. 6 (1986): 1–5. ISEAS, NLB, NUS.

1980. Milne, R.S. "Singapore's Exit from Malaysia: The Consequences of Ambiguity". *Asian Survey* 6, no. 3 (1966): 175–84. ISEAS, NLB, NTU, NTUNIE, NUS.

1981. Min Sai Siew. "Singapore in the Malay World: Building and Breaching Regional Bridges". *South East Asia Research* 18, no. 3 (September 2010): 609–13. NLB, NTUNIE, NUS.

1982. Mohd Nizam Ismail. "The Globalisation and the Malay/Muslim Community: Time for Closer Look Within". *Karyawan: Professionals for the Community* 8, issue 1 (December 2007): 23–25. ISEAS, NLB, NTUNIE, NUS.

1983. Ng Han Kwee, Robert. "Malaysia–Singapore Relations: A Malaysian Perspective". Academic exercise, Department of Political Science, National University of Singapore, 1991. 62 pp. NUS.

1984. Oummar Nor Aman Bin Othman. "Reactions and Attitude of the Malays towards the Separation of Singapore from Malaysia (1965–1972)". MA dissertation, Kulliyyah Islamic Reveled Knowledge and Human Sciences, International Islamic University, Malaysia, 2012. 108 pp. ISEAS.

1985. "Sidek Saniff Calls for Non-Interference". *Petir: Organ of the People's Action Party* (April 1987): 13. ISEAS, NLB, NTUNIE, NUS.

1986. Yeong Gah Hou. "Singapore–Malaysia Relations, 1984–88: Race, Religion and Foreign Relations". Academic exercise, Department of Political Science, National University of Singapore, 1989. 98 pp. NUS.

RELIGION

- *General Works*
- *Religious Relations and Tolerance*
- *Islam and Islamic Identity*
- *Islamic Revival and Radicalism*
- *Islamic Organizations and Leadership*
- *MUIS*
- *Mosques*
- *Religious Life*
- Da'wah *and Muslim Converts*
- *Waqf*

General Works

1987. Chatfield, Godfrey A. *The Religions and Festivals of Singapore.* Singapore: D. Moore for Eastern University Press, 1962. 28 pp. NLB, NUS.

1988. Kho Ee Moi. "Religion and State in Singapore, 1959–1978". Academic exercise, Department of History, University of Singapore, 1979. 78 pp. NUS.

1989. Kuo C.Y. (Chen-Yu), Eddie. *Religion in Singapore: An Analysis of the 1980 Census Data: Report.* Singapore: Ministry of Community Development, 1987. 61 pp. ISEAS, NLB, NTUNIE, NUS.

1990. Kuo C.Y. (Chen-Yu), Eddie and J.S.T. Quah. *Religion in Singapore: Report of a National Survey.* Singapore: Ministry of Community Development, 1989. 152 pp. ISEAS, NLB, NTUNIE, NUS.

1991. Kuo C.Y. (Chen-Yu), Eddie and Tong Chee Kiong. *Religion in Singapore.* Census of Population 1990 Monograph, no. 2. Singapore: Department of Statistics, 1995. 74 pp. ISEAS, NLB, NTUNIE.

1992. Lee Hwee Hoon. "Religion and Politics in a Secular State: A Case Study of Singapore". Academic exercise, Department of Political Science, National University of Singapore, 1990. 65 pp. NUS.

1993. *Religions in Singapore: Speeches Delivered during a Seminar held at the Conference Hall Singapore, on 10th August 1966.* Singapore: Inter-Religions Organization, 1966. 48 pp. NUS.

1994. *Religions in Singapore.* Singapore: Inter-Religious Organisation of Singapore, 2002. 184 pp. NUS. First published: Singapore: Inter-Religious Organisation of Singapore, 1993. 125 pp. ISEAS, NLB, NUS.

1995. "Religious Fervour a Source of Fear". *Country Report (Singapore)* 2 (1989): 7–8. ISEAS, NLB, NUS.

1996. Semple, E.G. *Singapore Religions: A Summary of Great Oriental Faiths.* Singapore: Methodist Publishing House, 1927. 48 pp. NLB.

1997. Tamney, Joseph B. and Riaz Hassan. *Religious Switching in Singapore: A Study of Religious Mobility.* Singapore: Select Books, 1987. 63 pp. ISEAS, NLB, NUS.

Religious Relations and Tolerance

1998. Alsagoff, Syed Ibrahim Omar. "Inter Religious Organisation, Singapore and Johore Bahru". *Muslim World, Singapore* 2, no. 1 (January 1950): 22.

1999. Chai Chong Yii. "Religious Harmony Has Become Our Way of Life". *Speeches* 4, no. 9 (March 1981): 60–61. ISEAS, NLB, NTUNIE, NUS.

2000. Finlay, Matthew Henderson and Sumali Alwi. *A Christian-Muslim Dialogue between M.H. Finlay of New Zealand and Sumali Alwi of Singapore.* Johore Bahru: Omar Brothers Publications, 1979. 158 pp. ISEAS, NLB, NTUNIE, NUS.

2001. Goh Chok Tong. "Don't Take Racial Harmony for Granted: [Speech by Prime Minister Goh Chok Tong at the Official Opening of Khadijah Mosque Annexe on Wednesday, 1 January 2003]". *Inabah* 15, no. 1 (March 2003): 32–35. NLB.

2002. Mohamad Fadzrun Adnan. "Apathy and Ignorance in Religious Ties". *Karyawan: Professionals for the Community* 7, issue 1 (November 2006): ISEAS, NLB, NTUNIE, NUS.

2003. Mohamad Shamsuri Juhari. "Unity of Worldview as a Basis of Cooperation amongst Muslims in SEA: The Singapore Model". Paper presented at a Symposium on Islam and the New Era of ASEAN Countries: Unity of Worldview towards Shared Prosperity, organized by Institut Kefahaman Islam, Malaysia, 4–5 June 2013.

2004. Mohd. Jakfar Embek. "Islam and Religious Pluralism in Singapore since Independence (1965): Analysing Muslim Thoughts of Awareness, Responses and Challenges of Religious Pluralism". MA dissertation, Markfield Institute of Higher Education, University of Gloucestershire, UK, 2009. 71 pp. NLB.

2005. Mohd. Jakfar Embek. "Islam, Muslims and the Idea of Interfaith Relations in Singapore and Malaysia from Pre-Independence to Present Day". *Jurnal Dakwah* 4 (December 2014): 71–99. NLB.

2006. "Religious Tensions: Actual Examples". *Petir: Organ of the People's Action Party* (January 1990): 12–13. ISEAS, NLB, NTUNIE, NUS.

2007. Scott, Margaret. "Halting the Crusade: The Government Confronts Singapore's Church Activists: Proselytising Angers Muslims: Waging

Spiritual Warfare". *Far Eastern Economic Review* 137 (2 July 1987): 44, 61–65. ISEAS, NLB, NTUNIE, NUS.

2008.   See Guat Kwee. "History of Christian-Muslim Relations in Singapore since Country's Independence in 1965". MA dissertation, Hartford Seminary, 2007. 253 pp. NLB.

2009.   See Guat Kwee. "Building Bridges between Christians and Muslims: A Personal Journey". In *Religious Diversity in Singapore*, edited by Lai Ah Eng. Singapore: Institute of Southeast Asian Studies; Institute of Policy Studies, 2008. ISEAS, NLB, NTUNIE, NUS.

2010.   Semait, Syed Isa Mohamed. "A Time to Strengthen Inter-Religious Understanding: When Jihad is Not a War". *Warita Kita* 135 (September/October 2001): 16–17. ISEAS, NLB, NUS.

2011.   Siddique, Sharon. "Mutual Tolerance for Multicultural Singapore". *Karyawan: Professionals for the Community* 3 (September–November 1997): 6–7. ISEAS, NLB, NTUNIE, NUS.

2012.   Sinha, Vineeta. "Scrutinizing the Themes of 'Sameness' and 'Difference' in the Discourse on Multireligiousity and Religious Encounters in Singapore". In *Asian Interfaith Dialogue: Perspectives on Religion, Education and Social Cohesion*, edited by Syed Farid Alatas, Lim Teck Ghee, and Kazuhide Kuroda. Singapore: RIMA; Washington, D.C.: The World Bank, 2003. ISEAS, NLB, NTUNIE, NUS.

Islam and Islamic Identity

2013.   Abdul Rahman Mohamed Said. "Tarekats in Singapore: An Ethnographic Study". Academic exercise, Department of Sociology, University of Singapore, 1975. 63 pp. NUS.

2014.   Abdullah Alwi Haji Hassan. "Islam di Singapura: Satu Pengenalan". In *Islamika: Esei-Esei Sempena Abad ke 15 Hijrah dengan Sumbangan Khas dari Kakitangan Akademik Jabatan Pengajian Islam, Universiti Malaya*, edited by Lutpi Ibrahim. Kuala Lumpur: Sarjana Enterprise, 1981. ISEAS, NLB.

2015.   Abu Talib Ahmad. "Japanese Policy towards Islam in Malaya during the Occupation: A Reassessment". *Journal of Southeast Asian Studies* 33, no. 1 (February 2002): 107–22. ISEAS, NTUNIE.

2016. Ahmad Ibrahim. "Islam in Singapore". In *Religions in Singapore: Speeches Delivered during a Seminar Held at the Conference Hall, Singapore, on 10th August 1966 under the auspices of Inter-Religious Organization, Singapore*. Singapore: Inter-Religious Organization, 1966. NUS.

2017. Ahmad Mattar. "Beware of False Teachings". *Speeches* 4, no. 7 (January 1981): 45–46. ISEAS, NLB, NTUNIE, NUS.

2018. Ahmad Mattar. "The Islamic Way to a Progressive Society". *Speeches* 16, no. 4 (July/August 1992): 39–41. ISEAS, NLB, NTUNIE, NUS.

2019. Ahmad Mattar. "No Place for Ignorance or Fanaticism". *Speeches* 4, no. 9 (March 1981): 53–54. ISEAS, NLB, NTUNIE, NUS.

2020. Ahmad Mattar. "Promoting a Community with High Morals". *Speeches* 4, no. 10 (April 1981): 33–34. ISEAS, NLB, NTUNIE, NUS.

2021. Ahmad Mattar. "Religion and Social Cohesion". *Speeches* 2, no. 4 (October 1978): 31–33. ISEAS, NLB, NTUNIE, NUS.

2022. Ahmad Mattar. "The Teachings of Islam". *Speeches* 3, no. 5 (November 1979): 34–35. ISEAS, NLB, NTUNIE.

2023. *Al-Risalah: Majalah Warga PERGAS*. Singapore: Jabatan Dakwah PERGAS, 2000–. NLB.

2024. Alatas, Syed Farid. *Covering Islam: Challenges & Opportunities for Media in the Global Village*. Singapore: Centre for Research on Islamic and Malay Affairs, Konrad-Adenauer-Stiftung, 2005. 181 pp. ISEAS, NLB, NUS.

2025. Alatas, Syed Farid. "Islam and Modernization". In *Islam in Southeast Asia: Political, Social and Strategic Challenges for the 21st Century*, edited by K.S. Nathan and Mohammad Hashim Kamali. Singapore: Institute of Southeast Asian Studies, 2005. 362 pp. ISEAS, NLB, NTUNIE, NUS.

2026. Al-Attas, Syed Muhammad Naguib. "A Study of Sufism in Present-Day Malaya and Singapore". Academic exercise, University of Malaya, Singapore, 1959.

2027. Al-Attas, Syed Muhammad Naguib. "Sufi Orders in Malaya". In *Some Aspects of Sufism as Understood and Practised among the Malays*, edited by Shirley Gordon. Singapore: Malaysian Sociological Research Institute, 1963. ISEAS, NLB, NUS.

2028. Albakri Ahmad. "Muslims in Multicultural Singapore". *Warita Kita* 131 (February 2001): 14–15. ISEAS, NLB, NUS.

2029. Aljunied, Syed Muhd Khairudin. "From Noble Muslims to Saracen Enemies: Thomas Stamford Raffles' Discourse on Islam in Malay World". *Sari* 21 (2003): 13–29. ISEAS, NLB, NUS.

2030. Aljunied, Syed Muhd Khairudin. *Raffles and Religion: A Study of Sir Stamford Raffles' Discourse on Religions amongst Malays.* Kuala Lumpur: The Other Press, 2004. 124 pp. ISEAS, NLB, NTUNIE, NUS.

2031. Aljunied, Syed Muhd Khairudin. *Rethinking Raffles: A Study of Stamford Raffles' Discourse on Religions amongst Malays.* Singapore: Marshall Cavendish Academic, 2005. 107 pp. ISEAS, NLB, NTU, NTUNIE, NUS.

2032. Asad Latif. "The Many Faces of Islam". *Warita Kita* 125 (January/ February 2000): 14–15. ISEAS, NLB, NUS.

2033. Azhar Ibrahim (Alwee). "Discourses on Islam in Southeast Asia and Their Impact on the Singapore Muslim Public". In *Religious Diversity in Singapore*, edited by Lai Ah Eng. Singapore: Institute of Policy Studies, 2008. 723 pp. ISEAS, NLB, NTUNIE, NUS.

2034. Azhar Ibrahim Alwee and Mohamed Imran Mohamed Taib, eds. *Islam, Religion and Progress: Critical Perspectives.* Singapore: The Print Lodge Pte. Ltd. [for] The Reading Group Singapore, 2006. 185 pp. ISEAS, NLB, NTUNIE, NUS.

2035. Babu Sahib and M.H. Moulavi. "Islam in the Context of a Multi-Racial and Multi-Religious Society as that of Singapore". *Al-Islam* 4, no. 2 (April/June 1973): 19–21. NLB, NUS.

2036. Barr, Michael D. "Muslims in Singapore". *NIAS Nytt* 3 (December 2008): 20–24. ISEAS, NUS.

2037. "Cabaran Sekularisasi dan Globalisasi Barat kepada Harakah Islamiyyah Nusantara: Perspektif Singapura". Kerjas kerja untuk Kongress Ulama Asia Tenggara, Universiti Malaya, Kuala Lumpur, Malaysia, 23 Jun 2001. *Al-Risalah: Majalah Warga PERGAS* 4 (July–September 2001): 5–8. NLB.

2038. Chomil Kamal. "Secularization among the Muslims in Singapore: Myth or Reality? An Exploratory Study". Academic exercise, Department of Sociology, National University of Singapore, 1982. 100 pp. NUS.

2039. Dodsworth, Marmaduke. "The Assimilation of Christianity by the Malays of the Malay Peninsula". Dissertation, University of Chicago, 1928. 1 microfilm reel. NUS.

2040. *Fajar Islam.* Singapore: MUIS, 1970–88. ISEAS, NLB, NUS.

2041. *Fikrah: Shaping the Future.* Singapore: MUIS, 1995. 62 pp. ISEAS, NTUNIE.

2042. *The Fount Journal.* Singapore: NUS Muslim Society, 1993–2001. ISEAS, NUS.

2043. Funston, John. "Country Overview: Singapore". In *Voices of Islam in Southeast Asia: A Contemporary Sourcebook*, edited by Greg Fealy and Virginia Hooker. Singapore: Institute of Southeast Asian Studies, 2006. ISEAS, NTUNIE.

2044. *Genuine Islam: Organ of the All Malaya Muslim Missionary Society.* Singapore: All Malaya Muslim Mission Society, 1936– [194–?]. 1 microfilm reel. ISEAS, NLB.

2045. Hikmatullah Babu Sahib. "Islamic Studies in Singapore: Past Achievements, Present Dilemma and Future Directions". In *Islamic Studies in ASEAN: Presentations of an International Seminar*, edited by Isma-ae Alee et al. Pattani, Thailand: College of Islamic Studies, Prince of Songkla University, Pattani Campus, 2000. ISEAS, NUS.

2046. *Himmah Mastika.* Singapore: Pusat Pendidikan Islam, Muhammadiyah, 1988–. NLB.

2047. Hussin Mutalib. "The Islamic Movement in Singapore: Organization, Activities and Challenges". Paper presented at a Conference on Islamic Movements in the Malay World, organized by ABIM, Kuala Lumpur, Malaysia, 1986. 17 pp. NUS.

2048. Hussin Mutalib. "Minority Muslims and Islam in Modern, Secular Singapore". Paper presented at the Panel on "Islam in Southeast Asia" in the Annual Asian Studies Association Conference, Washington D.C., U.S., April 2002.

2049. Hussin Mutalib. "Pergerakan Islam di Singapura: Sumbangan dan Cabaran". In *Islam: Cabaran dan Isu Semasa*, edited by Ismail Abdul Rahman dan Mohd. Nasir Omar. Kuala Lumpur: Dewan Bahasa dan Pustaka, 1991. NLB, NUS.

2050. Hussin Mutalib. "Religious Diversity and Pluralism in Southeast Asian Islam: The Experience of Malaysia and Singapore". In *Religious Pluralism in Democratic Societies: Challenges and Prospects for Southeast Asia, Europe, and the United States in the New Millennium*, edited by K.S. Nathan. Singapore: Konrad-Adenauer-Stiftung; Kuala Lumpur: Malaysian Association for American Studies, 2007. ISEAS, NLB, NUS.

2051. *Insaf.* Singapore: University of Singapore Muslim Society, 1969–. ISEAS, NLB, NUS.

2052. "Islam in Singapore". *Mirror* 16, no. 9 (May 1980): 2. ISEAS, NLB, NTUNIE, NUS

2053. Jalil Miswardi. "The Structure of an Islamic Religious Movement". Academic exercise, Department of Sociology, University of Singapore, 1979. 52 pp. NUS.

2054. Lily Zubaidah Rahim. "Governing Islam and Regulating Muslims in Singapore's Secular Authoritarian State". Working Paper, no. 156. Asia Research Centre, Murdoch University, Australia, 2009. 27 pp. NLB, NUS.

2055. Lindsey, Timothy and Kerstin Steiner. *Islam, Law and the State in Southeast Asia. Volume 2, Singapore.* London: I.B. Tauris, 2011. 314 pp. ISEAS, NLB, NUS.

2056. Mak Lau-Fong. *Modeling Islamization in Southeast Asia: Brunei and Singapore.* PROSEA Research Paper, no. 29. Taipei: Academia Sinica, Program for Southeast Asian Area Studies, 2000. 49 pp. ISEAS.

2057. Marcinkowski, Christoph. "Facets of Shi'ite Islam in Contemporary Southeast Asia (II): Malaysia and Singapore". IDSS Working Paper, no. 121. Singapore: Institute of Defence and Strategic Studies, 2006. 41 pp. ISEAS, NTUNIE.

2058. Mariam Mohamed Ali. "Uniformity and Diversity among Muslims in Singapore". MSocSc dissertation, Department of Sociology, National University of Singapore, 1989. 179 pp. NUS.

2059. Mohammad Hisham Amat. "Islam in Question: The Position of Islam and Muslims in Singapore and Malaysia since the September 11 Tragedy". Academic exercise, Department of Southeast Asian Studies Programme, National University of Singapore, 2002/3. 63 pp. ISEAS, NUS.

2060. Mohd. Jakfar Embek. "Tauhid Worldview in Malay Archipelago". *Jurnal Dakwah* 1 (December 2010): 40–54. NLB.

2061. Mohd Shuhaimi Haji Ishak and Osman Chuah Abdullah. "World Journal of Islamic History and Civilization: Islam and the Malay World: An Insight into the Assimilation of Islamic Values". *Borneo Research Bulletin* 43 (2012): 312. ISEAS, NTUNIE, NUS.

2062. Muhammad Haniff Hassan. "Contextualizing Political Islam for Minority Muslims". RSIS Working Paper, no. 138. Singapore: S. Rajaratnam School of International Studies, Nanyang Technological University, 2007. 31 pp. ISEAS, NLB, NTUNIE, NUS.

2063. Muhammad Haniff Hassan. "Interpreting Islam on Plural Society". RSIS Working Paper, no. 159. Singapore: S. Rajaratnam School of International Studies, Nanyang Technological University, 2008. 24 pp. ISEAS, NLB, NTUNIE, NUS.

2064. Muhammad Haniff Hassan. *Muslim ... Moderate ... Singaporean = Muslim ... Moderat ... Warga Singapura*. Singapore: Perdaus and Al-Khair Management Board, 2003. 42 pp. NTUNIE, NUS, NLB.

2065. Muhammad Haniff Hassan. "War, Peace or Neutrality: An Overview of Islamic Polity's Basis of Inter-State Relations". RSIS Working Paper, no. 130. Singapore: S. Rajaratnam School of International Studies, Nanyang Technological University, 2007. 19 pp. ISEAS, NLB, NTUNIE, NUS.

2066. Muhammad Nor Hasbun. "Pengajaran Agama Islam di Singapura". Dissertation, Kolej Islam Malaya, 1969. 42 pp. NUS.

2067. *Muharram Annual 1975*. Singapore: Muslim Missionary Society, 1976. 1 vol. ISEAS, NLB, NUS.

2068. *Muslim Messenger: A Monthly Magazine Published in the Interests of Islam and the Muslims*. Singapore: [s.n.], 1936–. Microfilm reels. NUS.

2069. *The Muslim: The Organ of the Anjuman-i-Islam, Singapore*. Singapore: [s.n.], 1923–27. 1 microfilm reel. NUS.

2070. *Muslim World: Islamic Quarterly in English*. Singapore: All-Malaya Muslim Missionary Society, 1949. 1 microfilm reel. ISEAS.

2071. *The Muslims' Digest*. Singapore: Ze Majeed's Pub., 1999–2000. ISEAS, NLB.

2072. *Nadi: Pulse of the Singapore Muslim Community*. Singapore: Majlis Ugama Islam Singapura, 2005–. NUS. Available at <http://www.muis.gov.sg/cms/publications/newsletters.aspx?id=2396>.

2073. Naimah Said Talib. "British Policy towards Islam in the Straits Settlements (1867–1941)". Academic exercise, Department of History, National University of Singapore, 1982. 73 pp. NUS.

2074. *Noktah Hitam: Ajaran Sesat di Singapura*. Singapore: MUIS dengan kerjasama PERDAUS, 2001. 535 pp. NLB.

2075. Norhairen Amer. "Adat and Islam: Tension and Accommodation in Contemporary Malay-Muslim Society in Singapore". Research exercise, Department of Malay Studies, National University of Singapore, 1996. 50 pp. NUS.

2076. Norshahril Saat. "Constructing 'Muslimness': The State and Religiosity in Singapore and Malaysia". Academic exercise, Department of Political Science, National University of Singapore, 2007. 62 pp. NUS.

2077. Norshahril Saat. *Faith, Authority and the Malays: The Ulama in Contemporary Singapore*. Singapore: The Malay Heritage Foundation and Select Publishing, 2015. 111 pp. ISEAS, NLB, NUS.

2078. *NUSMS Souvenir Magazine*. Singapore: National University of Singapore Muslim Society, 1982–. NUS.

2079. Pasuni Maulan. "Masharakat Islam Singapura". Latihan ilmiah, Kolej Islam Malaya, 1967. 51 pp. NUS.

2080. *PERGAS Ulama Convention (2003: Singapore). Moderation in Islam in the Context of Muslim Community in Singapore*. Singapore: PERGAS, 2004. 370 pp. ISEAS, NUS. Also published in Malay under the title: *Kesederhanaan dalam Islam dalam Konteks Masyarakat Islam Singapura*. Singapore: PERGAS, 2004. 422 pp. NLB.

2081. *Progressive Islam and the State in Contemporary Muslim Societies: Report on a Conference Organised by the Institute of Defence and Strategic Studies (IDSS), 7th–8th March 2006, Marina Mandarin*

Singapore. Singapore: Institute of Defence and Strategic Studies, Nanyang Technological University, 2006. 24 pp. NTUNIE, NUS.

2082. "Religion and Modernization". Paper presented at a Seminar on Modernization, organized by the Current Affairs Club, Sang Nila Utama Secondary School, 20 March 1971. 4 pp. ISEAS.

2083. Rizwana Abdul Azeez. "Creating a Modern Singapore Muslim Community: A Tale of Language Dissonances". ISEAS Working Papers no. 2 (2014). Singapore: Institute of Southeast Asian Studies, 2014. 18 pp. ISEAS, NUS. Available at <http://www.iseas.edu.sg/documents/publication/ISEAS_Working%20Paper_%20No%202.pdf>.

2084. Roff, William R. "The Malayo-Muslim World of Singapore at the Close of Nineteeth Century". *Journal of Asian Studies* 24, no. 1 (1964): 75–90. ISEAS, NLB, NTUNIE, NUS.

2085. Saeda Buang. "Islamic Issue of Interest to the Malays in Malaysia and Singapore since Independence". MA dissertation, Department of Malay Studies, National University of Singapore, 1985. 164 pp. NUS.

2086. Sallim Jasman. *Perkembangan Islam di-Singapura.* Petaling Jaya: Kolej Islam Malaya, 1968. 72 pp. NUS.

2087. Sayuti, Hendri. *Islamika Pergumulan Melayu-Islam di Singapura: Antara Identitas dan Loyalitas.* Pekan Baru: IKAPI and the Ford Foundation, 2007. 118 pp. NLB.

2088. Seah Chee Meow. "The Muslim Issue and Implications for ASEAN". *Pacific Community* 6, no. 1 (October 1974): 139–60. ISEAS, NLB, NTUNIE, NUS.

2089. *Sedar: A Journal of Islamic Studies.* Singapore: University of Singapore Muslim Society, 1960–80. ISEAS, NLB, NUS.

2090. "Seminar Bahaya Ajaran Sesat: [Kertas Kerja]". Anjuran Jawatankuasa Dakwah MUIS, di Auditorium Pusat Islam Singapura, 21 & 22 Januari 1989. 1 vol. NLB.

2091. Shaik A. Kadir. *Commanding a Dynamic Islamic Personality.* Singapore: Islamic Theological Association of Singapore, 2000. 157 pp. NLB.

2092. Shamsul Amri Baharuddin. "Islam Embedded: 'Moderate' Political Islam and Governance in the Malay World". In *Islam in Southeast Asia: Political, Social and Strategic Challenges for the 21st Century*, edited by

K.S. Nathan and Mohammad Hashim Kamali. Singapore: Institute of Southeast Asian Studies, 2005. ISEAS, NTUNIE, NUS.

2093.   Siddique, Sharon. "The Administration of Islam in Singapore". In *Islam and Society in Southeast Asia*, edited by Taufik Abdullah and Sharon Siddique. Singapore: Institute of Southeast Asian Studies, 1986. ISEAS, NLB, NTUNIE, NUS.

2094.   Siddique, Sharon. "Islam and Civil Society: A Case Study from Singapore". In *Islam & Civil Society in Southeast Asia*, edited by Nakamura Mitsuo, Sharon Siddique and Omar Farouk Bajunid. Singapore: Institute of Southeast Asian Studies, 2001. ISEAS, NLB, NTUNIE, NUS

2095.   *Sinar: Risalah yang Mengandungi Berita dan Pengetahuan Tentang Islam.* Singapore: PERGAS, 1980–81. NLB, NUS.

2096.   Sofiah Ismail. "Islam and Environmentalism: Greening Our Muslim Youths". In *Igniting Thought, Unleashing Youth: Perspectives on Muslim Youth and Activism in Singapore*, edited by Mohamed Nawab and Farhan Ali. Singapore: Select Pub. in association with Young AMP, 2009. ISEAS, NLB, NTUNIE, NUS.

2097.   Stauth, Georg. "Slave Trade, Multiculturalism and Islam in Colonial Singapore: A Sociological Note on Christian Snouck Hurgronje's 1891 Article on Slave Trade in Singapore". *Southeast Asian Journal of Social Science* 20, no. 1 (1992): 67–79. ISEAS, NLB, NTUNIE, NUS.

2098.   Suzaina Kadir. "Islam, State and Society in Singapore". *Inter-Asia Cultural Studies* 5, no. 3 (2006): 357–71. NTU, NTUNIE, NUS.

2099.   Tan K.B., Eugene et al. *To Post or Not to Post? Multiculturalism in the Social Media.* Occasional Paper Series, no. 1-2012. Singapore: Centre for Research on Islamic and Malay Affairs, 2012. 40 pp. ISEAS, NUS.

2100.   Tham Seong Chee. *Islam and Secularism: Dynamics of Accommodation.* Seminar Papers, no. 14. Singapore: Department of Malay Studies, National University of Singapore, 1993. 30 leaves. ISEAS, NLB, NTUNIE, NUS. Also published under the same title in: *Jurnal Pengajian Melayu* 5 (1993): 18–34. NLB.

2101.   Tisdall, C.E.G. "Singapore as a Centre for Moslem Work". *Moslem World* 8 (January 1918): 5–9. NUS.

2102.   *Utusan Islam = Muslim Messenger*. Singapore: [s.n.], 1971–75. ISEAS, NUS.

2103.   Weyland, Petra. "International Muslim Networks and Islam in Singapore". *Sojourn: Social Issues in Southeast Asia* 5, no. 2 (August 1990): 219–54. ISEAS, NLB, NTUNIE, NUS. Also published in Indonesian under the title: "Jaringan-Jaringan Umat Islam Internasional dan Islam di Singapura". In *Asia Tenggara Konsentrasi Baru Kebangkitan Islam*, edited by Moeflich Hasbullah. Bandung: Fokusmedia, 2003. ISEAS.

2104.   Wu, Ridzuan Abdullah. "Erosion of Islamic Identity: The Singapore Challenge". *Fajar Islam* 1, no. 1 (1988): 69–78. ISEAS, NLB, NUS.

2105.   Yang Razali Kassim. "Islam in Southeast Asia: Analysing Recent Developments — Singapore's Muslim Community". In *Islam in Southeast Asia: Analysing Recent Developments*, by Harold Crouch et al. Singapore: Institute of Southeast Asian Studies, 2002. ISEAS, NLB, NTU, NUS.

2106.   Yegar, Moshe. *Islam and Islamic Institutions in British Malaya: Policies and Implementation*. Jerusalem: Magnes Press, 1979. 302 pp. ISEAS, NLB, NUS.

2107.   Yeo Wee Ming. "Malay Animism and Islamic Orthodoxy in Singapore". Academic exercise, Department of Sociology, National University of Singapore, 1989. 57 pp. NUS.

2108.   Zaki, Mohamed Aboulkhir. "Modern Muslim Thought in Egypt and Its Impact on Islam in Malaya". PhD dissertation, University of London, 1966. 1 microfilm reel. 424 pp.

Islamic Revival and Radicalism

2109.   Abdul Halim Kader, comp. & ed. *Countering Radicalism: The Next Generation and Challenges Ahead*. Singapore: Taman Bacaan Pemuda Pemudi Melayu Singapura, 2009. 169 pp. ISEAS, NLB.

2110.   Abdul Halim Kader, comp. *Fighting Terrorism: Preventing the Radicalisation of Youth in a Secular and Globalised World*. Singapore: Taman Bacaan Pemuda Pemudi Melayu Singapura, 2007. 288 pp. NLB, NUS.

2111.   Alatas, Syed Hussein. "Perceptions of Muslim Revival". *The Muslim World* 97, no. 3 (2007): 377–384. NTUNIE, NUS.

2112. Azhar Ibrahim Alwee. "The Idea of Religious Reform: Perspectives of Singapore Malay-Muslim Experiences". In *Muslim Reform in Southeast Asia: Perspectives from Malaysia, Indonesia and* Singapore, edited by Syed Farid Alatas. Singapore: Majlis Ugama Islam Singapura, 2009. ISEAS, NLB.

2113. Bilveer Singh. "Singapore's Policy Toward Islamic Militant Groups". In *Militant Islamic Movements in Indonesia and South-East Asia*, by S. Yunanto et al Jakarta: Friedrich-Ebert-Stiftung, Ridep Institute, 2003. 310 pp. ISEAS, NLB.

2114. Bohari Jaon. "Reconsiderations: An Introspection on the Islamic Revival in Contemporary Singapore: Its Genesis and Orientation". *Sedar* (1983): 18–38. ISEAS, NLB, NUS.

2115. Bohari Jaon. "The Reawakening of Islam in Singapore". *Assyahid: Journal of the Muslim Youth Assembly* 1, no. 1 (1983): 86–111. ISEAS, NLB, NUS.

2116. Desker, Barry H.P. "The Jemaah Islamiyah (JI) Phenomenon in Singapore". *Contemporary Southeast Asia* 25, no. 3 (December 2003): 489–507. ISEAS, NLB, NTUNIE, NUS.

2117. Djamal Tukimin. *Beberapa Pemikiran tentang Reformasi Islam dan Hubungannya dengan Muhammadiyah*. Singapore: Masjid Jihad, 1977.

2118. Foo Chai Kwong, Alan. "Countering Radical Terrorism in Southeast Asia — A Case Study on Jemaah Islamiyah (JI) Network". *The Pointer* 35, no. 2 (2009): 32–44. NLB, NTUNIE.

2119. Heng Ju-Li. "Countering Radicalization in Singapore: Commonalities and Discourse". In *Countering Radicalism: The Next Generation and Challenges Ahead*, compiled and edited by Abdul Halim Bin Kader. Singapore: Taman Bacaan Pemuda Pemudi Melayu Singapura, 2009. 169 pp. ISEAS.

2120. Hussin Mutalib. "Islamic Revivalism in ASEAN States: Political Implications". *Asian Survey* 30, no. 9 (1990): 877–91. ISEAS, NLB, NTU, NTUNIE, NUS.

2121. Lee Kuan Yew. "We Can Overcome". *Speeches* 26, no. 1 (January–February 2002): 13–16. ISEAS.

2122. "Mas Selamat bin Kastari". In *Wikipedia: The Free Encyclopedia.* [U.S.]: Wikimedia Foundation, Inc., 2008. Available at <http://en.wikipedia.org/wiki/Mas_Selamat_Kastari>.

2123. Md. Kamal Hasan. "Revolusi dan Ledakan Rohani Barat". *Budaya: Penyambung Lidah Majlis Pusat* Bil 2 (1983): 25–30. NLB, NUS.

2124. Mohamed Nawab Mohamed Osman. "Countering Extremism amongst Muslim Youth in Singapore". In *Igniting Thought, Unleashing Youth: Perspectives on Muslim Youth and Activism in Singapore,* edited by Mohamed Nawab and Farhan Ali. Singapore: Select Publishing in association with Young AMP, 2009. ISEAS, NLB, NTUNIE, NUS.

2125. Muhammad Haniff Hassan. "Counter Ideological Work: Singapore Experience". In *The Ideological War on Terror: Worldwide Strategies for Counter-Terrorism,* edited by Anne Aldis and Graeme P. Herd. London; New York: Routledge, 2007. NLB, NTUNIE, NUS.

2126. Muhammad Haniff Hassan and Tuty Raihanah Mostarom. *A Decade of Combating Radical Ideology: Learning from the Singapore Experience (2001–2011).* RSIS Monograph, no. 29. Singapore: S. Rajaratnam School of International Studies, Nanyang Technological University. 84 pp. ISEAS, NLB, NTUNIE, NUS.

2127. Muhammad Mubarak Habib Mohamed. "Religious Rehabilitation Group — RRG". *Inabah* 25 (January 2014): 22–27. NLB.

2128. Omar Farouk Bajunid. "Malaysia's Islamic Awakening: Impact on Singapore and Thai Muslims". In *Muslim Social Science in ASEAN,* edited by Omar Farouk Bajunid. Kuala Lumpur: Yayasan Penataran Ilmu, Penerbit Universiti Malaya, 1994. ISEAS, NLB, NUS. Also published under the same title in: *Conflict* 8, no. 2/3 (1988): 157–68. ISEAS, NUS.

2129. Ramakrishna, Kumar. "The Case of DIY Radical Abdul Basheer: The Blind Path to Radicalism". In *Countering Radicalism: The Next Generation and Challenges Ahead,* compiled and edited by Abdul Halim Bin Kader. Singapore: Taman Bacaan Pemuda Pemudi Melayu Singapura, 2009. ISEAS, NLB.

2130. Ramakrishna, Kumar. "Self-Radicalization: The Case of Abdul Basheer Abdul Kader". In *Strategic Currents: Emerging Trends in Southeast Asia,* vol. 2, edited by Yang Razali Kassim. Singapore: Institute of Defence and Strategic Studies, 2008. ISEAS, NTUNIE.

2131. Roff, William R. "Kaum Muda-Kaum Tua, Innovation and Reaction amongst the Malays, 1900–1941". In *Papers on Malayan History*, edited by K.G. Tregonning. Singapore: University of Malaya Press, 1961. ISEAS, NLB, NTUNIE, NUS.

2132. Saat A. Rahman, ed. *Winning Hearts and Minds, Promoting Harmony: A Decade of Providing Care and Support*. Singapore: RRG, 2013. 191 pp. NLB.
(Commemorating the 10th Anniversary of the Religious Rehabilitation Group).

2133. Saywell, Trish. "Common Ground". *Far Eastern Economic Review* 165, no. 3 (24 January 2002): 20–22. ISEAS, NLB, NTUNIE, NUS.

2134. Singapore. Committee of Inquiry on the Escape of Jemaah Islamiyah Detainee, Mas Selamat bin Kastari, From the Whitley Road Detention Centre. "Report of the Committee of Inquiry on the Escape of Jemaah Islamiyah Detainee, Mas Selamat bin Kastari, From the Whitley Road Detention Centre: Executive Summary". The Committee submitted its report to the Minister for Home Affairs on 10 April 2008. Available at <www.channelnewsasia.com/annex/ms-summary.pdf>.

2135. Singapore. Parliament. *The Jemaah Islamiyah Arrests and the Threat of Terrorism: White Paper*. Singapore: Ministry of Home Affairs, 2003. 50 pp. ISEAS, NTUNIE.

2136. Tan, Andrew. "The Singapore Experience". In *Terrorism in the Asia-Pacific: Threat and Responses*, edited by Rohan Gunaratna. Singapore: Eastern Universities Press, 2003. ISEAS, NLB, NTUNIE, NUS.

2137. Zainuddin Mchd. Ismail. *The Making of a Singapore Fundamentalist: Post Sept. 11 Ramblings of Mangkaka Boy*. Pittsburgh, PA: Red Lead Press, 2007. 259 pp. ISEAS.

Islamic Organizations and Leadership

2138. *75 Years of Jamiyah Singapore (1932–2007): Deeds Inspired Hopes Exalted = Menjana Bakti Menjulang Harapan*. Singapore: Jamiyah, 2007. 160 pp. NLB.

2139. Abdul Rahman Basrun. "The AI-Arqam Movement in Singapore". Research exercise, Department of Malay Studies, National University of Singapore, 1994. 65 pp. NUS.

2140. Ahmad Mattar. "Elected Officials of Organizations Must Be Dedicated". *Speeches* 4, no. 9 (March 1981): 55–56. ISEAS, NLB, NTUNIE, NUS.

2141. Aljunied, Syed Muhd Khairudin. "The 'Other' Muhammadiyah Movement: Singapore 1958–2008". *Journal of Southeast Asian Studies* 42, no. 2 (2011): 281–302. ISEAS, NLB, NTUNIE, NUS.

2142. *Ashshahid: Jernal Himpunan Belia Islam.* Singapore: HBI, 1985–. NLB. Continues *Assyahid: Journal of the Muslim Youth Assembly.* Singapore: Himpunan Belia Islam, 1976–85. ISEAS, NLB.

2143. Azhar Ibrahim (Alwee). "Malay-Muslim Religious Discourse in Singapore: The Assertions of Religious Elites and Dakwah Activists in the Public Spheres". In *Contemporary Islamic Discourse in the Malay-Indonesian World: Critical Perspectives*, by Azhar Ibrahim. Petaling Jaya: Strategic Information and Research Development Centre, 2014. ISEAS, NLB, NUS.

2144. *Cenderahati 50 tahun Persatuan Muhammadiyah Singapura: 1957–2007.* Singapore: Persatuan Muhammadiyah Singapura, Jabatan Penerangan dan Penerbitan, 2007. 58 pp. NLB.

2145. "Donation for the Islamic Centre Jamiyah, Singapore: Shaikh AI- Azhar's Visit to the Centre". *The Muslim World League Journal* 14, no. 1 (October 1986): 15. NUS.

2146. Husain Haikal and Atiku Garba Yahaya. "Muslim Organizations in Singapore: An Historical Overview". *Islamic Studies* 35, no. 4 (1996): 435–47. ISEAS, NTUNIE, NUS.

2147. Jamari Mohtar. "Uhud: Lessons for Leaders in the 21st Century". *Nadi* 2 (October 2005): 4–6. NLB, NUS.

2148. *Jamiyah Bulletin.* Singapore: Muslim Missionary Society of Singapore, 1982–. NLB, NUS.

2149. "Jamiyah's Brief History". In *The Honourable Mr. Lee Kuan Yew, Prime Minister of Singapore, 1959–1990: Your Deeds Remembered, Your Services Appreciated.* Singapore: Muslim Missionary Society Singapore (Jamiyah), 1990. NLB, NUS.

2150.   "Introduction to Muslim Youth Assembly Himpunan Belia Islam (HBI): An Observation by Research Committee". In *Assyahid: Journal of the Muslim Youth Association* 1, no. 1 (1983): 172–79. ISEAS, NLB.

2151.   Mohamed Nawab Mohamed Osman. "The Religio-Political Activism of Ulama in Singapore". *Indonesia and the Malay World* 40, no. 116 (March 2012): 1–19. ISEAS, NLB, NUS.

2152.   Mohd. Ali Mahmood et al., eds. *Lighting Lives: The PPIS Story*. Singapore: Persatuan Pemudi Islam Singapura (PPIS), 2008. 115 pp. NLB.

2153.   Mohd. Daud Hashim. "Religious Institutions amongst the Malays of Singapore: A Comparison Study of a Rural and Urban Area". Academic exercise, Department of Social Studies, University of Malaya, 1958. 62 pp. NUS.

2154.   Muhammad Mubarak Habib Mohamed. "Religious Rehabilitation Group — RRG". *Inabah* 25 (January 2014): 22–27. NLB.

2155.   Noor Aisha Abdul Rahman. "The Muslim Religious Elite of Singapore". In *Religious Diversity in Singapore*, edited by Lai Ah Eng. Singapore: Institute of Policy Studies, 2008. ISEAS, NLB, NTUNIE, NUS.

2156.   Norshahril Saat. *Faith, Authority and the Malays: The Ulama in Contemporary Singapore*. Singapore: The Malay Heritage Foundation and Select Publishing, 2015. 111 pp. ISEAS, NLB, NUS.

2157.   Peacock, James L. "Singapore". In *Muslim Puritans: Reformist Psychology in Southeast Asian Islam*, by James L. Peacock. Berkeley: University of California Press, 1978. ISEAS, NLB, NUS.

2158.   Persekutuan Seruan Islam Singapura. *Annual Report*. Singapore: Muslim Missionary Society of Singapore, 1933–. NLB, NUS.

2159.   Persekutuan Seruan Islam Singapura. *Sejarah dan Kegiatan-Kegiatan Jamiyah Singapura = History and Activities of Jamiyah Singapore*. Singapore: Persekutuan Seruan Islam Singapura, [1985?]. 92 pp. ISEAS.

2160.   "Pertubuhan Islam di Singapura (JAMIYAH)". In *Ensiklopedia Sejarah dan Kebudayaan Melayu*, vol. 3, pp. 1929–30. Kuala Lumpur: Dewan Bahasa dan Pustaka, 1994. NLB, NTUNIE, NUS.

2161.   *Souvenir Magazine for Opening Ceremony of the Islamic Centre, Jamiyah Singapore & Commemoration of the 50th Anniversary of Jamiyah*. Singapore: Muslim Missionary Society Singapore, 1985. 307 pp. NLB, NUS.

2162. *Suara Muhammadiyah = The Voice of Muhammadiyah.* Singapore: Muharnmadiyah Singapura, 1970–. ISEAS, NLB, NUS.

2163. Sundusia Rosdi. "Menelusuri 60 Tahun Hijrah PERGAS". In *Gema Kesyukuran: Perjalanan 60 Tahun Hijrah.* Singapore: Persatuan Ulama dan Guru-Guru Agama Singapura, 2014. NLB.

2164. Tan Hui Sen, Robert. "The Cultural Landscape of Singapore: A Study of the Growth and Distribution of Religious Institutions on the Island (1819–1961)". Academic exercise, University of Malaya, Singapore, 1963. Microform. NUS.

2165. Tuty Raihanah Mostarom. "The Political in 'De-Politicization': The Role of the *Ulama* in Singapore". Paper presented at a [Seminar on] Muslim Religious Authority in Contemporary Asia, organized by Asia Research Institute, National University of Singapore, 24–25 November 2011. Its abstract is available at <http://www.ari.nus.edu.sg/showfile. asp?eventfileid=663>.

2166. Tuty Raihanah Mostarom. "The Singapore Ulama Religious Agency in the Context of a Strong State". *Asian Journal of Social Science* 42, issue 5 (2014): 561–83. ISEAS, NLB, NTUNIE, NUS.

2167. *Voice of Islam = Suara Islam = Sawt al-Islam.* Singapore: Muslim Missionary Society Singapore, [1970]–. Title varies slightly. ISEAS, NLB, NUS. Available at <http://www.jamiyah.org.sg/edisi/data/voi/>.

2168. W.K. Che Man (Wan Kadir Che Man). *The Administration of Islamic Institutions in Non-Muslim States: The Case of Singapore and Thailand.* Teaching and Research Exchange Fellowship, no. 10. Singapore: Southeast Asian Studies Program, Institute of Southeast Asian Studies, 1991. 25 pp. ISEAS, NLB, NUS.

MUIS

2169. Ahmad Mattar. "10 Years of Majlis Ugama Islam". *Speeches* 2, no. 2 (August 1978): 27–29. ISEAS, NLB, NTUNIE, NUS.

2170. Abdullah Tarmugi. "Challenging Times for MUIS". *Speeches* 24, no. 4 (July–August 2000): 64–67. ISEAS, NLB, NTUNIE.

2171. Ahmad Mattar. "Functions of MUIS". *Speeches* 3, no. 10 (April 1980): 80–82. ISEAS, NLB, NTUNIE, NUS.

2172.   Ahmad Mattar. "Need for Innovative Thinking". *Speeches* 1, no. 5 (November 1977): 63–69. ISEAS, NLB, NTUNIE, NUS.

2173.   Green, Anthony. *Honouring the Past, Shaping the Future: The MUIS Story: 40 Years of Building a Singapore Muslim Community of Excellence.* Singapore: Majlis Ugama Islam Singapura, 2009. 148 pp. ISEAS, NLB, NTUNIE, NUS.

2174.   Majlis Ugama Islam Singapura. *Annual Report.* Singapore: Majlis Ugama Islam Singapura, 1973–2006. ISEAS, NLB, NTU, NTUNIE, NUS. Available from 1998 onwards at <http://www.muis.gov.sg/cms/aboutus/annual.a\ spx?id=444>.

2175.   "Moving with the Times" *Warita Kita* 133 (May/June 2001): 3–6. ISEAS, NLB, NUS.

2176.   "MUIS: Detik-Detik Bersejarah". *Warita Kita* 116 (Mei–Ogos 1998): 6–7. ISEAS, NLB, NUS.

2177.   Mutahar, Sayyid Hassan. "Muslim Religious Council of Singapore". *Muslim World League Journal* 8 (June 1981): 53–55. NUS.

2178.   *Pusat Islam Singapura = Islamic Centre of Singapore: Official Opening, Sunday 13 Syawal 1408H. 29 May 1988.* Singapore: MUIS, 1988. 59 pp. NUS.

2179.   Ramlah Rahmat. "Majlis Ugama Islam Singapura: 1968–1977". Academic exercise, Jabatan Sejarah, Universiti Kebangsaan Malaysia, 1978. 203 pp. NUS.

2180.   Shahril Mohd Shah. "From the Mohammedan Advisory Board to the Muslim Advisory Board". In *Malays/Muslims in Singapore: Selected Readings in History, 1819–1965*, edited by Khoo Kay Kim, Elinah Abdullah and Wan Meng Hao. Subang Jaya, Selangor: Pelanduk Publications in cooperation with Centre for Research on Islamic and Malay Affairs, Singapore, 2006. ISEAS, NLB, NTUNIE, NUS.

2181.   Shahril Mohd. Shah. "The Muslim Advisory Board of Singapore, 1947–1968". Academic exercise, Department of History, National University of Singapore, 1990. 71 pp. NUS.

2182.   *Singapore Muslim Religious Council.* Singapore: MUIS, 1977. 12 pp. ISEAS, NLB.

2183. *Warita Kita*. Singapore: Majlis Ugama Islam Singapura, 1998–. ISEAS, NLB, NUS. Continues *Warita Majlis Ugama Islam*. Singapore: Majlis Ugama Islam Singapura, 1978–98. ISEAS, NLB, NUS.

2184. Zainul Abidin Rasheed. "MUIS and MENDAKI: Current and Future Challenges". Seminar Papers, no. 5. Singapore: Department of Malay Studies, National University Singapore, 1992. 18 pp. NTUNIE, NUS.

Mosques

2185. Abaza, Mona. "A Mosque of Arab Origin in Singapore: History, Functions and Networks". *Archipel* 53 (1997): 61–83. ISEAS, NLB, NUS.

2186. Abbas Kechik. "Mosque: A Comparative Study of a Sub-Urban and a City Mosque". Academic exercise, Department of Social Studies, University of Malaya, Singapore, 1962. 56 pp. NUS.

2187. *Abdul Gaffoor Mosque Preservation Guidelines*. Singapore: Preservation of Monuments Board, 1991. 2 vols. NLB, NUS.

2188. A. Ghani Hamid (Abdul Ghani Hamid). *Seni Indah Masjid di Singapura*. Singapore: Angkatan Pelukis Aneka Daya, 1990. 43 pp. NLB, NUS.

2189. Ahmad Mattar. "The Mosque Building Programme Exemplifies Self-Help". *Speeches* 5, no. 6 (October 1981): 58–60. ISEAS, NLB, NTUNIE, NUS.

2190. Ahmad Mattar. "Nine More Mosques in Public Housing Estates". *Speeches* 5, no. 1 (July 1981): 66–68. ISEAS, NLB, NTUNIE, NUS.

2191. *Al-Abrar Mosque Preservation Guidelines*. Singapore: Preservation of Monuments Board, 1991. 2 vols. NLB, NUS.

2192. Aljunied, Syed Muhd Khairudin. "AMLA, Mosques, and Madrasahs in Contemporary Singapore". *Karyawan: Professionals for the Community* 9, issue 2 (January 2009): 11–13. ISEAS, NLB, NTUNIE, NUS.

2193. Alsagoff, Syed Abubakar bin Mohamad bin Ali, comp. *Masjid-Masjid di Singapura 1413 = Mosques in Singapore 1992*. Singapore: Muslim Advancement Systems, 1992. 40 pp. NLB.

2194. Alsagoff, Syed Omar. "Masjid-Masjid di Republik Singapura". *Fajar Islam* 2 (November 1970): 29–30. ISEAS, NLB, NUS.

2195. "Anugerah CIDB untuk Masjid". *Warita* 94 (May–June 1994): 3. ISEAS, NLB, NUS.

2196. "The Assyafaah Mosque". *Architecture Asia: A Journal of the Architects Regional Council Asia* 1 (March–May 2005): 36–41. NLB, NUS.

2197. *Assyakirin.* Singapore: Lembaga Masjid Assyakirin, 1979–. NLB.

2198. "Enhancing Mosque Maintenance". *Warita Kita* 136 (November/December 2001): 26–27. ISEAS, NLB, NUS.

2199. *Fatimah Mosque Preservation Guidelines.* Singapore: Preservation of Monuments Board, 1991. 2 vols. NLB, NUS.

2200. "First for a Restored Mosque". *Skyline* (November/December 2003): 2–4. NLB, NTUNIE, NUS.

2201. Green, Anthony. *Continuing the Legacy: 30 Years of the Mosque Building Fund in Singapore.* Singapore: Majlis Ugama Islam Singapura, 2007. 136 pp. NLB, NUS.

2202. Hadijah Rahmat et al., eds. *The Last Kampung Mosque in Singapore: The Extraordinary Story and Legacy of Sembawang.* Singapore: Masjid Petempatan Melayu Sembawang in collaboration with Berita Harian/ SPH, 2007. 186 pp. NLB, NTUNIE, NUS.

2203. Hassan Selamat. "Masjid Khadijah". *Fajar Islam* 5 (1985): 46–50. ISEAS, NLB, NUS.

2204. "A Historical Landmark Serving Religious Needs". *Warita Kita* 136 (November/December 2001): 23. ISEAS, NLB, NUS.

2205. "History of Khadijah Mosque". *Inabah* 25 (January 2014): 46–50. NLB.

2206. Imran Tajudeen. "Adaptation and Accentuation: Type of Transformation in Vernacular Nusantarian Mosque Design and Their Contemporary Significance in Melaka, Minangkabau and Singapore". In *ISVS IV: Pace or Speed? 4th International Seminar on Vernacular Settlement, Ahmedabad, India, February 14–17, 2008: Proceedings*, pp. 143–62. Ahmedabad: Faculty of Architecture, CEPT University, 2008.

2207. *Jamae Mosque Preservation Guidelines.* Singapore: Preservation of Monuments Board, 1991. 2 vols. NLB, NUS.

2208. *Management of Mosque Rules, 1978.* Singapore: Majlis Ugama Islam Singapura, 1978. 8 pp. NLB, NUS.

2209. Mansor Haji Sukaimi, ed. *Dynamic Functions of Mosques: The Singapore Experience.* Singapore: Majlis Ugama Islam Singapura, 1982. 40 pp. ISEAS, NLB, NTUNIE, NUS.

2210. Maryam Yong. "Malabar Muslim Jama-ath Mosque". *Vizier Singapore* (Shawwal 1433): 16–17. NLB.

2211. "Masjid al-Ansar, Bedok". *SIAJ* 110 (January/February 1982): 26–27. NLB, NUS.

2212. "Masjid Alkaff Kampong Melayu: JPM Gembira dengan Reka Bentuk Masjid". *Warita* 92 (January–February 1994): 5. ISEAS, NLB, NUS.

2213. "Masjid al-Muttaqin, Ang Mo Kio". *SIAJ* 110 (January/February 1982): 24–25. NLB, NUS.

2214. "Masjid Jamiyah al-Rabitah". *Fajar Islam* 3 (1984): 34–37. ISEAS, NLB, NUS.

2215. "Masjid Kebun Limau". *Fajar Islam* 2 (1983): 44–49. ISEAS, NLB, NUS.

2216. "Masjid-Masjid Singapura Nadi Kegiatan Dakwah". *Al Islam* (April 2002): 44–47. NLB.

2217. "Masjid Mujahidin (Queenstown Mosque)". *SIAJ* 88 (May/June 1978): 6–9. NLB, NUS.

2218. "Masjid Memenuhi Keperluan Ummah". *Warita Kita* 132 (March–April 2001): 22–23. ISEAS, NLB, NUS.

2219. "Masjid Sultan". *Fajar Islam* 4 (1984): 44–50. ISEAS, NLB, NUS.

2220. "Masjid Sultan". In *Ensiklopedia Sejarah dan Kebudayaan Melayu*, vol. 3, pp. 1471–72. Kuala Lumpur: Dewan Bahasa dan Pustaka, 1994. NLB, NTUNIE, NUS.

2221. "Masjid Wak Tanjong". *Fajar Islam* 1 (1983): 38, 44. ISEAS, NLB, NUS.

2222. "MBMF (Mosque Building and Mendaki Fund)". *Nadi* 1 (June 2005): 23. NLB, NUS.

2223. Melati Haji Salleh. "Mosques in Singapore". Academic exercise, University of Singapore, 1979. 143 pp. NUS.

2224. Mosque Convention (2005: Singapore). *Remodelling Mosques*. Singapore: Islamic Religious Council of Singapore, 2005. 279 pp. NLB.

2225. Mosque Convention (2011: Singapore). *Enhancing Spirituality, Guiding Community, Changing Lives*. Singapore: Majlis Ugama Islam Singapura, 2011. 128 pp. Available at <http://www.muis.gov.sg/cms/uploadedFiles/MuisGovSG/Mosque/MC11.pdf>.

2226. Mosque Seminar (2000: Singapore). *Strengthening Mosque Effectiveness in the 21th Century = Pengukuhan Keberkesanan Masjid di Abad ke 21*. Singapore: Majlis Ugama Islam Singapura, 2000. 128 pp. NLB.

2227. "Mosques as Centres of Excellence". *Warita Kita* 135 (September/October 2001): 22–23. ISEAS, NLB, NUS.

2228. "Mosques Built by HDB". *SIAJ* 110 (January/February 1982): 19–27. NLB, NUS.

2229. "Mosques Need Trained Counsellors". *Warita Kita* 133 (May/June 2001): 10–11. ISEAS, NLB, NUS.

2230. "Mosques of the New Millennium". *Warita Kita* 133 (March/April 2001): 8–11. ISEAS, NLB, NUS.

2231. *New Generation Mosques and Their Activities Bringing Back the Golden Era of Islam in Singapore*. Singapore: Majlis Ugama Islam Singapura, 1991. 48 pp. NUS. Previous ed. published under the title: *New Generation Mosques in Singapore and Their Activities*. Singapore: MUIS, 1986. 44 pp. ISEAS, NLB, NTUNIE, NUS.

2232. Razak Mohd Lazim. "Our Mosques: The Next Phase". *Nadi* 2 (October 2005): 7–11. NLB, NUS.

2233. Razali Abdullah. "Masjid Aminah: Tempat Jatuh Lagi Dikenang". *Fajar Islam* 8 (1986): 49–51. ISEAS, NLB, NUS.

2234. Ritawillis Selamat. "The Mosque as a Focal Point of Malay Religious Life, with Reference to the Al-Ansar Mosque". Research exercise, Department of Malay Studies, National University of Singapore, 1994. 40 pp. NUS.

2235. S. Markasan (Suratman Markasan). "Surau, Masjid dan Madrasah Adalah Sebahagian Daripada Identiti Bangsa Melayu Singapura". In *Bangsa Melayu Singapura dalam Transformasi Budayanya*. Singapore: Anuar Othman & Associates Media Enterprise, 2005. NLB, NTUNIE, NUS.

2236. Salmah Buang. "The Extension of Sultan Mosque — An Islamic Centre". Academic exercise, National University of Singapore, 1989. 95 pp. NUS.

2237. *Sambutan Ulangtahun ke-15 Masjid Muhajirin 1977–1992.* Singapore: Lembaga Pentadbiran Masjid Muhajirin, 1992. 52 pp. NLB, NUS.

2238. *Sejarah Ringkas Masjid Sultan, Singapura.* Singapore: Trustees of Masjid Sultan, 1968. 38 pp. NUS.

2239. *Sempena Majlis Perasmian Masjid Alkaff Kampung Melayu, 1 Rabiulawal 1416H Bersamaan 29 Julai 1995.* Singapore: Jawatankuasa Buku Cenderamat, Masjid Alkaff Kampung Melayu, 1995. 56 pp. NLB.

2240. Seward, Pat. "New Mosques: Old Traditions". *Beam* 31, no. 1 (May 1987): 22–24. NLB, NUS.

2241. Siddique, Sharon. "Singapore's New Generation Mosques". *Petir: Organ of the People's Action Party* (July 1986): 18. ISEAS, NLB, NUS.

2242. Singapore. Media Development Authority. *Places & Faces. Episode 3, A House of Prayer.* Series producer, Lee Chang Yong; editor, Rizal Mattar; directors, Melissa Ong and Samantha Sng. Singapore: MediaCorp TV12 Singapore Pte. Ltd., 2003. 1 videocassette (VHS, PAL). 30 min. NUS.

2243. *Sultan Mosque Preservation Guidelines.* Singapore: Urban Redevelopment Authority for Preservation of Monuments Board, 1991. 2 vols. NLB, NUS.

2244. Suratee, Muhammad Faishal Ibrahim Khan. "Towards a Better Maintenance Management of Mosques in Singapore". Academic exercise, National University of Singapore, 1993. 184 pp. NUS.

2245. Syed Zakir Hussain. "New-Look Mosques Take on Varied Roles". In *Countering Radicalism: The Next Generation and Challenges Ahead,* compiled and edited by Abdul Halim Kader. Singapore: Taman Bacaan Pemuda Pemudi Melayu, 2009. ISEAS, NLB, NUS.

2246. Tan Wee Kiat. *Singapore Heritage: Places of Worship.* Singapore: Singapore Philatelic Museum, 2012. 15 pp. NLB, NTUNIE.

2247. Taufeeq Mohd. "Ba'alwi Mosque". *Vizier Singapore* 03/2012 = *Dhul-qa'dah* 1433: 9. NLB.

2248. Ten Leu-Jiun. "The Invention of a Tradition: Indo-Saracenic Domes on Mosques in Singapore". *BiblioAsia* 9, no. 1 (April–June 2013): 16–23. NLB, NTUNIE, NUS.

2249. Teo Chee Hean. "Roles of Mosque in the Information Age". In *Jendela Kata: Kumpulan Ucapan Muis Siri ke-3*. Singapore: Majlis Ugama Islam Singapura, 2000. ISEAS, NLB, NUS.

2250. Zhuang, Justin. "Carving Back Air: Kampung Siglap Mosque". *Singapore Architect* 256 (2010): 90–95. NLB, NUS.

2251. Zuraidah Abdul Karim. "Kepelbagaian Peranan Masjid di Singapura". Academic exercise, Department of Malay Studies, National University of Singapore, 1991. 50 pp. NUS.

Religious Life

2252. A. Rahim Ishak (Abdul Rahim Ishak). "Teachings of Islam". *Speeches* 2, no. 9 (March 1979): 46–49. ISEAS, NTUNIE.

2253. Abdul Majid Zainuddin. "A Malay's Pilgrimage to Mecca". *JMBRAS* 4, no. 2 (October 1927): 269–87. ISEAS, NLB, NTUNIE, NUS.

2254. Abu Bakar Hashim. "Wang CPF dan Hukum Zakat: Satu Tinjauan". Paper presented at a Regional Islamic Convention, arranged by the Islamic Centre, Jamiyah Singapore, 24–27 April 1986. 7 pp. ISEAS, NUS.

2255. Ahmad Mattar. "Harmonious and Co-operative Living". *Speeches* 4, no. 10 (April 1981): 43–44. ISEAS, NLB, NTUNIE, NUS.

2256. Ahmad Mattar. "Lessons from the Fast". *Speeches* 17, no. 2 (March–April 1993): 27–31. ISEAS, NLB, NTUNIE, NUS.

2257. Ahmad Mattar. "Looking after Welfare of Muslims". *Speeches* 2, no. 6 (December 1978): 26–28. ISEAS, NLB, NTUNIE, NUS.

2258. Alatas, Syed Hussein. *Biarkan Buta: Sekitar Perbahasan Ilmiah Mengenai Derma Cornea-Mata dengan Majlis Ugama Islam, Singapura, 10 Ogos-7 September 1973*. Singapore: Pustaka Nasional, 1974. 101 pp. ISEAS, NLB, NUS.

2259. Alfred, E.R. "The Pilgrim Ships of Singapore". *Heritage* 10 (1988): 20–24. ISEAS, NLB, NUS.

2260. Channel NewsAsia. *Essence of Faith. Episode 2, Hari Raya Haji Special.* Singapore: MediaCorp News, 2002. 1 videodisc (DVD). 24 min. NUS.

2261. Channel NewsAsia. *Essence of Faith. Episode 3, Hari Raya Puasa Special.* Singapore: MediaCorp News, 2002. 1 videodisc (DVD). 24 min. NUS.

2262. Firdaus Yahya. "LGBT: Critical Study". *Jurnal Dakwah* 3 (December 2012): 69–99. NLB.

2263. Gabrielpillai, Matilda. "Patriarchal Politics and the Singaporean Tudung Fetish". *Focas: Forum on Contemporary Art & Society* 5 (January 2004): 260–85. ISEAS, NLB, NTU, NTUNIE, NUS.

2264. Green, Anthony. *Our Journey: 30 Years of Haj Services in Singapore.* Singapore: Majlis Ugama Islam Singapura, 2006. 132 pp. ISEAS, NLB, NTUNIE, NUS.

2265. "Halal Certificate". *Warita Kita* 138 (March/April 2002): 138. ISEAS, NLB, NUS.

2266. *Halal Food: A Guide to Good Eating Singapore.* Kuala Lumpur: Kaseh Dia Publication, 2003–. NLB.

2267. Hoe, Irene. "Spotlight on Singapore: A Call to Prayer". *Silver Kris* 13, no. 7 (July 1988): 54–57. NLB, NUS.

2268. *Inabah: Kembali ke Jalan Allah.* Singapore: Lembaga Pentadbir Masjid Khadijah, 2000–. NLB.

2269. Julaina Kamarudin. "The Sheikh System in Singapore". *Journal of the South Seas Society* 28, no. 1/2 (December 1973): 79–105. ISEAS, NLB, NTUNIE, NUS.

2270. Kamisah Ismail. "The Haj and Singapore: A Historical and Biographical Study of Its Effects". Academic exercise, Department of Sociology, National University of Singapore, 1987. 54 pp. NUS.

2271. Law Kam Yee. "The Myth of Multiracialism in Post-9/11 Singapore: The Tudung Incident". *New Zealand Journal of Asian Studies* 5, no. 1 (June 2003): 51–71. NUS.

2272. "The Magnet of the East". *Inter-Ocean: A Dutch East Indian Magazine Covering Malaysia and Australasia* 8, no. 2 (February 1927): 83–86. NLB.

2273. Marranci, Gabriele. "Defensive or Offensive Dining? Halal Dining Practices among Malay Muslim Singaporeans and Their Effects on Integration". *The Australian Journal of Anthropology* 23, issue 1 (April 2012): 84–100. NTUNIE, NUS.

2274. Marsh, Robert M. "Muslim Values in Islamic and Non-Islamic Societies". *Comparative Sociology* 11, no. 1 (2012): 29–63. NUS.

(Singapore has been cited as one of the non-Islamic societies).

2275. Melor Ralif. *Melor di Pusara: Aman dan Abadi*. Penyunting, Hartinah Ahmad. Singapura: Pusara Warisan, 2015. 142 pp. NLB.

2276. Miller, Harry. "Singapore – The Greatest Pilgrim Port in Asia". *The Straits Times Annual* (1938): 91, 93, 96. NLB, NUS.

2277. Mohamad Fadzly Samsuri. "Is There Such a 'Thing' as 'Culture'? A Study on the Singapore Muslim Culture and the New Generation Mosques". Academic exercise, Department of Geography, National University of Singapore, 2007. 86 pp. NUS.

2278. Mohamad Hasbi Hassan. "Masyarakat Melayu Singapura: Kehidupan Kerohanian". *Jurnal Dakwah* 4 (December 2013): 40–70. NLB.

2279. Mohamed Kamil Suhaimi. "Peranan dan Keupayaan Institusi Zakat dalam Pembangunan Islam (dari Kontek Singapura)". Paper presented at a Regional Islamic Convention, arranged by the Islamic Centre, Jamiyah Singapore, 24–27 April 1986. 26 pp. ISEAS, NUS.

2280. Mohamedzen Idris. "Our Journey: The Growth of the MUIS Haj Services". *Nad* 2 (April 2006): 20–21. NLB, NUS.

2281. Mohammad Yusri Yubhi Md. Yusoff. "Amalan Bacaan Solat Berdasarkan Sunnah Rasulullah s.a.w.: Satu Kajian di Kalangan Masyarakat Islam Singapura". *Jurnal Dakwah* 3 (December 2012): 42–68. NLB.

2282. Mohd Ikram Mohd Ariff et al. *Boy Meets Tekong: NS Guidebook for Muslims*. NLB, NTUNIE, NUS.

2283. Mohd Jakfar Embek. *Menunggak Nilai, Melurus Faham: Koleksi Rencana di Berita Harian & Berita Minggu dari 1997–2007*. Singapore: Pustaka Nasional, PERGAS, 2008. 192 pp. NLB.

2284. Muhammad Nuruddin Muhammad Yunus. "Mecca Pilgrim Traffic, 1868–1873". Academic exercise, Department of History, University of Malaya, Singapore, 1956. 84 pp. NUS.

2285. Muhammad Soffian Abdul Rahim. "A Thesis on the Institution of the Haj among the Malays in Singapore: A Study of the Expectations of the Pilgrims and the Consequences such Expectations have on Their Lives". Academic exercise, Department of Social Studies, University of Singapore, 1963. 1 vol. (various pagings). NUS.

2286. Mukhlis Abu Bakar. "Going Back to Our Root". *Karyawan: Professionals for the Community* 3 (September–November 1997): 26–27. ISEAS, NLB, NTUNIE, NUS.

2287. *The Muslim Ummah: Challenges, Directions & Reflections.* Singapore: NUS Muslim Society, 2000. 132 pp. NLB.

2288. *Muslims in Singapore: Beliefs and Practices.* Singapore: Islamic Religious Council of Singapore, 2003. 1 CD-ROM. ISEAS.

2289. Noorman Abdullah. *(Re)Thinking the Categories of Halal and Haram: Notes on Islamic Food Rules in Singapore.* Working Papers, no. 168. Singapore: Department of Sociology, National University of Singapore, 2004. 37 pp. ISEAS, NUS.

2290. Nor-Afidah Abdul Rahman. "Journeys of Faith: Haj Pilgrimage in the Malay Archipelago before the 20th Century". *BiblioAsia* 2, no. 3 (October 2006): 6–11. NLB, NTUNIE, NUS.

2291. Nor Ashikin Kader Saheer. "Organ Transplantation, Islamic Banking, Takaful: Contemporary Issues in Islam which are Concerned with the Practicalities of the Daily Lives of the Malay-Muslims in Singapore". Research exercise, Department of Malay Studies, National University of Singapore, 1995. 39 pp. NUS.

2292. "Nurturing Strong, Righteous & Contributing Muslims". *Warita Kita* 137 (January/February 2002): 3–6. ISEAS, NLB, NUS.

2293. *Pemindahan Organ di dalam Islam: Fiqh dan Perlaksanaan di Singapura.* Singapore: Majlis Ugama Islam, [2009?]. 12 pp. NLB.

2294. Rajendran, N. "Notes on Haji Labour in Early Singapore". *Malaysia in History* 25 (1982): 123–25. NLB, NUS.

2295. *Report [on] Feedback on Pilgrimage Services, 1984.* Singapore: MUIS, [1984?]. 19 pp. NUS.

2296. *Risalah for Building a Singapore Muslim Community of Excellence.* Singapore: Office of the Mufti, Majlis Ugama Islam Singapura, 2006. 104 pp. NLB.

2297. Salim Osman. "The Haj Business". *Inabah* 8, no. 1 (February 2001): 72–73. NLB.

2298. Sanusi Mahmood, Haji. "Adakah Wang Tabung Simpanan Pekerja (CPF) Dikenakan Zakat". Paper presented at a Regional Islamic Convention, arranged by the Islamic Centre, Jamiyah Singapore, 24–27 April 1986. 3 pp. ISEAS, NUS.

2299. Semait, Syed Isa Mohamed. "Adakah Wang Simpanan Pekerja (CPF Wajib Dizakatkan?" Paper presented at a Regional Islamic Convention, arranged by the Islamic Centre, Jamiyah Singapore, 24–27 April 1986. 6 pp. ISEAS, NUS.

2300. Shahlan, Hairalah. "Eat, Drink and be Muslim: How the Muis Halal Label is Given". *Nadi* 1 (January 2006): 22–23. NLB, NUS.

2301. Stimpfl, Joseph Richard. "Veiling and Unveiling: Reconstructing Malay Female Identity in Singapore". In *Undressing Religion: Commitment and Conversion from Cross-Cultural Perspectives.* New York: Berg, 2000. NLB, NTUNIE, NUS.

2302. Tham Seong Chee. *Religion and Modernization: A Study of Changing Rituals among Singapore's Chinese, Malays and Indians.* Singapore: Graham Brash, 1985. 186 pp. ISEAS, NLB, NTUNIE, NUS.

2303. Tschacher, Torsten. "From Local Practice to Transnational Network — Saints, Shrines and Sufis among Tamil Muslims in Singapore". *Asian Journal of Social Science* 34, no. 2 (2006): 225–42. ISEAS, NLB, NTUNIE, NUS.

2304. *Tudung: Beyond the Face Value.* Singapore: Bridges Books, 2002. 94 pp. ISEAS, NLB, NTUNIE, NUS.

2305. Yohanna Abdullah. "Beyond the Veil: The Case of Muslim Women in Singapore". Academic exercise, Department of Sociology, National University of Singapore, 1990. 89 pp. NUS.

2306. Zalman Putra Ahmad Ali. "Dynamic Faith — Reflections on Moral Guidance and Social Transformation". *MENDAKI Policy Digest* (2008): 97–105. ISEAS, NLB, NTUNIE, NUS.

Da'wah and Muslim Converts

2307. Abu Bakar Maidin. "Gerakan Dakwah di Singapura". Paper presented at a Kongres Dakwah Se-Malaysia Kali Kedua, Yayasan Dakwah Islamiah Malaysia, Kuala Lumpur, Malaysia, 10–12 Ogos, 1990. NUS.

2308. Fatimah Eunos. "Muslim Converts in Singapore: The Experience of Transition". Academic exercise, Department of Sociology, National University of Singapore, 1988. 82 pp. NUS.

2309. *Jurnal Dakwah.* Singapore: Persatuan Ulama dan Guru-Guru Agama Islam, 2010–. NLB.

2310. Maarof Salleh. "Aspects of Dakwah in Singapore". *Sedar* (1975/7): 18–25. ISEAS, NLB, NUS.

2311. Mohd Dzulfiqar Mohammad. "Dakwah Movement in Singapore: Its Social and Political Orientations". Academic exercise, University of Singapore, 1980. 80 pp. NUS.

2312. Muhd. Fazalee Ja'afar and Jamari Mokhtar. "Riding Modernisation Wave with Strong Islamic Values". *Nadi* 2 (October 2005): 12–13. NLB, NUS.

2313. *Muktamar Dakwah: Kertas Kerja.* Anjuran Jawatankuasa Haiah Dakwah Singapura, Majlis Ugama Islam Singapura. Singapore: MUIS, 1986. 102 pp. ISEAS, NLB, NUS.

2314. *Muslim Reader.* Singapore: Kumpulan Saudara Baru, 1978–96. NUS.

2315. *The Muslim Reader.* Singapore: Muslim Converts' Association of Singapore, 1978–. ISEAS, NLB.

2316. Ravenhill, John. *The Role of Saudara Baru in Ethnic Relations: The Chinese Converts in Singapore.* PROSEA Research Paper, no. 55. Taipei: Academia Sinica Program for Southeast Asian Area Studies, 2001. 37 pp. ISEAS.

2317. Saleem, H.M. "Modern Method of Da'wah: A Case Study of Jamiyah Singapore". Presented at a Three-Day Seminar on the Role of Muslim Organizations in Promoting Development and Human Fellowship in

Muslim Minority Countries in Asia, organized by Jamiyah Singapore in cooperation with the Islamic Educational Scientific and Cultural Organization and the Ministry of Awqaf, Kuwait, 24–26 September 2004. NLB.

2318.   *Singapore Islamic Missionary Committee = Jawatankuasa Haiah Dakwah Islamiah (JHD)*. Singapore: MUIS, 1985. 38 pp. NLB, NUS.

2319.   Sundusia Rosdi. "Pergerakan Jama'at Tabligh di Singapura: Sejarah, Inspirasi, Kesan dan Cabarannya". *Jurnal Dakwah* 3 (2012): 69–99. NLB.

2320.   Wu, Ridzuan Abdullah. *The Call to Islam*. Singapore: Muslim Converts Association of Singapore, 1991. 35 pp. NTUNIE. Previous ed. published under the title: *The Call to Islam: A Contemporary Perspective*. Singapore: Muslim Converts Association of Singapore, 1990. 103 pp. NUS.

Waqf

2321.   "Building a Heritage". *Warita Kita* 137 (January/February 2002): 18–19. ISEAS, NLB, NUS.

2322.   Brown, Rajeswary Amplavanar. "Islamic Endowments and the Land Economy in Singapore: The Genesis of an Ethical Capitalism, 1830–2007". *South East Asia Research* 16, no. 3 (November 2008): 343–403. ISEAS, NLB, NTUNIE, NUS.

2323.   Md. Zahid Yacob. "Waqf Development in Singapore: Sharing Our Experiences". Paper presented at a Singapore International Waqf Conference 2007, jointly organized by MUIS at the Fullerton Hotel, Singapore, 6–7 March 2007.

2324.   Mirza Namazie. "Wakaf Administration and Finance". In *Theory and Practice of Islamic Finance*, edited by Saw Swee-Hock and Karyn Wong. Singapore: Saw Centre for Financial Studies, 2008. NLB, NUS.

2325.   Shamsiah Abdul Karim. "Contemporary Waqf Administration and Development in Singapore: Challenges and Prospects". Paper presented at a Singapore International Waqf Conference 2007, jointly organized by MUIS at the Fullerton Hotel, Singapore, 6–7 March 2007. 15 pp. Available at <http://www.muis.gov.sg/cms/uploadedFiles/MuisGovSG/Wakaf/Contemporary%20Waqf%20In%20singapore.pdf>.

SOCIOLOGY

- *Social Structure*
- *Family, Kinship and Marriage*
- *Women*
- *Youth*
- *Children and the Elderly*
- *Social Integration*
- *Social Policy and Conditions*
- *Social Problems and Services*
- *Self-Help Groups*

Social Structure

2326. Chen S.J., Peter. *Social Stratification in Singapore.* Singapore: Department of Sociology, University of Singapore, 1973. 99 pp. ISEAS, NLB, NTUNIE, NUS.

2327. Chiew Seen Kong. "Ethnic Stratification". In *Social Class in Singapore,* edited by Stella R. Quah et al. Singapore: Times Academic Press for Centre for Advanced Studies, National University of Singapore, 1991. ISEAS, NLB, NTUNIE, NUS.

2328. Hashimah Johari. "The Emerging Malay Social Structure in Singapore". MA dissertation, National University of Singapore, 1985. 179 pp. NUS.

2329. Hassan, Riaz. "Class, Ethnicity and Occupational Structure in Singapore". *Civilisations* 20 (1970): 496–515. NUS. Also published under the same title in: *Studies on Social Stratification in Southeast Asia,* edited by Hans-Dieter Evers and Riaz Hassan. Singapore: Department of Sociology, University of Singapore, 1974. ISEAS, NLB, NUS.

2330. Hassan, Riaz. "Occupational and Class Structure of Singapore Malays". *Suara Universiti* 2, no. 1 (October 1971): 29–32. ISEAS, NUS.

2331. Pang Keng Fong. "The Malay Royals of Singapore". Academic exercise, Department of Sociology, National University of Singapore, 1983. 130 pp. ISEAS, NUS.

2332. Sharif Ismail. "The Social Structure of a Block of Singapore Police Quarters". Academic exercise, University of Malaya, Singapore, 1961. 138 pp. NUS.

2333. Suen Johan Mohd Zain. "Gambling in 'Multi-Racial' and 'Middle Class' Singapore: Exploring Class Realities, Religious Orientations and Racial Discourses among Male Lower-Income Malay-Muslim Gamblers". Paper presented at a Graduates Seminar on Nation-building in the Malay World, held at The Shaw Foundation Building, AS7 Auditorium, National University of Singapore, 28–29 October 2009. ISEAS, NUS.

2334. Zarina Hashim. "The Malay Middle Class in Singapore: A Study of Its Origin, Perception and Values on Education, Family Life and Work". Research exercise, Department of Malay Studies, National University of Singapore, 1992. 55 pp. NUS.

Family, Kinship and Marriage

2335. Abdul Rahim Ahmad. "A Study of Kinship Relations of Some Nuclear Malaysian Families in Singapore, including the Study of the Degree, to which Social Ties are Maintained with the Other Members or Branches of the Family and to What Extent do Factors Such as Occupation, Type of Education, etc., Affect these Relationships". Academic exercise, Department of Social Studies, University of Malaya, Singapore, 1961. 111 pp. NUS.

2336. Abduyah Ya'akub. "Pandangan Ibu Tunggal Terhadap Sokongan Keluarga". Research exercise, Department of Malay Studies, National University of Singapore, 1993. 42 pp. NUS.

2337. Abdullah Tarmugi. "Avoid Teen Marriages". *Speeches* 26, no. 1 (January–February 2002): 58–61. ISEAS, NLB, NTUNIE.

2338. Ahmad Mattar. "Responsibilities of Marriage". *Speeches* 3, no. 8 (February 1980): 53–55. ISEAS, NLB, NTUNIE.

2339. "Brides by Age Group". In *Yearbook of Statistics, Singapore, 2015*. Singapore: Department of Statistics, 2015. ISEAS, NLB, NTU, NTUNIE, NUS. Available at <http://www.singstat.gov.sg/docs/default-source/default-document-library/publications/publications_and_papers/reference/yearbook_2015/yos2015.pdf>.

2340. Chang Chen Tung. "Nuptiality Patterns among Women of Childbearing Age". In *The Contemporary Family in Singapore: Structure and Change*, edited by Eddie Kuo and Aline Wong. Singapore: Singapore University Press, 1976. ISEAS, NLB, NTUNIE, NUS.

2341. Cheong, Felix. "The Matchmaker". *The Edge Singapore* 319 (May 2008): OP5. NLB.

2342. Chew Sock Foon and John A. MacDougall. *Forever Plural: The Perception and Practice of Inter-communal Marriage in Singapore*. Athens, Ohio: Southeast Asia Program, Center for International Studies, Ohio University, 1977. 61 pp. ISEAS, NLB, NTUNIE, NUS.

2343. Chung Sang Hao. "Inter-ethnic Marriage in Singapore". Academic exercise, Department of Sociology, National University of Singapore, 1991. 82 pp. NUS.

2344. Djamour, Judith. *The Family Structure of the Singapore Malays: Report to the Colonial Social Science Research Council*. London: Colonial Office, 1953. 141 pp. NLB, NUS.

2345. Djamour, Judith. "The Malay Family and Marriage in Singapore". PhD dissertation, London School of Economics, 1955. 159 pp. NLB.

2346. Djamour, Judith. *Malay Kinship and Marriage in Singapore*. London: Athlone Press and Humanities Press, 1965. 155 pp. ISEAS, NLB, NTUNIE, NUS. Also published in Malay under the title: *Kekeluargaan dan Perkahwinan Orang Melayu Singapura*. Kuala Lumpur: Dewan Bahasa dan Pustaka, 1979. 206 pp. NLB, NTUNIE, NUS.

2347. Fadilah Hassan. "Siswazah Wanita Melayu: Perkahwinan dan Kekeluargaan di Kalangan Siswazah Wanita Melayu". Research exercise, Department of Malay Studies, National University of Singapore, 1992. 58 pp. NUS.

2348. *Family Life among the Malays of Singapore*. Geneva: International Union for Child Welfare, 1958. 83 pp. NLB, NUS. Also published under the same title in: *International Child Welfare Review* 12, no. 2 (1958): 51–83. NUS.

2349. Fazlinda Faroo. *I'm Getting Married ... Again!: Exploring Children's Understanding and Experience of Parental Remarriage*. Singapore: Persatuan Pemudi Islam Singapura (PPIS), c2012. 81 pp. NLB.
(A research sponsored by the National Council of Social Services and supported by the Ministry of Community Development, Youth and Sports).

2350. Fazlinda Faroo. *Remarriage in the Malay Community: An Exploration of Perceptions, Expectations and Adjustments to Stepfamily Living*. Singapore: Persatuan Pemudi Islam Singapura, 2012. 178 pp. NLB.

2351. *General Household Survey 1995: Socio-Demographic and Economic Characteristics*. Singapore: Department of Statistics, 1996. 224 pp. ISEAS, NLB, NTUNIE, NUS.

2352. *General Household Survey 1995: Transport Mode, Households and Housing Characteristics*. Singapore: Department of Statistics, 1997. 230 pp. ISEAS, NLB, NTUNIE, NUS.

2353. *General Household Survey 2005: Socio-Demographic and Economic Characteristics.* Singapore: Department of Statistics, 2006. 228 pp. ISEAS, NLB, NTUNIE, NUS.

2354. *General Household Survey 2005: Transport, Overseas Travel, Households and Housing Characteristics.* Singapore: Department of Statistics, 2006. 194 pp. ISEAS, NLB, NTUNIE, NUS.

2355. Gordon, Shirley. "Malay Marriage and Divorce in the 11 States of Malaya & Singapore". *Intisari* 2, no. 2 (1965): 23–32. ISEAS, NLB, NUS.

2356. "Grooms by Age Group". In *Yearbook of Statistics, Singapore, 2015.* Singapore: Department of Statistics, 2015. ISEAS, NLB, NTU, NTUNIE, NUS. Available at <http://www.singstat.gov.sg/docs/default-source/default-document-library/publications/publications_and_papers/reference/yearbook_2015/yos2015.pdf>.
(*Source*: Registry of Muslim Marriages).

2357. Hafiza Aseken. "Poligami: Pengalaman dan Anggapan di Kalangan Masyarakat Melayu Singapura". Research exercise, Department of Malay Studies, National University of Singapore, 1992. 55 pp. NUS.

2358. Hasanul Arifin. "Nikah Gantung: A 'Halal' Alternative to 'Unlawful' Dating?" *Karyawan* 9, issue 1 (July 2008): 31–34. ISEAS, NLB, NTUNIE, NUS.

2359. Hassan, Riaz. "Interethnic Marriage in Singapore: A Sociological Analysis". *Sociology and Social Research* 55, no. 3 (April 1971): 305–23. NLB, NUS.

2360. Hassan, Riaz. *Interethnic Marriage in Singapore: A Study in Interethnic Relations.* Singapore: Institute of Southeast Asian Studies, 1974. 85 pp. ISEAS, NLB, NTUNIE, NUS.

2361. Hassan, Riaz. "The Religious Factor in Interethnic Marriage in Singapore". *Sedar* 2 (1969/70): 47–52. ISEAS, NLB, NUS.

2362. Hassan, Riaz and Geoffrey Benjamin. *Ethnic Outmarriage Rates in Singapore: The Influence of Traditional Socio-cultural Organization.* Singapore: Department of Sociology, University of Singapore, 1972. 20 pp. ISEAS, NLB, NUS. Also published under the same title in: *Journal of Marriage and the Family* 35, no. 4 (1973): 731–38. NTUNIE, NUS.

2363. "Inter-ethnic Marriages under the Administration of Muslim Law Act by Educational Qualifications of Grooms and Brides, 2014". In *Statistics on Marriages and Divorces, Singapore, 2014*. Singapore: Department of Statistics, 2015. NLB. Available at <http://www.singstat.gov.sg/docs/default-source/default-document-library/publications/publications_and_papers/marriages_and_divorces/smd2014.pdf>.

2364. "Inter-Ethnic Marriages under the Administration of Muslim Law Act by Ethnic Group of Grooms and Brides, 2014". In *Statistics on Marriages and Divorces, Singapore, 2014*. Singapore: Department of Statistics, 2015. NLB. Available at <http://www.singstat.gov.sg/docs/default-source/default-document-library/publications/publications_and_papers/marriages_and_divorces/smd2014.pdf>.

2365. *Jalur Hidayah: Persiapan Berumah Tangga*. Singapore: Majlis Ugama Islam Singapura, 2004. 12 pp. NLB.

2366. Kuo C.Y., Eddie and Riaz Hassan. "Ethnic Intermarriage in a Multiethnic Society". In *The Contemporary Family in Singapore: Structure and Change*, edited by Eddie Kuo and Aline Wong. Singapore: Singapore University Press, 1979. ISEAS, NLB, NTUNIE, NUS.

2367. Kuo C.Y., Eddie and Riaz Hassan. *Some Social Concomitants of Interethnic Marriage in Singapore*. Singapore: Department of Sociology, University of Singapore, 1974. 28 pp. ISEAS, NLB, NTUNIE, NUS.

2368. Lee Geok Bee. "Inter-ethnic Marriage in the Islamic Religion". Academic exercise, Department of Sociology, University of Singapore, 1979. 67 pp. NUS.

2369. Lim Yuen Kheng, Janet. "Interethnic Marriage in Singapore". Academic exercise, University of Singapore, 1975. 1 microform. NUS.

2370. Lulu Marlya Abdul Rahim. "Marrying Mr. Right: Experiences of Educated Singaporean Malay Women in 'Masuk Melayu' Marriages". Academic exercise, Department of Sociology, National University of Singapore, 2010. 64 pp. NUS.

2371. Mardiana Abu Bakar. "Of Hopes, Needs and Reality". *Karyawan: Professionals for the Community* (December 1994): 8–9, 13. ISEAS, NLB, NTUNIE, NUS.

2372.   "Marriages Registered by Ethnic Group of Couple". In *Yearbook of Statistics, Singapore, 2015*. Singapore: Department of Statistics, 2015. NLB, NTU, NTUNIE, NUS. Available at <http://www.singstat.gov.sg/docs/default-source/default-document-library/publications/publications_and_papers/reference/yearbook_2015/yos2015.pdf>.
        (Statistics for 2008 to 2014 from Registry of Muslim Marriages).

2373.   "Marriages under the Administration of Muslim Law Act by Age Group and Educational Qualification of Grooms and Brides, 2014". In *Statistics on Marriages and Divorces, Singapore, 2014*. Singapore: Department of Statistics, 2015. ISEAS, NLB, NTU, NTUNIE, NUS. Available at <http://www.singstat.gov.sg/docs/default-source/default-document-library/publications/publications_and_papers/marriages_and_divorces/smd2014.pdf>.

2374.   "Marriages under the Administration of Muslim Law Act by Age Group and Ethnic Group of Grooms and Brides, 2014". In *Statistics on Marriages and Divorces, Singapore, 2014*. Singapore: Department of Statistics, 2015. ISEAS, NLB, NTU, NTUNIE, NUS. Available at <http://www.singstat.gov.sg/docs/default-source/default-document-library/publications/publications_and_papers/marriages_and_divorces/smd2014.pdf>.

2375.   "Marriages under the Administration of Muslim Law Act by Age Group and Educational Qualification of Resident Grooms and Brides, 2014". In *Statistics on Marriages and Divorces, Singapore, 2014*. Singapore: Department of Statistics, 2015. ISEAS, NLB, NTU, NTUNIE, NUS. Available at <http://www.singstat.gov.sg/docs/default-source/default-document-library/publications/publications_and_papers/marriages_and_divorces/smd2014.pdf>.

2376.   "Marriages under the Administration of Muslim Law Act by Age Group and Occupation of Grooms and Brides, 2014". In *Statistics on Marriages and Divorces, Singapore, 2014*. Singapore: Department of Statistics, 2015. ISEAS, NLB, NTU, NTUNIE, NUS. Available at <http://www.singstat.gov.sg/docs/default-source/default-document-library/publications/publications_and_papers/marriages_and_divorces/smd2014.pdf>.

2377. "Marriages under the Administration of Muslim Law Act by Age Group of Brides, 1965–2014". In *Statistics on Marriages and Divorces, Singapore, 2014*. Singapore: Department of Statistics, 2015. ISEAS, NLB, NTU, NTUNIE, NUS. Available at <http://www.singstat.gov.sg/docs/default-source/default-document-library/publications/publications_and_papers/marriages_and_divorces/smd2014.pdf>.

2378. "Marriages under the Administration of Muslim Law Act by Age Group of Grooms, 1965–2014". In *Statistics on Marriages and Divorces, Singapore, 2014*. Singapore: Department of Statistics, 2015. ISEAS, NLB, NTU, NTUNIE, NUS. Available at <http://www.singstat.gov.sg/docs/default-source/default-document-library/publications/publications_and_papers/marriages_and_divorces/smd2014.pdf>.

2379. "Marriages under the Administration of Muslim Law Act by Ethnic Group of Couple, 1965–2014". In *Statistics on Marriages and Divorces, Singapore, 2014*. Singapore: Department of Statistics, 2015. ISEAS, NLB, NTU, NTUNIE, NUS. Available at <http://www.singstat.gov.sg/docs/default-source/default-document-library/publications/publications_and_papers/marriages_and_divorces/smd2014.pdf>.

2380. "Marriages under the Administration of Muslim Law Act by Occupation of Grooms and Brides, 2014". In *Statistics on Marriages and Divorces, Singapore, 2014*. Singapore: Department of Statistics, 2015. ISEAS, NLB, NTU, NTUNIE, NUS. Available at <http://www.singstat.gov.sg/docs/default-source/default-document-library/publications/publications_and_papers/marriages_and_divorces/smd2014.pdf>.

2381. "Median Age of Brides Married under the Administration of Muslim Law Act by Ethnic Group of Brides, 2004–2014". In *Statistics on Marriages and Divorces, Singapore, 2014*. Singapore: Department of Statistics, 2015. ISEAS, NLB, NTU, NTUNIE, NUS. Available at <http://www.singstat.gov.sg/docs/default-source/default-document-library/publications/publications_and_papers/marriages_and_divorces/smd2014.pdf>.

2382. "Median Age of Grooms Married under the Administration of Muslim Law Act by Ethnic Group of Brides, 2004–2014". In *Statistics on Marriages and Divorces, Singapore, 2014*. Singapore: Department of Statistics, 2015. ISEAS, NLB, NTU, NTUNIE, NUS. Available at <http://www.singstat.gov.sg/docs/default-source/default-document-library/publications/publications_and_papers/marriages_and_divorces/smd2014.pdf>.

2383. Mohamed Fauzi Yusof. "Expectations towards Marriage: A Study of Malay Undergrads in NUS". Research exercise, Department of Malay Studies, National University of Singapore, 1995. 57 pp. NUS.

2384. Mohd. Maliki Osman. "Marriage: Are You Man Enough to Think Out of the Box?" *Warita Kita* 132 (March–April 2001): 14–15. ISEAS, NLB, NUS.

2385. Mohd. Maliki Osman. "The Male in the Malay Family". Academic exercise, Department of Social Work and Psychology, National University of Singapore, 1990. 128 pp. NUS.

2386. Mohd. Rafiz Hapipi. "Mis(yar)-Marriages". *Karyawan: Professionals for the Community* 7, issue 1 (November 2006): 35–36. ISEAS, NLB, NTUNIE, NUS.

2387. Muhammad Ariff Ahmad and Mohd Raman Daud. "To Bind & to Bond — Family Ties". In *Malay Heritage of Singapore*, edited by Aileen T. Lau and Bernhard Platzdasch. Singapore: Suntree Media in association with Malay Heritage Foundation, 2010. ISEAS, NLB, NTUNIE, NUS.

2388. Muhammad Khalil M. Nasir. "Divorce and the Muslim Husband". Academic exercise, Department of Social Work and Social Administration, University of Singapore, 1969. 114 pp. NUS.

2389. Noor Aisha Abdul Rahman. "Muslim–Non-Muslim Marriage in Singapore". In *Muslim–Non-Muslim Marriage: Political and Cultural Contestations in Southeast Asia*, edited by Gavin W. Jones, Chee Heng Leng and Maznah Mohamad. Singapore: Institute of Southeast Asian Studies, 2009. ISEAS, NLB, NUS.

2390. Noor Aisha Abdul Rahman. "Teenage Marriage in the Malay/Muslim Community of Singapore: Problems, Perceptions and Programmes". *Asian Journal of Social Science* 37, no. 5 (2009): 738–56. ISEAS, NLB, NTU, NTUNIE, NUS.

2391. Noor Tahirah Selamat. "Suatu Kajian Mengenai Beberapa Kes Wanita yang Dicerai Suami di Dalam Masyarakat Melayu Singapura". Research exercise, Department of Malay Studies, National University of Singapore, 1996. 39 pp. NUS.

2392. Noraslinda Muhamad Zuber. "Malay Families and the Development of the Malay Community". Research exercise, Department of Malay Studies, National University of Singapore, 1996. 54 pp. NUS.

2393. Nur Aini Mubarak. "Marriage Relationships in the Malay Community". Academic exercise, Department of Applied Social Studies, University of Singapore, 1967. 113 pp. NUS.

2394. Ong Kah Kok. "The Practice of Adoption within and as between Different Communities in this Country, the Policy of the Government and the Extent and Effectiveness of Its Intervention". Academic exercise, University of Malaya, Singapore, 1954. 78 pp. NUS.

2395. Othman Haron Eusope. "Family Development Programmes to Reduce Divorces". In *Jendela Kata: Ucapan-Ucapan Muis* 2 (1998–99): 16–18. ISEAS, NLB, NTUNIE, NUS.

2396. *Report on Survey of Households*, April 1977. Singapore: Department of Statistics, 1978. 84 pp. NLB.

2397. "Resident Marriages under the Administration of Muslim Law Act by Ethnic Group of Couple, 2004–2014". In *Statistics on Marriages and Divorces, Singapore, 2014*. Singapore: Department of Statistics, 2015. ISEAS, NLB, NTU, NTUNIE, NUS. Available at <http://www.singstat.gov.sg/docs/default-source/default-document-library/publications/publications_and_papers/marriages_and_divorces/smd2014.pdf>.

2398. Saw Swee-Hock. "Divorce Trends and Patterns". In *The Population of Singapore*. Singapore: Institute of Southeast Asian Studies, 2012. ISEAS, NLB, NTUNIE, NUS.

2399. Saw Swee-Hock. "Marriage Trends and Patterns". In *The Population of Singapore*. Singapore: Institute of Southeast Asian Studies, 2012. ISEAS, NLB, NTUNIE, NUS.

2400. Saw Swee-Hock. "Muslim Divorce Trends and Patterns in Singapore". *Genus* 48, nos. 3–4 (1992): 29–34. NUS.

2401. Shariffah Bahyah Syed Ahmad. "A Study on the Effectiveness of the Pre-marriage Course". Research exercise, National University of Singapore, 1991. 62 pp. NUS.

2402. Singapore. Registry of Muslim Marriages and the Shariah Court. *Annual Report of the Registry of Muslim Marriages and the Shariah Court*. Singapore: Registry of Muslim Marriages and the Shariah Court, 1960–63. ISEAS, NLB, NUS.

2403. Siraj, Mehrun. "Muslim Marriages in Singapore". *World Muslim League Magazine* 1, no. 3 (1964): 41–50. NLB, NUS.

2404. *Statistics on Marriages and Divorces.* Singapore: Department of Statistics, 1985–. Title varies slightly. ISEAS, NLB, NTU, NTUNIE, NUS. Available at <http://www.singstat.gov.sg/publications/publications-and-papers/marriages-and-divorces/marriages-and-divorces>.

2405. *A Study on Widowed Families.* Singapore: Singapore Council of Social Service, 1986. 30 pp. NUS.

2406. Suriani Suratman. *Studies on Malay Families and Households in Singapore: A Critical Assessment.* Seminar Papers, no. 35. Singapore: Department of Malay Studies, National University of Singapore, 2002. 23 pp. ISEAS, NLB, NUS.

2407. Suriyadarma Adi. "Hantaran and Its Possible Influence on Divorce amongst the Malay Community in Singapore". Research exercise, Department of Malay Studies, National University of Singapore, 1994. 46 pp. NUS.

2408. Swift, M.G. "A Note on the Durability of Malay Marriages". *Man* 58 (October 1958): 155–59. NLB, NUS.

2409. Tay J.S.H., William and C.L. Yip. "Teenage Marriages in Singapore". *Singapore Medical Journal* 25, no. 3 (1984): 216–24. NLB, NUS.

2410. Tham Seong Chee. *Malay Family Structure: Change and Continuity with Reference to Singapore.* Seminar Papers, no. 13. Singapore: Department of Malay Studies, National University of Singapore, 1993. 31 pp. ISEAS, NLB, NUS.

2411. Tham Seong Chee. "Social Change and the Malay Family". In *The Contemporary Family in Singapore*, edited by Eddie C.Y. Kuo and Aline Wong. Singapore: Singapore University Press, 1979. ISEAS, NLB, NTUNIE, NUS.

2412. Wahidah A. Jalil. "Study of Muslim Divorce in Singapore". Academic exercise, Department of Sociology, National University of Singapore, 1980. 107 pp. NUS.

2413. Wu, Daven. "Family Ties". *Salt* 3 (May–June 2004): 11. NLB.

2414. Zainab Atan. "The Tali, the Cross and the Crescent Moon: Religion and Marriage in an Indian Community: A Comparative Analysis of the

Three Religious Groups of the Malayali Community". Academic exercise, Department of Sociology, National University of Singapore, 1991. 82 pp. NUS.

2415.   Zaleha Ahmad. "Is the Malay Family Breaking Down?" *Karyawan: Professionals for the Community* 6, issue 1 (November 2005): 6–8. ISEAS, NLB, NTUNIE, NUS.

Women

2416.   *An-nisaa: Official Newsletter of the Young Women Muslim Association = An-nisaa': Majalah Rasmi Persatuan Pemudi Islam Singapura.* Singapore: PPIS, 1983–96. ISEAS, NLB, NUS.

2417.   Asiah Abu Samah. "Emancipation of Malay Women, 1945–1957". Academic exercise, Department of History, University of Malaya, 1960. 87 pp. NUS.

2418.   Cheng Siok Hwa. *Women in Singapore: Legal, Educational and Economic Aspects.* Singapore: Institute of Humanities and Social Sciences, College of Graduate Studies, Nanyang University, 1976. 32 pp. ISEAS, NLB, NUS.

2419.   Chung Yuen Kay. "Gender, Work and Ethnicity: An Ethnography of Female Factory Workers in Singapore". PhD dissertation, National University of Singapore, 1989. 316 pp. NUS.

2420.   Fazida Mohd Alim Khan. "Ibu-ibu Tunggal di Singapura". Research exercise, Department of Malay Studies, National University of Singapore, 1991. 50 pp. NUS.

2421.   Loo Kim Pheck. "The Influence of Ethnicity and Other Factors on Women's Perceptions of Their Roles in Society". Academic exercise, Department of Sociology, National University of Singapore, 1986. 77 pp. NUS.

2422.   Noor Aisha Abdul Rahman. "Convention on the Elimination of Discrimination against Women and the Prospect of Development of Muslim Personal Law in Singapore". *Journal of Muslim Minority Affairs* 34, no. 1 (March 2014): 45–65. ISEAS, NTUNIE, NUS.

2423.   Norliza Mohd Ali. "Malay Attitudes towards Working Mothers". Research exercise, Department of Malay Studies, National University of Singapore, 1995. 48 pp. NUS.

2424. Norshidah Muhammad Amin. "The Woman Criminal". Academic exercise, Department of Social Studies, University of Malaya, Singapore, 1961. 107 pp. NUS.

2425. Nur'adlina Maulod. "Woman Like a Man: Negotiating Female Masculinity in the Malay/Muslim Community of Singapore". Academic exercise, Department of Sociology, National University of Singapore, 2007. 52 pp. NUS.

2426. Nuraisyah Mohamed Rashid et al. *Lighting Lives: The PPIS Story.* Editor, Mohd Ali Mahmood; consulting editor, Saat A. Rahman. Singapore: Persatuan Pemudi Islam Singapura, 2008. 115 pp. NLB, NTUNIE, NUS.

2427. Nurhannah Irwan. "Living on the 'Edge': Malay Single Mothers and Their Coping Strategies". Academic exercise, Department of Sociology, National University of Singapore, 2011. 56 pp. NUS.

2428. *Obor.* Singapore: Persatuan Wanita dan Teruna, 1976–. NLB.

2429. Persatuan Pemudi Islam Singapura. *Laporan Dwitahunan = Biennial Report.* Singapore: Persatuan Pemudi Islam Singapura, 1988–2006. ISEAS, NLB, NUS.

2430. "Report and Recommendation of Women's Seminar on Women: Commitment and Contribution to Family, Community and Nation". Jointly organized by KGMS and STU and held at the Teacher's Centre on 15 May 1982. 32 pp. NLB.

2431. Seminar Penyertaan Wanita Melayu dalam Pembangunan Masyarakat (1974: Singapura). *Laporan Seminar Penyertaan Wanita Melayu dalam Pembangunan Masyarakat.* Anjuran Jabatan Wanita Majlis Pusat. Singapore: Majlis Pusat, 1974. 34 pp. ISEAS, NLB, NUS.

2432. Siti Ruziya Nasir. "Three Generations of Singapore Malay Women". Academic exercise, Department of Sociology, National University of Singapore, 1988. 72 pp. NUS.

2433. Suriani Suratman. "Tudung Girls: Unveiling Muslim Women's Identity in Singapore". In *Melayu: The Politics, Poetics and Paradoxes of Malayness,* edited by Maznah Mohamad and Syed Muhd. Khairudin Aljunied. Singapore: NUS Press, 2011. 370 pp. ISEAS, NLB, NTU, NTUNIE, NUS.

2434. Suzaina Kadir. 'When Gender is Not a Priority: Muslim Women in Singapore and the Challenges of Religious Fundamentalism". In *Muslim Women and the Challenge of Islamic Extremism*, edited by Norani Othman. Petaling Jaya, Selangor: Sisters in Islam, 2005. 215 pp. ISEAS, NLB, NUS.

2435. Tan Mei Chang. "Female Population of Singapore, 1980". Academic exercise, Department of Geography, National University of Singapore, 1986. 135 pp. NUS.

2436. Wong K., Aline *Women in Modern Singapore*. Singapore: University Education Press, 1975. 137 pp. ISEAS, NLB, NTUNIE, NUS.

2437. Wong K., Aline and Leong Wai Kum, eds. *A Woman's Place: The Story of Singapore Women*. Singapore: PAP Women's Wing, 1993. 120 pp. ISEAS, NLB, NTUNIE, NUS.

Youth

2438. *4PM: Dian Masyarakat, 1948–1998*. Singapore: Persatuan Persuratan Pemuda Pemuda Melayu, 1999. 134 pp. ISEAS, NLB.

2439. Adli Yashir Kuchit et al. *Remaja: Salah Siapa?* Penasihat, Haji Pasuni Maulan & Saat A. Rahman. Singapore: Pejabat Pendaftaran Pernikahan Orang-orang Islam Singapura dengan kerjasama Berita Harian, 2004. 117 pp. ISEAS, NLB.

2440. Ahmad Mattar. "Inculcating Right Values in Our Youths". *Speeches* 4, no. 10 (April 1981): 38–39. ISEAS, NLB, NTUNIE, NUS.

2441. Ahmad Mattar. 'Malay Youths Must Upgrade Their Education Levels". *Speeches* 5, no. 11 (May 1982): 48–50. ISEAS, NLB, NTUNIE, NUS.

2442. Azhar Ibrahim Alwee. 'Progressive Youth and Transformative Social Thought". *MENDAKI Policy Digest* (2007): 113–25. ISEAS, NTUNIE, NUS.

2443. *Bingkisan 1948–1984: dari Jalan Eunos ke Bedok Reservoir*. Singapore: Persatuan Persuratan Pemuda Pemudi Melayu, 1985. 48 pp. NLB.

2444. *Chenderamata Dewasa: 20 Tahun, 1948–1968*. Singapore: Persatuan Persuratan Pemuda Pemudi Melayu Singapura, 1968. 36 pp. NLB, NUS.

2445. Dayanullah Ohorella Othman. "The Trouble with Our Boys". *Buletin Saujana* 1 (2000): 42–50. NLB, NUS.

2446. Farhan Ali. "Developing the Next Generation of Malay/Muslim Youth". *Karyawan: Professionals for the Community* 8, issue 1 (December 2007): 2–4. ISEAS, NLB, NTUNIE, NUS.

2447. Farhan Ali. "Setting the Agenda for Progress: Muslim Youths in Research, Science and Technology". In *Igniting Thought, Unleashing Youth: Perspectives on Muslim Youth and Activism in Singapore*, edited by Mohamed Nawab and Farhan Ali. Singapore: Select Publishing in association with Young AMP, 2009. ISEAS, NLB, NTUNIE, NUS.

2448. Farhan Ali and Mohamed Nawab Mohamed Osman. "Thought-leadership and Malay/Muslim Youths". In *Igniting Thought, Unleashing Youth: Perspectives on Muslim Youth and Activism in Singapore*, edited by Mohamed Nawab and Farhan Ali. Singapore: Select Publishing in association with Young AMP, 2009. ISEAS, NLB, NTUNIE, NUS.

2449. Fathiah Edrus. "A Study of Young Adult Malay Residents of a Housing Estate". Academic exercise, Department of Social Work and Social Administration, University of Singapore, 1972. 129 pp. NUS.

2450. Humaira Zainal. "The 'Happiness' Quotient: A Summary of Policies Affecting Singaporean Youth". *MENDAKI Policy Digest* (2012): 39–56. NLB.

2451. Johann Johari. "Youth and Development – A Positive Potential". *MENDAKI Policy Digest* (2008): 37–44. ISEAS, NLB, NUS.

2452. Kamaludeen Mohamed Nasir. *Globalized Muslim Youth in the Asia Pacific: Popular Culture in Singapore and Sydney*. Houndmills, Basingstoke, Hampshire; New York, N.Y.: Palgrave MacMillan. 231 pp. NLB.

2453. "Khadijah Youth: Excellence in Conduct, Perfect in Built". *Inabah* 16, no. 2 (August 2003): 54–59. NLB.

2454. Lim, David. "Youth Involvement in Community Could Shape Nation". In *Jendela Kata: Ucapan-Ucapan Muis Siri ke-2*. Singapore: Majlis Ugama Islam Singapura, 1999. ISEAS, NLB, NTUNIE, NUS.

2455. Mardiana Abu Bakar. "Pedagogy of Hope – Singapore Malay Youths and Our Educational Future". *MENDAKI Policy Digest* (2012): 149–57. NLB.

2456. Mohamad Shamsuri Johari. "Building Capacities for Critical Thinking among Malay-Muslim Youths in Singapore". Paper presented at a Graduates Seminar on Nation-building in the Malay World, held at The Shaw Foundation Building, AS7 Auditorium, National University of Singapore, 28–29 October 2009. ISEAS, NUS.

2457. Mohamed Nawab Mohamed Osman and Farhan Ali, eds. "The Future of Muslim Youths in Singapore". In *Igniting Thought, Unleashing Youth: Perspectives on Muslim Youth and Activism in Singapore*, edited by Mohamed Nawab and Farhan Ali. Singapore: Select Publishing in association with Young AMP, 2009. ISEAS, NTUNIE, NUS.

2458. Mohamed Nawab Mohamed Osman and Farhan Ali, eds. *Igniting Thought, Unleashing Youth: Perspectives on Muslim Youth and Activism in Singapore*. Singapore: Select Publishing, 2009. 164 pp. ISEAS, NLB, NTUNIE, NUS.

2459. Murshidah Hassan and K. Mehta. "Grief Experience of Bereaved Malay/ Muslim Youths in Singapore: The Spiritual Dimension". *International Journal of Children's Spirituality* 15, no. 1 (2010): 45–57. NTUNIE, NUS.

2460. Ng T.P. et al. "Ethnic Differences in Quality of Life in Adolescents among Chinese, Malay and Indians in Singapore". *Quality of Life Research* 14, no. 7 (2005): 1755–68. NTUNIE, NUS.

2461. Nur Azha Putra. "The Guilt of Ignorance: Youths & Sexual Promiscuity". *Karyawan: Professionals for the Community* 6, no. 1 (November 2005): 9–10. ISEAS, NLB, NTUNIE, NUS.

2462. Nursila Senin and I.Y.H. Ng. "Educational Aspirations of Malay Youths from Low-income Families in Singapore". *Asia Pacific Journal of Social Work and Development* 22, no. 4 (2012): 253–65. NTUNIE, NUS.

2463. *Persatuan Persuratan Pemuda Pemudi Melayu Singapura 10 tahun 1948-1958: Chendera mata*. Singapore: 4PM, [1958-63?]. 3 vols. in 1. NUS.

2464. Rafiz Mohyi Hapipi. "Through the I's of Youth – Identity, Independence, Individuality". *MENDAKI Policy Digest* (2007): 63–70. ISEAS, NLB, NTUNIE, NUS.

2465.   Rahil Ismail. "Critical Multiculturism in Changing Global Landscapes: Youth Citizenship in the Age of Insecurity". *MENDAKI Policy Digest* (2012): 159–91. NLB.

2466.   *Remaja Salah Siapa?: Panduan Didikan Ibubapa dan Remaja*. Singapore: ROMM dengan Berita Harian, 2004. 120 pp. ISEAS, NLB.

2467.   Rizwana Begum. "Singapore Youths and Internet-Mediated Muslim Identities". In *Igniting Thought, Unleashing Youth: Perspectives on Muslim Youth and Activism in Singapore*, edited by Mohamed Nawab and Farhan Ali. Singapore: Select Publishing in association with Young AMP, 2009. ISEAS, NLB, NTUNIE, NUS.

2468.   Saw Swee-Hock and Aline K. Wong. *Youths in Singapore: Sexuality, Courtship and Family Values*. Singapore: Singapore University Press for Family Planning Association of Singapore, 1981. 88 pp. ISEAS, NLB, NTUNIE, NUS.

2469.   Shazana Mohd Anuar. "Muslim Youths in a Multi-Cultural Society". *Karyawan: Professionals for the Community* 7, issue 1 (November 2005): 2–5. ISEAS, NLB, NTUNIE, NUS.

2470.   Sharifah Maisharah Mohamed. "Are Our Muslim Youths Becoming Extinct?" *Karyawan: Professionals for the Community* 6, issue 1 (November 2006): 11–12. ISEAS, NLB, NTUNIE, NUS.

2471.   Shirlene Noordin. "Mat Rockers: An Insight into a Malay Youth Subculture". Academic exercise, Department of Sociology, National University of Singapore, 1992. 72 pp. NUS.

2472.   "Singapore Malay Youth Library Association". *Citizen* (August 1989): 18. NLB.

2473.   Siti Hazirah Mohamad. "'...We Talk Like Normal People': Contesting Representations of Malay Youth Delinquency in Singapore". MA dissertation, National University Singapore, 2014. NUS.

2474.   *Suara 4PM*. Singapore: Persatuan Persuratan Pemuda Pemudi Melayu, [1970?]–. NUS. Continues *Suara Belia = Voice of Youth*. Singapore: Persatuan Persuratan Pemuda Pemudi Melayu, 1966– [1970?]. NUS.

2475. Tan Jun Yuan, Jeremy Lim Zi Kai, and Low Choon Peng. "Contemporary Model of Mentorship: Addressing the Malay's Youth Conundrum". In *Issues Facing the Malay/Muslims Community in Singapore*. Singapore: Lembaga Biasiswa Kenangan Maulud, 2010. NLB.

2476. Tan Su Ling, Susan. "Travel, Language and National Identity among Young Singaporeans". Academic exercise, Department of Sociology, National University of Singapore, 1994. 61 pp. NUS.

2477. Thomas, Elwyn. "Filial Piety, Social Change, and Singapore Youth". *Journal of Moral Education* 19, no. 3 (1990): 192–205. NTUNIE, NUS.

Children and the Elderly

2478. Anwar Yahya. "The Home Environment and the Inculcation of the Reading Habit among Malay Children". Research exercise, Department of Malay Studies, National University of Singapore, 1994. 42 pp. NUS.

2479. *Bengkel Bacalah Bersama Anak Anda*. Anjuran Yayasan MENDAKI dan Perpustakaan Negara. Singapore: Fajar video Baru, 1985. 1 videocassettes (VHS, PAL). 155 min. NLB.

2480. Blake, Myrna L. (Myrna Louise). "The Sick Child in Singapore Malay and Malaysian Families". Academic exercise, Department of Social Studies, University of Malaya, Singapore, 1959. 147 pp. NUS.

2481. Blake, Myrna L. (Myrna Louise) and Enon Mansur. *Growing Old in the Malay Community*. CAS Occasional Paper, no. 10. Singapore: Times Academic Press for the Centre for Advanced Studies, Faculty of Arts and Social Sciences, National University of Singapore, 1992. 144 pp. ISEAS, NLB, NTU, NTUNIE, NUS.

2482. Djamour, Judith. "Adoption of Children among Singapore Malaysians". *The Journal of the Royal Anthropological Institute of Great Britain and Ireland* 82, no. 2 (July–December 1952): 159–68. NLB, NUS.

2483. Hashim Ali. "Cognitive Development among Malay Children in Singapore". MA dissertation, Department of Malay Studies, National University of Singapore, 1984. 178 pp. NUS.

2484. Heng Hong Ngoh. "The Adopted Child, with Particular Reference to the Child Adopted into a Family of a Different Race". Academic exercise, Department of Social Studies, University of Malaya of Singapore, 1957. 141 pp. NUS.

2485. Khrishnan, Deby Sarojiny. "Young Children's Fears: A Study of Young Children's Fears in the Indian and Malay Community". Academic exercise, Department of Social Work and Social Administration, University of Singapore, 1967. 70 pp. NUS.

2486. Lee K.M., William. "Ethnicity and Ageing in Singapore". *Asian Ethnicity* 2, no. 2 (2001): 163–76. NUS.

2487. Lee K.M., William. "Income Protection and the Elderly: An Examination of Social Security Policy in Singapore". *Journal of Cross-Cultural Gerontology* 13, issue 4 (December 1998): 291. 17 pp. NUS.

2488. Lim Choon Geok. "Problem-solving Approaches of Families with Young Down Syndrome Children". Academic exercise, Department of Social Work and Psychology, National University of Singapore, 1992. 69 pp. NUS.

2489. Lina Simuan. *Pengorbananku (videorecording)*. Produced by Mohd Iqbal. 2009. 1 DVD. 13 min. NLB.

2490. *Mengubah Kehidupan pada Usia: Warga Tua Bahagia, Sihat, Aktif.* Singapore: MCYS, 2009. 50 pp. NLB.

2491. Mohamad Shafee Khamis. "Grandparents as Child Care-takers in Contemporary Singapore Malay Society". Research exercise, Department of Malay Studies, National University of Singapore, 1994. 76 pp. NUS.

2492. Mohamed Zain Mohamed. "The Aged and Family Support in the Malay Community". Research exercise, Department of Malay Studies, National University of Singapore, 1996. 67 pp. NUS.

2493. Mohammad Nizam Noordin. "Child Upbringing in Present Day Singapore Malay Society". Research exercise, Department of Malay Studies, National University of Singapore, 1996. 41 pp. NUS.

2494. Mohammed Hassan Ngah Mahmud. "Patterns of Child Rearing Practices among the Malays: A Study of Patterns of Child Rearing Practices Based on 49 Malay Families in Kampong Wak Hassan, Sembawang and Kampong Radin Mas". Academic exercise, Department of Social Work and Social Administration, University of Singapore, 1967. 147 pp. NUS.

2495. Norlaily Ahmad. "Penyertaan Suami dalam Kerja Rumah dan Pengasuhan Anak". Research exercise, Department of Malay Studies, National University of Singapore, 1991. 46 pp. NUS.

2496. Punna Cheruvori, Sushama. "Pregnancy and Infant-Care Beliefs and Practices among Some Singapore Malays". Academic exercise, University of Malaya, Singapore, 1955. 79 pp.

2497. Rohaizan Mustaffa. "Value of Children among the Poor: A Case Study of Low SES Malays". Academic exercise, Department of Sociology, University of Singapore, 1979. 75 pp. NUS.

2498. Shamsuddin Abu Samah. "Pattern of Child Rearing in Malay Families: A Study of Bringing up of Malay Children in Pasir Panjang Village, Singapore, with Particular Reference to Discipline and Authority". Academic exercise, Department of Social Studies, University of Malaya, 1957. 125 pp. NUS.

2499. Siti Hanifah Mustapha. "MENDAKI Foundation Home Library and Reading Project". *Singapore Libraries* 13 (1983): 25–27. ISEAS, NLB, NTUNIE, NUS.

2500. Siti Sohanah Kasmani and Rosaleen Ow. "Worldviews and Resilience in Children of Divorced Families". *Asia Pacific Journal of Social Work* 11, Special Issue (July 2001): 37–50. NLB, NTUNIE.

2501. Syahirah Nazimuddeen. "The Amplification of Child Abuse among Malays in Singapore: Folk Devils, Moral Panics and Institutional Response". Academic exercise, Department of Sociology, National University of Singapore, 2003. 83 pp. NUS.

2502. Tan Soo Khing. "Life Space of the Aged in Singapore". Academic exercise, Department of Geography, National University of Singapore, 1991. 142 pp. NUS.

2503. Teo P. "Aging in Singapore". *Journal of Cross-Cultural Gerontology* 11, no. 3 (1996): 269–86. NTUNIE, NUS.

2504. Tham Seong Chee. "Child-Rearing in the Malay Business Family: A Study in Change and Continuity". *Journal of the South Seas Society* 28, no. 1/2 (December 1973): 106–18. ISEAS, NLB, NUS.

2505. Tham Seong Chee, comp. & ed. *Study of Aging and Retirement in Singapore: Preliminary Report.* Singapore: National University of Singapore, 1989. 138 pp. NLB, NUS.

2506. Zahidi Abdul Rahman. "Muslim Child Development Centre at Punggol High Density Village". Academic Exercise, National University of Singapore, 1986. 106 pp. NUS.

2507. Zarinah Mohamed. "Parenting in Singapore: Father's Attitudes Towards Involvement in Childcare". Academic exercise, Department of Sociology, National University of Singapore, 1989. 76 pp. NUS.

Social Integration

2508. A.F. Yassin. "Reality Melayu Kini: Orang Melayu Singapura Tidak Leka, Tidak Mengharap dan Lebih Banyak Berdikari". In *Dewan Budaya*, no. 8 (August 2004): 18–20. ISEAS, NLB, NTUNIE, NUS.

2509. "At Successful Malay Level, Integration is Good". *Far Eastern Economic Review* 109, no. 32 (August 1980): 74–76. ISEAS, NLB, NTUNIE, NUS.

2510. "Bagaimana Hendak Menarik Orang Melayu Bergiat?" *Citizen* (June 1987): 21. NLB, NUS.

2511. Chang Chen Tung. "A Sociological Study of Neighbourliness". In *Public Housing in Singapore: A Multi-Disciplinary Study*, edited by Stephen H.K. Yeh. Singapore: Singapore University Press, 1975. ISEAS, NLB, NTUNIE, NUS.

2512. Chong, Terence. "Asian Values and Confucian Ethics: Malay Singaporeans' Dilemma". *Journal of Contemporary Asia* 32, no. 3 (2002): 394–406. ISEAS, NLB, NTUNIE, NUS.

2513. Choo, Anne Marie. "Ethnicity and Neighbouring Activities". Academic exercise, Department of Sociology, University of Singapore, 1976/77. 89 pp. ISEAS, NUS.

2514. Hanif, Nafis Muhamad. "Prison's Spoilt Identities: Racially Structured Realities Within and Beyond". *Current Issues in Criminal Justice* 20, no. 2 (2008): 243–64. NTUNIE, NUS.
("Prison culture is able to articulate and elaborate on the processes of social exclusion faced by ethnic Malay minorities and male transvestites in Singapore society.")

2515. Lee Hsien Loong. "Maintaining Social Cohesion and Racial Harmony". *Speeches* 22, no. 5 (September/October 1998): 42–47. ISEAS, NLB, NTU, NTUNIE.

2516. Lily Zubaidah Rahim. "Perceptions of the Malay Marginality". In *The Singapore Dilemma: The Political and Educational Marginality of the Malay Community*. Kuala Lumpur: Oxford University Press, 1998. ISEAS, NLB, NTU, NTUNIE, NUS.

2517. Rahil Ismail. "Muslims in Singapore as a Case Study for Understanding Inclusion/Exclusion Phenomenon". Paper presented at a Fulbright Symposium [on] Muslim Citizens in the West: Promoting Social Inclusion, Perth August 2007.

2518. Rahman, N.A.A. "The Dominant Perspective on Terrorism and Its Implication for Social Cohesion: The Case of Singapore". *Copenhagen Journal of Asian Studies* 27, no. 2 (2009): 109–28. ISEAS, NLB, NUS.

2519. Rozi Rahmat. "A Focus Study Malay Participation in Community Centre (Boon Lay CC)". Research exercise, Department of Malay Studies, National University of Singapore, 1995. 104 pp. NUS.

2520. Sharom Ahmat and James Wong, eds. *Malay Participation in the National Development of Singapore*. Singapore: Eurasia Press, 1971. 25 pp. ISEAS, NLB, NTUNIE, NUS. Also published in Malay under the title: *Penyertaan Masyarakat Melayu dalam Pembangunan Nasional Singapura*. Singapore: Central Council of Malay Cultural Organisations Singapore, 1971. 50 pp. ISEAS, NLB.

Social Policy and Conditions

2521. Aidaroyani Adam. "Moving Forward — Striding through 2007". *MENDAKI Policy Digest* (2006): 83–91. ISEAS, NLB, NTUNIE, NUS.

2522. Ahmad Mattar. "Changes in the Social and Economic Status of the Malays". In *People's Action Party, 1954–1984: Petir 30th Anniversary Issue*. Singapore: Central Executive Committee, People's Action Party, 1984. ISEAS, NLB, NTUNIE, NUS. Also published in Malay under the title: "Perubahan dalam Taraf Sosial dan Ekonomi Orang-Orang

Melayu". In *People's Action Party, 1954–1984: Petir 30th Anniversary Issue*. Singapore: Central Executive Committee, People's Action Party, 1984. ISEAS, NLB, NTUNIE.

2523.   A. Rahim Ishak. "Muslims: Challenge of the 80's". *Speeches* 3, no. 11 (May 1980): 54–59. ISEAS, NLB, NTUNIE, NUS.

2524.   Abdullah Tarmugi. "Cabaran Melayu". *Petir: Organ of the People's Action Party* (May 1986): 19. ISEAS, NLB, NTUNIE, NUS.

2525.   Abdullah Tarmugi. *Development of the Malay Community in Singapore: Prospects and Problems*. Seminar Papers, no. 9. Singapore: Department of Malay Studies, National University of Singapore, 1993. 9 pp. ISEAS, NLB, NUS.

2526.   Abdullah Tarmugi. "The Malay Challenge: Where Do We Go from Here?" *Petir: Organ of the People's Action Party* (June 1986): 17. ISEAS, NLB, NTUNIE, NUS. Also published in Malay under the title: "Cabaran untuk Orang Melayu: ke Mana Arah yang Dituju?" *Petir: Organ of the People's Action Party* (June 1986): 18. ISEAS, NLB, NTUNIE, NUS.

2527.   Ahmad Mattar. "Malay Participation in Singapore's Development". *Petir: Organ of the People's Action Party* 4 (March 1980): 24–26. ISEAS, NLB, NTUNIE, NUS. Also published in Malay under the title: "Penyertaan Orang Melayu dalam Pembangunan Singapura". *Petir: Organ of the People's Action Party* 2 (June 1980): 24–26. ISEAS, NLB, NTUNIE, NUS.

2528.   Ahmad Mattar. "Religion and Socio-Economic Development". *Speeches* 1, no. 5 (November 1977): 57–62. ISEAS, NLB, NTUNIE.

2529.   Alatas, Syed Farid. *Keadaan Sosiologi Masyarakat Melayu = The State of Malay Sociology in Singapore*. Occasional Paper Series, no. 5-97. Singapore: Association of Muslim Professionals, 1997. 50 pp. ISEAS, NLB, NTUNIE, NUS.

2530.   Alatas, Syed Hussein. *The New Malay: His Role and Future*. Occasional Paper Series, no. 2-96. Singapore: Association of Muslim Professionals, 1996. 34 pp. ISEAS, NLB, NTUNIE, NUS.

2531.   Aljunied, Syed Hassan. "Melayu Singapura Sepintas Lalu". In *Utusan Melayu 10 Tahun*. Singapore: Utusan Melayu, 1949. ISEAS, NLB.

2532. Aljunied, Sharifah Alwiyah. "Minority Dilemmas: The Malay Community in Singapore". Academic exercise, Department of Sociology, National University of Singapore, 1991. 86 pp. NUS.

2533. *Aspirasi = Aspire: Bi-monthly Publication of Yayasan MENDAKI.* Singapore: Yayasan MENDAKI, 1990–. ISEAS, NLB, NUS.

2534. Azhar Ibrahim Alwee. *Narrating Presence: Awakening from Cultural Amnesia.* Singapore: Malay Heritage Foundation and Select Publishing, 2014. 116 pp. ISEAS, NLB, NTUNIE, NUS.

2535. Azhari Zahri. "Urbanization and Malay Society in Singapore". *Suara Universiti* 2, no. 1 (January 1971): 56–59. ISEAS, NUS.

2536. Bambang Sugeng Kajairi. "Into the 1990s: The Organisational Challenge for Singapore Muslims". *Fajar Islam* 1, no. 1 (1988): 79–86. ISEAS, NLB, NUS.

2537. Benjamin, Geoffrey. *The Cultural Logic of Singapore's Multiracialism.* Working Papers, no. 44. Singapore: Department of Sociology, University of Singapore, 1975. 34 pp. ISEAS, NLB, NTUNIE, NUS. Also published under the same title in: *Singapore: Society in Transition*, edited by Riaz Hassan. Kuala Lumpur: Oxford University Press, 1976. ISEAS, NLB, NTUNIE, NUS.

2538. *Building a Muslim Community of Excellence.* Singapore: Majlis Ugama Islam Singapura, 2001. 15 pp. ISEAS.

2539. Chan Heng Chee. "Need for Higher Level Community Research". *Karyawan: Professionals for the Community* (June 1995): 2. ISEAS, NLB, NTUNIE, NUS.

2540. Chen S.J., Peter and Tai Ching Ling. *Social Ecology of Singapore.* Singapore: Federal Publications, 1977. 112 pp. ISEAS, NLB, NTU, NTUNIE, NUS.

2541. Clammer, John. "Malay Society in Singapore: A Preliminary Analysis". *Southeast Asian Journal of Social Science* 9, no. 1/2 (1981): 19–32. ISEAS, NLB, NTU, NTUNIE, NUS.

2542. Clammer, John. *Singapore: Ideology, Society, Culture.* Singapore: Chopman Publishers, 1985. 169 pp. ISEAS, NLB, NTU, NTUNIE, NUS.

2543. *Community of Excellence: Nurturing a Conscientized Generation = Masyarakat Cemerlang Menjana Generasi Peduli.* Singapore: Yayasan Mendaki, 2010. ISEAS, NLB, NTU, NTUNIE, NUS.

2544. "Driven and Directed Amidst Anxiety". *Suara MP* 1 (December/March 2000/1): 8–9. NLB.

2545. "Facing Future Problems Together". *Karyawan: Professionals for the Community* (July 1996): 4–5. ISEAS, NLB, NTUNIE, NUS.

2546. Fredericks, Mariam Eve. "Social Aspects of Malay Society, 1819–1874". Academic exercise, Department of History, University of Malaya, Singapore, 1961. 72 pp. NUS.

2547. *Global Minds, Global Strides.* Singapore: [Publisher not identified], 2007. 25 pp. NLB.
        ("Celebrating Excellence, Community Leaders' Forum" — Cover).

2548. Goh Chok Tong. "Focus on Larger Issues". *Speeches* 17, no. 3 (May/June 1993): 23–27. ISEAS, NLB, NTUNIE, NUS.

2549. Goh Chok Tong. "A Key Pillar of Singapore". In *Jendela Kata: Ucapan-Ucapan Muis Siri ke-2.* Singapore: Majlis Ugama Islam Singapura, 1999. ISEAS, NLB, NTUNIE, NUS.

2550. Goh Chok Tong. "Malays have Made Progress: [Speech at the Malay/Muslim Organisation's Tribute to Prime Minister's 10 Years of Leadership on 21 January 2001]". *Speeches* 25, no. 1 (January/February 2001): 1–8. ISEAS, NLB, NTU, NTUNIE, NUS.

2551. Goh Chok Tong. "Take the Initiative". *Speeches* 15, no. 1 (January/February 1991): 11–16. ISEAS, NLB, NTUNIE, NUS.

2552. Goh Keng Swee. "The Dilemma of the Malay". *Suara Merdeka* 2, no. 2 (July–September 1951): 11–15. NLB.

2553. Hadijah Rahmat. "Motivasi dalam Masyarakat Melayu". *Analisa* (1981): 22–30. NLB, NUS.

2554. Hadijah Rahmat. "Kilat Senja: Sebuah Pendekatan Bersepadu dalam Kajian Sejarah Sosial Budaya Kampung-Kampung di Singapura". Paper presented at a Persidangan Antarabangsa Bahasa, Sastera dan Kebudayaan Melayu ke 2, anjuran Jabatan Bahasa dan Kebudayaan Melayu, Kumpulan Akademik Bahasa dan Kebudayaan Asia, Institut Pendidikan Nasional,

Universiti Teknologi Nanyang, Singapura, 1–3 September 2002. 19 pp. ISEAS, NLB.

2555. Hadijah Rahmat. *Kilat Senja: Sejarah Sosial dan Budaya Kampung-Kampung di Singapura.* Singapore: HSYang Publishing, 2005. 463 pp. ISEAS, NLB, NTUNIE, NUS.

2556. Harun Ghani. *Cabaran-Cabaran yang dihadapi oleh Masyarakat Melayu Singapura dalam Pembangunan Sosial.* Seminar Papers, no. 17. Singapore: Department of Malay Studies, National University of Singapore, 1995. 15 pp. ISEAS, NLB, NUS.

2557. Hassan, Riaz. *Families in Flats· A Study of Low Income Families in Public Housing.* Singapore: Singapore University Press, 1977. 249 pp. ISEAS, NLB, NTUNIE, NUS.

2558. "Home is Where the Heart is: Trends". *Asiaweek* 15, no. 5 (February 1989): 42. ISEAS, NLB, NTUNIE, NUS.

2559. Hussin Mutalib. "Cabaran dan Wawasan Bangsa Melayu Singapura". Paper presented at the International Seminar on the Malay Mind, organized by the Institute of Language and Literature Malaysia and the Malaysian Malay Studies Society, National University of Malaysia, Selangor, Malaysia, 26–27 October 1995.

2560. Hussin Mutalib. "Challenges and Prospects of Singaporean Malays". *Mirror* 25, no. 17 (September 1989): 10–11. ISEAS, NLB, NTUNIE, NUS.

2561. Hussin Mutalib. "Future Challenges Confronting Singapore". Paper presented at the Singapore Conference: Future Challenges, Washington, D.C., USA, organized by Johns Hopkins University, October 2002.

2562. Hussin Mutalib. "Issues Facing Muslims in This Modern Era, with Special Reference to Singapore". Paper presented at a Regional Islamic Convention, arranged by the Islamic Centre, Jamiyah Singapore, 24–27 April 1986. 13 pp. ISEAS, NUS.

2563. Hussin Mutalib. "Malays' Concept of Progress". Paper presented at the Conference on Challenges Facing Malays/Muslims in Singapore, organized by the National University of Singapore Muslim and Malay Language Society, 1986. 15 pp. NUS.

2564.   Hussin Mutalib. "Masyarakat Melayu Singapura Sejak Dua Dekad Lalu". *Jurnal Pengajian Melayu* 7 (1997): 104–16. NLB, NUS.

2565.   Hussin Mutalib. "Malays/Muslims in 21st Century Singapore: Prospects, Challenges and Directions: (Theme Paper)". In *Malays/Muslims in 21st Century Singapore: Prospects, Challenges & Directions: National Convention of Singapore Malay/Muslim Professionals, 6–7 October 1990, NPB Auditorium, Singapore*. Singapore: Organising Committee, National Convention of Singapore Malay/Muslim Professionals, 1990. ISEAS, NLB, NUS.

2566.   Hussin Mutalib, ed. *Malays/Muslims in 21st Century Singapore: Prospects, Challenges & Directions: National Convention of Singapore Malay/ Muslim Professionals, 6–7 October 1990, NPB Auditorium, Singapore*. Singapore: Organising Committee, National Convention of Singapore Malay/Muslim Professionals, 1990. 233 pp. ISEAS, NLB, NUS.

2567.   "An Image of Disunity". *Asiaweek* 18, no. 38 (September 1993): 28. ISEAS, NLB, NUS.

2568.   Iskander Mydin. "The Singapore Malay/Muslim Community: Nucleus of Modernity". In *Malays/Muslims in Singapore: Selected Readings in History 1819–1965*, edited by Khoo Kay Kim, Elinah Abdullah and Wan Meng Hao. Subang Jaya, Selangor: Pelanduk Publications in cooperation with Centre for Research on Islamic and Malay Affairs, Singapore, 2006. ISEAS, NLB, NTUNIE, NUS.

2569.   *Issues Facing the Malay/Muslim Community in Singapore: A Collection of Essays Submitted by University Students in Conjunction with the Socialive! Challenge 2010*. Organized by PMBM Scholarship Fund Board (LBKM) & Berita Harian. Singapore: Lembaga Biasiswa Kenangan Maulud, 2010. 146 pp. NLB.

2570.   Jaffar Haron. "Satu Kajian Pembaruan Semula Bandar di Singapura dengan Penglibatan Orang Melayu Khasnya". BA dissertation, Jabatan Antropologi dan Sosiologi, Universiti Malaya, 1973. Kuala Lumpur: Universiti Malaya, Unit Mikrofilem, 1994. 3 microfiches. NUS.

2571.   Kamaludeen Mohamed Nasir. "Rethinking the 'Malay Problem' in Singapore: Image, Rhetoric and Social Realities". *Journal of Muslim Minority Affairs* 27, no. 2 (August 2007): 309–18. ISEAS, NTUNIE, NUS.

2572. Kamaruddin Ngah. "A Study of an Urban Pile Village and Those Who Live There". Academic exercise, Department of Social Studies, University of Malaya, Singapore, 1962. 167 pp. NUS.

2573. *Karyawan: Professionals for the Community.* Singapore: Association of Muslim Professionals, 1994–2010. ISEAS, NLB, NTUNIE, NUS.

2574. *Kongres Pembangunan Masyarakat Melayu-Islam Singapura 19–21 Mei 1989: [Kertaskerja].* Singapore: Yayasan MENDAKI, 1989. 116 pp. NLB, NUS.

2575. Lee Hsien Loong. "A New Optimism for the Future". *Karyawan: Professionals for the Community* (October 1995): 8–9. ISEAS, NLB, NTUNIE, NUS.

2576. Lee Hsien Loong. "Singapore in the 21st Century: Challenges Facing the Malays and Other Races". *Speeches* 13, no. 6 (November/December 1989): 48–55. ISEAS, NLB, NTUNIE, NUS.

2577. Lee Hsien Loong. "Sustaining Progress of the Singaporean Malay Community". *Speeches* 20, no. 6 (November–December 1996): 53–62. ISEAS, NLB, NTUNIE, NUS.

2578. Lee Kuan Yew. "Confidence in Malay Progress". *Petir: Organ of the People's Action Party* (July 1990): 47. ISEAS, NLB, NTUNIE, NUS. Also published in Malay under the title: "Yakin akan Kemajuan Orang Melayu". *Petir: Organ of the People's Action Party* (July 1990): 55. ISEAS, NLB, NTUNIE, NUS.

2579. Lim Boon Heng. "Malay/Muslim Singaporeans Make Progress". *Petir: Organ of the People's Action Party* (April/May 1989): 2. ISEAS, NLB, NTUNIE, NUS.

2580. MacIntyre, Maureen Elizabeth. "Study of Malay Family Life-Styles in High-Rise and Low-Rise Homes". Academic exercise, Department of Sociology, University of Singapore, 1976. 93 pp. NUS.

2581. Mafoot Simon. "The Go(h)lden Age for Muslim". *Inabah* 19, no. 2 (August 2004): 30–32. NLB.

2582. Majlis Ugama Islam Singapura. *Charting the Course: For a Muslim Community of Excellence.* Singapore: Islamic Centre of Singapore, 2000. 1 CD-ROM. ISEAS, NTUNIE.

2583. "Malay/Muslims in the 90s: Key Trends, with Reference to the Census of Population 1990 Data". AMP Inaugural Seminar held at Regional English Language Centre on 5 February 1994. 11 pp. NUS.

2584. Mansor Haji Sukaimi. "Pertubuhan-Pertubuhan Melayu dan Pembangunan Singapura: Points for Discussion". Paper presented at the Camping-In Seminar organized by Persekutuan Bahasa Melayu, Universiti Singapura, 20 June 1977. 8 pp. ISEAS.

2585. Manger, Leif O. "Singapore: Making Muslim Space in a Global City". In *The Hadrami Diaspora: Community-Building on the Indian Ocean Rim*, by Leif O. Manger. New York: Berghahn Books, 2010. 201 pp. ISEAS, NLB.

2586. Mariam Mohamed Ali. "'Orang Baru' and 'Orang Lama': Ways of Being Malay on Singapore's North-Coast". Academic exercise, Department of Sociology, National University of Singapore, 1984. 226 pp. NUS.

2587. Mastura Manap. "The Interplay of Structure and Culture in Intergenerational Underdevelopment: The Case for Working Poor Malays in Singapore". MSc dissertation, Department of Sociology, National University of Singapore, 2010. 218 pp. NUS.

2588. MENDAKI (Organization). *MENDAKI's Corporate Plan*. Singapore: Council for the Development of Singapore Muslim Community, 1990–92. ISEAS, NUS.

2589. *MENDAKI Policy Digest*. Singapore: Yayasan MENDAKI, 2002–. ISEAS, NLB, NTUNIE, NUS.

2590. Mohd. Maidin Packer Mohamad. "Kolektivisme: Kekuatan Menghadapi Masa Depan". *Petir: Organ of the People's Action Party* (February 1990): 46–47. ISEAS, NLB, NTUNIE, NUS.

2591. Mohd. Maidin Packer Mohamad. "Pencapaian Orang Melayu Sepanjang 25 Tahun". *Petir: Organ of the People's Action Party* (September 1990): 51–53. ISEAS, NLB, NTUNIE, NUS.

2592. Mohd. Maidin Packer Mohamad. "Progress: Between Hopes and Reality". *Petir: Organ of the People's Action Party* (June 1990): 6–7. ISEAS, NLB, NTUNIE, NUS. Also published in Malay under the title: "Kemajuan: antara Harapan dan Kenyataan". *Petir: Organ of the People's Action Party* (May 1990): 46–47. ISEAS, NLB, NTUNIE, NUS.

2593. Mohd Raman Daud. "Dilema?" *Analisa* (1981): 16–21. NLB, NUS.

2594. Muhammad Nadim Adam. "Singapore's 'New Normal' Socio-economic Paradigm: Navigating Needs, Expectations and Aspirations". *Mendaki Policy Digest* (2012): 83–131. ISEAS, NLB, NTUNIE, NUS.

2595. Muhammad Nadim Adam. "Social Aspirations, Community Needs, Relevant Social Safety Nets & Its Implications for Vulnerable Malay/ Muslim Families in Singapore". *MENDAKI Policy Digest* (2013): 27–43. ISEAS, NLB, NTUNIE, NUS.

2596. Neville, Warwick. "Patterns of Change in a Plural Society: A Social Geography of the City State of Singapore". PhD dissertation, London School of Economics, University of London, 1967. 934 pp. NUS.

2597. *The Next Decade: Strengthening Our Community's Architecture*. Singapore: Association of Muslim Professionals, 2012. 220 pp. ISEAS, NLB.

2598. Nur Amali Ibrahim. "Moving to a New Past: Unmasking the Mission Civilisatrice". *Buletin Saujana* 1 (2000): 30–35. NLB, NUS.

2599. Nur Aqilah Suparti. "'The Two-Thirds Challenge': The MMC's Race of the Next Two Decades". *MENDAKI Policy Digest* (2013): 45–57. ISEAS, NLB, NTUNIE, NUS.

2600. *Perubahan Kemasharakatan di Singapura*. Singapore: Kementerian Kebudayaan, 1964. 146 pp. NLB, NUS.

2601. Pung, Lynden H.S. "The Malays in Singapore: Political Aspects of the 'Malay Problem'". MA dissertation, McMaster University, 1993. 136 pp. NLB, NUS.

2602. Rafiz Mohyi Hapipi. "Changing Boundaries: Symbolic Power and Malay Community Empowerment". *MENDAKI Policy Digest* (2007): 1–15. ISEAS, NLB, NTUNIE, NUS.

2603. Rafiz Mohyi Hapipi. "Re©entering the Mobility Agenda" Lessons from Grameen". *MENDAKI Policy Digest* (2008): 87–95. ISEAS, NLB, NTUNIE, NUS.

2604. Ramachandran, Somasundram. "A Social and Economic Study of Residents of a Suburban Kampong Scheduled for Demolition". Academic exercise, Department of Social Work and Social Administration, University of Singapore, 1970. 168 pp. NUS.

2605. Richards, Denise Nicole. "Study on the Social Issues Brought Up by the Malays and Published in the Berita Harian". Research exercise, Department of Malay Studies, National University of Singapore, 1992. 55 pp. NUS.

2606. *Risalah Membangun Masyarakat Islam Cemerlang Singapura*. Singapore: MUIS, 2006. 104 pp.

2607. *Risalah Membangun Masyarakat Islam Cemerlang Singapura: Dokumen Kerja*. Singapore: Islamic Religious Council of Singapore, 2005. 1 CD-ROM. ISEAS.

2608. Robert, Cecilia Inparani. "The Social and Economic Implications of Relocation on Squatter Settlements: A Case Study of Kebun Bugis". Academic exercise, University of Singapore, 1973. Microform. NUS.

2609. Roff, William R. "Murder as an Aid to Social History: The Arabs in Singapore in the Early Twentieth Century". In *Transcending Borders: Arabs, Politics, Trade and Islam in Southeast Asia*, edited by Huub de Jonge and N.J.G. Kaptein. Leiden: KITLV Press, 2002. ISEAS, NLB, NUS.

2610. Rohayati Rahim. "Socio-economic Profile of the Malays in Singapore". Academic exercise, Department of Economics & Statistics, National University of Singapore, 1984. 75 pp. NUS.

2611. Roziah Ismail. "Adjustment to High Rise Living: A Case Study of the Malays in Clementi New Town". Academic exercise, Department of Geography, National University of Singapore, 1983. 148 pp. NUS.

2612. Saat A. Rahman et al., eds. *In Quest of Excellence: A Story of Singapore Malays*. Co-writer, Thusitha de Silva. Singapore: Yayasan MENDAKI, 2002. 204 pp. ISEAS, NLB, NTUNIE, NUS.

2613. Saktiandi Supaat. "The Globalisation Wave: Challenges and Risks for the Malay/Muslim Community". *Karyawan: Professionals for the Community* 8, issue 1 (December 2007): 19–22. ISEAS, NLB, NTUNIE, NUS.

2614. "Seminar on Challenges Facing the Malay-Muslim Community in Singapore". Organized by National University of Singapore Muslim Society and Malay Language Society, 13 September 1986. 53 pp. NUS.

2615.   "Seminar on Muslim Communities in Singapore". Organized by Islamic Fellowship Association at the RELC Auditorium, 1988.

2616.   Sha'ari Tadin. "Reserving a Place on the Sun". *New Directions* 1, no. 4 (December 1974): 41–43. ISEAS, NLB, NTUNIE, NUS.

2617.   Sharifah Mohamed. *Kenapa Saya Menulis.* Singapore: Sharifah Mohamed, 2014. 183 pp. NLB.

2618.   Sharom Ahmat. "The Singapore Malay Community". *Journal of the Historical Society* (1971): 39–46. ISEAS, NLB, NUS. Also published under the same title in: *NYLTI Journal* (September 1972): 44–53. ISEAS, NLB, NUS.

2619.   Sharom Ahmat and James Wong, eds. *Malay Participation in the National Development of Singapore.* Singapore: Eurasia Press, 1971. 25 pp. ISEAS, NLB, NTUNIE, NUS. Also published in Malay under the title: *Penyertaan Masyarakat Melayu dalam Pembangunan Nasional Singapura.* Singapore: Central Council of Malay Cultural Organisations Singapore, 1971. 50 pp. ISEAS, NLB.

2620.   Siddique, Sharon. "Being Muslim in Singapore: Change, Community and Consciousness". Paper presented at Conference on Islam and Society in Southeast Asia, Jakarta, Indonesia, 29–31 May 1995. 1 microfiche. ISEAS.

2621.   Siddique, Sharon. "Some Malay Ideas on Modernization, Islam and Adat: An Analysis of Certain Attitudes and Ideas Concerning Modernization, Islam and Adat and Their Interrelationship in the Context of Malay Social Life". MA dissertation, Department of Malay Studies, University of Singapore, 1973. 201 pp. ISEAS, NUS.

2622.   *Singapore Malay/Muslim Community: Vision of a Learning, Creative, Confident Community.* Singapore: Regional Training and Publishing Centre, 1999. 49 pp. NLB, NTUNIE, NUS.

2623.   "Singapore: Malays". *The Asiatic Journal and Monthly Miscellany* 6, no. 23 (November 1831): 129–130. NLB.

2624.   Sitiurika Ahmad. "Strategising for Social Progression and Strengthening of Malay/Muslim Families". *MENDAKI Policy Digest* (2007): 17–31. ISEAS, NLB, NTUNIE, NUS.

2625.   Suniwati Suni. "Isu-Isu Penting yang Dihadapi oleh Masyarakat Melayu/ Islam di Singapura Sekitar 1990–1991". Academic exercise, Department of Malay Studies, National University of Singapore, 1992. 94 pp. NUS.

2626.   Swettenham, F.A. "Malay Problems, 1926". *British Malaya* 1, no. 1 (May 1926): 7–14. NLB, NUS.

2627.   *Tanahairku: Singapura Malay/Muslims 1991–1996.* Singapore: Association of Muslims Professionals, 1996. 96 pp. NLB, NTUNIE, NUS.

2628.   Teh Cheang Wan. "Public Housing: A Powerful Melting Pot". *Speeches* 5, no. 8 (February 1982): 23–28. ISEAS.

2629.   Tham Seong Chee. "Pembangunan Masyarakat Melayu Singapura: Dahulu dan Sekarang". *Analisa* (1981): 1–4. NLB, NUS.

2630.   *Tinjauan.* Singapore: Perbadanan Penyiaran Singapura, 1984–. Videocassettes (VHS, PAL). NLB.

2631.   *Vision 2010: Setting the Community Agenda in 21st Century Singapore: 2nd National Convention of Singapore Malay/Muslim Professionals, 4–5 November 2000, Singapore.* Singapore: Steering Committee, National Convention of Singapore Malay/Muslim Professionals, 2000. 199 pp. ISEAS, NUS, NTUNIE.

2632.   Walter, Michael A.H.B. and Riaz Hassan. *An Island Community in Singapore: A Characterization of a Marginal Society.* Sociology Working Paper, no. 61. Singapore: Chopmen Enterprises for Department of Sociology, University of Singapore, 1977. 41 pp. ISEAS, NLB, NTUNIE, NUS.

2633.   Wan Hussin Zoohri. *The Singapore Malays: The Dilemma of Development.* Singapore: Kesatuan Guru-Guru Melayu Singapura, 1990. 94 pp. ISEAS, NLB, NTUNIE, NUS.

2634.   Wan Hussin Zoohri. "Socio-economic Problems of the Malays in Singapore". *Sojourn: Social Issues in Southeast Asia* 2, no. 2 (August 1987): 178–203. ISEAS, NLB, NTUNIE, NUS. Also published under the same title in: *Fajar Islam* 1, no. 1 (1988): 1–23. ISEAS, NLB, NUS.

2635.   Yaacob Ibrahim. "What Makes a 'New Malay': [Speech at Department of Malay Studies Seminar, 18 April 2002]". *Speeches* 26, no. 2 (March–April 2002): 88–100. ISEAS, NTUNIE, NLB.

2636. Yaacob Ibrahim, Halijah Mohamad, and Jumari Naiyan. "Dimensions of the Malay 'Dilemma'". *Commentary* 11, no. 2 (1993): 91–110. ISEAS, NLB, NTUNIE, NUS.

2637. Yang Razali Kassim. "Why There is Still a Malay Problem?" In *Singapore 25 Years: A Straits Times Special, National Day, 9 Aug 1990*, edited by Leslie Fong. Singapore: Straits Times Press, 1990. ISEAS, NLB, NUS.

2638. Yeo Cheow Tong. "Social Problems among Malays". *Speeches* 16, no. 4 (July/August 1992): 73–76. ISEAS, NLB, NTUNIE, NUS.

2639. Yeo Yong Boon, George. "The Malay/Muslim Community in the Next Lap". *Speeches* 15, no. 5 (September/October 1991): 95–101. ISEAS, NLB, NTUNIE, NUS. Also published under the same title in: *Singapore Professional* 16, no. 1 (March 1992): 13–17. NLB, NUS.

2640. Yeo Yong Boon, George. "Our Modern, Scientific and Dynamic Singapore Malay Community". *Speeches* 13, no. 2 (March/April 1989): 63–65. ISEAS, NLB, NTUNIE, NUS.

2641. Zahrah Munir. "The Experience of Being Rehoused: Malay Families in Singapore". Academic exercise, Department of Social Studies, University of Singapore, 1965. 101 pp. NUS.

2642. Zaid Hamzah. "Dynamics of Strategic Change among the Malays in Singapore". *Fajar Islam* 1, no. 1 (1988): 25–31. ISEAS, NLB, NUS.

2643. Zainul Abidin Rasheed. *Collection of Speeches*. Singapore: [s.n.], 1991–. 1 vol. (loose-leaf). NUS.

2644. Zaki Amrullah. "Good Enough?" *Nadi* 2 (April 2006): 18–19. NLB, NUS.

2645. Zuraidah Ibrahim. "Malay Experience". *Accent* (December 1990): 70–78. NLB, NUS.

2646. Zuraidah Ibrahim. *Muslims in Singapore: A Shared Vision*. Singapore: Published for Majlis Ugama Islam Singapura by Times Editions, 1994. 123 pp. ISEAS, NLB, NTUNIE, NUS. Also published in Malay under the title: *Orang Islam di Singapura: Visi Bersama*. Penterjemah Bahasa Melayu, Nik Safiah Nik Karim. Singapore: Diterbitkan untuk Majlis Ugama Islam Singapura oleh Times Edition, 1994. 123 pp. ISEAS, NLB.

Social Problems and Services

2647. A. Rahim Ishak. "Drug Abuse among Malay Youth Shows a Downward Trend". *Speeches (SANA)* (January/March 1979): 21–22. NLB, NTUNIE, NUS.

2648. Abdullah Tarmugi. "Working for Social Progress". *Karyawan: Professionals for the Community* (July 1996): 10–11. ISEAS, NLB, NTUNIE, NUS.

2649. Ahmad Burok. "Najis Dadah dan Masyarakat Melayu Islam Singapura". *Petir: Organ of the People's Action Party* (March 1988): 28–29. ISEAS, NLB, NTUNIE, NUS.

2650. Ahmad Mattar. "Muslims' Community Services". *Speeches* 4, no. 7 (January 1981): 42–44. ISEAS, NLB, NTUNIE, NUS.

2651. Ahmad Mattar. "Muslims Urged to Volunteer Their Service". *Speeches* 14, no. 4 (July/August 1990): 44–46. ISEAS, NLB, NTUNIE, NUS.

2652. Ahmad Mattar. "Young Muslim Professionals Urged to Take Part in Community Activities". *Speeches* 5, no. 3 (September 1981): 94–95. ISEAS, NLB, NTUNIE, NUS.

2653. Ahmad Mattar. "Problems Faced by Malays Can Be Progressively Overcome". *Petir: Organ of the People's Action Party* (July 1990): 48–49. ISEAS, NLB, NTUNIE, NUS. Also published in Malay under the title: "Masaalah Masyarakat Melayu Kian Dapat Diatasi". *Petir: Organ of the People's Action Party* (July 1990): 57. ISEAS, NLB, NTUNIE, NUS.

2654. Ahmad Mattar. "Society's Well-Being Depends on Mutual Concern". *Speeches* 4, no. 11 (May 1981): 69–70. ISEAS, NLB, NTUNIE.

2655. Baey Lian Peck. *Drug Abuse: The Singapore Experience.* Singapore: Singapore Anti-Narcotics Association, 1980. 21 pp. NLB, NUS.

2656. Baey Lian Peck. "Female Drug Takers". *Speeches (SANA)* (April/June 1979): 45–47. NLB, NUS.

2657. Baey Lian Peck. "Social Service within the Drug Rehabilitation Centres". *Speeches (SANA)* (July/September 1979): 26–31. NLB, NUS.

2658. *The Beam: Directory of Social Services.* Singapore: Majlis Ugama Islam Singapore, 2002–. NLB.

2659. Blake, Myrna. "Building Independence among the Disadvantaged". *Karyawan: Professionals for the Community* (July 1996): 6–7. ISEAS, NLB, NTUNIE, NUS.

2660. Chan Wing-Cheong. "Juvenile Offenders in Singapore". *British Journal of Community Justice* 8, no. 3 (2010): 63–77. NUS.

2661. Cheong Bee Lay, Janice. "The Family Service Centre: YWMA-MENDAKI FSC (PPIS) as a Service Provider in the Malay-Muslim Community". Research exercise, Department of Malay Studies, National University of Singapore, 1996. 50 pp. NUS.

2662. *Directory of Social Services*. Singapore: National Council of Social Services, 2003. 732 pp. ISEAS, NLB, NTUNIE, NUS. Available at <http://www.ncss gov.sg/VWOcorner/members_list.asp>.

2663. Enon Mansor and Amali Ibrahim. "Muslim Organizations and Mosques as Social Service Providers". In *Religious Diversity in Singapore*, edited by Lai Ah Eng. Singapore: Institute of Southeast Asian Studies; Institute of Policy Studies, 2008. ISEAS, NLB, NTUNIE, NUS.

2664. *The Helping Hand: Singapore Council of Social Service Directory of Voluntary Welfare Organizations 1961*. Singapore: Singapore Council of Social Service, 1962. 152 pp. NLB, NUS.

2665. Ho, Stephanie and Jamie Koh, eds. *Many Roads Home: Stories from the Muhammadiyah Welfare Home*. Singapore: Muhammadiyah Welfare Home, 2009. 187 pp. NLB

2666. Jumari Naiyan. "Adding Value to the Community". *Karyawan: Professionals for the Community* (March 1995): 4–5. ISEAS, NLB, NTUNIE, NUS.

2667. Jumari Naiyan. "Blueprint for the Disadvantaged". *Karyawan: Professionals for the Community* (December 1994): 4–5. ISEAS, NLB, NTUNIE, NUS.

2668. Kadir Jamaludin. "Tackling Drug Problem among the Malays". *Petir: Organ of the People's Action Party* (March 1988): 21. ISEAS, NLB, NTUNIE, NUS.

2669. Lim Chee Onn. "The Vital Role Played by the Muslim Counselling Service for the Malays". *Speeches (SANA)* (January/March 1977): 20. NLB, NUS.

2670. *List of Registered Societies: Supplement to the Republic of Singapore Government Gazette.* Singapore: Singapore National Printer, 1978–. ISEAS, NLB, NTUNIE, NUS.

2671. Mohana Rani Suppiah. "The Road from Dope to Hope: Drug Recidivism in the Context of Ethnicity in Singapore". Academic exercise, National University of Singapore, 1989. 62 pp. NUS.

2672. Mohd Ali Mahmood. *Jurnal Kaunseling: Menghurai Dilema Remaja Hamil.* Singapore: Darby Media, 2010. 142 pp. NLB.

2673. Mohd Maliki Osman. "Predicting Rehabilitated or Relapsed Status of Malay Drug Addicts in Singapore: The Role of Familial, Individual, Religious, and Social Support Factors". PhD dissertation, University of Illinois, 1998. 287 pp. NLB, NTUNIE.

2674. Mohd. Yusoff Ahmad. "Presentation of Certificates of Muslim Registered Volunteer Aftercare Officers". *Speeches (SANA)* (April/June 1979): 43–44. NLB, NUS.

2675. Mohd. Yusoff Ahmad. "SANA Muslim Aftercare (Counselling) Service". *Speeches (SANA)* (April/June 1979): 15–16. NLB, NUS.

2676. *MTFA 80th Anniversary: 80 Years of Welfare Services, 1904–1984.* Singapore: Muslim Trust Fund Association, 1984. 124 pp. NUS.

2677. Ng Tai Phong. "Delinquency Problems in the Malay Society". Research exercise, Department of Malay Studies, National University of Singapore, 1996. 43 pp. NUS.

2678. Noraidee Abd Sukor. "Profile on Malay Female Drug Offenders". Research exercise, National University of Singapore, 1991. 62 pp. NUS.

2679. Ong Teck Hong. "The Attitudinal and Psychological Characteristics of Drug Abusers in Singapore". PhD dissertation, University of Wales, 1986. 442 pp. NUS.

2680. Rafiz Mohyi Hapipi. "Social Intervention and the Underclass Worry". *MENDAKI Policy Digest* (2008): 9–25. ISEAS, NTUNIE, NUS.

2681. Raihan Yusof. "Cadangan Tindakan Berkesan untuk Membasmi Penyalahgunaan Dadah di Kalangan Belia Islam". *Petir: Organ of the People's Action Party* (March 1988): 30–31. ISEAS, NLB, NTUNIE, NUS.

2682. Rasman Saridin. *Nilai-nilai Islam dalam Membentuk Keperibadian Islam*. Singapore: Persatuan Hira, 2015.

2683. Saini Salleh et al., eds. *Of Heroes and Heroin: How the Singapore Malay-Muslim Community Waged War Against Drug Abuse*. Singapore: Harun Ghani Education Fund, 2007. 168 pp. ISEAS, NLB, NTUNIE, NUS.

2684. Salahudin Chee Yahya. "Drug Abuse: A Sociological Study of Malay Drug Addicts in Singapore". Academic exercise, National University of Singapore, 1991. 80 pp. NUS.

2685. Salleh Md. Piah. "The Ex-Drug Taker Deserves the Right to be Assisted". *Speeches (SANA)* (October/December 1979): 9–10. NLB, NUS.

2686. Sha'ari Tadin. "Fighting Crime and Drug Abuse in Bedok Constituency". *Speeches (SANA)* (October/December 1978): 31–32. NLB, NUS.

2687. Sha'ari Tadin. "How Volunteer Aftercare Officers and Parents can Help in Rehabilitating the Ex-Drug Taker". *Speeches (SANA)* (April/June 1978): 7–9. NLB, NUS.

2688. Sha'ari Tadin. "Some Expectations of the SANA Muslim Aftercare (Counselling) Service". *Speeches (SANA)* (April/June 1979): 19–21. NLB, NUS.

2689. Sidek Saniff. "Drug Abuse and Crime". *Speeches (SANA)* (July/September 1979): 32–34. NLB, NUS.

2690. *Social and Health care Service Directory: A Resource Directory for Persons Needing Care and Their Caregivers*. Singapore: Agency for Integrated Care, Centre for Enabled Living, 2012–. NLB.

2691. Teo S.H. et al. "Heroin Abuse in Singapore: A Profile and Characteristics Study". *Singapore Medical Journal* 19, no. 2 (1978): 65–70. NLB, NUS.

2692. *Voice of MUJADACC* = Suara MUJADACC. Bimonthly. Singapore: Yayasan MENDAKI, 1993–99. NUS.

2693. Wan Peck Yuet and Au Yong Hou Khuan. "Drug Addiction amongst Youths in Singapore". Academic exercise, Department of Sociology, University of Singapore, 1973. 29 pp. NUS.

2694. Woon Chu Meng. "Drug Abuse among Female Addicts". Academic exercise, Department of Sociology, University of Singapore, 1976. 83 pp. NUS.

2695.   Yeo Yong Boon, George. "Civic Society in Singapore". *Karyawan: Professionals for the Community* 5 (January–April 1999): 12–15, 18–20. ISEAS, NLB, NTUNIE, NUS.

2696.   Zailinah Haji Safiee. "Drug Abuse: A Social Phenomenon?" Research exercise, Department of Malay Studies, National University of Singapore, 1991. 46 pp. NUS.

2697.   Zakaria Buang. "Drugs: The War is Not Over". *Mirror* 24, no. 1 (January 1988): 8–10. ISEAS, NLB, NUS.

Self-Help Groups

2698.   *20th AMP Singapore Anniversary 1991–2011: Celebrating 20 Years of Progress with Community Annual Report 2011.* Singapore: Association of Muslim Professionals, 2011. 176 pp. NUS.

2699.   Afiza Hashim. "Civil Society in Singapore: Case Study of AMP". Academic exercise, Department of Sociology, National University of Singapore, 2002. 50 pp. NUS.

2700.   Ahmad Mattar. "Muslim Community Practices Self-Reliance". *Speeches* 4, no. 4 (October 1980): 74–75. ISEAS, NLB, NTUNIE, NUS.

2701.   Aida Khalid. "MENDAKI Headquarters: A Council for the Development of Singapore Malay/Muslim Community". Academic exercise, National University of Singapore, 1991. 1 vol. NUS.

2702.   Aljunied, Syed Muhammad Raziff. "MENDAKI: Its Aims, Development and the Masses Perceptions". Research exercise, Department of Malay Studies, National University of Singapore, 1991. 36 pp. NUS.

2703.   "AMP 2010". *Karyawan: Professionals for the Community* (August 1994): 8–9. ISEAS, NLB, NTUNIE, NUS.

2704.   "AMP Goes Regional". *Karyawan: Professionals for the Community* (August 1994): 4–5. ISEAS, NLB, NTUNIE, NUS.

2705.   *AMP Inaugural Souvenir Magazine.* Singapore: AMP, 1991.

2706.   "AMP Project Crisis Centre Seminar, 27 & 28th June 1992". 72 pp. NUS.

2707.   "AMP Report Card". *Karyawan: Professionals for the Community* (February 1996): 14–15. ISEAS, NLB, NTUNIE, NUS.

2708. *AMP Singapore 1ˢᵗ Anniversary*. Singapore: Association of Muslim Professionals, 1992. 40 pp. NLB.

2709. "AMP Singapore 1st Anniversary Charity Dinner, 8 November 1992". Singapore: Asssociation of Muslim Professionals, [1992?]. 33 pp. NUS.

2710. *AMP Singapore: Launch*. Singapore: AMP, 1991. 103 pp. NLB.

2711. "Association of Muslim Professionals". *Singapore Professionals* 16, no. 1 (March 1992): 18–19. ISEAS, NLB, NTUNIE, NUS.

2712. *Association of Muslim Professionals (Singapore). Annual Report*. Singapore: Association of Muslim Professionals, 1996/97–. ISEAS, NTUNIE, NUS.

2713. *Bingkisan 1948–1984: dari Jalan Eunos ke Bedok Reservoir*. Singapore: Persatuan Persuratan Pemuda Pemudi Melayu, 1985. 48 pp. NLB.

2714. *Buku Penerangan mengenai Yayasan MENDAKI*. Singapore: Yayasan MENDAKI, 1986. 19 pp. NLB, NUS.

2715. *Chenderamata Dewasa: 20 Tahun, 1948–1968*. Singapore: Persatuan Persuratan Pemuda Pemudi Melayu Singapura, 1968. 36 pp. NLB, NUS.

2716. "First Class, Please: Minority Malays Band Together to Help Themselves". *Asiaweek* 20, no. 49 (7 December 1994): 29. ISEAS.

2717. *Information on Yayasan MENDAKI*. Singapore: Yayasan MENDAKI, 1986. 19 pp. NLB, NUS.

2718. Isa Kamari. "Wisma MENDAKI". Academic exercise, National University of Singapore, 1988. 98 pp. NUS.

2719. Kamaroonnisa Mohamed "Association of Muslim Professionals: Origins & Role in the Development of the Malay/Muslim Community". Research exercise, Department of Malay Studies, National University of Singapore, 1995. 84 pp. NUS.

2720. Lee Hsien Loong. "Maximum Community Involvement: The Way to Uplift the Malays". *Speeches* 15, no. 3 (May/June 1991): 25–31. ISEAS, NLB, NTUNIE, NUS.

2721. Lee Hsien Loong. "Self-Help and Community Effort among Malays". *Speeches* 15, no. 6 (November/ December 1991): 34–37. ISEAS, NLB, NTUNIE, NUS.

2722. Lily Zubaidah Rahim. "The Inherent Limitations of Mendaki". In *The Singapore Dilemma: The Political and Educational Marginality of the Malay Community*, by Lily Zubaidah Rahim. Kuala Lumpur: Oxford University Press, 1998. ISEAS, NLB, NTUNIE, NUS.

2723. *Making the Difference: Ten Years of MENDAKI*. Singapore: Yayasan Mendaki, 1992. 251 pp. ISEAS, NLB, NTUNIE, NUS.

2724. *Memorandum and Articles of Association of Yayasan MENDAKI: Incorporated in Singapore on 28th June 1989*. Singapore: Yayasan MENDAKI, 1989. NLB, NUS.

2725. *MENDAKI Genap Setahun*. Singapore Yayasan MENDAKI, 1983. 28 pp. NLB.

2726. MENDAKI (Organization). *Annual Report = Laporan Tahunan*. Singapore: Yayasan MENDAKI, 1990–. ISEAS, NTUNIE, NUS.

2727. MENDAKI (Organization). *Penyata Tiga Tahunan*. Singapore: Yayasan MENDAKI, 1985–. NLB, NUS.

2728. "MENDAKI: Pertubuhan Orang Melayu Singapura". In *Ensiklopedia Sejarah dan Kebudayaan Melayu*, vol. 3, p. 1518. Kuala Lumpur: Dewan Bahasa dan Pustaka, 1994. NLB, NTUNIE, NUS.

2729. Mohamed Faizal Ahmad. "Of Fishes, Fisherman and Social Enterprises". *MENDAKI Policy Digest* (2007): 93–102. ISEAS, NTUNIE, NUS.

2730. Mohd. Maidin Packer Mohamad. "MENDAKI: Self-help Progress". *Petir: Organ of the People's Action Party* (September 1989): 33. ISEAS, NLB, NTUNIE, NUS.

2731. Mohd. Maidin Packer Mohamad. "MENDAKI: Senama Tapi Tak Sama". *Petir: Organ of the People's Action Party* (September 1989): 40–41. ISEAS, NLB, NTUNIE, NUS.

2732. "The National Convention of Singapore Malay/Muslim Professionals: Communique". *Karyawan* (October 1995): 14–15. ISEAS, NLB, NTUNIE, NUS.

2733. Persatuan Pemudi Islam Singapura. *Laporan Dwitahunan = Biennial Report*. Singapore: Persatuan Pemudi Islam Singapura, 1988–2006. ISEAS, NLB, NUS.

2734. *Persatuan Persuratan Pemuda Pemudi Melayu Singapura 10 tahun 1948-1958: Chendera mata.* Singapore: 4PM, [1958–63?]. 3 vols. in 1. NUS.

2735. *PM at the Association of Muslim Professionals Convention.* Broadcasted on 8/11/2000. Singapore: Television Corporation of Singapore, 2000. 1 videocassette. 30 min. NUS.

2736. Ramthan Hussain. "Room for Total Commitment". *Karyawan: Professionals for the Community* (December 1994): 14–15. ISEAS, NLB, NTUNIE, NUS.

2737. "Singapore Malay Youth Library Association". *Citizen* (August 1989): 18. NLB.

2738. Tay, Simon et al. *Self-Help and National Integration.* Occasional Paper Series, no. 3-96. Singapore: Association of Muslim Professionals, 1996. 50 pp. ISEAS, NLB, NTUNIE, NUS.

2739. Wan Hussin Zoohri. "MENDAKI Making the Grade". *Mirror* 25, no. 5 (March 1989): 10–11. ISEAS, NLB, NTUNIE, NUS.

2740. Yang Razali Kassim. "AMP as Problem-Solver, Mobiliser and Think Tank". *Karyawan: Professionals for the Community* 6, issue 1 (November 2005): 8. ISEAS, NLB, NTUNIE, NUS.

2741. *Yayasan MENDAKI: Scaling Greater Heights.* Singapore: Media Arts, 1997. 1 CD-ROM. NTUNIE, NUS.

2742. Yeo Yong Boon, George. "Towards a Caring Society". *Speeches* 22, no. 6 (November–December 1998): 46–47. ISEAS, NLB, NTUNIE.

2743. Yusman Ahmad. "Square Peg in a Round Hole? MENDAKI is Hard Put to Repeat Its Success with Education in Other Areas". *Malaysian Business* (November 1992) 55. ISEAS, NLB, NTUNIE, NUS.

2744. Zuraidah Ibrahim. "Sustaining the Pioneering Spirit". *Karyawan: Professionals for the Community* 2 (October 1995): 12–13. ISEAS, NLB, NTUNIE, NUS.

SPECIAL LOCALITIES

- *Geylang Serai*
- *Kampong Glam*
- *Islands*
- *Other Localities*

Geylang Serai

2745.   Adli Yashir Kuchit et al. *The Heart of Geylang Serai*. Editor, Saat A. Rahman. Singapore: Kampong Ubi Citizens' Consultative Committee, 2005. 170 pp. ISEAS, NLB, NTUNIE, NUS.

2746.   Baey Yit Mei. "The Malay Village". *Chinese Women's Association Journal* (May/June 1990): 14–17. NLB, NUS.

2747.   *Changing Landscapes: Geylang*. Producer, Zainab Rahim. Singapore: Singapore Broadcasting Corporation, 1988. 1 videocassette (VHS, PAL). 50 min. NLB.

2748.   Devasahayam, Patricia. "Geylang Serai: The Malay Emporium of Singapore". Academic exercise, Department of Sociology, National University of Singapore, 1985. 141 pp. NUS.

2749.   *Geylang Serai, Down Memory Lane = Geylang Serai, Kenangan Abadi*. Singapore: Heinemann Asia; National Archives, 1986. 92 pp. ISEAS, NLB, NTUNIE, NUS.

2750.   Ong Boon Geok. "Social Structure of the Resettled Malay Community in Geylang Serai, Singapore". Academic exercise, Department of Sociology, University of Singapore, 1974. 50 pp. ISEAS, NUS. Also published under the same title in: *Review of Southeast Asian Studies* 4, no. 1–2 (June 1974): 44–63. ISEAS, NLB, NUS.

2751.   "Preserving Our Heritage: 2 Projects, Kerbau Redevelopment [and] Geylang Serai Malay Village". *SIAJ* 157 (November/December 1989): 15–23. NLB, NUS.

2752.   *Secondary Settlements: Conservation Guidelines for Geylang Conservative Area*. Singapore: Urban Redevelopment Authority, 1991. 67 pp. ISEAS, NLB, NUS.

2753.   Shahrin Mohd. Shahir. "Development Potential and Value Trends (Geylang Serai Area)". Academic exercise, National University of Singapore, 1987. 132 pp. NUS.

2754.   Shaik Kadir. *A Kite in the Evening Sky*. Singapore: EPB Publishers, 1989. 115 pp. ISEAS, NLB, NTUNIE, NUS.
        ("… first hand account of kampung life in Geylang Serai during the late 1950s and 1960s" — Pref.).

Kampong Glam

2755. Ahluwalia, S.S. "Royal Wrangle". *New Straits Times Annual* (1982): 88–94. ISEAS, NLB, NUS.

2756. Ali, Z. "The Istana at Kampong Gelam: From Royal Ground to National Heritage". Academic exercise, Department of Southeast Asian Studies Programme, National University of Singapore, 2002. NUS.

2757. Ambiga Raju. "Old Glam Tree ... Where Malay History was Made". *Young Families* (January/February 2005): 12–14. NLB.

2758. Barry, Jennifer. *Istana Kampong Glam: Archaeological Excavations at a Nineteenth Century Malay Palace in Singapore.* Stamford: Rheidol Press, 2009. 166 pp. NLB.

2759. Barry, Jennifer. *Istana Kampong Glam: European Ceramic from Archaeological Excavations at a Nineteenth Century Malay Palace in Singapore.* Stamford: Rheidol Press, 2007. 84 pp. NLB.

2760. Boey Yut Mei. "Kampong Glam: A Community". Academic exercise, University of Singapore, 1975. 80 pp. NUS.

2761. Fachry, Eva. "Malay Heritage Center". *Singapore American* 50, no. 8 (August 2006): 18. NLB.

2762. Goh Lee Eng. "Conservation and Redevelopment of Kampung Glam". Academic exercise, School of Architecture, National University of Singapore, 1977. 1 microfilm reel. NUS.

2763. Hadijah Rahmat. "Portraits of a Nation: The British Legacy for Malay Settlements in Singapore". *Indonesia and the Malay World* 36, no. 106 (2008): 359–74. ISEAS, NLB, NTUNIE, NUS.

2764. Hidayah Amin. *Gedung Kuning: Memories of a Malay Childhood.* Singapore: Singapore Heritage Society; Helang Books, 2010. 227 pp. ISEAS, NLB, NTUNIE, NUS.

2765. *Historic Districts in the Central Area: A Manual for Kampong Glam Conservative Area.* Singapore: Urban Redevelopment Authority, 1988. 100 pp. ISEAS, NLB, NUS.

2766. Hussin Mutalib. "Kampung Glam". In *Ensiklopedia Sejarah dan Kebudayaan Melayu,* vol. 2, edited by Safian Hussain. Kuala Lumpur: Dewan Bahasa dan Pustaka, 1994. NLB, NTUNIE, NUS.

2767. Imran Tajudeen. "Kampong Gelam, Rochor & Kallang – The Old Port Town". In *Malay Heritage of Singapore*, edited by Aileen T. Lau and Bernhard Platzdasch. Singapore: Suntree Media in association with Malay Heritage Foundation, 2010. ISEAS, NLB, NTUNIE, NUS.

2768. Imran Tajudeen. "Reading the Traditional City in Maritime Southeast Asia: Reconstructing the 19th Century Port Town at Gelam-Rochor-Kallang, Singapore". *Journal of Southeast Asian Architecture* 8 (2005): 1–25. ISEAS, NLB, NUS.

2769. *Kampong Glam*. Singapore: Television Corporation of Singapore, 1987. 1 videocassette. 22 min. NUS.

2770. *Kampong Glam: Historic District*. Singapore: Urban Redevelopment Authority, 1995. 88 pp. ISEAS, NLB, NTUNIE.

2771. Khadijah Yaakub. "Conservation of Kampong Glam: Towards a Successful Implementation". Academic exercise, National University of Singapore, 1989. 91 pp. NUS.

2772. Khong Swee Lin and Carl-Bernd Kaehlig. *Sari, Sarong and Shorts: Singapore's Kampong Glam & Little India*. Singapore: SNP Editions, 2008. 167 pp. NLB, NTUNIE.

2773. Ler Seng Ann. "The Restoration of Two Pilot Blocks of Conservation Shophouses in Kampong Glam and Little India: A Practical Experience". *Singapore Architect* 185 (July/August 1994): 38–40. NLB, NUS.

2774. Lim Say Liang. "Remembering Gedung Kuning". *Singapore* (October–December 2009): 20–21. NLB.

2775. Norhayati Ahmad. "Kampong Glam: The Genre de Vie of Urban Malays". Academic exercise, Department of Geography, National University of Singapore, 1987. 104 pp. NUS.

2776. Perkins, Jane. *Kampong Glam: The Spirit of a Community*. Singapore: Times Publishing for Kampong Glam Citizens' Consultative Committee, 1984. 77 pp. ISEAS, NLB, NUS.

2777. Siti Habibah Siraj. "The Conservation of Kampong Glam & Kampong Glam Heritage Centre". Academic exercise, National University of Singapore, 1987. 151 pp. NUS.

Islands

2778. Chen Bosheng and Lee Leong Sze. *A Retrospect on the Dust-laden History: The Past and Present of Tekong Island in Singapore*. Singapore; Hackensack, N.J.: World Scientific Pub. Co., 2012. 121 pp. ISEAS, NLB, NTUNIE, NUS.

2779. Chew Soo Beng. *Fishermen in Flats*. Monash Papers on Southeast Asia no. 9. Clayton, Vic.: Centre of Southeast Asian Studies, Monash University, 1982. 151 pp. ISEAS, NLB, NTUNIE, NUS.

2780. Normala Manap. "Pulau Seking: Social-History and an Ethnography". Academic exercise, Department of Sociology, National University of Singapore, 1982. 214 pp. NUS.

2781. Osman Sidek. "Rehabilitation of Pulau Seking: Legitimate Interpretation of a Cultural Symbol Using the Malay House and Village as Illustration". Academic exercise, National University of Singapore, 1989. 217 pp. NUS.

2782. Png San-San, Carmen. "The Malays in Pulau Ubin". Research exercise, Department of Malay Studies, National University of Singapore, 1995. 34 pp. NUS.

2783. Tan Im Kian, Frederick. "The Fishing Settlements of Pulau Semakau". Academic exercise, Department of Geography, University of Singapore, 1966. 1 microfilm reel. NUS.

Other Localities

2784. Chan, Loke Ming, ed. *A Report on the Fishermen of Siglap*. Singapore: Siglap Community Centre, 1977. 50 pp. NLB.

2785. Goh Si Guim. "Twilight for Bidadari". *Nature Watch* 10, no. 1 (January–March 2002): 14–15. NLB.

2786. Hadijah Rahmat. *Kilat Senja: Sejarah Sosial dan Budaya Kampung-Kampung di Singapura*. Singapore: HSYang Publishing, 2005. 463 pp. ISEAS, NLB, NTUNIE, NUS.

2787. Hafiza Talib. *Nostalgia Kampung Padang Terbakar*. Singapore: Hafiza Talib, 2013. 165 pp. NLB.

2788. Henry, J.S. "A Visit to Telok Blangah". *Malaysia in History* 14, no. 1 (October 1971): 32–36. ISEAS, NUS.

2789. Hon, Joan. *Tidal Fortunes: A Story of Change: The Singapore River and Kallang Basin*. Singapore: Landmark Books, 1990. 164 pp. ISEAS, NLB, NTUNIE, NUS.

2790. Ibrahim Tahir, ed. *A Village Remembered: Kampong Radin Mas, 1800s–1973*. Singapore: OPUS Editorial Private Limited, 2013. 248 pp. NLB, NTUNIE, NUS.

2791. *Jalan Kayu 1964: A Survey on the Living Conditions of the Hokkien, Malay and Tamil Communities*. Singapore: Child Welfare & Social Work Section of Stella Girls' School, 1964. 60 pp. ISEAS, NLB.

2792. Julita Mohd Hussein. "A Study of an Urban Malay Village: Jalan Eunos Malay Settlement". Academic exercise, Department of Sociology, National University of Singapore, 1981. 110 pp. NUS.

2793. "Kampong Ubi Celebrates 25 Years". *Citizen* (February 1994): 12–13. NLB.

2794. Kartini Saparudin. "Digging Bidadari's Past: From Palace to First Muslim State Cemetery". *BiblioAsia* 8, no. 4 (January–March 2013): 26–33. NLB, NTUNIE, NUS.

2795. Kartini Yayit. "Vanishing Landscapes: Malay Kampongs in Singapore". Academic exercise, Department of Geography, National University of Singapore, 1986. 158 pp. NUS.

2796. Koh May May, Madeline. "Kampong Teban: A Study of a Village Community in Northeast Singapore". Academic exercise, University of Singapore, 1967. 23 pp. NUS.

2797. Kucinta Setia. *The Bidadari Cemeteries and Their Surroundings: The First Formal Report on the Bidadari Region to the Historic Sites Unit of the National Heritage Board for the Proposed Bidadari Memorial Garden*. Singapore: [s.n.], 2002. 23 pp. NLB.

2798. Miksic, John N. *Archaeological Research on the "Forbidden Hill" of Singapore: Excavations at the Fort Canning, 1984*. Singapore: National Museum, 1985. 143 pp. ISEAS, NLB, NUS.

2799. Mohd Ali Mohd Baksh. "The Jalan Eunos Malay Settlement of Singapore: Geographical Survey". Academic exercise, University of Singapore, 1966. 25 pp. NUS.

2800. Mohd. Anis Tairan. *Kampungku Siglap: Memoir Mohd. Anis Tairan.* Singapore: Majlis Pusat Pertubuhan-Pertubuhan Budaya Melayu Singapura, 2010. 182 pp. NLB, NUS.

2801. Phua, Ann. *Once Upon a Tai Seng Village.* Singapore: Hemisphere Foundation, 2015. 164 pp. NLB.

2802. Rohani Baharin. "Malay Kampong Houses in Singapore with Reference to the Jalan Eunos Malay Settlement". Academic exercise, University of Singapore, 1979. 120 pp. NUS.

2803. Sundusia Rosdi. "Menyingkap Kenangan Kampung Pasiran dan Sekitarannya". *BiblioAsia* 8, no. 2 (2012): 39–45. NLB, NTUNIE, NUS.

2804. Tan Choon Kiat. "A History of Tanjong Pagar, 1823–1911". Academic exercise, Department of History, National University of Singapore, 1989. 75 pp. NUS.

2805. Umi Kalthom Abdul Karim. "The Social and Economic Study of the Residents of Kampong Amber Which is Due for Demolition". Academic exercise, Department of Social Work and Social Administration, University of Singapore, 1970. 139 pp. NUS.

NAME INDEX

LIST OF JOURNALS CITED

Accent
Singapore: World Publications Distributors, [1993]–.

Acta Psychiatrica Scandinavica
Copenhagen: Munksgaard, 1961–.

Akademika
Kuala Lumpur: Universiti Kebangsaan Malaysia, 1973–.

Al-Mahjar: A Publication of the Arab Association of Singapore
Singapore: Al Wehdah Al Arabiah, 1996–.

Al-Risalah: Majalah Warga PERGAS
Singapore: Jabatan Dakwah PERGAS, 2000–.

Analisa
Singapore: Persekutuan Bahasa Melayu Universiti Singapura, 1970–.

Annals of the Academy of Medicine, Singapore (online)
Singapore: Academy of Medicine, 1972–.

Annals of the Association of American Geographers
[Washington: Association of American Geographers], 1911–.

Architecture Asia: A Journal of the Architects Regional Council Asia (ARCASIA)
Kuala Lumpur: Pertubuhan Akitek Malaysia on behalf of ARCASIA, 1997–2006.

Archives of Ophthalmology
Chicago: American Medical Association, 1960–2012.

Archives of Suicide Research: Official Journal of the International Academy for Suicide Research (online)
Dordrecht; Boston: Kluwer Academic Publishers, 1995–.

Armed Forces & Society
New Brunswick, NJ: Transaction Periodicals Consortium, 1974–.

Arts Magazine
Singapore: Singapore Arts Centre Company, 1997–2003.

ASEAN Review
[Kuala Lumpur: Wedgwood Sdn. Bhd.], 1976–.

Asia Europe Journal
[Berlin; New York]: Springer; [Singapore: For the Asia Europe Foundation], 2003–.

Asia Magazine
Hong Kong: Asia Magazines Ltd., 1961–98.

Asia Pacific Journal of Education
Singapore: Published for the National Institute of Education by Oxford University Press, 1996–.

Asia-Pacific Journal of Public Health (online)
Hong Kong: SAGE Publications, 1987–.

Asia Pacific Journal of Social Work
Singapore: Department of Social Work and Psychology, National University of Singapore, 1991–2003.

Asia Pacific Journal of Social Work and Development (online)
Singapore: Department of Social Work and Psychology, National University of Singapore, 2004–.

Asia Pacific Viewpoint
Oxford; Cambridge, MA: Blackwell, 1996–.

Asian Ethnicity
Basingstoke, Hants, UK: Carfax Publishing, Taylor & Francis Ltd., 2000–.

Asian Folklore Studies (online)
Nagoya: Asian Folklore Institute, 1963–2007.

Asian Journal of Political Science
Singapore: Times Academic Press for Department of Political Science,
National University of Singapore, 1993–.

Asian Journal of Social Science
Leiden: Brill, 2001–.

Asian Journal of Sports Medicine (online)
[S.l.: s.n.], 2010–.

Asian Survey
Berkeley, California: University of California Press, 1961–.

The *Asiatic Review*
London: Westminster Chamber, 1914–52.

Asiaweek
[Hong Kong: Asiaweek Ltd.], 1975–2001.

Assyahid: Journal of the Muslim Youth Assembly
Singapore: Himpunan Belia Islam, 1976–85.

The *Australian Journal of Anthropology* (online)
Sydney: The Anthropological Society of New South Wales, 1990–.

Bahasa
Singapore: Persekutuan Bahasa Melayu University Malaya, 1957–68.

Beam
Singapore: British European Association, 1957–.

BeMuse
Singapore: Education and Outreach Division, National Heritage Board, 2007–.

Beriga
Brunei: Dewan Bahasa dan Pustaka, 1967–.

BiblioAsia
Singapore: Publishing and Research Services, National Library Board, 2005–.

Bijdragen tot de Taal-, Land-en Volkenkunde
s'Gravenhage: M. Nijhoff, 1949–.

Borneo Research Bulletin (online)
Williamsburg, Va.: Borneo Research Council, 1969–.

Breast Cancer Research and Treatment
The Hague; Boston: M. Nijhoff, 1981–.

British Journal of Community Justice (online)
Sheffield, England: Sheffield Hallam University Press, 2002–.

British Malaya
London: Association of British Malaya, 1926–51.

Buletin Saujana
Singapore: Persatuan Pengajian Melayu, Universiti Nasional Singapura, 2000–.

Chinese Women's Association Journal
Singapore: Chinese Women's Association, 1978–.

Citizen
Singapore: People's Association, 1972–2000.

Civilisations
Bruxelles: Institut International des Civilisations Differentes, 1951–.

Clinical & Experimental Ophthalmology (online)
Victoria, Australia: Blackwell Science Asia Pty Ltd., 1997–.

Commentary
Singapore: University of Singapore Society, 1968–.

Community Dental Health
London: John Libbey, 1984–.

Community Genetics (online)
[Basel, Switzerland]: Karger, 1998–2008.

Contemporary Southeast Asia
Singapore: Singapore University Press for the Institute of Southeast Asian Studies, 1979–.

The *Copenhagen Journal of Asian Studies*
Copenhagen: Museum Tusculanum, 1995–.

Crossroads: An Interdisciplinary Journal of Southeast Asian Studies
DeKalb, Ill.: Centre for Southeast Asian Studies, Northern Illinois University, 1983–2008.

Current Issues in Criminal Justice
Sydney: Institute of Criminology, 1989–.

Development
Rome: Society for International Development, 1981–.

Dewan Bahasa
Kuala Lumpur: Dewan Bahasa dan Pustaka, 1999–.

Dewan Budaya
Kuala Lumpur: Dewan Bahasa dan Pustaka, 1979–.

Dewan Masyarakat
Kuala Lumpur: Dewan Bahasa dan Pustaka, 1962–.

Dewan Sastera
Kuala Lumpur: Dewan Bahasa dan Pustaka, 1971–.

Digestive Diseases and Sciences
New York: Plenum Pub. Corp., 1956–.

Discourse: Studies in the Cultural Politics of Education (online)
[London]: Carfax, 1980–.

Economic Bulletin
Singapore: Singapore International Chamber of Commerce, 1974–2003.

Educational Research for Policy and Practice (online)
Dordrecht; New York: Kluwer, 2002–.

Ethnic and Racial Studies
London; New York: Routledge & Kegan Paul, 1978–.

Ethnicity & Health
Abingdon, Oxfordshire; Cambridge, MA: Carfax, 1996–.

The *Expat*
Singapore: The Expat, 2002–6.

Far Eastern Economic Review
Hong Kong: [Review Publishing Co. Ltd., etc.], 1946–2009.

Focas: Forum on Contemporary Art & Society
Singapore: The Necessary Stage, 2001–.

The *Fount Journal*
Singapore: NUS Muslim Society, 2000–1.

Fundsupermart
Singapore: iFast Financial, 2001–11.

Genuine Islam (microform)
London: British Library, Reprographic Section, 1981. Reproduction of:
Singapore: All Malaya Muslim Missionary Society, 1936– [194–?].

Geriatric Nursing (online)
[St. Louis, Mo.: Mosby, Inc., etc.], 1980–.

Global Networks: A Journal of Transnational Affairs [online]
Oxford, UK; Malden, MA: Blackwell, 2001–.

Goodwood Journal
Singapore: Goodwood Hotels Corp., 1975–94.

Health Promotion International (online)
Oxford, U.K.: Oxford University Press, 1986–.

Her World
Singapore: Straits Times Press, 1960–.

Heritage
Singapore: National Museum, 1977–.

Heritage Journal (online)
Singapore: National Heritage Board, 2004–.

The *History Journal*
Singapore: National University of Singapore, History Society, 1994–.

Human Heredity
Basel, New York: Karger, 1969–.

Identities: Global Studies in Culture and Power
Yverdon, Switzerland: Gordon and Breach Publishers, 1994–.

The *Illustrated London News*
[London: The Illustrated London News & Sketch Ltd.], 1842–.

Ilmu Masyarakat: terbitan Persatuan Sains Sosial Malaysia = *Malaysian Social Science Association Publication*
Kuala Lumpur: Persatuan Sains Sosial Malaysia, 1983–92.

Immigrants & Minorities
London: Crown House, Frank Cass, 1982–.

Inabah: kembali ke jalan Allah
Singapore: Lembaga Pentadbir Masjid Khadijah, 2000–.

Indonesia and the Malay World
Oxford: Oxford University Press for the School of Oriental and African Studies, 1997–.

In step: with NAC and the arts
Singapore: The National Arts Council, 1999–.

Inter-Asia Cultural Studies
London: Taylor & Francis, 2000–.

Intercultural Education (online)
London: Carfax Pub., 2000–.

International and Comparative Law Quarterly
[London]: British Institute of International and Comparative Law, [etc.], 1952–.

International Child Welfare Review
Geneva, Switzerland: The Union, 1947–85.

International Journal of Children's Spirituality (online)
Oxfordshire, England; Cambridge, Mass.: Carfax, [1996?]–.

International Journal of Educational Reform (online)
Lancaster, PA: Technomic Pub., 1992–.

International Journal of Geriatric Psychiatry
Chichester, Sussex, England; New York: Wiley, 1986–.

International Journal of Urban and Regional Research
[London]: E. Arnold, 1977–.

International Labour Review
Geneva: International Labour Office, 1921–.

International Psychogeriatrics (online)
New York: Springer Pub. Co., 1939–.

Inter-Ocean: A Dutch East Indian magazine covering Malaysia and Australasia
Weltevreden (Batavia): G. Kolff, 1920–32.

Intisari
Singapore: Malaysian Sociological Research Institute, 1962–.

Investigative Ophthalmology & Visual Science
[Hagerstown, MD: Association for Research in Vision and Ophthalmology],
1977–.

Islamic Studies
Islamabad, Pakistan: Islamic Research Institute, 1962–.

Jamiyah Bulletin
Singapore: Muslim Missionary Society of Singapore, 1982–.

Journal of Affective Disorders (online)
Amsterdam: Elsevier, 1979–.

Journal of Beliefs and Values (online)
Abingdon, Oxfordshire: Carfax Publishing, 1984–.

Journal of Biosocial Science (online)
Oxford: Blackwell Scientific Publications for the Galton Foundation, 1969–.

Journal of Contemporary Asia
London: Journal of Contemporary Asia, 1970–.

Journal of Developing Societies
Leiden: Brill, 1985–.

Journal of Epidemiology and Community Health (eResource)
London: British Medical Association, 1978–.

Journal of Institute of Muslim Minority Affairs
London: Umran Publications, 1979–96.

Journal of the Historical Society
Singapore: University of Singapore Historical Society, 1966–79.

Journal of the Indian Archipelago and Eastern Asia (microform)
Singapore: University of Singapore Library, 1980. Reproduction of: Singapore:
Printed at Mission Press, 1847–63.

Journal of the Malayan Branch of the Royal Asiatic Society (JMBRAS) (microform)
Singapore: University of Singapore Library, 1977. Reproduction of: Singapore:
Malayan Branch, Royal Asiatic Society, 1923–64.

Journal of the Malaysian Branch of the Royal Asiatic Society (JMBRAS)
Singapore: Malaysian Branch of the Royal Asiatic Society, 1964–.

Journal of Management Education (eResource)
London: Sage Publications, 1975–.

Journal of Marriage and the Family
Menasha, Wis.: National Council on Family Relations, 1939–.

Journal of Moral Education
Abingdon, Oxfordshire, [etc.]: Carfax Pub. Co. [etc.], 1971–.

Journal of Multilingual and Multicultural Development
Clevedon, Somerset: Tietro Ltd., 1980–.

Journal of Muslim Minority Affairs
Abingdon, Oxfordshire: Carfax Publishing Company, 1996–.

Journal of Southeast Asian Architecture
Singapore: School of Architecture, National University of Singapore, 1996–.

Journal of Southeast Asian Studies
Singapore: Cambridge University Press for the Department of History,
National University of Singapore, 1970–.

Journal of the Straits Branch of the Royal Asiatic Society (JSBRAS)
Singapore: Straits Branch, Royal Asiatic Society, 1878–1922.

Journal of the South Seas Society
Singapore: The South Seas Society, 1959–.

Journal of Southeast Asian History
Singapore: Department of History, University of Malaya in Singapore, 1960–69.

Jurnal Pengajian Melayu
Kuala Lumpur: Akademi Pengajian Melayu, Universiti Malaya, 1989–.

Jurnal Biografi Malaysia
Kuala Lumpur: Arkib Negara Malaysia, 2005–.

Jurnal Dakwah
Singapore: Persatuan Ulama dan Guru-guru Agama Islam Singapura
(PERGAS), [2010]–.

Jurnal Dewan Bahasa
Kuala Lumpur: Dewan Bahasa dan Pustaka, 1989–99.

Karyawan: Professionals for the Community
Singapore: Association of Muslim Professionals, 1994–.

Kekal Abadi: Berita Perpustakaan Universiti Malaya
Kuala Lumpur: Perpustakaan Universiti Malaya, 1982–.

Law Times
[Singapore]: University of Singapore Law Society, 1966–83.

Malaya
London: Association of British Malaya, 1952–63.

Malaya Law Review
Singapore: Faculty of Law, University of Singapore, 1962–90.

The *Malayan Economic Review*
Singapore: Malayan Economic Society, 1956–82.

Malayan Historical Journal
[Kuala Lumpur: Malayan Historical Society], 1954–56.

The *Malayan Law Journal*
Singapore: Malaya Pub. House, 1932–.

Malaysia in History
Kuala Lumpur: Malaysian Historical Society, 1967–85.

Man
London: Royal Anthropological Institute of Great Britain and Ireland, 1901–94.

Mastika
[Kuala Lumpur: Utusan Melayu (Malaysia) Berhad, etc.], [19–]–.

Mekar
Singapore: Kementerian Pelajaran, 1980–81.

Mendaki Policy Digest
Singapore: Yayasan MENDAKI, 2003–.

The *Mirror: A Weekly Almanac of Current Affairs*
Singapore: Ministry of Culture, 1965–91.

The *Muslim World* (eResource)
[Hartford, Conn.]: Hartford Seminary Foundation, 1948–.

Muslim World League Journal
[Makkah al-Mukarramah, Saudi Arabia: Press and Publications Department, Muslim World League], 1973–92.

Nadi: Pulse of the Singapore Muslim Community
Singapore: Islamic Religious Council of Singapore (Muis), 2005–.

Nature Watch: Official Magazine of the Nature Society (Singapore)
Singapore: Nature Society (Singapore), 1993–.

Nephrology, Dialysis, Transplantation: Official Publication of the European Dialysis and Transplant Association – European Renal Association
[Berlin; New York, NY]: Springer International, 1986–.

New Directions
Singapore: Times Publishing, 1973–78.

Ophthalmic Epidemiology (eResource)
Buren, The Netherlands: Aeolus Press, 1994–.

Pacific Affairs (eResource)
Vancouver: University of British Columbia, 1928–.

Pacific Community
[Tokyo: Pacific News Commonwealth], 1969–78.

Pacific Rim Law and Policy Journal
Seattle, Washington: Students of the University of Washington School of Law, 1992–2014.

Parkinsonism & Related Disorders (eResource)
[Kidlington, Oxford]: Elsevier Science Ltd., 1995–.

The *Parliamentarian: Journal of the Parliaments of the Commonwealth*
London: General Council of the Commonwealth Parliamentary Association, 1966–.

Petir: Organ of the People's Action Party
Singapore: People's Action Party, 1956–.

The *Pointer*
Singapore: School of Methods of Instruction, SAFTI, 1975–.

Population Studies
London: University Press, 1947–.

Procedia – Social and Behavioral Sciences (eResource)
[New York]: Elsevier, 2009–.

Quality of Life Research (eResource)
[Boston]: Kluwer Academic Publishers Group, 1992–.

Race & Class
[London: Institute of Race Relations], 1974–.

RELC Journal
Singapore: Oxford University Press for Regional English Language Centre, 1970–.

Review of Indonesian and Malayan Affairs (RIMA)
Sydney, Australia: Department of Indonesian and Malayan Studies, University of Sydney, 1967–82.

Review of Indonesian and Malaysian Affairs (RIMA)
Sydney, Australia: Department of Indonesian and Malayan Studies, University of Sydney, 1983–.

Review of Southeast Asian Studies
Singapore: South Seas Society, 1974–.

Round Table: Commonwealth Journal of International Affairs
London: Round Table, 1910–.

SALT
Singapore: National Volunteer & Philanthropy Centre, 2004–9.

Sari
Bangi, Selangor: Institut Bahasa, Kesusasteraan dan Kebudayaan Melayu, Universiti Kebangsaan Malaysia, 1983–2012.

Sedar: A Journal of Islamic Studies
[Singapore: Muslim Society, University of Singapore], 1968–.

Sekata
Singapore: Jawatankuasa Bahasa Melayu, Singapura, Kementerian Kebudayaan, 1984–.

SIAJ: Journal of the Singapore Institute of Architects
[Singapore]: Graphic Publications, 1966–94.

Silver Kris
Singapore: MPH Magazines for Singapore Airlines, 1975–.

The *Singapore Architect*
Singapore: Singapore Institute of Architects, 1994–.

The *Singapore Artist*
Singapore: Singapore Art Society, 1954–55.

Singapore Book World
[Singapore]: National Book Development Council of Singapore, 1970–.

Singapore Business
[Singapore: Times Periodicals Pte. Ltd.], 1977–98.

Singapore Journal of Education
Singapore: Federal Publications for the Institute of Education, 1978–95.

Singapore Journal of Legal Studies
Singapore: Faculty of Law, National University of Singapore, 1991–.

Singapore Libraries
Singapore: Library Association of Singapore, 1971–98.

Singapore Law Gazette: An Official Publication of the Law Society of Singapore
Hong Kong: Asia Law & Practice Ltd., 1992–.

Singapore Medical Journal
Singapore: Singapore Medical Association, 1960–.

Singapore Nursing Journal
Singapore: Singapore Nurses Association, 1998–.

Singapore Paraplegics
Singapore: Calton, 1976–96.

The *Singapore Professionals*
[Singapore]: Singapore Professional Centre, 1976–2003.

The *Straits Times Annual*
Singapore: Straits Times, 1905–82.

Singapore: Year in Review
Singapore: Times Academic Press [for] Institute of Policy Studies, 1991–98.

Skyline
Singapore: Urban Redevelopment Authority, 1982–.

Social Dimension
Singapore: Singapore Association of Social Workers, 1978–.

Social Science & Medicine
Oxford; New York: Pergamon, 1982–.

Sociology and Social Research
[Los Angeles: University of Southern California], 1927–.

Sojourn: Social Issues in Southeast Asia
Singapore: Institute of Southeast Asian Studies, 1986–.

South East Asia Research
Brighton, UK: In Print for the School of Oriental and African Studies,
University of London, 1993–.

Southeast Asian Affairs
Singapore: Institute of Southeast Asian Studies, 1974–.

Southeast Asian Journal of Social Science
[Singapore: University Education Press], 1973–2000.

Southeast Asian Journal of Sociology
Singapore: University of Singapore Sociology Society, 1968–71.

Speeches
Singapore: Publicity Division, Ministry of Culture, 1977–2002.

Speeches: A Quarterly Collection of Speeches (SANA)
Singapore: Singapore Anti-Narcotics Association, 1979–.

Studies in Ethnicity and Nationalism (eResource)
London: Association for the Study of Ethnicity and Nationalism, 2001–.

Studies in Family Planning
[New York: Population Council], 1963–.

Suara Merdeka: Organ of the Malayan Forum (microform)
Singapore: National Library Microfilms Units, [197–?]. Reproduction of:
London: Malayan Forum, 1955–62.

Suara Muhammadiyah
Singapore: Jabatan Penerangan dan Penerbitan Muhammadiyah Singapura,
1970–.

Suara Universiti
Singapore: [Kesatuan Akademis, Universiti Singapura], 1964–72.

Tissue Antigens (eResource)
Copenhagen: Munksgaard, 1971–.

Traditional Dwellings and Settlements Review
Berkeley, Calif.: International Association for the Study of Traditional
Environments, 1989–.

Treasures of Time
Singapore: Historic Sites and Public Education Units of National Archives of Singapore, [19–]–.

Tropical and Geographical Medicine
Amsterdam: Foundation Tropical and Geographical Medicine [etc.], 1949–95.

Urban Affairs Review
Thousand Oaks, Calif.: Sage Publications Inc., 1995–.

University of Malaya Law Review
Singapore: Law Department, University of Malaya in Singapore, 1959–61.

The *Veteran*
Singapore: SAF Veteran League, 1996–.

Vizier Singapore
Singapore: Wazir Media, 2012–.

Visual Anthropology Review (eResource)
Los Angeles: Center for Visual Anthropology, University of Southern California, 1991–.

Vox Sanguinis
Basel, Switzerland; New York [etc.]: S. Karger, 1956–.

Warita Kita
Singapore: Majlis Ugama Islam Singapura, 1998–2003.

World Englishes (eResource)
Oxford; New York: Pergamon Press, 1985–.

World Muslim League Magazine
Singapore: World Muslim League, 1963–68.

Young Families
Singapore: Times Periodicals for the PAP Community Foundation, 1990–.

DIRECTORY OF SINGAPORE MALAY/MUSLIM ORGANIZATIONS

ADAM Association
An Association for Devoted and Active Men / Sebuah Persatuan Lelaki Setia dan Aktif
Blk 3 Queen's Road #01-169, Singapore 260003
Tel: 64715446
<http://adamassociation.sg>

AIN Society / Persatuan Ain
Blk 2 Eunos Crescent #01-2545, Singapore 400002
Tel: 68485166
<http://ainsociety.org sg>

Akademi Peningkatan Keluarga Islam (APKIM)
134 Arab Street, Singapore 199824
Tel: 62951011
<http://www.apkim.sg>

Alwehdah
Arab Association of Singapore
11 Lorong 37, Geylang Road, Singapore 387908
Tel: 67475590
<http://alwehdah.org>

Angkatan Pelukis Aneka Daya (APAD) / Association of Artists of Various Resources
28 Aliwal Street #02-01, WS09, Aliwal Arts Centre, Singapore 199918
<http://apad.org.sg>

Angkatan Sasterawan '50 (ASAS '50) / Association of 1950 Malay Writers
Goodman Arts Centre, 90 Goodman Road, Blk B #05-12,
Singapore 439053
Tel (hp): 96652644
<http://asas50.com>

Association of Muslim Professionals (AMP) / Angkatan Karyawan Islam Singapura
1 Pasir Ris Drive 4 #05-11 Singapore 519457
Tel: 64163966
<http://www.amp.org.sg>

Association of Muslim Travel Agents (Singapore) (AMTAS) / Persatuan Agensi Pelancongan Islam Singapura
723A North Bridge Road, Singapore 198691
Tel: 62972861
<http://www.amtas.sg>

Badan Agama & Pelajaran Radin Mas (BAPA) / Religious & Educational League of Radin Mas
Kembangan Court, 5 Jalan Masjid #01-15, Singapore 418924
Tel: 62787750
<http://www.bapa.org.sg>

Bayaan Association
P.O. Box 451, Singapore 914016
<http://www.bayaan.org.sg>

Casa Raudha Women Home
Jurong Point Post Office P.O. Box 455, Singapore 916416
Fax: 68981376
<http://www.casaraudha.org>

Club HEAL (Hope, Empowerment, Acceptance & Love) / Kelab HEAL
244 Bukit Batok East Ave 5 #01-02, Singapore 650244
Tel: 68993463
<http://www.clubheal.org.sg>

Darul Arqam Singapore
Muslim Converts' Association of Singapore
32 Onan Road, The Galaxy, Singapore 424484
Tel: 63488344
<http://www.darul-arqam.org.sg>

Darul Ihsan
Darul Ihsan Orphanage (Boys)
5 Mattar Road, Singapore 387713
Tel: 67477556
<http://www.mtfa.org/index.php/darul-ihsan>

Darul Ihsan Lilbanat
Darul Ihsan Orphanage (Girls)
23 Wan Tho Ave, Singapore 347552
Tel: 62852973
<http://www.mtfa.org/index.php/darul-ihsan>

Darul Islah
Jamiyah Halfway House
352 Pasir Panjang Road, Singapore 118694
Tel: 67769101
<http://jhh.jamiyah.org.sg>

Darul Ma'wa
Jamiyah Children's Home
15 Guillemard Crescent, Singapore 399910
Tel: 63449533
<http://jch.jamiyah.org.sg>

Darul Syifaa
Jamiyah Nursing Home
130 West Coast Drive, Singapore 127444
Tel: 67768575
<http://jnh.jamiyah.org.sg>

Darul Takrim
Jamiyah Home for the Aged
1 Tampines Ave 3, Singapore 529707
Tel: 67837071
<http://jha.jamiyah.org.sg>

Dewan Perniagaan & Perusahaan Melayu Singapura (DPPMS) /
Singapore Malay Chamber of Commerce & Industry (SMCCI)
15 Jalan Pinang, Singapore 199147
Tel: 62979296
<http://www.smcci.org.sg>

HIRA Educational & Social Services
Hira Society
303 Woodlands Street 31 #01-197, Singapore 730303
<https://www.facebook.com/HIRAedu>

Jamiyah Singapore
Muslim Missionary Society of Singapore
31 Lorong 12 Geylang, Singapore 399006
Tel: 67431711
<http://www.jamiyah.org.sg>

Just Parenting Association
Blk 3 Queens Road #01-169, Singapore 260003
Tel: 64715448
<http://justparenting.org.sg>

Kesatuan Guru Melayu Singapura (KGMS) / Singapore Malay Teachers' Union
587 Geylang Road #04-01, Singapore 389526
Tel: 64407952
<http://www.kgms.org.sg>

Kumpulan Angkatan Muda Sastera (KAMUS)
60 Sims Drive #08-1275, Singapore 380060
<https://www.facebook.com/Kamus.Singapura>

Kumpulan Orang Cacat Muslim Singapura
218E Changi Road #03-06 PKMS Building, Singapore 419737
Tel: 63124054
<https://www.facebook.com/kcms.org.sg>

Lembaga Biasiswa Kerangan Maulud (LBKM) / Prophet Muhammad's
Birthday Memorial Scholarship Fund Board
448 Changi Road #04-01 Wisma Indah, Singapore 419975
Tel: 64474770
<http://lbkm.org.sg>

Lembaga Khairat Muslimin (LKM) Polis Repablik Singapura
175A Bencoolen Street #12-05 Burlington Square, Singapore 189650
<http://lkm.org.sg>

Majlis Bahasa Melayu Singapura (MBMS) / Malay Language Council,
Singapore
National Heritage Board c/o 61 Stamford Road, #03-08 Stamford Court,
Singapore 178892
Tel: 63323832
<http://www.mbms.sg>

Majlis Pusat
93 Toa Payoh Central #06-01, Toa Payoh Central Community Building,
Singapore 319194
Tel: 62514458
<http://majlispusat.org>

Majlis Ugama Islam Singapura (MUIS) / Islamic Religious Council of Singapore
273 Braddell Road, Singapore 579702
Tel: 63591199
<http://www.muis.gov.sg>

Malabar Muslim Jama-ath
471 Victoria Street, Singapore 198370
Tel: 85695082
<http://mmj.org.sg>

Malay Language Centre of Singapore (MLCS) / Pusat Bahasa Melayu Singapura
13 Bishan Street 14, Singapore 579787
Tel: 63546961
<http://www.malaylanguagecentre.moe.edu.sg>

Malay Youth Performing Art (MyPart)
Blk 102 Yishun Ave 5 #04-121, Singapore 760102
<http://www.mypart.org.sg>

MESRA
People's Association Malay Activity Executive Committees Council (MAECs)
People's Association
9 King George's Avenue, Singapore 208581
Tel: 63405346
<https://www.facebook.com/MESRA.PA>

Muhammadiyah Association / Persatuan Muhammadiyah
14 Jalan Selamat, Singapore 418534
Tel: 62427388
<http://www.muhammadiyah.org.sg>

Muhammadiyah Welfare Home (MWH) / Rumah Kebajikan
Muhammadiyah (RKM)
58 Bedok North Street 3, Singapore 469624
Tel: 63447551
<http://www.mwh.muhammadiyah.org.sg>

Muslim Financial Planning Association (MFPA)
55 Market Street #08-01, Singapore 048941
<http://muslimfinancialplanning.org.sg>

Muslim Healthcare Professionals Association (MHPA)
1 Pasir Ris Drive 4 #05-11, Singapore 519457
<http://www.mhpa.org.sg>

Muslim Kidney Action Association (MKAC Association)
122 Telok Kurau Road, Singapore 423806
Tel: 64407390
<http://www.mkac.sg>

Muslim Welfare Association of Singapore (MWAS)
77 High Street #03-02, High Street Plaza, Singapore 179433
<https://www.facebook.com/mwas.sg>

Muslimin Trust Fund Association (MTFA) / Pertubuhan Derma Amanah
Muslimin Singapura
Darul Ihsan Orphanage Building, 5 Mattar Road, Singapore 387713
Tel: 67477556
<http://www.mtfa.org>

NTU Muslim Society (Nanyang Technological University Muslim Society)
Nanyang Technological University, 50 Nanyang Avenue,
Singapore 639798
<https://www.facebook.com/groups/NTU.NIEmuslimsociety>

NUS Muslim Society (National University of Singapore Muslim Society) (NUSMS)
NUSMS c/o NUSSU Secretariat, 31 Lower Kent Ridge Road #05-02 Yusof
Ishak House, Singapore 119078
<http://nusms.org.sg>

Perbayu NTU
Persatuan Bahasa dan Budaya Melayu Universiti Teknologi Nanyang /
Nanyang Technological University (NTU) Malay Language and
Cultural Society
<https://www.facebook.com/perbayuNTU>

Perdaus
Blk 364 Bukit Batok Street 31 #01-259, Singapore 650364
Tel: 65132300
<http://perdaus.org.sg>

Perkumpulan Seni (PS) Singapura / Arts Group
126 Cairnhill Road, Singapore 229707
Tel: 62356674
<https://www.facebook.com/perkumpulanseni.org>

Persadamu
Persatuan Bahasa dan Budaya Melayu Universiti Pengurusan Singapura /
Singapore Management University (SMU) Malay Language & Cultural Club
Singapore Management University, Administration Building, 81 Victoria
Street, Singapore 188065
<http://persadamu.weebly.com>

Persatuan Bahasa Melayu Universiti Kebangsaan Singapura (PBMUKS) /
National University of Singapore (NUS) Malay Language Society
Office of Student Affairs, 31 Lower Kent Ridge Road #05-02 Yusof Ishak
House, Singapore 119078
<http://pbmuks.org>

Persatuan Bawean Singapura / Singapore Baweanese Association
757A North Bridge Road, Singapore 198725
Tel: 63445738
<http://persatuanbaweansingapura2012.blogspot.sg>

Persatuan Guru-Guru Al Quran Singapura (PERGERAQ)
218E Changi Road #03-10 PKMS Building, Singapore 419737
<http://www.pergeraq.net>

Persatuan Hadrah Kompang Singapura (PEHAKS)
<https://www.facebook.com/hadrah.kompang>

Persatuan Ikatan Ria Bersama (Singapura) (IKRAB)
Street 24 Bukit Batok, Singapore
Tel: 94837153
<http://ikrabs.com>

Persatuan Islam Singapura (Persis)
598C Sembawang Road, Singapore 758456
Tel: 64812056
<http://persissingapore.weebly.com>

Persatuan Islam dan Pencak Silat Singapura (PERIPENSIS) / The Singapore Islamic and Pencak Silat Association
35 Onan Road, Singapore 424436
<http://www.peripensis.org>

Persatuan Pemudi Islam Singapura (PPIS) / Young Women Muslim Association
Blk 1 Eunos Crescent #01-2509, Singapore 400001
Tel: 67440258
<http://web.ppis.sg>

Persatuan Persuratan Pemuda Pemudi Melayu (4PM) / Malay Youth Literary Association
Blk 606 Bedok Reservoir Road #01-716, Singapore 470606
Tel: 62426288 / 62426381
<http://www.4pm.org.sg>

Persatuan Ulama dan Guru-Guru Agama Islam (Singapura) (PERGAS) / Singapore Islamic Scholars & Religious Teachers Association
448 Changi Road #03-01, Wisma Indah, Singapore 419975
Tel: 63469350
<http://pergas.org.sg>

Persekutuan Sepaktakraw Singapura (PERSES) / Singapore Sepaktakraw Federation
7 Bedok North Street 2 #02-02, Singapore 469646
Tel: 64498963
<http://www.perses.org>

Persekutuan Silat Singapura (PERSISI) / Singapore Silat Federation
Silat Centre of Excellence, 7 Bedok North Street 2 #01-01, #02-01,
Singapore 469646
Tel: 67418837
<http://www.persisi.org>

Pertapis
Blk 1 Joo Chiat Road #04-1001 Joo Chiat Complex, Singapore 420001
Tel: 67453969
<http://pertapis.sg>

Pertapis Centre for Women and Girls
42 Surin Avenue, Singapore 535638
Tel: 62844707
<http://pertapis.sg/centre-for-women-and-girls>

Pertapis Children's Home
993B Kovan Road (off Yio Chu Kang Road), Singapore 545676
Tel: 63830914
<http://pertapis.sg/children-s-home>

Pertapis Halfway House
50 Lorong 34 Geylang Road, Singapore 398239
Tel: 67464752
<http://pertapis.sg/halfway-house>

Pertapis Senior Citizen Fellowship Home
Blk 222 Lorong 8 Toa Payoh, Singapore 310222
Tel: 62521159
<http://pertapis.sg/senior-citizen-fellowship-home>

Perwanit Singapore
300 Whampoa Drive, #02-06, Singapore 327737
Tel: 63566253
<http://pertapis.sg/senior-citizen-fellowship-home>

Rahmatan Lil 'Alamin Foundation
Singapore Islamic Hub
273 Braddell Road, Singapore 579702
Tel: 63591199
<http://rlafoundation.org.sg>

Religious Rehabilitation Group (RRG)
Khadijah Mosque, 583 Geylang Road, Singapore 389522
Tel: 67475607
<http://rrg.sg>

RIMA
Centre for Research on Islamic and Malay Affairs
1 Pasir Ris Drive 4 #05-11, Singapore 519457
Tel: 64163966
<http://www.rima.sg>

SGM Singapura Koperatif Bhd / Singapore Malay Teachers' Co-operative Ltd.
Wisma SGM, 785 Geylang Road, Singapore 389673
Tel: 67439595
<http://www.sgmcoop.org.sg>

SIM (Singapore Institute of Management) Malay Cultural & Muslim Society (SIMCMS)
<http://www.sim-mcms.com>

Singapore Kadayanallur Muslim League (SKML)
Blok 65 Telok Blangah Drive #01-166, Singapore 100065
Tel: 62744161
<http://www.skml.sg>

Singapore Muslim Students Overseas (SMSO)
<https://www.facebook.com/mysmso>

Singapore Tenkasi Muslim Welfare Society
Blk 334 Kreta Ayer Road #02-02, Singapore 080334
Tel: 63271296
<http://www.tenkasi.org>

Sri Warisan
Som Said Performing Arts Ltd.
47 & 59 Kerbau Road, Singapore 219173
Tel: 62256070
<http://www.sriwarisan.com>

Sriwana
90 Goodman Road, Blk D #01-25, Goodman Road Arts Centre, Singapore
439053
<http://www.sriwana.com>

Taman Warisan Melayu / Malay Heritage Centre
85 Sultan Gate, Singapore 198501
Tel: 63910450
<http://tamanwarisan.org.sg>
<http://malayheritage.org.sg>

Taman Bacaan (Singapore Malay Youth Library Association)
Blk 136, Bedok Reservoir Road #01-1423, Singapore 410136
Tel: 67448457
<http://www.uima.org.sg>

United Indian Muslim Association (UIMA)
587 Geylang Road #03-01, Singapore 389526
Tel: 67486187
<http://www.uima.org.sg>

Yayasan MENDAKI
Council for the Development of Singapore Muslim Community
51 Kee Sun Ave, Wisma Mendaki, Singapore 457056
Tel: 62455555
<http://www.mendaki.org.sg>

www.ingramcontent.com/pod-product-compliance
Lightning Source LLC
Chambersburg PA
CBHW072044020426
42334CB00017B/1383